Information

A SHORT HISTORY

EDITED BY ANN BLAIR,
PAUL DUGUID,
ANJA-SILVIA GOEING, &
ANTHONY GRAFTON

T0324632

PRINCETON UNIVERSITY PRESS
PRINCETON & OXFORD

Copyright © 2024 by Princeton University Press

Princeton University Press is committed to the protection of copyright and the intellectual property our authors entrust to us. Copyright promotes the progress and integrity of knowledge. Thank you for supporting free speech and the global exchange of ideas by purchasing an authorized edition of this book. If you wish to reproduce or distribute any part of it in any form, please obtain permission.

Requests for permission to reproduce material from this work should be sent to permissions@press.princeton.edu

Published by Princeton University Press
41 William Street, Princeton, New Jersey 08540
99 Banbury Road, Oxford OX2 6JX

press.princeton.edu

All Rights Reserved

ISBN (pbk.) 9780691261553
ISBN (e-book) 9780691263694

British Library Cataloging-in-Publication Data is available

Editorial: Anne Savarese and James Collier
Production Editorial: Natalie Baan
Cover Design: Karl Spurzem
Production: Erin Suydam
Copyeditor: Karen Verde

This book has been composed in Arno

Printed in the United States of America

10 9 8 7 6 5 4 3 2 1

CONTENTS

INTRODUCTION

Paul Duguid

EARLY IN THIS CENTURY, a colleague and I made a change from jobs in Silicon Valley to teach in the School of Information at the University of California, Berkeley. Surrounded in our old and new positions by invocations of information, we both felt that a useful contribution to the School might be to teach a course on information's history. As is not uncommon for people proposing to teach a course for the first time, we took to the library and the World Wide Web to see how others taught this subject. To our surprise, we couldn't find any courses on the topic. There were courses on the history of "communications," and on the history of "information and library science," each from within those academic fields. But information itself did not seem to be a critical subject for history or historians.

Much has changed since then. Courses and books on aspects of information's history abound. An insightful "History of Information" website has been running since 2011, and an illustrated *History of Information: A Visual History of Communication* will soon be available for children.[1] Indeed, the topic might be approaching what James Gleick in his book *The Information* (2011) calls "a flood," irrigating a fertile, if still rather disjointed, field. As more people turn to this area, it seemed appropriate to the editors of this volume to bring together a group of historians to write about how the discipline was approaching information's history. This resulting book seeks to provide useful insight into this still-evolving area not only for historians, but also for teachers and students more generally, and for members of the public.

Today's technologies and the discussions they provoke about machine learning, information processing, data mining, artificial intelligence, bots,

---

1. For the website, organized by Jeremy Norman, see HistoryofInformation.com. The book, by Chris Haughton, is due to be published by Dorling Kindersley in 2024.

and the like make information appear to most people to be not only a very contemporary subject, but also a highly visible one. This might suggest that where, in past societies, information was not the center of attention, it was not significant. To resist such assumptions, the contributors to this volume explore the various ways information raised important issues for earlier societies. They also explore how information can provide a useful means to understand those societies. Collectively, then, the essays explore information through the lens of history, while illuminating history through the lens of information. Thus, as new AI-related technologies and practices seem to be transforming society, heralding significant future changes that people are still trying to fathom, so the following chapters show how earlier "revolutions," from printing to the computer, forced earlier societies to address for themselves challenges of change.

Without denying the profundity of these changes, the chapters also reveal continuities. The desire for ever-more information to help answer questions and resolve problems, for example, runs throughout these essays. But so, too, do attendant concerns about the ever-increasing volume of information these desires produced and problems that the resulting accumulation of information introduces rather than resolves. When the Roman scholar Pliny compiled his 37-volume *Natural History* in the first century of the Common Era, he was happy to point out that he had followed the call of his friend Domitius Piso to offer not a "book" but a "store-house." Today, in a similar vein, many information-focused corporations describe a central challenge to be the management of *"data warehouses."

The title of this book does not assume that the history of information is short. Rather, it reflects the attempt to encompass central topics of its long history in a manageable form: to present a suitable selection rather than a Pliny-like collection. The "short" title also indicates that these chapters originally appeared as part of a much larger volume, *Information: A Historical Companion*, which in some ways reflected the encyclopedic structure of Pliny's work, with thirteen "long" and more than one hundred "short" entries on topics that are key to understanding information history. This collection extracts the long entries from that collection to provide a composite, shorter account.

The essays gathered here collectively seek, in particular, to show the value of a continuous historical narrative, tracking the evolution of information technologies, practices, and attitudes over time. With any such narrative, one of the most challenging questions is "where to begin?" To keep the book manageably short, while bringing its continuous narrative up to the present, choosing an appropriate starting point was critical. The editors decided to begin in what historians designate the "early modern period," starting in the middle of the fifteenth century. Thus, the first essay opens the book with an account of Columbus crossing the Atlantic, thereby setting exploratory travel of the time in the context of the gathering and circulation of information. (Starting in that time and place, this essay and several others nonetheless find that to go forward, they also need to look back, to Greece, Rome, and China, and from the Atlantic routes across the sea to land routes to the Pacific.) Succeeding essays take the overall narrative forward from the early modern era to the present. The final essays bring us to the gathering and distribution of information around the world today via such means as the internet and Google, setting issues concerning search, artificial intelligence, and machine learning in historical context.

Inevitably, the attempt to achieve both continuity and diversity across a "short history" can make no claim to comprehensiveness. All contributors are aware of inevitable gaps. We hope, nevertheless, that the collection, as a whole, can reveal how missing topics might nonetheless be illuminated by a shared, information-centered perspective.

Across the thirteen essays that present this history, authors introduce not only the technologies of the time, but also the practices and politics that surround them. From the opening account of Columbus and the Silk Road, chapters engage with the topic of globalization, represented by emerging networks of travel and communication across Asia, the Islamic world, and Europe. Informational connections inevitably shaped the roads taken as not only silk and spices but also word of supply and demand and technologies such as paper and forms of writing passed back and forth, opening new worlds, both literally and metaphorically, to recipients. These exchanges also fostered spiritual and scientific engagements, as intrepid Buddhists, Muslims, and Christians traveled in opposite directions along these interconnecting pathways, appearing in new environments and before new audiences, then sending back information about the encounters and what might be learned from them.

The collection also shows how devices, from stone to silicon, that capture and circulate information created underlying information infrastructures. Chapters explore innovative communication systems such as land and ocean navigation, letters and postal services, telegrams and telephones. With these, we see complex sets of social structures emerge in response to growing demand for and supply of information. And given the inevitable limitations of the devices for capture and circulation (and of the people who use them), issues recur about what information to keep and to share, and what to let go; about how to assimilate different kinds of information; about how to arrange what is assimilated; and about how to navigate and interpret resulting private and public collections. Throughout, challenges of authentication and validation are constant as people encountered then, as they do now, different kinds of mis- and disinformation.

The search for reliable information turns attention in particular to institutions that both shape and are shaped by the information devices of their day. Thus, for instance, printing, though invented centuries before in China, is shown to be transformed and also transforming when developed within the institutions of early modern Europe. Analyses of such interactions and the information practices that emerge with them challenge simple yet pervasive accounts that too readily assume technologies will change every society that adopts them in the same way.

The volume also explores in several settings the development of commercial relations and new information techniques around, for example, pricing, budgeting, exchange rates, and payment systems that spread with them. These accounts show increasing use of information to control and stabilize markets, as well as attempts by markets to control information in order to commodify and commercialize it.

One of the most significant developments explored across the volume is the rise of the "information state" and its bureaucratic informational apparatus—including chanceries, embassies, secretaries, surveillance systems, and government archives—designed to help assert political control over populations. States were often the source of innovative attempts to standardize information through forms, questionnaires, the census, cadastres, registries, and the like. The authors also reveal challenges that such attempts at quantification faced as, for example, different governments assembled and quantified such data in different ways for different reasons. The passport, as one article shows, offers an unexpected but illuminating view of states' attempts to control both information and population and of the normative effects of standardization.

A particularly notable development across the period surveyed herein involves the rise of, for example, "public information" in Japan and the "public sphere" in the West. Chapters show how the development of new information technologies and practices, among them the printing press, the newspaper, and the "news," helped transform relations between nation-states and the public. The book explores rising optimism about information's potential to create efficient and effective democracies. Nonetheless, themes of unequal distribution, propaganda, commodified information, and antidemocratic practices also run throughout.

Some chapters explore how evading restrictions on the circulation of information allowed people to resist government control. Thus, it is shown that when in some societies print became subject to government censorship, manuscript communication became particularly helpful as a way to evade control. In this and similar examples, these essays challenge the common assumption that new technologies and practices will simply replace the old.

Resistance to control is also evident in the accounts of scientific groups that sought autonomy for members and also for their information so both could circulate across national, political, and religious boundaries. In this way, the book follows the development and spread of new forms of scholarly information and the rise of scholarly institutions.

The final group of chapters examines another wave of political optimism and its challenges with the development of new devices and infrastructures (such as transoceanic cables) that freed information to travel independent of and at far greater speeds than human travel, from the telegraph, telephone, and radio into the modern age of the internet and the cell phone. This technologically driven optimism confronts the rise of state and corporate monopolistic control of these technologies and, by extension, their hold on the information carried and stored in the process.

Information's complex character presents challenges to anyone trying to undertake this sort of historical enquiry. As noted above, it is easy to assume that information is a feature of the current age alone. In contrast to that view, all the authors of this volume seek the presence of information in the period that they examine. But in so doing, they face questions about whose notion of information is at stake. Is it the historian's notion or that of the subjects of historical study? The latter perspective is explained in relation to knowledge by the historian Peter Burke, whose *Social History of Knowledge* (2000) seeks to trace "what early modern people—rather than the present author or his readers—considered to be knowledge." This is an important distinction. The chapters in this volume seek to highlight people becoming aware of information as a critical aspect of their lives. But the alternative view, allowing examination of historical actors who did not have the term or the concept but whose behavior can nonetheless be illuminated with insight from current perspectives of information, is equally important. Contributors have taken what they believed to be the appropriate approach for the time and topic they address.

The term *information* presents further problems. Not only does the word favor particular (i.e., Latinate) languages, but even within those languages, *information* is used quite differently in different times and contexts, and the different uses have distinct histories. Given these complexities, it might seem plausible for the editors to define *information* as a technical term to be shared among the book's contributors, putting to one side both historical and contemporary variations. But, as Marcia Bates wrote in the *Encyclopedia of Library and Information Science* (2009), which also had to wrestle with the term, "any claim to present a unified, singular vision of the topic would be disingenuous."

Indeed, attempts at a definition are as likely to generate as to resolve difficulties. For instance, it seems unexceptional to take "information" as a carrier of meaningful ideas between people. Such views, however, must confront the pioneering information theorist Claude Shannon, whose work probably did more than any other to promote ideas of an "information age." Shannon's theory held meaning as irrelevant to information. Many also assume that information is an objective entity. Yet Gregory Bateson's famous account of information as "a difference that makes a difference" assumes information to be personally subjective, the differences made being dependent on what each recipient knew before.

Similarly, some take information as an autonomous entity that can be removed from one context and unproblematically presented in another. In contrast, the media theorist Marshall McLuhan was celebrated for arguing that in the "age of information" "the medium is the message," suggesting that context is an inescapable component of informational content.

Contributors to this volume addressed their topics using their own understandings rather than subordinating themselves to a single definition. Their contributions reveal both common and distinctive threads across the volume. Nonetheless, one aim of the book has been, where possible, to encourage contributors (and readers) to weave these threads together. While following the development of current scholarship, another goal of this book, as noted above, is to engage readers outside the academy. Consequently, the book eschews scholarly footnotes and long bibliographies, offering instead short "further reading" lists. For those seeking more depth, the editors have built a fuller bibliography of works explicitly and implicitly invoked in articles, available on this project's website.[2] Throughout the book, words marked with an asterisk (*) on

2. For the website, see https://infohist.fas.harvard.edu, and for the bibliography, see https://infohist.fas.harvard.edu/further-reading-bibliography.

first mention within a chapter can be found in the *glossary at the end of the book. This defines terms used in specific ways by the authors.

Overall, the chapters work both individually and together to illustrate, across a limited period, key facets of information's *longue durée* and wide reach from a range of information-based perspectives. Again, the book makes no claim to be comprehensive but rather aspires to be illustrative. Its contributors hope to provide a range of audiences with useful and reliable insights, but also to prompt readers in the evolving field of information history to pursue new questions and fill gaps made evident by this attempt.

ACKNOWLEDGMENTS

THE EDITORS WOULD LIKE TO EXTEND deepest thanks to the contributors to this volume for their individual work and for their collective cooperation. They would also like to extend similar thanks for their oversight to the members of the project's advisory board, Jean Bauer, Arndt Brendecke, Peter Burke, Michael Cook, Richard Drayton, Markus Friedrich, Randolph Head, Matthew Kirschenbaum, Carla Nappi, Daniel Rosenberg, and Jake Soll. The editors are also deeply grateful to Princeton University Press and Anne Savarese and her colleagues, in particular James Collier, Natalie Baan, and Karen Verde, for the extraordinary support and responsiveness provided throughout the process of assembling this book and its antecedent volume and to Steven Moore for making a new index.

INFORMATION

1

Premodern Regimes and Practices

Anthony Grafton

ON THE SIXTH OF NOVEMBER 1492, Christopher Columbus was exploring Cuba. In his journal, he recorded what the native inhabitants told him: information that filled him with excitement. They "said, by signs," that he could find plenty of cinnamon and pepper—samples of which he had brought and showed them—nearby. A couple of days before, old men had reported that locals wore gold "on their necks, ears, arms, and legs, as well as pearls." True, he also learned that "far away, there were men with one eye, and others with dogs' noses who were cannibals, and that when they captured an enemy, they beheaded him and drank his blood, and cut off his private parts." Even this unpromising report did not dismay Columbus. On the contrary, it confirmed what he had believed and hoped since he reached land in October: that he had arrived, by traveling west across the Atlantic, at the Indies, near China, "the land of the great Cham."

Columbus knew where he was: at or near the eastern sources of the two great sets of trade routes that brought luxuries from the East to Latin Christendom and trade goods and money from Latin Christendom to the East: the Silk Road and the Spice Route. Both had functioned, more or less regularly, since the early centuries of the Common Era. Both had generated wealth for those who created silk and harvested spices to sell and for the numerous intermediaries who brought them to market. And both had been the sources of information of many kinds, about everything from distant lands to the properties of foods and spices. But both routes had been disrupted, in the thirteenth century and after, by the rise of Mongol power in the steppes of central Asia. In Columbus's day, both were dominated by Muslim merchants and powers, whom most Christians regarded as enemies—but from whom they bought, indirectly or directly, glossy consumer goods. When he heard tales of gold, pearls, and monsters in his vicinity, he knew he had arrived at the place where luxuries of many kinds originated. Immediately he inferred that he could enrich his masters, the Catholic Kings, both by eliminating middlemen and by domesticating the natives and putting them to productive work.

Columbus was wrong, of course, about the geographical facts. He was in the Caribbean, not the Pacific, the very existence of which was unknown to him and all other Europeans. And the local knowledge that he gleaned from the Cubans was inaccurate as well. Accounts of gold, pearls, and spices in Cuba proved to be greatly exaggerated. Investigation—as Columbus later informed the Catholic Kings—uncovered no men of monstrous form. This comes as no great surprise, since Columbus seems to have extracted these reports from the signs made by Cubans with whom he shared no language. Yet he had some reason to think as he did. An imaginary map of the world and its resources had formed over the centuries, as sailors and travelers told, and later wrote, tales. Monsters appeared on it, at the far end—from a European perspective—of the world, next to the lands from which silks and pepper were imported to Europe. These ancient images loomed before Columbus's eyes and shaped and colored what he saw.

After Columbus, travel—and the collection of information about the world—underwent a transformation. The Catholic Kings established permanent colonies and trade networks. They sponsored continuing, systematic collection of information, recorded and transmitted by pilots with formal training and credentials and military commanders with royal commissions. They and their rivals worked with sailors, merchants, and soldiers to begin the process that historians refer to as globalization: the uniting of the globe by institutions, sometimes paper thin but still constructed for the long term (Ghobrial, chap. 5).

Information travels: it moves, often unpredictably, with the people or the mediums that carry it. Information matters: states need reliable ways to collect, store, and access information and to provide it to their subjects, and merchants and bankers need it to serve their customers and outwit their rivals. Information abides: so long as its owners also possess a medium that can store it. This chapter sketches three histories of information. It follows the trading routes that brought luxuries from China and India across the world. It re-creates the information regimes that were created to govern the Roman Empire. And it examines the history of paper, a single medium for writing that had a powerful impact. The result will not be a survey but a sketch map of some of the ways in which information was collected and stored, transmitted and accessed, before the full process of globalization began.

Silk Road and Spice Route

Exchange of goods and ideas is as old as human settlement. By 3000 BCE, caravans connected cities and markets across the Fertile Crescent and beyond. But the forms of trade that took shape early in the Common Era—and that eventually connected two great but distant empires, China and Rome—differed in scale, as well as distance covered, from anything that had preceded them. In the third century BCE, the Qin dynasty, based in the wealthy state of the same name, conquered the other six Warring States and created a unified government with a powerful military and civil service. It and its successor, the Han dynasty, ruled from 221 BCE to 220 CE. Always confronted by the obligation to feed their large population, China's rulers had to encourage agriculture. To do so it was necessary to protect their farmers from the Xiongnu, horse-riding nomad archers who lived on the steppes to their north and defeated them in 200 CE. Early military expeditions were unsuccessful. Gradually, the Chinese realized that the silk that they had learned to produce, in the Yangtze valley and elsewhere, was unique and desirable. The heavier and more complex brocades, produced by specialists for the imperial court, were reserved for the Chinese elite. But farming families also cultivated mulberry trees, grew silkworms, and produced thin, simple silks, with which they paid their taxes to the state. These silks, the Chinese found, could be traded to the nomads of the steppes in return for horses, which they needed for agriculture. The Han extended the walls that protected China from the nomads. But they also pierced them with gates, which in turn became the centers of trading stations. From these sprang the immense trade network conventionally called the Silk Road.

Across Eurasia, meanwhile, Rome developed great military power, which enabled it to defeat the trading power Carthage in the third and second centuries BCE. In the next century, Rome conquered Gaul and Britain, establishing farms and founding new cities, and took Egypt, which had been ruled since the time of Alexander by a Greek-speaking dynasty, the Ptolemies. Roman rule stretched from North Africa to Gaul and from Syria to Britain. New cities were founded, and older Greek cities prospered under imperial authority. As the elite of aristocrats and entrepreneurs who dominated Rome under the emperors became increasingly wealthy, new luxuries, arriving from China and elsewhere in the East, found an eager market. Silk shocked Roman traditional-ists, who complained that dresses made from it were immodest. But it became fashionable nonetheless. Roman merchants began to look for larger supplies. Fleets sailed from Alexandria to the eastern Mediterranean. Other traders trav-eled down the Nile and across land to the Red Sea coast, from which point they could sail to India in search of silk and other goods.

Contacts between Rome and China were not direct. Intermediaries ruled the thousands of miles of territory between them. Alexander the Great's ex-pedition from Persia across Afghanistan and the Hindu Kush in the fourth century BCE did not extend his empire to the ends of the earth, as he may have hoped it would. But it transformed much of the world nonetheless. Alexan-der's conquest of Persia and looting of the immense royal treasury spread pre-cious materials through the known world, making possible the creation of more coined money than had ever existed before. His hard-fought journey to India and back proved in the most dramatic way possible that large numbers of people and animals could move from the Mediterranean to Asia. The Greek-speaking cities that he founded across central Asia and the spread of the Greek language and Greek styles in art and religion, finally, brought lands and peoples that had previously existed in separation into contact with one another—contact that became more intense and regular as his successors invested in massive port facilities that supported trade.

Other intermediaries, equally vital, worked on a more local level. In the first century BCE the Yuezhi, another nation of steppe-dwelling nomads, founded the Kushan Empire in Bactria and India. They created cities modeled, in their layout and architecture, on those of the Greek world. Trade generated new forms of settlement, and these, in turn, perpetuated the trade. Caravan routes developed, which came to dominate central Asian trade. They also sponsored the growth of what became a new brand of Buddhist religion: one centered on monasteries, gifts to which were strongly encouraged, and which soon col-lected massive endowments. Further west, the Nabateans—an Arab people who lived in northern Arabia and the Levant—engineered water systems that enabled them to settle in the desert. They built caravan cities, whose traders moved silk into Parthian and Roman territory, and ports. Though the Nabate-ans were conquered by the Romans, the wealth that trade generated for them enabled the creation of Petra, a city cut from the rocks of a gorge in Jordan. Sculpted façades deftly combined Greek and Roman architectural forms with local ones. By the third century the Sogdians—an Iranian people whose lands were centered on Samarkand, in modern Uzbekistan—were also actively engaged in commerce along the Silk Road. They set up trading zones everywhere from the Byzantine Empire to China itself, where they settled in large numbers. These and other nations created the aggregate of trading routes that made up the Silk Road.

Meanwhile a second set of trade routes developed—one that intersected with the first but involved maritime as well as overland trade. For centuries, the inhabitants of southern Arabia—Arabia Felix—had tapped trees that flourished in their desert habitat for aromatic resins like frankincense and myrrh—the gifts that the Magi, wise men from the East, bring to the baby Jesus in the Gospel of Matthew. Employed in the creation of incense, perfumes, and medicaments, the oil from these resins came to be valued from China to Greece. Traders who used camels as their beasts of burden (since they could cross the desert on their thickly padded feet and required far less water than horses) formed caravans to carry it to Parthia and Rome. The Nabateans and other intermediaries offered vital help and shelter. As Roman sailors based in Egypt mastered the prevailing winds of the Indian Ocean, they moved back and forth between East Africa and western India, where they could exchange these precious resins and other products for the even more precious spices made in India and beyond: pepper above all.

The silk and spice trades linked China, Rome, and many lands between in a complicated but effective system of exchanges, one that brought gold and silver, slaves, and other products from the lands to the west and exchanged them for pepper and incense as well as fine silks. These systems were supported more by self-interest and curiosity than government policy, more by traders cooperating than by formal institutions. Yet they proved flexible and resilient. As the western Roman Empire weakened after the fourth century, the new city founded by Constantine at the meeting point of Asia and Europe, New Rome (later Constantinople), turned into one of the great entrepôts for trade in luxury goods between the edges of the world. Even the Mongol invasions of the thirteenth century and after did not cut these trade routes, though they changed them in important ways. While the techniques used by traders and the sailors who transported their goods changed over time, these long-distance trade routes proved strikingly durable.

Information and its transmission were woven into these trade routes from the start. The Han emperor Wudi (147–87 BCE) called for an official to undertake an embassy to the Yuezhi, in the hope of allying with them against the Xiongnu. Only Zhang Qian, a minor official, proved willing. His embassy turned into an epic. It lasted for thirteen years, most of which he spent in captivity. He failed to make the treaty Wudi had sought. But he succeeded in something of much greater import in the long run. His reports, preserved in later Chinese histories, show that he was a sharp observer with an eye and ear for detail, who used his time in foreign lands to learn a great deal. He drew up crisp ethnographies, replete with information about resources, crops, and potential trading conditions.

> *An-si* [Parthia] may be several thousand *li* west of the Ta-yue-chi. The people live in fixed abodes and are given to agriculture; their fields yield rice and wheat; and they make wine of grapes. Their cities and towns are like those of Ta-yuan. Several hundred small and large cities belong to it. The territory is several thousand *li* square; it is a very large country and is close to the K'ui-shui [Oxus]. Their market folk and merchants travel in carts and boats to the neighboring countries, perhaps several thousand *li* distant. They make coins of silver; the coins resemble their king's face. Upon the death of a king the coins are changed for others on which the new king's face is represented. They paint [rows of characters] running sideways on [stiff] leather, to serve as records. West of this country is T'iau-chï; north is An-ts'ai.

One observation in particular reveals the quality of attention that Zhang Qian brought to observing everyday life: "When I was in Ta-hia [Bactria]," he told the king, "I saw there a stick of bamboo of Kiung [Kiung-chóu in Ssï-ch'uan] and some cloth of Shu [Ssï-ch'uan]. When I asked the inhabitants of Ta-hia how they had obtained possession of these, they replied: 'The inhabitants of our country buy them in Shon-tu [India].'" Wudi, impressed by the active trading systems and range of goods that Zhang Qian's report described, tried to follow his recommendation and forge routes to India and Bactria that did not pass through the lands controlled by the steppe nomads. This enterprise failed, but Wudi extended the northern wall far to the west and founded garrisons and trading posts. As trade expanded, the Chinese obtained Indian spices and cloth, Roman glass, and other exotic goods—as well as further knowledge about the kingdoms that produced them. Embassies also continued to be organized and dispatched. As Xin Wen has shown, they too formed networks that transported material gifts and useful knowledge across boundaries, often confronting great hardships. Information made the Silk Road.

It also traveled. Languages and knowledge of languages expanded. Chinese, for example, rapidly became a language of world trade. Trading centers became zones where several languages might be in use. Palmyra, for example, was a caravan oasis northeast of Damascus. Once Petra was conquered by Rome, Palmyra became a dominant node in the caravan routes that brought goods to and from the Persian Gulf. The city established garrisons and trading sites in other cities. Many Palmyrenes spoke Aramaic, the lingua franca of the eastern Mediterranean, and wrote it in a distinctive alphabet. Others used Arabic, and still others were conversant in Greek and the Iranian language of the Parthians. In Dunhuang, a city of some thirty thousand inhabitants near the border with Tibet, forty thousand surviving scrolls reveal that the languages used there included Tibetan, Sanskrit, Chinese, Sogdian—and, as attested by one scroll, Hebrew. In this small but cosmopolitan community, as Jacob Mikanowski has noted, "Buddhists rubbed shoulders with Manicheans, Christians, Zoroastrians, and Jews, and Chinese scribes copied Tibetan prayers that had been translated from Sanskrit by Indian monks working for Turkish khans."

Cultural practices and styles moved as far—and as erratically—as words, transmitted by the artisans who made them, by the products that embodied them, and, above all, by missionaries and other migrants. Palmyra was constructed as a magnificent Greek city. Its main trading street ran between immense colonnades built in three stages, more than a kilometer long, supported by several hundred Corinthian columns. At its core were an agora, a theater, and a senate house. The reliefs on the sarcophagi of its wealthy inhabitants showed them reclining, like Greeks, on couches and drinking from goblets. They were following the practices of the Greek symposium, a fundamental part of social life. Yet they dedicated their main temple to Bel, a Semitic god, and—unlike the cities of Hellenistic and Roman Egypt and Syria—never developed a local culture based on the Greek language; nor did they build the gymnasium that was as central to Greek cities as the agora was. Followers of Nestorius, a fifth-century theologian, carried Christianity all the way to China; fleeing condemnation by the church council of Ephesus in 431, they established a separate church in Persia. In 781, Nestorians described the history of their church in China in a long inscription on a stele in the inland city of Xi'an, which was both the terminus of the Silk Road and the capital of the ruling Tang dynasty. They told their story in Chinese and placed special emphasis on both the imperial favor that had allowed them to proselytize and the pursuit of perfection and purity, which they treated as the core of Christianity. Yet even they were no more skillful in portraying themselves in the languages of distinct cultures than the Sogdian officials in sixth-century Xi'an, whose families commemorated them with monuments in both Sogdian and Chinese, which emphasized completely different traits and accomplishments. It is often hard to know what a particular style of building or sculpture, hair or clothing, or a particular turn of phrase in a second or third language, meant to those who enthusiastically adopted them.

Technical information—especially about the goods traded on the silk and spice routes—traveled these roads as well. Surviving letters written by Sogdian traders in the fourth century offer little information about markets beyond brief lists of goods for sale in a particular locality. It seems that trade on the Asian silk routes was often relatively modest in scale, conducted by peddlers. But monks also traveled these routes, as we have seen, bringing elaborate scriptures and complex doctrines with them. Sometimes their packs may have included much more. In the middle of the sixth century, according to the Byzantine historian Procopius, "there came from India certain monks; and when they had satisfied Justinian Augustus that the Romans no longer should buy silk from the Persians, they promised the emperor in an interview that they would provide the materials for making silk so that never should the Romans seek business of this kind from their enemy the Persians, or from any other people whatsoever" (*History of the Wars* VIII.xvii.1–2). Justinian had long planned to cultivate silk, and archaeological evidence suggests that sericulture, like the fashion for silk garments, had spread from China over the centuries. Once the monks—or someone else—provided the silkworm eggs, the emperors made Byzantium a western center of silk manufacture, which remained an imperial monopoly. Brilliantly colored silks, stitched with gold designs, served for centuries to come as material for court garments and as gifts to foreign powers. Like the transfer of religions, the transfer of technologies was often encouraged by royal authority.

The trade routes that carried spices—and, eventually, silks—across the Indian Ocean and up the Red Sea were also polyglot and cosmopolitan. They carried the spices that gave food in Rome and medieval and *early modern Europe its sharp, varied flavors. At first, spices arrived with little cultural framework. The Roman natural historian Pliny, writing in the first century CE, complained that "pepper has nothing in it that can plead as a recommendation to either fruit or berry, its only desirable quality being a certain pungency; and yet it is for this that we import it all the way from India" (*Natural History* XII.xiv.29)—though even Pliny recommended it for many medicinal uses. The scale of the trade, at its height, was immense. A single ship, the *Hermapollon*, which sailed from India to Alexandria in the second century CE, carried more than 500 tons of pepper, as well as Gangetic nard, ivory tusks, and other goods. Over time, spices were discovered to have multiple preferred functions, as Greek and Arabic medical writers observed their effects. By the eleventh century, Constantine the African—a Muslim physician from Tunisia, steeped in the traditions of Arabic medicine, who ended his life as a Benedictine monk at Monte Cassino in Italy—revealed to readers in the Latin world that cloves, ginger, cinnamon, anise, and several other spices could remedy sexual impotence.

Those who traveled the long distances of the spice trade collected technical information, to an extent not documented for their counterparts in central Asian caravans. In the middle of the first century CE, a Greek-speaking merchant captain based in Egypt took the time to write down, in spoken rather than literary Greek, a record of the useful knowledge he had accumulated in his time as a trader. The *Periplus [Coasting Voyage] of the Erythraean Sea* is, first and foremost, a practical guide to navigation and trade. It moves from the Egyptian ports where the author was based south along the Red Sea. The author describes natural features, ports, and markets on the Horn and southeast coast of Africa, in Arabia, and in the Indian subcontinent. He also makes clear how dangerous expeditions across the oceans that separated them could be. A captain had to be in command not only of the prevailing winds, which carried ships across the Indian Ocean in both directions, but also of the challenging geography of many coasts: "To set a course along the coast of Arabia is altogether risky, since the region with its lack of harbors offers poor anchorage, is foul with rocky stretches, cannot be approached because of cliffs, and is fearsome in every respect." Even major ports could be dangerous. At Barygaza, a major entrepôt on the west coast of India, the tides "are much more extreme . . . than elsewhere." The flood tide, which was so powerful that it made the seafloor visible, overturned small ships and grounded larger ones on the shoals.

But the *Periplus* spends much more time on the opportunities for trade available in the "designated harbors"—the cities where established trade routes met and permanent markets flourished. To reach Barygaza from Egypt, one had to set sail in July. There one could sell wine from Italy, Laodicea, and Arabia; copper, tin, and lead; coral; and textiles and clothing; as well as silverware, unguent, and female slaves for the ruler. Exports included ivory, onyx, Chinese silk and silk yarn, and pepper, but "Roman money, gold and silver, which commands an exchange at some profit against the local currency," could also be traded. Passages like these make clear how rich and varied the major markets were: Barygaza served both the silk and the spice trades and many others. Such passages also reveal the striking range of knowledge a trader needed: mastery of exchange rates and knowledge of both valuable exports and desirable imports in multiple different trading zones.

Above all, the trader had to be able to make expert judgments of a vast range of goods. In the course of the *Periplus*, the author evaluates the quality of cloth, garments, nard, incense, tortoise shell, and slaves available in different markets. Evidently, he and his colleagues had to cultivate skilled eyes and hands in order to learn the preferred colors, weights, and textures of many forms of goods and to subject the goods offered them for sale to expert scrutiny. When Columbus interrogated the inhabitants of Cuba and scrutinized their ornaments and the plants they brought him, he was practicing skills and depending on knowledge developed long before in the silk and spice trades.

Traders were curious. In the course of their voyages, they learned something of the methods used to create the products they bought and sold. The *Periplus*, which devotes close attention to the "frankincense-breeding land" of Yemen and the resins produced there, describes their production in grim, unsparing detail: "The frankincense-bearing trees are neither very large nor tall: they give off frankincense in congealed form on the bark, just as some of the trees we have in Egypt exude gum. The frankincense is handled by royal slaves and convicts. For the districts are terribly unhealthy, harmful to those sailing by and absolutely fatal to those working there—who, moreover, die off easily because of the lack of nourishment." This is probably accurate. Even now the desert highlands where frankincense is harvested are forbidding, and those engaged in the harvesting are said to live ascetic lives while at work. Pearl diving in India, the *Periplus* notes, was also "carried out by convicts."

Occasionally, the text provides information that is not strictly practical. For example, it describes an Indian shrine: "men who wish to lead a holy life for the rest of their days remain there celibate; they come there and they perform ablutions. Women, too, do the same. For it is said that at one time the goddess remained here and performed ablutions." More often, the author reports information about inland markets and the trades performed there, which could derive from conversations in the port city markets he frequented rather than direct experience. For example, he describes the yearly fair held at the border between northeastern India and Tibet, attended by people whom he calls Sêsatai, who "come with their wives and children bearing great packs resembling mats of green leaves and then remain at some spot on the border between them and those on the Thina side, and they hold a festival for several days" and provide the locals with the materials for making malabathrum, balls of dried leaves from cinnamon-like plants, in three distinct grades. Officials and merchants from other societies had eyes as sharp as those of the author of the *Periplus*. In southern India, in the years when he was plying the Indian Ocean, a literary work recorded the striking presence at Arikamedu, near modern Pondicherry, of "abodes of [Romans], whose prosperity was never on the wane. On the harbor were to be seen sailors come from distant lands, but for all appearance they lived as one community."

Much remained unknown. The author of the *Periplus* broke off his account after describing the Tibetan fairs: "What lies beyond this area, because of extremes of storm, bitter cold, and difficult terrain, and also because of some divine power of the gods, has not been explored." He thought of China as a land to the north of India and mistakenly believed that the Greek kingdom of Bactria still existed in his time. Misinformation derived from tradition as well as from misunderstood experience. Ancient myths survived into modern collections of information. The monsters that Columbus expected to find in the Indies had first been described not by traders or soldiers but by Greek writers, Ctesias and Megasthenes, from whom a Roman authority on natural history and ethnography, the elder Pliny (d. 79 CE), took them over into his own compendium, the *Natural History*. Yet as Columbus's interest in them suggests, traders and sailors undoubtedly included such creatures, as well as information about winds and coasts, currencies and goods for sale, when they told tales and advised the young. To put the information that moved down these networks to practical use always required a critical mind and a quick wit.

Empire and Information: The Case of Rome

The description of the kingdom of Da Qin—possibly Rome—in the Chinese dynastic histories includes some striking details. Da Qin has four hundred walled towns and many dependent kingdoms. The walls are made of stone. More impressive still, "at regular intervals, it has built postal relay stations, which are all plastered and whitewashed." The king moves every day from one of his five palaces to another, giving justice, and "each palace has a staffed archive." In these passages at least, the kingdom in question sounds like Rome. It is a massive empire, a mosaic of towns and nations under the rule of a single monarch. And it makes provision—extensive provision—for receiving inquiries and pleas from the citizens of those lands and communicating its decisions to them. A postal service and a system of archives are both in place, to conserve and move the documents on which this kingdom seems to run. The Chinese— who built their own formidable road system and bureaucracy, which managed immense amounts of information—were naturally sensitive to these features of Roman life. But they were not the only observers to note the sheer mass of record keeping that Roman government required. A Jewish scholar who lived in the Babylonian town of Sura, under Roman rule, is reported to have made the same observation: "Rav said: Even if all the seas were ink, and the reeds were quills, and the heavens were parchment, and all the people were scribes; all these are insufficient to write the intricacies of governmental authority" (*Babylonian Talmud Shabbat* 11a). Chinese and Jewish observers were both right. Rome functioned as much by its systems of records and communication as by its armies and navies.

The Roman Empire—which grew, first through Italy and then, in the last century BCE and the first century CE, into Gaul, Egypt, England, and beyond—covered a staggeringly large and varied territory. At its height, according to the Stanford ORBIS project, which has created "a geospatial network model of the Roman world," it "ruled a quarter of humanity through complex networks of political power, military domination and economic exchange" that covered one-ninth of the world's surface. These vast land holdings were wrapped around an enormous inland sea. As Fernand Braudel, a pioneering historian of the Mediterranean, argued long ago, distance was the enemy: it constantly hindered the exertion of political power and military force in predictable time spans.

Rome's leaders fought distance from the start of the city's rise to power. They constructed a system of roads that eventually extended from the city of Rome east to Constantinople and then to Trebizond; to the west across Gaul to London and then to northern Britain, and across Iberia to Gades, at the entrance to the Mediterranean. Across from Gades, another road system began in Banasa, in what is now Morocco. This ran eastward, along the southern shore of the Mediterranean, to the Levant, and joined the northern system of roads in Syria. Republican magistrates had begun constructing the Italian part of the system, not only building roads but also lining them with milestones to mark distances. But the emperors built the great roads that connected the parts of the empire. The system consisted, at its peak, of 372 roads, more than 400,000 kilometers in total length. (By way of comparison, the American Interstate Highway System is 78,465 kilometers long.)

Though forms of paving varied, tens of thousands of kilometers were paved with cut blocks of stone or lava resting on layers of earth and rubble. Roads were cambered—made convex—so that water would run off into the drainage ditches that flanked them. Rows of curbstones held the layers of pavement in place. Oak pilings made it possible to build roads across marshy land. Stone bridges supported by piers carried roadways directly across rivers and valleys. The longest of these runs 2,437 meters. The section of it that spans the bed of the Danube is 1,137 meters long. Roads were built, largely, by the Roman armies, using the same engineering skills seen in their camps, pontoon bridges, and siege weapons, but slaves and prisoners of war were also conscripted to work on them. Once these vast projects had been completed, local magistrates were responsible for maintaining them from their own funds or by raising taxes. This system functioned well for centuries. Many of the roads survive to this day.

Roman roads were open to all: to the Roman military and officials, but also to merchants and ordinary citizens. From the start, though, they existed to carry information, as well as to project military power and support trade and travel. Suetonius, the biographer of the early Roman emperors, records that the first of them, Augustus, systematically reorganized the *cursus publicus*, or postal service: "First he set young men at reasonable intervals on the military roads, then he placed vehicles there, so that what was happening in each province could be known as swiftly as possible." He added the vehicles in order to receive and analyze important news as soon as possible: "This seemed the most convenient way, so that those who brought a letter from a given place could be questioned about it, if necessary" (*Life of Augustus* 49.3). When the system was complete, couriers (*tabellarii*) riding horses or post carts carried the news, changing horses at designated changing places (*mutationes*), ten to twenty kilometers apart. Full rest stops (*mansiones*), set a day's journey from one another, offered lodging, artisans, veterinary surgeons, and police, to support the couriers.

Imperial power also depended on travel by water. The empire included navigable rivers and canals that stretched some 28,000 kilometers, and its oceangoing ships followed hundreds of routes in the summer sailing season. Roman ships could carry substantial cargoes—up to three thousand amphoras, or 150 metric tons. Thanks to Rome's hold on the Mediterranean littoral and to its vast naval power, travel by ship was safe and, by historical standards, inexpensive. Emperors, accordingly, often chose to send crucial dispatches and instructions by ship. Fleets carried hundreds of thousands of tons of Egyptian grain to Pozzuoli in Campania: the philosopher Seneca describes the eager crowds, greeting the mailboats that arrived first and announced the coming of the larger fleet.

Imperial authority rested on this immense communications network. Political changes and military developments in, around, and outside the

Roman world had to be observed. Decrees, legislation, and verdicts that affected the empire's immense and scattered body of citizens and subjects had to be circulated. From the time of Julius Caesar, scribes prepared and posted the *Acta diurna*: an official record of important events. This began as a record of deliberations in the Senate and the assemblies of the people but expanded to include news of major bequests, prodigies of nature, and victories of gladiators. When Cicero was away from Rome, he followed events in the *Acta*, complaining that they contained too much trivial matter. He was not wrong. A century later, the emperor Caligula not only recorded good and bad ratings for the married women with whom he had sex but in some cases made out bills of divorce in their husbands' names and "ordered that they be inserted into the *Acta*" (Suetonius, *Life of Caligula* 36.2). Still, the *Acta* did much to make the operations of government visible, if not transparent.

Roman emperors did not provide, or promise to provide, much of what even an austere modern government might offer: public education for all, health care, security in old age. But they did need to maintain armed forces around the empire: soldiers had to be equipped and paid. Citizens of Rome, moreover, were entitled to "bread and circuses"—a ration of wheat and free entertainment. Citizens and subjects across the immense empire had to be taxed to cover this vast expense. Surviving documents from Egypt show that local officials kept careful registers of landownership, which noted the legal status and state of cultivation of each plot. *Coded marginal annotations—a single letter or a pen stroke—indicate that these records were consulted and used, though their exact meaning is unclear. When an official suspected that a given landowner was not paying a proper share, he could check the tax return in question against census records. The same officials also recorded troop movements and accommodations and ordered shipments of the materials they needed.

At a higher level, the imperial government in Rome regularly promulgated edicts, issued other official documents, and provided verdicts on legal cases appealed to the highest authority. Archives in Rome and in the provinces stored these documents. Requests for new copies regularly reached Rome and shed light on the procedures used to produce and validate them. In 39 BCE the city of Aphrodisias in Anatolia sent an ambassador to Rome, partly in order to obtain copies of four distinct documents. Octavian—not yet Augustus— replied, sending a letter to which the copies were attached. When the city government received the emperor's communication, it gave orders that both Octavian's reply and a senatorial decree should be recorded in public inscriptions.

The whole system required the employment of many scribes, as well as skilled artisans who could inscribe texts on stone or bronze tablets.

Given the distances between cities—and between the provinces and Rome—such documents had to bear clear signs of their authenticity. References to archival practices were common. Octavian, writing to Aphrodisias, noted that the copies he forwarded came "from the public records," and he expressed his "wish" that the citizens of Aphrodisias would "register them among your public records." Many surviving documents contain declarations that they were "copied and approved," or statements that "I have signed it. I have approved it"—presumably to be attributed, as Clifford Ando has shown, not to the emperors who appear as the authors of the decrees in question but to the scribes who copied them. Roman magistrates also took responsibility for making new legislation known to the empire's subjects. Gradually, uniform procedures developed. Even in the Republican period, the governors of the vast Roman provinces sent copies of decrees or instructions to all major cities, with orders that they be inscribed on stone pilasters "in the most conspicuous place, so that justice might be established for all time uniformly for all the province." Under the principate and empire, these became the norms for imperial decrees as well. Even matters not important enough to be preserved on stone had to be formally announced. A standard principle stated that no one could be held accountable to obey a new ordinance until it had been posted—normally in the form of a text on *papyrus or wood—for at least thirty days.

The empire, in short, built a sophisticated system for producing and distributing official documents—one whose vast Roman core was mirrored in part by local archives and workshops. Yet it would be wrong to imagine that this system embraced all the tasks of government. Around 110 CE, the emperor Trajan appointed the younger Pliny, the nephew of the natural historian, as governor of Bithynia in Asia Minor. Pliny repeatedly passed the buck, forwarding requests from the citizens of his province to the emperor: "It is my custom, Sire," he remarked, his tail wagging as he dictated his letter, "to refer to you in all cases where I am in doubt, for who can better clear up difficulties and inform me?" (*Letters* X.xcvi.1). Pliny would not give permission for Prusa to build a new bath or Nicomedia to create a fire department until he had asked Trajan's assent (which was forthcoming for the former, not for the latter). When he encountered followers of a new superstition, some of them denounced by informers, he reported in detail to the emperor. Pliny composed what remains the earliest description of a Christian service, which he confirmed by torturing two deaconesses: "they declared their guilt or error was simply this—on a fixed day they used to meet before dawn and recite a hymn among themselves to Christ, as though he were a god. So far from binding themselves by oath to commit any crime, they swore to keep from theft, robbery, adultery, breach of faith, and not to deny any trust money deposited with them when called upon to deliver it. This ceremony over, they used to depart and meet again to take food—but it was of no special character, and entirely harmless" (X.xcvi.7). What matters most about these letters, for our purposes, is the manner of their survival. The road system made it possible for the governor and the emperor to discuss official business, at the slow pace that distance required but still in detail, reflecting the granular, prosaic nature of everyday administrative work. These texts are cast in an economical, formulaic language, which enabled Pliny to report *facts, express his uncertainty about how to deal with difficult cases, and ask for advice. The emperor's replies include friendly if patronizing personal letters to his trusted governor and official rulings. "The correspondence between Pliny and Trajan," comments Kathleen M. Coleman, "lets us overhear two bureaucrats running the empire at an absolutely nuts-and-bolts level." But their surviving correspondence was not simply preserved—so far as we know—in an official archive. Pliny himself included it as the tenth book of his letters, which he may have collected and redacted from his own records, inserting the emperor's replies in the proper places, omitting many attachments mentioned in the texts, and deleting what he saw as superfluous or potentially awkward details. Some scholars have argued that Pliny assembled this collection, with Trajan's permission, to serve as a portrait of the empire in action. In this case—and in dozens of others—important documents were created and preserved in ways that suggest that important Romans saw them as their private property.

Information gathering in the empire as a whole, moreover, depended on multiple systems. The elder Pliny served the emperor Vespasian in multiple capacities. He died doing his job as prefect of the fleet, trying to rescue friends from the eruption of Mount Vesuvius—and to study it close up—in August 79 CE. He believed in seeing for himself. But in compiling his enormous *Natural History*, an *encyclopedic survey of the wonders of nature and art—especially those of the Roman Empire—he drew his information chiefly from written sources, which he listed. He probably worked from the immense notebooks full of excerpts that, the younger Pliny tells us, he assembled, using the help of enslaved scribes. Despite his official position, Pliny often compiled facts and traditions passed down in ordinary texts: for example, the descriptions of the monstrous races to be found in India. From Augustus on, Romans liked to suggest that they had conquered, and knew, the whole world. Yet Claudius Ptolemy, who folded thousands of place names and vast amounts of other information into the maps and text of his atlas, the *Geography*, in the second century CE, depended on written sources and his own conjectures for his knowledge of the Indian Ocean and seems to have had no access to military maps and itineraries, which often would have allowed him to correct his own work.

The efficiency and comprehensiveness of the Roman information state, in short, were anything but absolute. The entire corps of Roman officials numbered no more than thirty thousand to thirty-five thousand—just over a quarter as many as are employed by the US Department of Justice. Even the most important documents were not systematically classified and preserved. The first full collection of imperial edicts, the Theodosian Code, was not commissioned until 429 CE: it was promulgated nine years later. The Senate saw to it that carefully prepared official copies were dispatched to multiple archives. So far as its sources were concerned, though, it was a patchwork. The committee that composed it had to scour local as well as central archives, family papers, law school libraries, and other collections to find the texts of the emperors' proclaimed new laws. Transport of documents—though rapid by ancient standards—was often too slow and too unpredictable to have the desired effect. The last letter that the emperor Caligula sent to Publius Petronius, the governor of Syria, who had disobeyed what he thought an unreasonable command, threatened him with execution. Fortunately for Petronius, the Jewish historian Josephus explained, "It happened that the carriers of Caius [Caligula]'s letter were caught in a storm for three months on the ocean, while the others that brought the news of Caius's death had a good voyage. Accordingly, Petronius received the letter concerning Caius twenty-seven days before he received the one against himself" (*Jewish War* II.203).

Yet the system functioned for centuries. Early in the fourth century, Eusebius of Caesarea, a Christian bishop who had avoided martyrdom during the Great Persecution, wrote a triumphant history of the Christian Church. Later he would also write the life of the emperor Constantine, who had adopted the Christian God and religion. Both texts were unusual, because Eusebius filled them with documents quoted word for word—a violation of the normal conventions of narrative history in Greece and Rome. He drew them from both the archives of the more established Christian churches—especially those in Jerusalem, not far from him—and the official archives of the Roman Empire. Eusebius has been accused by more than one historian of passing off forgeries in the documents in his life of Constantine. Yet one of these has now turned up in an independent copy on papyrus, and current opinion is that it is genuine. In one case, Eusebius even stated that he was citing his text "from an authenticated copy of the imperial edict preserved in my possession, on which the personal subscription, by Constantine's right hand, signifies its testimony to the trustworthiness of my speech" (Eusebius, *Life of Constantine* II.23). Clifford Ando maintains that Eusebius saw himself as following Roman practice when he emphasized that his histories rested on authentic documents. And it is certain that he knew and used the imperial information system. When the emperor asked Eusebius to have his *scriptorium produce fifty large Bibles for the new churches of Constantinople, he sent the necessary *parchment—too much for even a rich bishop to provide—by the post carts of the *cursus publicus*. And when Eusebius himself compiled his work on the topography of Palestine, he drew on military records for the positions of towns and the directions of roads. No wonder that Chinese and Jewish observers, like Eusebius, found much to admire in Rome's imperial information culture.

In one respect, though, Eusebius's admiration was qualified. When he quoted his official copy of Constantine's letter, he explained that "I think it well to insert [it] here as connected with my present subject, in order . . . that a copy of this document may be recorded as matter of history, and thus preserved to posterity." The implicit point of this remark is clearly true. The archives that held the emperor's letters have disappeared, taking the vast majority of their contents with them. Yet Eusebius's literary work remains, attesting to the power of writing and the materials on which it is inscribed to preserve what governmental power could not.

Fragile Infrastructure: Paper

Writing materials, like trade, are ancient and varied. More than two thousand years ago, the Chinese were the first to realize that plant fibers, now known as cellulose, could be beaten, mixed with water, and then left on a screen to drain until a sheet of paper remained. This practical discovery changed the world. Millennia before anyone knew what cellulose was, papermakers separated it strand by strand from wood and silk, cotton and seaweed, and devised a writing material that is still cheaper and more adaptable than any other. The Chinese themselves had long since developed elaborate systems for incising their characters on bones and tortoiseshell, and for writing them with ink on strips of bamboo, as well as for inscribing them on bronze bells and cauldrons and on boulders. But paper rapidly showed its advantages. It could be created from different raw materials, from various plants to waste rags, and in many different forms and qualities. Brilliant white paper made from the bark of paper mulberry was used for the largest scrolls; bright green paper, perhaps from mulberry bark, for writing; white rattan paper for the Inner Chamber edicts of the Tang government. Paper could also be used for many purposes, from wiping the nose to doing the same for the rear—a use attested by the sixth century (for its later diffusion see Fitzgerald and Nappi, chap. 3).

Made from inexpensive materials, paper could be produced in sufficient quantities to be used for printing. For millennia the Chinese had used seals to make impressions of reverse images with ink. They also found paper useful for taking rubbings, for copies of reliefs, and inscriptions. By the beginning of the seventh century, carved woodblocks were in use to print images and characters on paper. During the Tang (618–906) and Song (960–1279) dynasties, woodblock printing became more widespread. At first it was used chiefly for practical works, such as medical texts and almanacs. By 868, a Chinese translation of the Diamond Sutra, a Buddhist text on the pursuit of perfection, had been printed. The only known copy of it, now in London, was found, appropriately, at Dunhuang. Over the centuries to come, wood-block printing would become the standard method for reproducing Chinese texts of every kind, from the classics and the commentaries on them to novels. At first, the government dominated production, but during the Song dynasty, commercial printers also appeared, competing to take over the market with what they and their editors described as critical editions, produced by comparing many versions of the classic texts, preserved in academy libraries. Though printing with movable metal type was also invented in China, in the eleventh century, wood-block printing, which was cheaper and made reprinting easy, remained the standard method. Printing moved from China to Korea and then to Japan. There too it sparked innovation. By the fourteenth century, Korean books were being printed with movable metal type.

"The Silk Road," as Lothar Müller observed, "was also a paper road." In the eighth and ninth centuries, Chinese paper texts bearing everything from inventories to short Buddhist scriptures traveled as far as the Caucasus Mountains, near the Black Sea. More important, the methods of papermaking also traveled. By the time the storeroom at Dunhuang was closed off, it contained thousands of documents, from astrological charts to scriptures: hundreds of them are written on paper. The new religion of Islam took shape—and its followers captured vast territories, from central Asia to Spain and Africa—in the seventh and eighth centuries. At first, Muslims used the writing materials that had been most common in the ancient Mediterranean. Scribes normally used parchment, the writing material made from the skins of sheep and calves, for the Quran. Egypt was the home of papyrus—the paper, made from reeds that grew in the Nile, that had been the standard writing material for ancient Greece as well as Egypt. It found use in bureaucratic documents, as the new government grew.

But paper had much to offer the followers of Islam. The Chinese had already found that rags, as well as bark, could be turned into paper. In central Asia and beyond, mulberry bark was not available. But used clothing and cordage were. As great new cities took shape at Baghdad, Damascus, and elsewhere, paper mills were created. They took advantage of a ready-made wealth of raw material. Cheaper than parchment, which depended on the availability of livestock and required intensive preparation, more flexible and durable than papyrus, paper could be used for many purposes. The fifteenth-century historian Ibn Khaldūn explained that a vizier who had served the caliph Hārūn al-Rashīd, eight hundred years before, sponsored the manufacture of paper in Baghdad because parchment was in short supply. His decision, Ibn Khaldūn held, had transformed politics and culture: "paper was used for government documents and diplomas. Afterwards, people used paper in sheets for government and scholarly writings, and the manufacture [of paper] reached a considerable degree of excellence."

Gradually paper did become the writing material of choice, for the Quran and other texts as well as for government registers and inventories. Paper mills spread across the Islamic world, all the way to Iberia. New techniques were developed. Rags had to be beaten before they could be spread across the racks to form paper. The mills of Samarkand, in modern Uzbekistan, used water to power mechanical hammers, known in the West as stampers, to carry out this part of the process.

The ready availability of paper, as Jonathan Bloom has shown, transformed possibilities in many fields. Though the Quran always remained as much an oral as a written text, meant for recitation, a world of commentaries and further traditions grew up alongside it, recorded—like the Quran itself—on paper. Another vast world of philosophy and *philology, based on translations from Greek into Syriac and from Syriac into Arabic, grew up in fields from medicine to metaphysics. Imaginative writers began to rework stories and fables into works on a grander and more elaborate scale—like the *Thousand and One Nights*, the title of which appears on one of the earliest Arabic documents to survive, a ninth-century fragment preserved in Chicago.

Muslims learned to compute, using Arabic numerals, with pen and ink on paper rather than an abacus or dust board. Cartographers who revived and expanded the techniques inherited from the Greek and Roman world made their maps on paper. Architects used paper to draw up formal plans for buildings. Paper, the nomadic medium, provided essential aid to societies that were remaking themselves in the pursuit of many forms of knowledge. It made possible the founding of libraries from Damascus to the Abbasid *"House of Wisdom" in Baghdad and the tenth-century library of Caliph al-Ḥakam II al-Mustanṣir in Cordoba, and the flourishing of book markets like the one that Ibn Baṭṭūṭa found in fourteenth-century Damascus, near the great Umayyad Mosque, and the one in Istanbul, still the largest in the Mediterranean world in the seventeenth century (see Muhanna, chap. 2). On a more basic level, it provided vital infrastructure for the growth of the trade networks documented by the thousands of letters and contracts, court documents, and pilgrim records, fragments of which were stored in the Cairo Genizah, the storeroom of the Ben Ezra Synagogue in Old Cairo—networks that stretched from Morocco to India.

Paper mills were not altogether good neighbors. They were noisy; they processed vast piles of dirty rags, collected by male and female ragpickers; and they stank of ammonia, often derived from human urine, which was used to break down the rags' fibers. Neighbors hated them. Yet their workers developed extraordinary skills, working "so quickly and with such agility that you can scarcely see their hands." More important, they produced something mysteriously strong and beautiful. As an observer wrote on visiting a paper mill in seventeenth-century Genoa: "the way paper is made is a marvelous thing, because, as we have said, the materials from which it is made are merely rags and water, which have no viscous or resistant qualities, and yet the sheets of paper made from them have such consistency that they are better than cloth."

Some early reactions to paper in Christian Europe were negative. Peter the Venerable complained around 1144 that Jews wrote on a material made not, as it should be, from animal skins, but from "scraps of old rags or even viler stuff." A century later Emperor Frederick II forbade its use in official records. Others, however, adopted it eagerly. Once King Jaume the Conqueror had fought his way to mastery of the Iberian coastal realm that he called the kingdom of Valencia, his government produced thousands of documents. More than ten thousand of them, written between 1257 and 1276, are now preserved in twenty-nine immense volumes. From the start he issued charters in paper as well as parchment, to Christians as well as Muslims, using the products of the Muslim paper mill at Játiva and then establishing his own mill. Soon paper mills opened in southern France and in Fabriano in the Italian Marches, where wire molds produced paper with handsome surface patterns and distinctive watermarks.

Innovation never stopped. European technology for making scissors improved in the fourteenth century, making it possible to cut the rags that went into paper more evenly. So did methods for wire drawing, which enabled papermakers to make finer sieves than ever before, with which they could produce an absolutely smooth form of paper. European papermakers devised a way to size paper with gelatin, giving it a smooth surface that was impervious to ink and resisted abrasion and soiling. Many grades of paper were available. When the Nuremberg printer Johannes Petreius was trying to convince Erasmus Reinhold to publish with him, he promised that his work would appear on "fine crown paper." Early printers used parchment for deluxe copies of particular books. But Vincenzo Conti, who owned the press at Cremona, did not need to have animals skinned when he brought out the first three-volume edition of the *Zohar*, the core text of the kabbalah from 1558 to 1560. Instead he followed a precedent set by Aldus Manutius and later applied to Jewish texts by Daniel Bomberg and used a rich blue paper for some copies.

By the fourteenth century, paper played a substantial role in book production in the Latin West. Most authors preferred parchment, especially for the fine presentation copies of their works destined for patrons. Some thirty extant documents contain Petrarch's handwriting. Only two are on paper. A generation later, Christine de Pizan still chose parchment for the splendid *illuminated copies of her French writings. In them she herself appeared, wielding the penknife with which she would have both sharpened her quill and scraped away slips of the pen. But secular scribal work was expanding, in city governments and state bureaucracies. *Vernacular literature of all kinds was being written and copied. The Latin literature of the humanists was also finding a larger market. Several of the translations and treatises of the most popular fifteenth-century humanist, Leonardo Bruni, are preserved in two or three hundred manuscript copies each, all, or all but a handful, written on paper. Paper production grew to meet the need, and more—so much so that it began to dominate the Muslim as well as the Christian market. In 1409 a worried client asked the Maghrebi jurist Ibn Marzūq for a formal opinion on whether a devout Muslim could use Christian paper—particularly Christian paper with a watermark that might include Christian symbols—for the Quran and other texts. In an elaborate fatwa, Ibn Marzūq argued that one could. The holy text, after all, transformed the mere medium that held it.

Paper made possible the rise of movable-type printing in Europe in the fifteenth century, which is treated in detail below (Blair, chap. 4). But it made other developments possible as well. A vast expansion of writing took place at the same time as printing, which became the dominant form of publication. Even as printers filled the world with books, governments invested in vast new paper management systems, diplomats filed endless reports in cipher, impresarios produced handwritten newsletters for select clients, and scholars devoted their lives to filling notebooks with excerpts taken from the vast production of the presses and systematically classified. The age of Gutenberg was also the age of the "paper king," Philip II of Spain, who took to signing documents with a stamp and waved them around at meetings like a *Renaissance Joseph McCarthy (Head, chap. 6).

It seems completely appropriate that Columbus, trying to understand what he was seeing in the Indies, used pen and paper as his tools. In this as in other ways, he was the heir of generations of travelers and traders, missionaries and skippers. Some of their ways would soon be transformed beyond recognition. Others continued to rest on foundations laid long before and far away.

Further Reading

Clifford Ando, *Imperial Ideology and Provincial Loyalty in the Roman Empire*, 2000; Timothy Barrett, "Early European Papers/Contemporary Conservation Papers," *Paper Conservator* 13 (1989): 1–108; Jonathan Bloom, *Paper before Print: The History and Impact of Paper in the Islamic World*, 2001; Fernand Braudel, *The Mediterranean and the Mediterranean World in the Age of Philip II*, 1949, translated by Siân Reynolds, 1973; Socha Carey, *Pliny's Catalogue of Culture: Art and Empire in the "Natural History,"* 2003; Kathleen M. Coleman, "Bureaucratic Language in the Correspondence between Pliny and Trajan," *Transactions of the American Philological Association* 142, no. 2 (2012): 189–238; Federico De Romanis, *The Indo-Roman Pepper Trade and the Muziris Papyrus*, 2020; Paul Freedman, *Out of the East: Spices and the Medieval Imagination*, 2008; Anthony Grafton and Megan Williams, *Christianity and the Transformation of the Book: Origen, Eusebius and the Library of Caesarea*, 2006; Valerie Hansen, *The Silk Road: A New History with Documents*, 2017; Friedrich Hirth, "The Story of Chang K'ien, China's Pioneer in Western Asia," *Journal of the American Oriental Society* 37 (1919): 89–152; Christopher Kelly, *Ruling the Later Roman Empire*, 2004; Xinrue Liu, *The Silk Road in World History*, 2010; John Matthews, *Laying Down the Law: A Study of the Theodosian Code*, 2000; Jacob Mikanowski, "A Secret Library, Digitally Excavated," *New Yorker*, October 9, 2023; Lothar Müller, *White Magic: The Age of Paper*, 2012, translated by Jessica Spengler, 2014; Walter Scheidel, "ORBIS; The Stanford Geospatial Network Model of the Roman World" (online); Romolo Augusto Staccioli, *The Roads of the Romans*, 2003; Xin Wen, *The King's Road: Diplomacy and the Remaking of the Silk Road*, 2022; Frances Wood, *The Silk Road: Two Thousand Years in the Heart of Asia*, 2002.

2

Realms of Information in the Medieval Islamic World

Elias Muhanna

THIS CHAPTER CONSIDERS THE HISTORY of information in the medieval Islamic world. First, a few remarks about the words *information* and *Islamic* are necessary. The diverse readings of the concept of information found in this volume testify to the difficulty of saying what it is, particularly outside the context of the information age. Scholars of historical civilizations are accustomed to thinking about the development of intellectual disciplines, scribal traditions, educational institutions, and other subjects related to the history of knowledge. But what about information? Are knowledge and information the same thing? Some have drawn on a familiar metaphor from structuralist anthropology to distinguish between the two concepts, suggesting that information is "raw" while knowledge is "cooked." Others describe information as free-floating and value-neutral, and knowledge as holistic and rooted within a particular *epistemological regime. Information is often said to be "harvested" or "gathered" while knowledge is "produced." Are these meaningful distinctions, or has knowledge been information all along?

In Classical Arabic and Persian, the literary languages of the contexts I will be exploring, a distinction is detectable between terms associated with knowledge (Arabic: *'ilm, ma'rifa, ḥikma*; Persian: *dānist, dānish, ma'rifat*), and a rich stock of words denoting a class of entities that, while related to knowledge, aren't quite the same thing. An important term in this regard is *khabar* (pl. *akhbār*), which Lane's *Arabic-English Lexicon* defines as "*a piece of information; a notification; intelligence; an announcement; news; tidings . . . what is related from*

24

another or others: to which authors on the Arabic language add, that it may be *true* or *false*." *Akhbār* is the stock-in-trade of historians; many chronicles have the word in their titles. Like information, a *khabar* may be disseminated, investigated, circulated, published, and suppressed. It can be scrutinized, falsified, deemed unreliable, taken out of context, or colored by bias, and it is sought out through reading and research (*muṭālaʿa*) or interrogation (*istifsār*). Information of this kind is often granular, described as a small particle, portion, or trace (*luṭkha, nubdha, athar*), and may take different shapes: a narrative (*riwāya*), an announcement (*nabaʾ*), or a strange report (*ṭurfa*).

Many of these Arabic terms are also found in Persian, where the word *khabar* is connected with a wide array of professions, from scholars to explorers, investigators, spies, historians, informers, and scouts. The methods of acquiring information are strongly associated with the five senses, reflected in the Persian word for "ear" (*gosh*), which may refer figuratively to a spy, sentinel (*goshchī*), rumor (*gosh-zad*); and "tongue" (*zabān*), which is connected with the act of taking a prisoner to gain information (*zabān giriftan*) about an enemy. Perhaps the most common word for spy in Arabic, Persian, and Turkish—*jāsūs*—derives from the Arabic verb *jassa* (to touch, feel, take the pulse of). All this is to say that while *information* is a term that has certainly been reshaped by developments in digital technology since the middle of the twentieth century, there is no shortage of concepts from medieval Islamicate languages pointing to a category that looks quite a bit like "information," in the looser sense of "reports supposed to be truthful or useful that could be spread in various media," as Ann Blair has written. This is the sense I will be using in this chapter.

So much for information—what about *Islamic*? A history of information in the medieval Islamic world is difficult to imagine in light of the great diversity of peoples, cultures, and languages encompassed by that term. It would include more than a millennium's worth of attitudes, artifacts, and practices across a large part of the earth, from Indian tax records and Syrian cookbooks to the teaching circles of medieval Fes and the libraries of Mamluk Cairo. In other words, too much information. How to go about synthesizing it into knowledge? And why would such an exercise be useful? I propose to address these questions by introducing some of the most important tokens of the creation, circulation, transmission, authentication, and interpretation of information in three historical contexts: ninth- and tenth-century Iraq, the heart of the Abbasid Empire; fourteenth-century Egypt and Syria, which were ruled by the Mamluk sultanate; and Timurid Iran and Khorasan in the fifteenth century. A history of information in just one of these contexts would fill an entire book. This discussion is, therefore, necessarily macroscopic and intended as a survey as well as an attempt to rethink the history of knowledge through the lens of information.

Iraq, Ninth and Tenth Centuries

In the late ninth century the city of Baghdad was a hundred years old, the capital of an empire that stretched from North Africa to Transoxania. Never again would a single Islamic polity exert its dominion—however tenuously in some territories—across such a wide span of the globe. When people today speak of the golden age of Islamic civilization, many have Abbasid Baghdad in mind, a glorious city inhabited by scientists, translators, poets, musicians, and philosophers. The stories of its rulers and their courts, their soirees filled with learned and witty conversation, would be told in the literature and lore of the Islamic world for centuries.

According to some early accounts of the city's founding, the specific time and place chosen for Baghdad's creation were decided by information. An ancient prophecy foretelling that the caliph al-Manṣūr would erect a great city on the banks of the Tigris was found in a Christian text. A Persian astrologer in al-Manṣūr's court cast a horoscope establishing that July 30, 762, was an opportune moment to commence work on the foundation. Alongside astrological information and prophecies, geopolitical concerns played a deciding role. The new city sat on a fertile plain where the Tigris and Euphrates Rivers were only thirty kilometers apart. Baghdad was positioned more centrally than the old Umayyad capital at Damascus with respect to the empire's expansion into Iran and central Asia. It sat along the road to Khorasan, serving as a way station for caravans from the East traveling to the Levant and Egypt, and for pilgrims making their way to Mecca for the annual hajj pilgrimage. In this respect, Baghdad was a place to and from which many things flowed: people, commodities, and information. The book markets of the city, like its palaces and gardens, would become proverbial in Islamic history. Before visiting them, it is worth considering the backdrop of Baghdad's bookish culture. Both before and after the arrival of paper in the eighth century, the world of information was profoundly shaped by knowledge practices rooted in orality.

Orality and Information

The origins of all the major disciplines of Islamic thought are connected to orality in some way, none so firmly as the area of prophetic tradition (hadith). In the years after the death of the Prophet Muḥammad in 632 CE, there emerged a large body of tradition about his biography. This took many shapes: narratives about his political career following the revelation of the Quran, details of his ethical views, anecdotes about his dealings with different groups of people, and general data about his life. Insofar as the Quran did not provide answers to every practical, legal, or theological question that medieval Muslims would meditate on in the centuries after the revelation, the traditions about Muḥammad's life and customs, as well as those of his closest companions, acquired tremendous significance.

At first, these traditions, like the Quranic revelations, circulated almost exclusively in oral form. Muḥammad's companions were the keepers of this data, but as they relayed it to their own disciples and followers in the growing Muslim community, the population of transmitters grew larger, as did the number of utterances and actions attributed to Muḥammad. By the ninth century, a *canon of authoritative selections was beginning to emerge in the form of respected compendia compiled by traditionists. Relying on a sophisticated methodology of authentication through the use of the isnād—or chain of transmitters—compilers like Muḥammad ibn Ismāʿil al-Bukhārī pulled together the hadiths that merited special status on the basis of the trustworthiness of their transmitters. This mode of authenticating information was initially associated with the hadith literature, but it would have an important impact on other forms of knowledge transmission throughout the Islamic world.

Even as the methodology for certifying the trustworthiness of information about the Prophet became more robust, the traditions that were deemed suspect (or even confirmed as forgeries) were not universally discarded. Many continued to be recorded and transmitted. Some scholars became specialists in compiling hadiths known to be problematic or abrogated by other, more reliable reports, as well as hadiths that were authenticated by only a single chain of transmission. This practice of preserving information even while recording its abrogation had parallels in the study of the Quran. The concept of abrogation (naskh) is one of the most important principles in Quranic *exegesis and Islamic legal theory. It offered to the exegete a way to harmonize and explain contradictions, inconsistencies, and ambiguities that emerged from the study of the Quran and the hadith canon, particularly when such problematic elements bore on legal issues.

In its most common form, the ruling expressed in one Quranic verse could be overruled or superseded by the ruling in a different verse. Such an approach to the Quran renders it a kind of divine *palimpsest, overwriting itself while continuing to preserve the abrogated verses. Sanction for a theory of abrogation comes from the Quran itself (Q 2:106, "And for whatever verse We abrogate [*nansakh*] or cast into oblivion, We bring a better or the like of it"). The verb *nasakha* has several meanings, among them: to obliterate, abandon, replace, nullify, erase, copy, transfer, and others. In interpreting Q2:106, the medieval exegetes explained the word *nansakh* in terms of either suppression or supersession. For the first meaning, scholars referred to Q13:39 ("God blots out and establishes what He pleases, and with Him is the Mother of the Book"), which suggests that God can (and does) erase or suppress parts of the Quran for unknown reasons. For the second meaning, the relevant verse adduced was Q16:101 ("When We replace one verse with another"), which suggests a process of divine "editing" or supersession within the revelation history of the Quran. These two processes are central to the history of Quran's reception in the medieval Islamic world and reveal how self-consciously preoccupied with issues of authentication, contradiction, and supersession Muslim learned cultures have been throughout history.

What were some of the other emerging disciplines influenced by the oral lifeworld of ninth-century Iraq? Even as the empire was becoming more ethnically and linguistically heterogeneous, there remained tremendous cachet associated with the Arabic language and the poetry of the pre-Islamic Bedouin tribes, who were thought to speak the purest and most eloquent form of the language. Beginning in the eighth century, *philologists from the emerging grammatical schools of Kufa and Basra began to systematize Classical Arabic. The medieval sources report that individuals like Sībawayh, a scholar of Persian extraction and the author of the first grammar of Arabic, *al-Kitāb* (The book), would go out into the desert and spend time with the Bedouins, observing their speech patterns and asking them questions about unusual expressions and rare words. The results of these exploratory missions found their way into grammars, word lists, dictionaries, and other philological texts. The earliest scholars of poetry built their corpora in similar ways, collecting their data—individual verses, fragments, and entire poems—from the mouths of tribal poets. The Arabic word for poetic criticism (*naqd*) derives from the idea of assaying currency to determine its authenticity. This is to say that the act of criticism was, from the start, concerned with determining the authenticity of poetic information.

The codification of Classical Arabic on the basis of what we might call today a form of ethnolinguistic dialectology would serve an infrastructural purpose for the apparatus of learned culture in the Islamic world for over a thousand years. Besides standardizing what would become one of the world's great cosmopolitan languages, the work of philology played an elemental role in a major cultural project: the exegesis of the Quran. The urban environments of Baghdad, Kufa, Basra, and Mosul were far removed from the Meccan setting in which the Quran had been revealed two centuries earlier, and the context for making sense of many of the Quran's references and its allusively evocative language was increasingly remote. As such, the ninth century witnessed the composition of some of the most influential works of exegesis (*tafsīr*) in Islamic history, none more important than Muḥammad ibn Jarīr al-Ṭabarī's thirty-volume work. The scholarship of al-Ṭabarī, a Persian *polymath who also authored the ninth century's most significant chronicle, the forty-volume *History of the Prophets and Kings* (*Tarīkh al-rusul wa-l-mulūk*), is an example of how different streams of information flowed together in the work of interpreting the Quran. Al-Ṭabarī's commentary brought together narratives of tribal exploits, linguistic analysis, accounts of prophetic history, and traditions about Muḥammad's life, all by way of stitching together the backdrop for the revelatory material.

A Well-Rounded Education

Al-Ṭabarī was in a class of his own in terms of the significance of his monumental works of history and exegesis, but ninth-century Baghdad was full of polymaths. The Abbasid Empire's secretarial class abounded in individuals well versed in a variety of disciplines, a quality seen as necessary for the duties of a scribal bureaucrat. A famous description of this many-sided competence is found in a manual on secretaryship by Ibn Qutayba, another ninth-century polymath:

> The Persians always used to say, "He who is not knowledgeable about diverting water into channels, digging out courses for irrigation streams and blocking up disused well-shafts; about the changes in the length of the days as they increase and decrease, the revolution of the sun, the rising-places of the stars and the state of the new moon as it begins to wax, and its subsequent phases; about the various weights in use; about the measurement of triangles, four-sided figures and polygons; about the construction of bridges and aqueducts, irrigation machines and water wheels; and about the materials used by various artisans, and the fine points of financial accounting—such a person must be considered only partly-qualified as a secretary." (Bosworth, "Pioneer")

Descriptions like this are plentiful in the historical sources, and while they smack of hyperbole and self-aggrandizement—after all, many of the authors of such descriptions were scribes themselves—there are a few important things to note in the description. One is the Persian connection: the secretarial tradition of the new Islamic empire was strongly shaped by the bureaucratic cultures of earlier polities. Under the Umayyads, who ruled from Damascus, many of the scribal families had come from the Byzantine Empire and brought with them a knowledge of Greek, Aramaic, and other languages of the Levant. In Iraq, most of the scribal elite had Persian ancestry, descending from families who had served the Sasanian Empire. This intermixing of cultures had an effect on the texts that circulated in the growing cities of Iraq. The ideal of encyclopedic education represented in Ibn Qutayba's description would, over time, come to apply to the materials of that education rather than just the ideal itself. The notion of *adab*—a term that means "good breeding," "good manners," a well-rounded education—emerged during this time as the name of a bibliographic *genre: an umbrella category that included poetry, belletristic prose narratives and reports about important historical figures, quotations from scripture and the hadith literature, proverbs, rare words and other lexicographical oddities, and materia medica (i.e., ingredients of medical recipes). One of the most important works in this genre, *Choice Reports* (*ʿUyūn al-akhbār*), was written by Ibn Qutayba himself and launched a tradition of adab *encyclopedias that aimed to provide an overview of the topics that any aspirant to a certain status of cultural literacy would be expected to know. *Choice Reports* contained ten chapters on the topics of sovereignty, war, governance, traits and morals, knowledge, piety, friends, achieving one's ends, food, and women. A few decades later, *The Unique Necklace* (*al-ʿIqd al-farīd*) of the Andalusian courtier and poet Ibn ʿAbd Rabbih (d. 328/940) had swelled to nearly twice the length of the *Choice Reports*. Following in the footsteps of these two foundational texts, adab encyclopedias proliferated throughout the Islamic world.

Classifying the Sciences

The explosion of books in the ninth century created a familiar problem: How to organize all this information? One solution took the shape of yet another bibliographical category, books on the classification of the sciences. Less voluminous than the adab encyclopedias, these texts included curricula of the disciplines like al-Fārābī's *Enumeration of the Sciences* (*Iḥṣāʾ al-ʿulūm*), dictionaries of technical terms such as al-Khwārizmī's *Keys of the Sciences* (*Mafātīḥ al-ʿulūm*), and programs for the integration of the rational and religious sciences, such as Abū ʿAlī Miskawayh's *The Classification of the Sciences and the Classification of Happiness* (*Tartīb al-ʿulūm wa-tartīb al-saʿādāt*). These works were the outcome of a larger process of consolidation that many disciplines would undergo, reflected in the growing conventionality of book arrangements, page layouts, tables of contents, and titles, and of generic categories. By this time, a canon was beginning to emerge in different disciplines, with respected oral authorities being replaced by textual sources. The textualization of information meant, among other things, that it could travel to places it hadn't before. Scholars with the means to devote all their time to study and teaching often moved from one city to another with their books. In their new homes, surrounded by new students, these books would serve as the progenitors of new textual seedlings, as the students copied texts from exemplar manuscripts. The oral tradition, however, never died away. Even in this new textualized form, remnants of the memory-based transmission of information persisted in the mechanisms by which information was passed along. Students earned the right to copy a text by reading it aloud to their master to ensure that there were no flaws in the process of copying. Once a perfect copy had been made, the student would receive a certificate (*ijāza*) to make additional copies of the text. This process of certification represented an essential mechanism for authenticating textualized information in the premodern Islamic world. It would last for centuries and was used in the madrasas of Pakistan and the Sufi lodges of Marrakesh.

One of the most important encyclopedic works produced in tenth-century Iraq was *The Epistles of the Sincere Brethren* (*Rasāʾil Ikhwān al-Ṣafāʾ*), a collection of letters on various philosophical themes including the "mathematical sciences," the "corporeal and natural sciences," the "sciences of the soul and of the intellect," and the "nomic, divine, and legal sciences." Who were the Sincere Brethren? The identity of this collective remains relatively obscure, but scholars believe that they were a group of Ismāʿīlī Shīʿī figures interested in Neoplatonic and Neopythagorean thought, with influences from other traditions such as Gnosticism and Hermeticism. Although the *Epistles* circulated widely, they did not exert much influence on the future of the philosophical encyclopedic tradition, which was dominated by Ibn Sīnā (d. 449/1037, also known as Avicenna) and his commentators. However, as we will see later in this chapter, the career of the Sincere Brethren would inspire other clandestine intellectual networks in the Turko-Persianate world.

Besides codicological means of consolidating knowledge, this era witnessed another important phenomenon: the emergence of knowledge practices concerned with the theoretical underpinnings of other disciplines. Characterized by the term *principles* or *origins* (*uṣūl*) in their titles, these fields sought to uncover the elemental assumptions and logical processes that lay at the basis of disciplines like grammar (*naḥw*), jurisprudence (*fiqh*), and lexicography (*lugha*). Today, we refer to information about information by the term *metadata*; by this token, one might call these knowledge practices *metadisciplines*. They sought to make sense of how disciplines operated and how they thought about their constitutive data.

The Paper Revolution

The transition from a culture in which information was transmitted orally to a written ecosystem was aided by the appearance of a revolutionary technology in the Islamic lands. Paper first arrived in Iraq in the eighth century, having been unknown in the lands governed by the Sasanian and Byzantine Empires before the rise of Islam. Prior to that, other materials had been used for record keeping. The Arabic word for account book, *daftar*, is derived from the Greek word *diphthera*, meaning "skin, hide," pointing to the practice of using prepared animal skins (parchment) as well as *papyrus for bureaucratic accounting. A paper mill was built in Baghdad in 794–95 CE, during the reign of the caliph Hārūn al-Rashīd, and paper began to replace more costly writing surfaces. Some reports suggest that the use of paper in al-Rashīd's administration was both a matter of cost savings and a safeguard against forgery, as writing on paper was more difficult to erase or scratch out than texts on parchment. From Iraq, paper would travel swiftly across the Islamic empire, reaching Spain within two hundred years of its discovery in central Asia.

The market for books in Baghdad meant that there was always a demand for the trade of the copyist (*warrāq*), who made copies of manuscripts that were in demand and sold them. The most famous bookseller in Islamic history was one such copyist: Abu l-Faraj Muḥammad ibn Isḥāq, known as al-Nadīm. Born in the first half of the tenth century in Baghdad, al-Nadīm was introduced to the trade at a young age. He traveled across Iraq, studying with notable teachers and frequenting the court circle of one of the grandees of the Abbasid Empire. His travels brought him to libraries and book markets, exposing him to the contours of the growing ocean of books. By way of mapping this ocean, al-Nadīm composed a work entitled *The Index* (*al-Fihrist*), a bibliographic compendium divided into ten chapters, cataloging all the Arabic books that he had come across during his travels. The chapters were organized thematically. The first six addressed subjects related to what were already, by then, considered to be the "traditional" subjects of the Arabic-speaking world (holy scriptures, grammar, historical works, genealogy, and belletristic prose, poetry, theology, and law). The last four chapters took up books translated from the "foreign" (mainly Greek) sciences, on subjects like philosophy, magic, fables, storytelling, syncretistic religions, and alchemy.

Al-Nadīm's *Index* provides an invaluable window into the culture of book-making in the tenth century, and also a sense of its bibliographic categories. He includes information about the length of books and their authors, and reports about well-known libraries and patrons of letters. The *Index* also provides rare insight into one of the most famous libraries in history, the *House of Wisdom (Bayt al-Ḥikma), an institution connected with the early Abbasid caliphs al-Rashīd and al-Ma'mūn. The House of Wisdom was a palace library staffed mainly by officials of Iranian descent, responsible for collecting books about Persian heritage and ancient Arabian lore. Among its holdings, al-Nadīm records, were old manuscripts written in different scripts and a book believed to be in the hand of Muḥammad's grandfather, ʿAbd al-Muṭṭalib ibn Hāshim. Al-Nadīm also mentions that some of the employees of the House of Wisdom were engaged in translating Persian books into Arabic. This report, along with another that connects the library's director, Salm, with a translation of Ptolemy's *Almagest*, fed the supposition among many scholars during the twentieth century that the House of Wisdom was a kind of research academy, the hub of a caliphate-sponsored project to translate Greek scientific and philosophical texts into Arabic. Recent scholarship has corrected that view; the name of the library was likely a translation of the Middle Persian term used for the palace libraries of the Sasanian empire of Iran, reflecting the influence of the bureaucratic traditions of Iran on the new Islamic empire.

The Abbasid translation movement was a watershed in the history of information. As Dimitri Gutas has written, "One can justly claim that the study of post-classical Greek secular writings can hardly proceed without the evidence in Arabic, which in this context becomes the second classical language, even before Latin." Beginning in the mid-eighth century, during the reign of al-Manṣūr, the builder of Baghdad, and reaching its apogee in the ninth century, the campaign to translate works of philosophy, medicine, mathematics, geometry, and other disciplines from Greek, Syriac, and Pahlavi would have a great impact on the transmission of these sciences throughout the Islamic world and into medieval Europe. The question of why translation was an imperial policy of the Abbasids is one that would require too much space to explore here, but, as we have already seen in the excerpt from Ibn Qutayba's manual on secretaryship, the benefits of astrology, geometry, arithmetic, and other sciences to the practice of statecraft are readily apparent. It is important to stress that this movement, which lasted more than two centuries, was supported not just by the political elite of Abbasid society but also by its scholars, bureaucrats, and merchants. It was a widespread cultural project that cut across different confessional, ethnic, and class lines.

During the ninth century, the most famous figure associated with the translation movement was Ḥunayn ibn Isḥāq, a Christian Arab from southern Iraq. Ḥunayn studied medicine in Baghdad at a young age and then traveled to the Byzantine lands—probably Constantinople—where he continued his studies and attained a mastery of Greek. His translations of the works of Galen from the Greek into Syriac and Arabic were commissioned by members of the Abbasid court and other wealthy patrons. Working with his son and nephew, he translated much of the Galenic corpus, along with works by Dioscorides, Artemidorus, and Aristotle, as well as the Old Testament. As a translator, Ḥunayn was a singular talent, but as a multilingual individual he was emblematic of the linguistic pluralism of Abbasid Iraq. The literate community of Iraq was familiar with Persian, Greek, and Syriac and almost certainly spoke a very different variety of Arabic than it wrote. The language of writing was what we today call Classical Arabic (al-ʿarabiyya, or al-ʿarabiyya al-fuṣḥā) while the languages of everyday speech—the dialects of Baghdad, Mosul, Basra, and Kufa, and all the subdialects within those *vernaculars—were grouped under the broad category of the demotic (lughat al-ʿāmm). Why should this matter to the history of information? Simply, because such a history is more than a catalog of official records and learned culture; information takes many forms. The existence of a prestige dialect in the Islamic lands served as a gatekeeper to the fields of privileged information. Like Latin in medieval and *Renaissance Europe, Classical Arabic predominated as the language of high culture, thus regulating the production of certain genres of information and delimiting the boundaries of the channels through which it flowed. In later centuries, evidence of information circulating in other registers of Arabic attests to the widening of those channels.

Egypt and Syria, Fourteenth Century

In 1258, the armies of the Mongol Ilkhanids led by Hülegü, a grandson of Genghis Khan, sacked the Abbasid capital at Baghdad and brought an end to a dynasty that had reigned for half a millennium. The Mongol conquests created great upheaval in the Near East, laying waste to cities and causing the deaths of millions through war, disease, and deprivation. The campaigns in the Russian steppe during the 1220s and 1230s transformed the slave trade and facilitated the rise of a regiment of slave-soldiers (*mamlūks*) who would overthrow their masters and rise to power, ruling over Egypt, Syria, and parts of northwest Arabia until 1517. Over the course of the fourteenth and fifteenth centuries, the territories of the Mamluk sultanate emerged as the intellectual and cultural hubs of the Arabo-Islamic world. Learned individuals emigrated from lands where bureaucratic and scholarly institutions had been thrown into upheaval by the invasions, and many of them found new homes in Cairo and Damascus, the flourishing school cities of the Mamluk realms.

Many of these immigrants were professional scholars, a vocation made possible by the rise of a relatively new institution: the madrasa. Formally colleges of jurisprudence, madrasas also offered instruction in the Quranic sciences, Prophetic traditions, Arabic grammar, rhetoric, theology, logic, mathematics, and other subjects. Students came from around the Islamic world to benefit from the hundreds of madrasas that had been established in Cairo and Damascus, endowed by wealthy members of the political and civilian elite. Many students sought careers as jurists, hoping to find employment as bureaucrats or judges in the imperial administration. Others intended to become madrasa professors themselves. Many made a living in the book trade, copying sought-after manuscripts and selling them to other scholars, interested laypeople, and the many libraries attached to the colleges. In these school cities, there was a large market for texts of a pedagogical character—commentaries, supercommentaries (i.e., commentaries on commentaries), glosses, digests, epitomes, abridgments—which offered guidance to the staples of a madrasa curriculum. A well-known work on the classification of the sciences by a fourteenth-century physician, Ibn al-Akfānī, entitled *Guiding the Seeker to the Most Splendid Destinations* (*Irshād al-qāṣid ilā asnā l-maqāṣid*), included descriptions of sixty disciplines and six hundred books associated with them. The fifteenth-century historian al-Sakhāwī prepared a list of texts mastered by graduates licensed to teach in madrasas, which included more than a thousand works. In comparison with other premodern societies, these numbers are striking. It is not uncommon to find accounts of libraries attached to Mamluk madrasas containing thousands of books. In a study of one such institution, the Ashrafiyya (an "average" Syrian library founded in the thirteenth century), Konrad Hirschler has suggested that its holdings were comparable in size to those of all the libraries of Cambridge University combined, two centuries later.

An Age of Compendia

This bookish environment not only facilitated the work of a compiler but also, in certain ways, engendered it. Insofar as the growing numbers of books and learned people circulating within the network of scholarly institutions created a sense of the expanding boundaries of knowledge, they also made it possible to envision a solution to the problem of too much information. This partly took the form of the capacious compilatory texts that began to appear in such profusion during this period. Anthologies, manuals, encyclopedias, dictionaries, commentaries, and chronicles all depended on the act of sorting and arranging existing information into new forms. The historical sources make it apparent that being a learned individual in this period meant devoting a great deal of time—perhaps a majority of one's working life—to copying, editing, abridging, commenting on, excerpting, anthologizing, and reorganizing information. Even texts that declared their own originality depended heavily on the work of earlier authors. As has been observed in other contexts, the importance of information-management techniques for gathering and sorting the textual materials that found their way into finished works was paramount. The historian and polymath al-Maqrīzī completed his many books by gathering his sources together, excerpting them, summarizing them, then composing them into rough drafts and then finished drafts. Some scholars kept a *commonplace book or aide-memoire (*tadhkira*) in which they made copies and excerpts of works they found to be useful in the course of their reading. The *Tadhkira* of Khalīl ibn Aybak al-Ṣafadī, a prolific author and bureaucrat of the fourteenth century, contained thirty volumes.

Among the many types of books that organized information in encyclopedic dimensions was the biographical dictionary. Compendia of famous individuals had been written in the Islamic world prior to this period, but the Mamluk realms saw an efflorescence and diversification of this genre. In its outlines, a biographical dictionary is a collection of biographies of famous individuals (mostly men, but famous women make appearances as well), grouped according to a theme. There are biographical dictionaries devoted to the members of a certain occupation (such as lawyers within a particular legal rite, musicians, hadith transmitters, Quran reciters, grammarians, etc.); people from a particular city; people born during a given century; and universal dictionaries that summed up all these other categories. It has been supposed that biographical dictionaries functioned as a kind of historiographical record, an alternative to the annalistic chronicle that served as a history of states.

Other types of compendia included enormous *lexicons, commentaries on the Quran and hadith, geographical works, cosmographical works, and universal histories. Similarly comprehensive in outlook, books on the classification of the sciences outlined a curriculum of study for the novice. Three of the most famous encyclopedias of the fourteenth and fifteenth centuries were composed by bureaucrats in the Mamluk administration. Shihāb al-Dīn al-Nuwayrī's thirty-one-volume work *The Ultimate Ambition in the Arts of Erudition* was a compendium of universal knowledge arranged into five divisions: (i) the cosmos, comprising the earth, heavens, stars, planets, and meteorological phenomena; (ii) the human being, containing material on physiology, genealogy, literature, music, proverbs, political rule, and chancery affairs; (iii) the animal world; (iv) the plant world; and (v) a universal history, beginning with Adam and Eve and continuing all the way through the events of al-Nuwayrī's life. To flip through *The Ultimate Ambition*'s pages is to encounter a dizzying array of subjects: poetry about the sleepiness of cheetahs; recipes for the production of aphrodisiacs; boilerplate legal language for marriage contracts; a biography of Muḥammad and the history of the Islamic world; anatomical and literary descriptions of electric eels, turtles, falcons, and cats; administrative minutiae concerning promissory notes, joint partnerships, commercial enterprises, loans, gifts, donations, charity, transfers of property; and much more.

Another fourteenth-century encyclopedia, Ibn Faḍl Allāh al-ʿUmarī's *Routes of Insight into the Civilized Realms*, was a geographical-historical compendium consisting principally of biographies of famous personages arranged by professional categories and organized to demonstrate the supremacy of the Islamic East vis-à-vis the Maghrib. Aḥmad ibn ʿAlī al-Qalqashandī, another Mamluk bureaucrat, composed a fourteen-volume scribal encyclopedia entitled *Dawn for the Night-Blind: On the Craft of Chancery Writing*. Although the main portion of his book was devoted to furnishing the aspiring clerk with sample letters and protocols of official address, it also covered such diverse topics as meteorological phenomena, foreign relations, the operation of water clocks, and the geography of the Mamluk Empire and neighboring realms.

It is in these encyclopedic texts that one best appreciates the wealth of information that circulated within the Mamluk cities. Some encyclopedists saw themselves primarily as compilers; others as synthesizers. Al-Nuwayrī and Ibn Faḍl Allāh are instructive examples in this regard. The former exhibits a mostly deferential attitude toward the information that he brings together. He makes a distinction, echoed in other sources, between different kinds of sciences—the traditional (al-ʿulūm al-naqliyya) and the rational (al-ʿulūm al-ʿaqliyya). His preference was for the former, favoring the authenticating transmission of traditional knowledge over the fickle, precarious operations of a single mind. Ibn Faḍl Allāh, by contrast, was more skeptical about time-honored knowledge. He writes in his preface that the books on geography are full of outdated information, and that he saw his role as an arbiter of fact: "Having consulted all of the books written about the states and contents of the terrestrial climes, I did not find any that scrutinized their conditions or depicted them accurately, for most of these books only contain old reports about the conditions of long-gone kings, extinct civilizations, and customs that have vanished along with their peoples. There is not much point in simply recounting them. The best statement is the truest one, and people resemble their own times more than they resemble their own ancestors" (Muhanna, *World*).

Information and Bureaucracy

It is no accident that many authors of encyclopedic texts and other compilations were employed in the Mamluk sultanate's administration. The bureaucracy, like the madrasas, cultivated a foundation in a range of disciplines and imparted many of the practical skills that proved essential to large-scale compilers, such as bookmaking, record keeping, and other forms of archival practice. The bureaucracy comprised an expansive network of learned individuals with diverse intellectual interests. Many of them spent time in the madrasas, studying jurisprudence and mastering the canons of traditional scholarship. But there are differences between the scholarly and bureaucratic realms that are worth paying attention to, not least because they help make vivid the distinction between "knowledge" and "information" at this time.

To put it simply, the information procured in the service of governance was of a different character than the knowledge imparted in a madrasa education. Gathered, recorded, and instrumentalized by the political administration, this bureaucratic information was almost exclusively contemporary in its outlook. Scribes collected information from visiting envoys about the conditions of other kingdoms. They toured the agricultural hinterlands outside the school cities and took notes on crop yields so as to make adjustments to their tax levies. They recorded the hiring and firing of provincial governors and other bureaucrats. While the path to scholarly excellence in the madrasa world involved, in its essence, the mastery of a curriculum of canonical texts, success in the bureaucratic sphere required an ability to negotiate the social, communal, and economic networks that constituted the contemporary sultanate. Al-Nuwayrī's and Ibn Faḍl Allāh's encyclopedias contain massive amounts of such data on the daily events of the Mamluk sultanate and the lives of its notable subjects. They detail the troop movements of the army as it went out to put down rebellions; financial information that emerged from cadastral surveys; and data about the flooding of the Nile, earthquakes, and other environmental phenomena.

These practices of record keeping were immensely important, and the historical sources testify to their sophistication and complexity. The administrative encyclopedias shed light on the structure of the administration and its various offices, which scholars have used to learn about how this society produced, disseminated, and preserved documents. While relatively few repositories have been found, there is ample evidence of an elaborate system used to keep track of the circulation of documents around a decentralized imperial administration, what Konrad Hirschler has called a "meta-layer" of indexes, lists, and registers that facilitated the retrieval of individual documents. Because such documents were not universally stored in a single state archive but rather in other locations such as regional bureaus and in the private papers of military officers, tax farmers, and provincial governors, this meta-layer provided a way to keep tabs on the circulation of information throughout the various branches of the bureaucracy.

Army secretaries, for example, were responsible for maintaining lists of all the soldiers and their commanding officers, the auxiliary troops from among the Turkoman and Bedouin tribesmen along with the number of horses and camels they contributed to the royal stables, and the details of their compensation through land grants, currency, or fungible commodities. Al-Nuwayrī tells us that the administrator in charge of the sultan's larder required accounting each day for all the "meats, seasonings, vegetables, spices, sweets, and nuts, as well as perfume, incense, fire logs, and other things" consumed by the royal kitchens, which received a continuous stream of shipments from around Egypt and Syria. In the sultan's buttery, the responsible official oversaw the preparation and stocking of "sugar drinks, theriacs, medicinal powders, pastes, pastilles, raisin drinks, near beer, dates, herbs, sweets, electuaries" and various other types of refreshments and restoratives. The treasury may have been the hardest office to keep track of, as al-Nuwayrī's description attests:

> Integrity and trustworthiness are the mainstays of this position, for the treasuries of kings in our age cannot be fully inventoried due to their size, abundant contents, and the immensity of their treasures. Were a scribe commissioned to prepare an account of the financial revenues of the sultan's treasury for a single year, he would have to be appointed solely to this task for an entire year without working on anything else. By the time the account was complete [at the end of the second year] and corrected by the secretary of the treasury [during the third year], its anticipated benefit would have long passed. Furthermore, the secretary of the treasury would have neglected the receipts of the third year, having been occupied with the first year's bookkeeping.

Procuring contemporary, reliable information in the service of the state was the common thread uniting the many professions that composed the administration—from financial comptroller to *notary to army secretary. There were similarities between the duties of the Mamluk bureaucrat and those of the scholarly compiler, which helps explain why so many learned individuals were active in both domains. Gathering large quantities of information from a wide range of sources, collating them and ensuring their authenticity, and distilling them into new forms represented the core activities of both professions. What set them apart, however, was the essential difference between what we have been calling information and knowledge.

Finally, it is worth noting that Mamluk Egypt and Syria, like Abbasid Iraq, were places of linguistic multiplicity. Even though Classical Arabic remained the preeminent language of literature, scholarship, and administration, other languages had begun to encroach on its domain. In the late thirteenth century, the North African judge Ibn Manẓūr composed a twenty-volume work entitled *The Arab Tongue* (*Lisān al-'Arab*), the largest Arabic dictionary written to date. Ibn Manẓūr was a tireless compiler; one of his biographers noted that his abridgments amounted to five hundred volumes. He had condensed Ibn 'Asākir's encyclopedic *History of Damascus* to a quarter of its size, and rearranged Abū Faraj al-Iṣfahānī's celebrated *Book of Songs* according to alphabetical order. In other words, Ibn Manẓūr had an immense stock of raw material with which to compose *The Arab Tongue*, in which individual entries spanned many pages, assaying the nuances of Arabic roots and their many shades of meaning. There is some irony in the fact that Ibn Manẓūr's desire to produce this book stemmed partly from a deep anxiety about Arabic's future, a belief that its position as the civilized world's language of social prestige, literary eloquence, and religious knowledge was under threat. Even within the Arab lands, Ibn Manẓūr saw signs of a looming threat. "In our time, speaking Arabic is regarded as a vice," he wrote in the dictionary's preface. "I have composed the present work in an age when men take pride in using languages other than Arabic, and I have built it like Noah built the Ark, enduring the sarcasm of his own people."

Which languages did Ibn Manẓūr have in mind? Persian and Turkish were becoming increasingly prestigious languages and would have been heard widely in the Mamluk territories, for reasons that will become clearer later in this chapter. But it's likely that Ibn Manẓūr was also thinking of the proliferation of literary production in Arabic vernaculars, an area that scholars have only lately begun to explore. Traditionally dismissed as the uncouth writings of semiliterate authors, this vernacular literature has begun to receive greater attention. It encoded spheres of contemporary information and subjective experience that were not often expressed in the high language, by individuals whose stories have been left out of traditional historiography. Given that Classical Arabic, as discussed earlier, has played a gatekeeping role in Islamic intellectual history, the inclusion of texts composed in nonstandard Arabic holds out the possibility of teaching us more about how information, and not just knowledge, circulated in the Islamic world.

Iran and Khorasan, Fifteenth Century

At the start of the fifteenth century, much of central Asia was ruled by Tīmūr Lang, the Turko-Mongol conqueror known to Europe as Tamerlane. Thirty-five years of military campaigning had knit together a vast patchwork of territories. Tīmūr's armies had reached as far west as Anatolia and as far east as northern India, and at the time of his death in 1405 CE Tīmūr was marching at the head of an army intent on invading China. The Timurid dynasty would rule over this domain—including most of modern-day Iran, Afghanistan, Iraq, Azerbaijan, Georgia, Turkmenistan, Uzbekistan, Kyrgyzstan, and Pakistan—until the end of the fifteenth century. Cities like Bukhara, Isfahan, Merv, Shiraz, Tabriz, Nishapur, and Balkh had produced some of the greatest thinkers of the Islamic world in earlier centuries, but the Mongol conquests of the 1200s coupled with Tīmūr's devastating campaigns in the 1300s had ravaged many of these historic centers of learning. During the fifteenth century, a period of relative stability, some of them would recover and flourish.

One of the distinctive features of intellectual and cultural production under the Timurids was its courtly context. As we have seen, patronage played an important role in the world of knowledge under the Abbasids. The translation movement was supported by the caliphs and their courts, who cultivated entourages of literati, scientists, philosophers, and musicians. In the Mamluk period, however, the sultan's court was eclipsed by the madrasa and the chancery as the preeminent spaces of intellectual exchange. These spaces were still, in most cases, financially supported by the political elite, but they were managed by networks of scholars and bureaucrats whose works were increasingly divorced from a strict relationship of patronage, and oriented toward other members of the network.

The Timurid period exhibits features of both these earlier contexts. Its princely courts were the sites of a cultural efflorescence often referred to as the Timurid Renaissance. The cities of Samarqand and Herat, in particular, witnessed an outpouring of royal patronage in the areas of astronomy, architecture, calligraphy, the occult sciences, miniature painting, and literature. They attracted some of the luminaries of the Persian world: Jāmī, the great Persian poet and Sufi scholar; Mīr ʿAlī Shīr Navāʾī, the father of Chagatay literature; Sharaf al-Dīn Yazdī, the historian and biographer of Tīmūr; Vāʿiẓ Kāshifī, the prominent preacher and occultist; and Bihzād, the most famous of Persian miniature painters. Some of the Timurid princes were themselves practitioners of the arts they patronized, such as Bāysunghur (d. 1433 CE), who oversaw the Herat *scriptorium (kitābkhāna) and was a talented calligrapher. The political economy of the Timurid dynasty, with its decentralized tax base, facilitated the independence of its different branches, allowing the courts to compete with each other in their patronage projects.

A second social feature of Timurid intellectual life was the importance of scholarly networks. As in the Mamluk sphere, these included formal networks of students who had studied with well-known teachers or who belonged to particular legal rites. The prominence of Sufi networks in both contexts has been noted by scholars, along with the extensive cultural contacts between the Timurid and Mamluk realms. There were also informal networks of individuals who were committed to, as Evrim Binbaş has written, "a specific political, ideological, and aesthetic view," and were often engaged in Neopythagorean philosophy and the occult sciences. The case of Sharaf al-Dīn Yazdī, the historian, provides an instructive example. He and his teacher, Ṣāʾin al-Dīn Turka, both traveled to Cairo at the end of the fourteenth century to study with Sayyid Ḥusayn Akhlāṭī, a well-known occultist. Akhlāṭī was a member of a clandestine network that called itself the Brethren of Purity (Ikhvān al-ṣafā, a nod to the famous tenth-century Ismāʿīlī collective that authored the encyclopedic *Epistles*), which extended across Egypt, Ottoman Anatolia, and the Balkans. Such interregional associations were important channels for the flow of information, which traveled through written correspondence (*munshāʾāt*)—a network that has been described as a fifteenth-century Islamicate *Republic of Letters.

Information and the Occult

The occult sciences were a chief interest of many scholars of this era. They included various forms of divination—for example, on the basis of dreams (oneiromancy), celestial phenomena (astrology), or sand (geomancy)—each with its own procedures and subsumed within a broader Neoplatonic and Neopythagorean philosophical framework. At the foundation of these divinatory methods was the science of letters or lettrism (ʿilm-i ḥurūf), a program for uncovering the secrets of the unified cosmos by studying the mystical properties of the Arabic alphabet. Similar in ways to kabbalistic traditions in Judaism, lettrism in fifteenth-century central Asia was used as a hermeneutic to interpret both the texts of sacred scripture as well as the hidden or interior nature of reality. Divinatory practices had existed for millennia, but the fifteenth-century Persianate world marked a golden age for this activity, attracting some of the period's foremost thinkers to its ranks. Astrologists, geomancers, and dream interpreters held high-ranking positions in Timurid courts. Some scholars eschewed these methods as heretical, but few discounted them as charlatanry. Ibn Khaldūn, the great fourteenth-century historian, famously denounced astrology and alchemy in his *al-Muqqadimah* (The Prolegomenon) (earning praise from nineteenth- and twentieth-century historians who cast him as a skeptical empiricist), but he was the exception that proved the rule. Furthermore, even Ibn Khaldūn did not doubt the reality and efficacy of magic and divination but rather categorized them as forms of illicit sorcery.

Why did the occult sciences attract so much interest? From our perspective, practices like alchemy, astrology, and geomancy (a form of "terrestrial astrology" similar to the *I Ching*) may not count as sciences at all, but it is necessary to recognize that these methods were enmeshed in a philosophical program that sought to explain the natural world by studying a code immanent in the

universe. Lettrist thought intersected with messianic, apocalyptic, and mystical thought, holding out the promise of prophetic intuition for those who
mastered its secrets. While historians have traditionally regarded such practices as belonging to a prescientific age, scholars such as Matthew Melvin-
Koushki have increasingly recognized the place of magic and esoteric practices
in the thought of many Renaissance and Enlightenment figures "from Pico to
Bruno and Kepler to Newton, [who have] been shown to be profoundly occultist in orientation and methodology—and profoundly dependent on Arabic sources in the same vein."

Astronomy and Mathematics

Alongside the copious writings devoted to astrology, the Timurid era witnessed
advances in the field of astronomical observation and measurement. One of
Tīmūr's grandsons, Ulugh Beg (d. 1449 CE), built a great observatory in Samarqand, the Timurid capital. At forty-eight meters wide, it contained an internal graduated trench that formed part of a massive sextant, which, because
of its size, could measure the angles between planets and stars with an unprecedented degree of accuracy. Ulugh Beg was a mathematician and astronomer
himself, and he brought together a large staff of scientists who taught at the
observatory and worked on devising new instruments and solving theoretical
astronomical problems. Around 1441, a set of star tables—the Zīj al-Ṣulṭānaʾī—
was completed and disseminated throughout the Islamic world, eventually also
translated into Latin. Such works, of which Ulugh Beg's was the last great example in the Ptolemaic tradition, were used to calculate the positions of the
planets, the sun, and the moon, as well as the time of the sunrise and sunset.

One of the significant theoretical advances made by astronomers at the
Samarqand observatory concerned the relationship of their discipline to
Aristotelian physics and metaphysics. Islamic astronomy had long been
grouped with the mathematical disciplines following Ibn Sīnā, but some
concepts from Aristotelian natural philosophy remained essential. The doctrine of the earth's stasis, for example, was held by Naṣīr al-Dīn al-Ṭūsī, the
thirteenth-century savant, to be unprovable solely on the basis of mathematical reasoning. Arguing against this long-standing view, one of the astronomers at the Samarqand observatory, ʿAlī Qūshjī (d. 1474 CE), would propose
that astronomy had no need of Aristotelian metaphysics and could rest
entirely on a mathematical foundation. As many of the Samarqand astronomers and mathematicians were themselves committed occultists, some have

speculated that this "mathematicization of astronomy" was itself strongly influenced by the occultist renaissance of the fifteenth century, which was rooted in Neoplatonic and Neopythagorean philosophy.

The Timurid Renaissance ended as the dynasty itself was brought down in the early sixteenth century. Many of the intellectuals and artists patronized by the Timurids left the glorious courts at Herat and Samarqand in search of new employers. Bābur, a fifth-generation descendant of Tīmūr (and of Genghis Khan, on his mother's side), would establish the Mughal sultanate in India, where the miniature painting traditions developed by Timurid artists would continue. The philosophical and scientific activities of the fifteenth century carried over into the Safavid and Ottoman Empires.

Conclusion

Nearly all the practices of disseminating, authenticating, and contesting information discussed here continued well up to the late nineteenth century. Under the Ottoman Empire, familiar institutions like the madrasa proliferated, along with public libraries, courts, and bureaucratic archives. Scholars continued to compose encyclopedic works and compilations of different kinds, relying on similar modes of textual reproduction. However, the early modern period brought with it new technologies of information management and publication. The arrival of print in the Ottoman lands in the late eighteenth century had a transformative effect, as might be expected, leading to the rise of newspapers and publishing houses, even if manuscript traditions did not disappear.

What has been left out of this survey of the history of information in the medieval Islamic world? I have not addressed the subject of hospitals as realms of medical information, or judicial courts as zones of legal information. What about markets, barracks, prisons, and private households? There has been no mention of postal systems, maps, diagrams, magic squares, or censuses. Some of the giants of Islamic thought—al-Ghazālī, Ibn Rushd, Fakhr al-Dīn al-Rāzī, and others—have not even made an appearance. This has to do with the contexts I have chosen to examine, but also my focus on information rather than knowledge. As should be apparent, the line between these two categories is difficult to draw. The purview of occult science was certainly considered by its practitioners to be *knowledge*, no less firmly rooted than any of the other disciplines I've addressed. Hadith collections, encyclopedic adab works, and astronomical tables were all seen as containing knowledge alongside information. Keeping both categories in mind as we study Islamic history attunes us to the processes by which knowledge and information were mutually constitutive and ever changing.

Further Reading

Jonathan P. Berkey, *The Transmission of Knowledge in Medieval Cairo: A Social History of Islamic Education*, 1992; İlker Evrim Binbaş, *Intellectual Networks in Timurid Iran: Sharaf al-Dīn ʿAlī Yazdī and the Islamicate Republic of Letters*, 2016; Ann Blair, "Managing Information," in *Oxford Illustrated History of the Book*, edited by James Raven, 2020; Jonathan Bloom, *Paper before Print: The History and Impact of Paper in the Islamic World*, 2001; C. E. Bosworth, "A Pioneer Arabic Encyclopedia of the Sciences: Al-Khwārizmī's Keys of the Sciences," *Isis* 54, no. 1 (1963): 97–111; Sonja Brentjes, "Teaching the Mathematical Sciences in Islamic Societies: Eighth–Seventeenth Centuries," in *Handbook on the History of Mathematics Education*, edited by A. Karp and G. Schubring, 2014, 85–108; Adam Gacek, "Tazwīr," in *Encyclopaedia of Islam*, 2nd ed., edited by P. Bearman, Th. Bianquis, C. E. Bosworth, E. van Donzel, and W. P. Heinrichs, 1960–2007; Dimitri Gutas, *Greek Thought, Arabic Culture: The Graeco-Arabic Translation Movement in Baghdad and Early ʿAbbāsid Society (2nd–4th/8th–10th Centuries)*, 1998; Konrad Hirschler, "From Archive to Archival Practices: Rethinking the Preservation of Mamluk Administrative Documents," *Journal of the American Oriental Society* 136, no. 1 (2016): 1–28; idem, *Medieval Damascus: Plurality and Diversity in an Arabic Library: The Ashrafiya Library Catalogue*, 2016; Ibn Qutayba, *Adab al-kātib*, edited by Max Günert, 1900; E. W. Lane, *Arabic-English Lexicon*, 1984; Matthew Melvin-Koushki, "Introduction: De-orienting the Study of Islamicate Occultism," *Arabica* 64, nos. 3–4 (September 13, 2017): 287–95; idem, "Powers of One: The Mathematicalization of the Occult Sciences in the High Persianate Tradition," *Intellectual History of the Islamicate World* 5 (2017): 127–39; Elias Muhanna, "Encyclopaedias, Arabic," *Encyclopaedia of Islam Three*, 2007–; idem, *The World in a Book: Al-Nuwayrī and the Islamic Encyclopedic Tradition*, 2018; Muḥsin Jāsim Mūsawī, *The Medieval Islamic Republic of Letters: Arabic Knowledge Construction*, 2015; Aḥmad ibn ʿAbd al-Wahhāb al-Nuwayrī, *The Ultimate Ambition in the Arts of Erudition: A Compendium of Knowledge from the Classical Islamic World*, translated by Elias Muhanna, 2016; Carl F. Petry, "Scholarly Stasis in Medieval Islam Reconsidered: Mamluk Patronage in Cairo," *Poetics Today* 14, no. 2 (Summer 1993): 323–48; F. Jamil Ragep, "Freeing Astronomy from Philosophy: An Aspect of Islamic Influence on Science," *Osiris* 16 (2001): 49–71.

3

Information in Early
Modern East Asia

Devin Fitzgerald and Carla Nappi

RECENT HISTORIES OF INFORMATION describing premodern East Asia have little to say about "revolutions" in information. The impact of the early invention of paper and printing has mostly been obscured, and while *"early modernity" has been a topic of great debate, there is little consensus about when or if the concept fits East Asia as a whole. That said, scholars of East Asia, particularly of Japan and China, have long focused their attention on histories of information circulation in the region during the "late imperial" period (roughly 1000–1840 CE). Structural shifts in China dating to the Song dynasty (960–1279), such as the popularization of printing, widespread proto-industrialization, the abolition of a landed aristocracy in favor of a bureaucratic elite, and the rise of autocratic governance, changed political and intellectual cultures across the region. The cosmopolitan Sinographic culture first developed in China during antiquity also extended throughout East Asia. However, in the fourteenth century after the collapse of the Mongol Empire the reconstitution of self-conscious, increasingly "ethnicized" culture undermined the universalist claims of the Sinitic tradition, as actors throughout the region began to clearly articulate what it meant to pass beyond the borders of one place into another cultural region. This survey of information in early modern East Asia aims to combine attention to transnational trends with attention to the impact of the Sinitic cultural model on local and regional scales.

From this perspective it is possible to argue that from roughly 1000 CE until the arrival of modern industrial technologies, a series of information revolutions continually remade East Asia, and these revolutions contributed to the rise of new concerns about the role information played in everyday life. In this essay we will proceed through five sections to consider how methods of disseminating, then storing, sorting, and controlling information interacted with the material and linguistic realities of the region.

Disseminating Information

China has a long history of written culture, dating back to the origins of writing in the early Shang dynasty circa 1700 BCE. Despite disruptions during periods of political instability and war, its linguistic and ideographic tradition has been continuously transmitted down to the present and widely dispersed geographically to neighboring areas. A few written artifacts (e.g., bamboo strips and scrolls) from ancient China survive thanks to modern archeological discoveries in caves at Dunhuang or tombs in Yinqueshan, but the bulk of the texts we have from ancient and medieval China survive only in later printed versions, produced during or after the great expansion of printing in the sixteenth century.

On Paper and Books

Unlike in the West, most premodern East Asian papers were made entirely from raw plant materials. East Asian paper production was therefore agrarian. Farmer-papermakers made paper to supplement household income during periods of agricultural quiet, although some regions produced year-round. In terms of material composition, it is almost impossible to speak of a "typical" paper. Chinese papers were highly local products, relying on plants endemic to the region of production. According to the *Tiangong Kaiwu* (The exploitation of the works of nature), a late Ming technological manual, to make paper from bamboo, young bamboo was harvested, cut into small sections, and soaked for several months in either a pool or running water. After soaking for roughly three months, the bamboo was ready to be processed by "killing its green." The phrase means that the husks of the plant were removed, and the remaining fibers were then combined with lime and either left to soak for up to a month or boiled for seven to eight days. Both methods weakened the long fibers so that they could be processed more efficiently.

Once the first boiling or monthlong soaking was done, the strands of bamboo were washed in clean water. The fibers were then recombined with ash, boiled, and strained in an almost-continual cycle for ten days. In some places, such as Jiangxi province, they were also left to bleach in the sun, sometimes for months. When the fibers had "ripened," they were drained and pulped by wooden beaters until they had a clay-like consistency. The pulped paper would have some form of sizing added to optimize its absorptive qualities (every region had its own preference), before being transferred to a vat. A vat man would then use a bamboo screen to pull individual sheets of paper from the slurry in the vat. As in Europe, the paper sheets would be couched in piles and pressed to remove moisture. In the final stage of drying, the paper would be brushed onto a wall for drying. A team of four, working the screens, couching, and drying, could produce over sixty pounds of paper in a day—which probably amounted to more than two thousand sheets. After the paper was dried, it would be assembled into bundles for transport to the market. It was at this time that the Chinese version of a "watermark" would be added, with an inked stamp noting the manufacturer's name.

The description of production above stems from the Ming dynasty (1368–1644), when Chinese papers were already common and inexpensive. In the earlier Song period (960–1279) paper was still scarce enough as to be frequently recycled, and few printed books from this period survive as a result. But in the fifteenth and sixteenth centuries paper became much cheaper and more widely available. Cheap paper meant that books, in both manuscript and print (by woodblock), were inexpensive in East Asia from a relatively early period.

After the medieval period, the most frequently encountered premodern East Asian books were codices, rather than scrolls (although scrolls never vanished). The *codex form emerged in the Tang dynasty (618–907), likely owing to the influence of palm-leaf (*pothi*) books entering China from Inner Asia. Pages, literally "leaves" (*yezi*), were new to the Chinese world, and they provided scholars with the unprecedented ability to randomly access bodies of texts. Codices became dominant almost simultaneously with the invention of printing by woodblock (or xylography). Scholars disagree over when to date the first use of wood-block printing in China, though it seems to have taken place sometime between the seventh and eighth centuries. A copy of the Diamond Sutra, published in 868 and found in a cave in the Buddhist monastic complex in Dunhuang in northwest China, is widely regarded as the world's oldest extant printed book. Unlike paper, however, printing was not widely adapted or sustained in regions outside China. Despite an initial burst of energy (we see printing in eighth-century Japan), the technology failed to win early popular support in Korea and Japan.

In China, population growth, commercialization, and urbanization that had begun in the late Tang dynasty continued through the Song dynasty, providing essential conditions for an early print revolution. The expansion of the elite class beyond hereditary nobility, along with the establishment of a standard curriculum for the imperial examinations, created a market eager to consume print. Scholars were not necessarily happy with the rise of printing. The eleventh-century thinker Cheng Ju (1078–1144) described the dangers of print to textual transmission, noting that

> earlier dynasties transmitted the Classics and Histories by transcribing them on paper and silk. Even though errors were made, still, the versions could be compared and collated. Then in the Five Dynasties, officials began to use inked-[wood]blocks to print the Six Classics. . . . With this, the manuscript versions of the Histories and Six Classics that had been transmitted down to that time were no longer used. Yet the inked-blocks were riddled with errors. They were never correct. . . . Later scholars will not be able to turn to other versions to discover and rectify the mistakes in them. (Cherniack, 34)

While print was not the actual cause of the loss of textual authority in the classics (similar concerns were present before the invention of printing), "inked-blocks" removed the agency of individual scholars, because their manuscripts could be corrupted by the processes of carving, printing, and circulating them.

The printed matter created to satisfy the Song market included works belonging to almost every *genre. Buddhist texts with elegant illustrations for lay devotees circulated next to cheap imprints from Jianyang Fujian, an early center of commercial publication. Song dynasty trends continued through the Mongol conquest in the thirteenth century and the early Ming (1368–1644). Government printing and commercial printing met most needs, but the volume of production seems to have remained relatively low until a second print revolution in the sixteenth century. The sixteenth-century Ming commercial boom—spurred in part by silver from the New World—heated the Chinese economy to the melting point. Costs for book production fell with the expansion of an available labor pool of people who could more cheaply transcribe and carve the script of a text into woodblocks. Several economic historians have recently shown that the cost of wood-block printing, while initially higher than the cost of printing with letterpress, was actually far lower than that of letterpress printing after print runs passed approximately fifteen hundred copies. Given that blocks could be used for hundreds of years if they were properly maintained, the economic benefits of East Asian printing made them a wise investment in several different regions around the empire. Ming and Qing printers grew into *publishers with transnational reach. By the middle of the seventeenth century, Chinese imprints could be found in Korea, Japan, Vietnam, and even Europe.

While print flourished early in China, it took a different trajectory in Korea, Japan, and Vietnam. After its early introduction to Korea and Japan, printing remained confined mostly to monasteries. Since the reproduction of Buddhist texts brought religious merit, print technology allowed for industrial-scale merit production. Alongside its Buddhist uses, printing emerged as the preferred mode of textual distribution only in conjunction with major shifts in the political cultures of each region.

In Korea, the long-lived Chosŏn dynasty (1392–1897) consolidated state ideologies around a Confucian *canon of classical texts and histories. While Buddhist printing continued in monasteries, the Chosŏn court became the primary producer of official calendars, texts required for education in the classics, and works promoting morality. The centralization of printing at the court had a notable influence on early Chosŏn print technology. While movable type had been invented in the twelfth century in East Asia, the level of resources required to print a wide range of texts in classical Chinese in movable type prevented its widespread adoption. When the Korean court asserted almost exclusive rights to print and distribute important texts, movable type became its preferred mode of textual production. In 1444, experiments with movable type for Chinese ideograms resulted in the emergence of one of the finest fonts ever created, the *kabin* type, which borrowed heavily from Song and Yuan aesthetics. The type was recast seven times over the course of the Chosŏn period. While the court promoted and used movable types given the predilection prevailing for an expensive luxury product, wood-block (or xylographic) printing remained the predominant form of printing in Korea. Popular texts— or texts that needed to be printed in especially high numbers—were usually printed via woodblocks. Moreover, the commercialization of print in the eighteenth and nineteenth centuries, when we see evidence of a popular market in Korea, was primarily a xylographic phenomenon.

As in China and Korea, in Japan the earliest printed matter consisted of Buddhist texts produced in temples. In the twelfth and thirteenth centuries the use of print in Buddhist institutions increased along with the geographical spread and range of those temples; at the same time the printing of secular works, such as the *Analects of Confucius*, began. But here too the success of printing depended on cultural factors in addition to technical know-how. The Tokugawa unification of the islands in the seventeenth century laid the foundation for a spectacular expansion of printing. Publication centers in Osaka, Kyoto, and Tokyo emerged to dominate a newly integrated state-scale market. Like late Ming China, where commercial print expanded rapidly, Tokugawa Japan also experienced a significant expansion in commercially published texts. As a result, a wide range of texts became newly available to urban readers. These included books, which were often beautifully illustrated, and news broadsides. The printed books ranged from classic Japanese texts to newer works like maps, travel guides, how-to manuals, picture books, and the ukiyo-e prints of the "floating world" that often depicted the entertainment and pleasure quarters and, with the advent of multicolor wood-block printing in the middle of the eighteenth century, could be cheaply mass-produced in vibrant colors (see figure 3.1). Printed books of non-Japanese authorship also circulated. By the end of the eighteenth century, these included imported and reprinted Chinese books, Dutch books and Dutch translations of books from other European languages, and Korean books.

Printing seems to have arrived in Vietnam sometime after the Song dynasty. As in other parts of East Asia, temples assumed a leading role in the publication of texts. However, the early history of printing is murky. The biography of Tín Học (d. 1190) noted that his family had been "carving blocks" for printing Buddhist scriptures for many generations. Despite this early reference, the high cost of printing and the tropical climate of Vietnam have left us with only a small amount of material dating to before the nineteenth century, with the earliest surviving printed text dating to 1665. While this early archive is fragmentary, a great deal of material testifying to potential productivity remains. Tens of thousands of blocks, as well as a large number of unstudied books, still survive from the Nguyen dynasty (1802–1945).

The rise of printing in East Asia never eclipsed manuscript production and transmission. As scholars have recently emphasized for early modern Europe, printing and manuscript production existed as mutually complementary modes of managing and circulating texts. In Japan, the system of manuscript publication allowed authors to carefully control the circulation of their works. Many of the works central to the Japanese literary canon, such as the *Tale of Genji*, were produced and transmitted via manuscript even after printed editions became common. Just as print never displaced manuscript in Europe, East Asian cultures continued to value manuscripts for a number of complicated reasons.

FIGURE 3.1. *Ehon azuma asobi*, 1802. A multicolor wood-block print of a shop selling ukiyo-e, illustrated by Hokusa. UCLA Library Special Collections.

The relationship between print and manuscript technology in China was regionally specific. (Indeed, throughout the history of books, print, and information, it is important to be wary of generalizations about large units like states, as there was a great deal of regional variation in the price, availability, medium, and distribution of books.) While the Song government sponsored massive printing initiatives in medicine, the classics, and official and government forms of all sorts, and in some areas of China, such as the economically prosperous regions around Hangzhou, print overtook manuscript as the form in which people read and collected books, elsewhere in the empire imprints began definitively to outnumber and replace manuscripts in popularity only in the sixteenth century. Regardless of locality, even at its height the popularity of print did not eclipse the production and use of manuscripts.

Commercialization and Vernacularization

As in other regions of the premodern world, the relationship between *vernaculars and written languages was complex in East Asia. One of the major changes that occurred during the early modern period was the widespread emergence of written and printed vernacular languages. Literary Sinitic (sometimes referred to as Classical Chinese, or simply Chinese) was the language of the educated elite throughout premodern East Asia. Although the language changed over time, when compared to the challenges posed by the paleographic and linguistic shifts in other parts of the world, Sinitic was remarkably stable, but like Latin in the West, its stability was imposed by the veneration of certain styles and grammars. This stability also applied to its grammatical difficulty, especially when studied by linguistic groups outside of the Sino-Tibetan family. Challenges to its hegemony began to emerge during the Song dynasty, when Inner Asian kingdoms such as the Khitan Liao (916–1125) and Tangut Xixia (1038–1227) invented their own scripts. At the same time, Japanese Kana (a phonetic syllabary derived from Sinitic) began to become more popular, partly because of the rise of late medieval literary culture. The rise of the Mongol Empire, with its policy of "divide and rule," continued to undermine claims of Sinitic centrality, as is demonstrated dramatically by the 1345 sexaglot inscriptions (Chinese, Tibetan, Mongolian, Uyghur, Sanskrit, and Tangut) of the Cloud Platform, near the Great Wall outside modern Beijing. Each of the inscriptions records a Buddhist text, and the platform is seen as an example of Mongol commitment to Buddhist rulership.

With the dissolution of Mongol imperial rule, East Asian multilingualism entered a new phase. While some scripts, such as semiphonetic Jurchen and character-based Tangut, faded, new scripts, such as the Korean alphabet, were invented (some of these languages belonged to the Sino-Tibetan family; others were Tungusic). When King Sejong (r. 1418–50) proposed promulgating the Korean alphabet for writing vernacular Korean, Choe Malli condemned the writing system because of the association of phonetic alphabets with "barbarians." He wrote: "Although winds and soils vary from region to region, there has been no separate writing system for local dialects. Only such peoples as the Mongolians, Tanguts, Jürchens, Japanese, and Tibetans have their own writings. But this is a matter that involves the barbarians and is unworthy of our concern. It has been said that the barbarians are transformed only by means of adopting Sinitic ways; we have never heard of Sinitic ways being transformed by the barbarians" (adapted from Lee, 519). For Choe, the problem at the root of the new script was that it promised to alter the nature of the relatively young Chosŏn state. While it may not seem so on first appearance, Choe's argument was fundamentally historical. Adopting "barbarian" ways, in this case a phonetic script, explicitly harkened back to the Yuan (Mongols), the Jurchen Jin, and the Tangut Xixia. Korea was different from these places *precisely* because it had never stepped away from Sinitic practices by adopting a "barbarian" script. Despite Choe's concerns, the Korean alphabet would eventually become an important script in Chosŏn Korea, particularly in later periods when *literacy expanded to include greater numbers of women and non-elite men (see figure 3.2). Sinitic remained the working language of state and scholarship until the modern period, but it coexisted alongside other forms of literacies.

Across the sea, Sinitic became less important to many readers in Japan after the Heian period (794–1185). Although the printing of Buddhist texts and some Confucian classics (as well as occasional monastic missions to China) kept Sinitic language alive, most Japanese literature, such as the *Tale of Genji*, was written in the vernacular. After the rise of the Tokugawa shogunate in the early seventeenth century, the fortunes of Sinitic improved, but it never displaced the dominance of texts written in colloquial Japanese—which included translations from Sinitic and semivernacular Chinese. In early modern Japan, the expansion of available texts that came with a burgeoning print market helped generate an increasingly accessible body of public information. According to Mary Elizabeth Berry's *Japan in Print*, this market helped to create a "library of public information," which manifested as something like an available pool of common knowledge and a collective memory. This "library" included *encyclopedic lists of flora and fauna, cookbooks, calendars, guides to etiquette, guidebooks for travel to various cities and localities, useful vocabularies for various circumstances and professions, and books on poetry composition, gardening, healing, the arts of the bedchamber, ritual and social customs of all sorts, and many other topics.

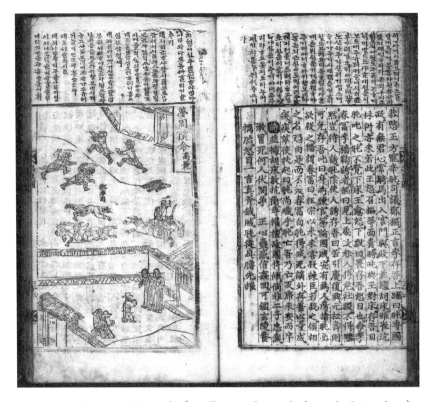

FIGURE 3.2. *Samgang Haengsilto* (An illustrated record of moral relationships), seventeenth century. A Korean morality primer in which the Chinese was printed with movable type, while the Korean alphabet was printed by xylography. UCLA Library Special Collections.

China, too, underwent a great vernacularization during the late Ming. During the sixteenth century commercial printers attracted new readers by issuing a wide variety of books for entertainment. Medieval stories were translated into *baihua*, semivernacular Chinese, which was more accessible to less educated readers. Under Manchu rule during the Qing dynasty (1644–1911), the print market expanded to include materials in non-Han languages. From the middle of the seventeenth century the Manchu language grew into a key language of empire, political instrument, and medium of translation and communication across eastern Eurasia. Manchu-language translations of Chinese poetry, fiction, history, and classic texts were printed alongside a growing library of original manuscript materials in a wide range of genres, both for the court and for a Manchu-reading public. Because not all Qing subjects had access to a Manchu-language education, composing a text in Manchu and refusing to translate it into Chinese was also a way to limit it to Manchu readers, like the Kangxi (r. 1661–1722) era *Dergici toktobuha ge ti ciowan lu bithe* (Complete record of the body, imperially commissioned, more commonly known as *The Manchu Anatomy*). This medical text combined East Asian and Western medical traditions into a hybrid style, allowing the Qing court to position itself as a center of cosmopolitan "imperial" science that existed only in Manchu. Tibetan monasteries were key sites of printing, storing, and making available works on religious, literary, medical, historical, and other topics, and the seventeenth and eighteenth centuries saw major shifts in Tibetan and Mongolian print cultures.

Similarly in Vietnam a distinctive script was developed for writing in the vernacular. Chữ Nôm script appeared sometime in the twelfth century, as a local adaptation of Chinese to represent Vietnamese pronunciation. The script gained in popularity during the Ming invasion of Vietnam in the early fifteenth century, eventually becoming the preferred language for literary composition. While Sinitic remained important in various Vietnamese courts, the elite composed and circulated (in manuscript and print) works in the vernacular.

Storing Information

Like any information culture, East Asian societies prioritized storing materials for later retrieval. For the most part, it is difficult to find firm distinctions between libraries and archives. Instead, repositories of books and manuscripts existed in a continuum. While archives (for which there was no single Sinograph, although many were "storehouses," e.g., Chinese *ku* / Japanese *ku* / Korean *ko* / Vietnamese *khố*) might be devoted exclusively to manuscript materials, they often held print as well. Nonetheless, in the following subsections we treat each separately.

Storing: Libraries

Libraries, by which we mean book collections that were accessible beyond the scale of a single individual or controlling family, became increasingly common in East Asia through the late imperial period. As book production increased, so did the number of libraries. Initially, most libraries were associated with institutions such as academies, government offices, or monasteries. But over time, libraries belonging to families that were accessible through personal introduction became important to scholarly communities.

Academies spread throughout East Asia (beginning in the 1200s in China, the 1400s in Korea, and after 1600 in Japan) as the principal institutions of higher education, each of which had its own books available for student perusal. Most academies owned standard works such as the Confucian classics and important historical chronicles but also displayed a great deal of regional variety. Since academies could often be traced to important intellectuals or specific lineages, they owned unique texts in manuscript or ones that had been produced in limited print runs (in some cases published by the academy) that differentiated their holdings from collections elsewhere. This meant that while scholars could use academy libraries to lay a common foundation, their more intensive research in a given library was often inflected by a particular intellectual tradition.

The academies of Chosŏn Korea are some of the best surviving institutions for understanding the nature of academy libraries. In the sixteenth and seventeenth centuries, Korean academies emerged as significant centers for both education and consolidation of their intellectual factions. Affiliation with a particular academy's educational lineage involved affiliation with a particular political faction. This was reflected not only in national politics, which began to divide around famous lineages and their teachings, but also in library collections. In a survey of thirty-three surviving collections, most of which were built in the eighteenth century, Yi Chun'hŭi has recently discovered that academies from the Namin faction held none of the collected works of the major thinkers from rival factions.

Like academies, monasteries also held significant collections of books. Veneration of the Buddhist canon played a major role in East Asian Buddhist piety. During both the Ming and the Qing dynasties, imperially printed editions of the Buddhist canon, in Mongolian, Tibetan, and Chinese, were disseminated to select monastic institutions to demonstrate imperial commitment to the faith. The presence of the canon attracted both scholars and lay devotees to monasteries and even contributed to the creation of a unique type of furniture: the rotating library case. Because "turning the wheel" of Buddhist doctrine was the metaphor for disseminating Buddhist teachings, it was seen as a devotional act to be able to literally rotate portions of the canon. Sometime in the late Tang dynasty, large rotating shelves containing the canon became popular features of some monasteries, and they became particularly popular in Japan during the Tokugawa period (and there are more than 110 rotating libraries in Japan today).

Private libraries also played a major role in the circulation of knowledge through the sharing of their holdings. The late Ming dynasty saw the emergence of several important private libraries in south China. The most famous library, the Tianyi ge library in Ningbo, was founded in 1561 by the bibliophile official Fan Qin. The library set new standards for book preservation and storage, becoming the model for other libraries, and it is still in use today with many of its original features. While not "public," the Fans permitted scholars with connections to the family (either directly or through social introduction) to access the seventy thousand or so books in the collection.

Government offices also maintained book collections. The collections developed by the Ming and Qing courts were especially large. Books printed in China were also central to government libraries in Korea and Japan. A memorial to the throne (a formal suggestion to the ruler) by the Korean official Kim Kŭnsa (d. 1539) on the importance of book collecting captured the role of books in government collections. He explained in his memorial to King Chungjong (r. 1506–44): "The collection of books dates to antiquity. . . . All governance, disorder, as well as the rise and fall of different historical periods are in them." Kim complained that collecting was unfortunately no longer a major priority: "That we have neglected books in this way, is it not heart breaking?" At the end of his memorial, he asked Chungjong not only to seek out old texts from among his subjects, but also to request books from the Ming.

A month after Kim's memorial, Chungjong released an official edict on the importance of books to the Korean throne. He reiterated Korea's commitment to books in a memorial to the Board of Rites:

Books are the abode of the way of governance. . . . Since the time of the ancestors of our dynasty, we have elevated the art of classicism, the sagely scriptures and traditions of the worthies, as well as all of the collections of the historical masters. We have done this so that we could gather all lost or neglected texts. We not only preserve them in secret government collections, but we also distribute them. . . . Today, we order our emissaries who go to the central court [of China] to seek books without limits . . . [and for those within Korea] to submit books, for which I will richly reward them.

This edict, which was circulated "domestically and abroad" made Chungjong's commitment to learning a matter of public record.

By 1600 the shogun of Japan, Tokugawa Ieyasu, had formed important collections of books produced abroad, often by relying on books looted from Korea, comprising both Chinese and Korean editions. Tokugawa Ieyasu collected books not only to bolster his legitimacy, but also to draw on the knowledge they contained as he patronized the new "Confucians" of Japan, the most famous of whom was Hayashi Razan (1583–1657). Razan looked at the Tokugawa collection in Sunpu with some ambivalence. He viewed himself as something of a hostage to the books in the shogunal collection for which he was responsible. The books, not the shogun, kept him loyal: "I myself feel as if I am [more and more] going in for fame and profit. . . . It is shameful. It is terrible. However, I hold the keys of the library in Sunpu. I try one of the buildings, and the boxes are filled [with books]. I leave it to my hand [which one] to pick. The happiness of reading a book I have not yet read. . . . My only pleasures are books. . . . This is a favour from my lord, and one thing that I have gained. Is it not also [a reason] to be glad?" (Boot, 236). As Razan's anxiety shows, collections of books were powerful enticements. Razan and his lineage founded one of the most impressive libraries in Tokugawa Japan. While printing enabled many scholars to amass impressive collections of their own, they could not hope to compete with the collecting agenda of the state. Royal collections, like those associated with the shogun Yoshimune (r. 1716–45), became centers for the creation of knowledge.

Over the course of the seventeenth century, the commercial production of books increased in Japan, fueling expanded individual collections but also new forms of access to books. By the end of the century, commercial lending libraries were open to readers who paid a subscription fee. By the end of the Tokugawa period in the nineteenth century, commercial libraries were common throughout Japan, and some domains could even boast entirely free "public" libraries housed in shrines. In Qing China there were commercial lending libraries, but the existence of "public" libraries is debated. Lending libraries for popular literature also became popular in nineteenth-century Korea.

Storing: Archives

Although premodern intellectuals in East Asia were keen collectors of information from all sources, when compared to libraries, archives were relatively less valued. Materials worth saving became parts of books, and it was presumed that ephemeral papers would vanish over time. Moreover, the presence of overwhelming amounts of paper made archives a focus of official anxiety. By the late sixteenth century, paperwork overload worried the Ming official Lu Kun. He blamed documentary disorder for the decline of the state:

"Methods of governance are in decline because of the flood of written text; the disaster has come from the overabundance of registers. . . . In their thousands, they pile up on hundreds of shelves, eaten by insects and rats, and inside they all contradict one another!" Lu Kun's concerns would have resonated at the time with readers in Europe struggling under similar archival burdens.

In Japan, archival practices and systems took a multitude of forms. Each domain and each office had its own particular modes of handling paperwork. The Nagasaki magistrates (*bugyō*), charged by the shogun with the management of the city and its extensive international trade, owned their own archival records. When they left office, they took their personal papers with them. Although archives moved with officials, continuity in practices was maintained because Japanese governance relied on networks of archives. Official translators in Nagasaki, for example, maintained their own archives, as did local neighborhood organizations. While there was disruption in the continuity of governance when officeholders left with their papers, vested subordinates could domesticate new officials to local practices and standards.

While the records of specific posts were often tied to the collections of the individuals who held them, various domains (which were controlled by lineage) maintained detailed archival records. The Tsushima domain, ruled by the Sō family (r. twelfth century–1871), managed trade between Chosŏn Korea and Tokugawa Japan. Its retainers kept records of both domain affairs and international relations in the family compounds on the island of Tsushima and in its estate in Edo. These chronologically organized registers were subdivided by topic, which could lead readers to full versions of documents. These records have been exploited by historians to great effect.

Governance by archive was also a characteristic of the Chosŏn and the Ming and Qing courts. In Ming and Qing China archival collections were essential tools for tracking government accountability, and registers linked readers in different offices with originals presumed to be in an archival collection. Unfortunately, our knowledge of the actual organization of archives of Chinese offices is anecdotal, since most were destroyed or reorganized in the twentieth century. One Ming compilation, a 1540s official manual for the Rear Lake Archive, where census records were stored, provides a sense of some of the changes in archival practices. For example, the manual explains a basic change in the material composition of registers. Early in the Ming, registers were bound in paper wraps, which were attached to the spine of the text using wheat paste. But the wheat paste attracted rodents and insects, and archival managers discovered extensive damage in the collection in the 1470s. This led to a debate about format—and a shift to the use of registers bound with paper twists and threads.

While preservation was clearly important in East Asian archives, destruction was also normal. In Chosŏn Korea, local-level government archives were routinely destroyed after they had been processed into summary registers. Only a small proportion of central-level archival documents survive from the Chosŏn period. But this was by design. Throughout East Asia, almost every member of society understood the power of political archives, and both states and their subjects knew better than to leave documents in archives "undomesticated" by historical narratives. History bureaus were formed by most courts to bring records into order. In Chosŏn Korea, historians were also officially prohibited from holding any other government positions, to ensure impartiality in processing records.

Officials were not the only collectors of papers. Family archives became increasingly important throughout the region as the state became increasingly capable of making its presence felt. Lineages in south China managed their archival materials with exceptional acuity in their efforts to manage their interactions with the state. In Huizhou, a commercially prosperous center of south China, many families held the Ming tax receipts into the twentieth century—even when the tax registers held by the state had long since been lost. In Korea and Japan family collections are some of our best-preserved collections for understanding and interpreting the premodern period. Although little has been written on these collections in English, East Asian scholars have long been aware of the importance of family archives for premodern history.

In addition to family collections, almost every corporate body in premodern East Asia maintained records of its activities. Large firms, such as those operating in the city of Chongqing during the Qing dynasty, kept their own records and also made sure to get important contracts on file in the county archives. Temples throughout East Asia kept collections of deeds and, in Tokugawa Japan, even assisted that state by holding records that were used to certify that no subject secretly harbored Christian beliefs.

Sorting Information

Since all premodern East Asian societies could boast sizable collections of texts, different methods for sorting and classifying information were created to manage materials. From a macro perspective, the tools available for managing information were similar on both ends of Eurasia. Library catalogs in codex form linked book locations to shelf numbers; paper files were organized according to paper registers; and filing systems used complicated taxonomies. Despite similarities in their technologies for information organization, the ways in which states and individuals interacted with materials created striking differences between premodern Asia and the West.

One easy example to consider is bibliographic classification. Most East Asian societies shared bibliographic categories that emerged during the medieval period of Chinese history, particularly as they were outlined in the "bibliography" section in the *History of the Sui* (compiled in the 620s). Libraries and catalogs in many parts of East Asia followed the order of categories outlined in the *History*—with the "classics, histories, masters, and compilations" as supercategories under which many subcategories were organized. However, the subcategories under each section were subject to regular change and debate. Books moved from "standard history" to "unofficial history" at the whims of bibliographers influenced by political changes. This could have social consequences beyond the library, as it led to the censorship of texts, and in some exceptional circumstances, the posthumous punishment of the earthly remains of their authors. In East Asia, as in other parts of the world, how things were sorted was political, and sorting was a major focus of intellectual activity.

Sorting Spaces

Sorting information was guided by any number of different priorities. One topic of great interest to East Asian intellectuals was sorting by place. In the Chinese context, this was exemplified in the transformation of a genre known as a *gazetteer (difang zhi)*, a textual compilation of information about the geography, peoples, history, and other features of a particular locality, culled from any combination of texts, in situ observations, and conversations. From their popularization in the Song period, there was a long-term rise in the production of local gazetteers, with periods of increased compilation during the founding and consolidation of dynasties and in the context of some imperial projects, and periods of decline during times of war.

Local gazetteers were crucial to the information history of China because they gathered local information in the material form in which it circulated to local and nonlocal readers. Gazetteers helped local elites connect to and influence central government officials and policy, and they helped a centralizing imperial state incorporate peripheral areas into the empire. Although they were intended primarily for an audience of officials and literati, the actual readership varied.

No two gazetteers are identical, but the genre is unified by similar topical arrangements. They often began with a series of maps, then related the administrative history of the area, and typically drilled down on further details about a locale. Gazetteers sorted the empire by contributing to court debates about how to classify regions according to their governability. Their functionality meant that in the borderland peripheries of the empire, gazetteers were perceived by Chinese officials as tools for assimilating native peoples into Chinese culture and political order. They were often the first Chinese-language literary projects in these places, and they helped facilitate the circulation and translation of information between Chinese and non-Chinese societies.

The influence of gazetteers extended far beyond China. The shogun Yoshimune viewed gazetteers as important tools to understand the politics of his Qing neighbor. This reading of Chinese gazetteers occurred alongside the continual production of gazetteers (*Fudoki* and other genres) in Japan, which had begun in the 700s. Tokugawa authors, like their Ming and Qing neighbors, also displayed an interest in classifying and sorting spaces on a local and global scale. In both East Asian contexts, attending to locality was bound up with attention to frontiers and boundaries, and much information was contained in gazetteers' discussions of border affairs, relations and networks across borders, and the characteristics that separated entities at various scales from one another.

Gazetteers were also a popular genre in Vietnam. The earliest surviving gazetteer was compiled in 1425. The Nguyen dynasty (1802–1945) sponsored a large number of gazetteer projects as it asserted rule over a united northern and southern Vietnam. Court enthusiasm for classifying the realm spurred individual scholar-officials, like Phạm Thận Duật (1825–85), to draw on their experience in border regions, as well as on their extensive reading in Chinese and Vietnamese sources, to compose their own local histories. Korea also inherited the gazetteer tradition. The Chosŏn court oversaw the production of gazetteers pertaining to important government offices. The *Gazetteer of the Translation Bureau* (T'ongmun'gwan chi), compiled in 1708, was a record intended to outline the duties and responsibilities of government translators. This kind of office gazetteer, which drew on earlier precedents, illustrates how officials could use textual genres to sort out bureaucratic responsibilities.

Stepping back from the issues associated with individual gazetteers, it is evident that the genre was essential for the transformation of space into specifically governed places. During the Qing dynasty, different counties throughout the empire were given "importance ratings" based on their governability. Although gazetteers were not directly mentioned in these ratings, the process that sorted the empire occurred at the gubernatorial level. The 1782 governor of Shandong county noted, for example: "Among the 110 districts, departments and garrisons [in Shandong], there are many where local conditions in the past and local conditions today are not the same. The importance ratings of such positions should be adjusted. One should go with the times and make changes. [It would be] for the sake of good government. . . . If we swap importance ratings [in the way outlined above], each place would end up with an appropriate label, human resources would be allocated according to local conditions and it would be to the benefit of local administration" (Koss, 166). Labeling counties with reference to archival and gazetteer-based reports sorted the empire in two ways. First, it made the state's difficulties legible by linking counties to particular problems of governance. Second, it allowed for the sorting of the people responsible for government. Counties ranked as "difficult" received more attention from more experienced magistrates than counties with few problems.

Sorting Sciences

The sorting of spaces went hand in glove with the sorting of human bodies and nature. Chinese natural historians in the late Ming period developed new methods for evaluating the many kinds of evidence available in the libraries, compendia, and collectanea of an expanded information economy. In addition to textual sources, scholars ascribed new evidentiary value to first-person witnessing of natural phenomena. Li Shizhen's *Bencao gangmu* (Systematic materia medica), first printed in 1596, exemplified this approach by drawing on poetry, dictionaries, histories, medical texts, first-person interviews, and self-experimentation to explain and organize the natural world. This work became one of the most influential works on natural history across East Asia. In the seventeenth and eighteenth centuries, natural history encyclopedias in China and Japan continued to combine lexicographical research and personal observation in descriptions of plants, animals, and other natural objects. The booming commercial market for these works in both places helped foster a concern for accuracy as a virtue and at the same time anxieties about identifying and assessing accuracy.

Like Li Shizhen, Hŏ Chun, a Chosŏn court physician active after the Japanese invasions of Korea (1592–98), compiled an encyclopedic collection of medical information that was both cosmopolitan and specific. It was cosmopolitan in its agreement with the basic practices of the Sinitic medical tradition, especially those in the *Bencao gangmu*. But like some before him, he also believed that a distinctly Korean body had emerged, along with distinctly Korean materia medica, which demanded special treatment and localized knowledge. The publication of his medical compendium in 1614 led to the work's eventual reprinting, in several editions, in both Qing China and Tokugawa Japan. His lessons about the specificity of the Korean body and Korean herbs placed the importance of locality at the center of increasingly transnational medical practices.

Throughout East Asia, the expanding print economy fostered methods of measuring, describing, and valuing natural objects that allowed for the further circulation of this information. Plants and animals became physical and intellectual commodities, and accounts of them strove for accuracy and precision. (Scholars and officials also learned to strategically deploy misinformation in order to further their political or social goals.) The commercialization also favored illustrations. A pictorial archive emerged as a result of the commodification of plants and animals, and with it connoisseurship practices around objects and images.

Images and accuracy not only were important in medical works but also played an important role in evidentiary scholarship. Like medical doctors, antiquarians valued the ability of print to reflect and circulate discoveries. One particularly stunning example of the speed with which such news traveled was the discovery of a Chinese Christian stele. In 1625, Chinese laborers excavated a nine-foot-tall, three-foot-wide limestone stele on the outskirts of Xi'an. The stone, dating to the late eighth century, was entitled *Jingjiao liuxing zhongguo bei* (A stele on the spread of Nestorianism in the Central Kingdom). It celebrated the progress of the Nestorian Church in China between 635 and 791. A rubbing of the stele was sent to Li Zhizao, who shared it with his *Jesuit colleagues. Li produced a xylographic edition and commentary of the text, while the Jesuits sent the inscription back to Europe with a translation. The inscription was eventually used as a basis for a copper-plate engraving of the monument when Athanasius Kircher published his *China monumentis qua sacris qua profanis nec non variis naturae et artis spectaculis aliarumque rerum memorabilium argumentis illustrata* (China illuminated by sacred and profane monuments, as well as varied spectacles of nature and art and tales of other remarkable matters) in 1667.

In the case of the Nestorian stele, the Jesuits were interlocutors in translating a Chinese archeological discovery for European readers, but in the case of calendrical sciences, they played a major role in transmitting Copernicanism and more accurate astronomy to East Asia. During the seventeenth and eighteenth centuries, Jesuit contributions to astronomical observation and recording, timekeeping, and mapmaking generated maps, charts, diagrams, and illustrations by wood-block printing for East Asian scholars. Their introduction of perspective to paintings also served informational purposes, notably when such paintings were designed to represent political reforms at the court or were exchanged in private communications as a form of social currency. One unintended consequence of the growing emphasis on observation, measurement, and identification was the emergence of anxieties about precision and accuracy in the production and circulation of such information across space and time.

Controlling Information

Sorting information inevitably involved selection and control. Compilers, librarians, and archivists were constantly making choices about what to keep and what to remove, and these choices were driven by political concerns. Even the grandest encyclopedia in world history, the imperially commissioned 1405 *Yongle Encyclopedia* (which, at the size of 370 million characters, was surpassed only by Wikipedia in 2007), was selective about which information to include. The act of selecting contributed directly to the standardization of information. In China and Korea, the predominance of court projects and the bureaucratic system of recruitment of officials ensured a relatively high level of central control of information cultures. Standardization and censorship were often closely related in the bureaucracies of East Asia. In China, the state's leadership in scholarly projects contributed to the creation of literary canons and allowed officials to check work for potential offenses to the throne.

Examinations and Standardizing Education

The civil service examination system stands out as one of the most remarkable features of premodern East Asian governments. While the examination system began in the Tang dynasty, it emerged as central to bureaucratic recruitment during the Song and Chosŏn dynasties in China and Korea, respectively. The premise of the system was simple enough: in order to earn appointment as a state official, scholars needed to pass a series of tiered examinations that would qualify them for office. This idea spawned massive investments by states and

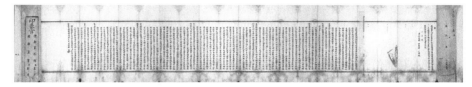

FIGURE 3.3. Palace Examination paper of Xiong Wentao, 1889. An example of a
Qing period examination paper. From the Han Yu-shan Collection, UCLA
Library Special Collections.

by aspiring officials. In China, by the thirteenth century there were already
tens of thousands of scholars competing in the triennial examination.

The examinations brought about different types of standardization. First,
they integrated the interests of state and society. Broad social networks were
necessary for a candidate to pass the exams and gain office (and this was increasingly the case already during the transition from the Tang to the Song
dynasty), and conversely exam credentials garnered social prestige and lucrative official appointments for successful candidates. An expansion of the exam
system in the late tenth century helped undermine long-standing social hierarchies for a time, but by the Ming period the exams were producing long-
lasting new literati groups. Competition for the civil exams created a status
group of degree holders who shared a common classical language that served
as a kind of lingua franca of classically educated men, a shared canon based on
Song "Confucian learning" that they memorized, and a shared literary writing
style (the eight-legged essay) (see figure 3.3).

Second, examinations contributed to the standardization of education.
One need look no further than the book market to see the impact of the examination system on reading and learning habits. Publishers around the empire all
sold their own editions of the core texts of the examination, the Confucian four
books and the Chinese classics. No scholar has attempted to estimate the total
number of distinct editions of these texts (attempting to count them would be
as bibliographically difficult as enumerating the number of Bible editions for
early modern Europe), and the commentarial tradition that developed to
make them accessible beggars comprehensive description. Already in the
southern Song, sample examination essays and discussions of examination
curricula formed an important part of the print market. By the Ming and Qing,
winning examination essays were frequently printed to serve as models for
the reading public. With the fall of the Ming and the rise of the Qing state,

examinations were adapted to further integrate the conquering Manchu and Mongolian soldiers. The state established special dynastic schools for the eight military banners (which comprised the Qing hereditary service elite), a school for the imperial Manchu family, and examinations in Manchu and Mongolian. Examinations for the banner men emphasized martial and translation skills, considered essential for those who would extend Qing rule over Inner Asia. The book market responded by making relevant textbooks available.

Examinations played an important part in Chosŏn Korea as well. The Chosŏn court limited participation in the civil service examinations to members of elite lineages (*yangban*). Scholar-bureaucrats, however, were unprepared for many of the more technical problems facing the state. Tackling those was the purview of *chungin* ("middle-people"), the technically trained classes of the Chosŏn government, including translators, scribes, doctors, and geomancy specialists. Like other members of the bureaucracy, they were recruited through examinations and trained for these in specialist schools that developed "practical" skills.

Vietnamese regimes were also early adopters of the examination system. By the 1230s, the Trần made examinations a regular part of bureaucratic recruitment. The first examinations recruited only small classes of bureaucrats, but by the middle of the sixteenth century, the examinations were routinely drawing thousands of candidates in the economic centers of the region. While later examinations would never prove as popular as they were during the sixteenth century, a strong test-taking culture ensured that a standard set of classics and texts unified "Confucian scholars" in China, Vietnam, and Korea.

In Japan the state was not powerful enough to impose such a system. Early Tokugawa Confucians admired the system, but the hereditary elite of various domains could never be abolished through shogunal fiat. Still, experiments with examinations were irresistible to the shogun's scholars. In 1792 the shogun began experimenting with educational reforms that culminated in a standardized examination. These experiments were inspired in part by fears of decline. The scholar Koga Seiri (1750–1817) noted these problems in the Saga domain: "As our country is under a regime of generals, the path of selection/election is closed. Particularly in domains [controlled by Daimyo] such as ours [Saga], the damage of the hereditary system is not to be avoided. Those with hereditary status are negligent, and those without it do not serve. This is why the spirit of the gentleman/samurai cannot be enacted and why custom can so degenerate" (Paramore, 88). The 1792 establishment of shogunal examinations based at the Shōheizaka Academy in Edo was one attempt to provide a new model for training scholars in the sorts of virtues necessary to prevent state decline. As with everywhere else in East Asia, Confucian books were at the center of the curriculum.

Throughout the region, the examination system contributed to the making and remaking of a Confucian canon tailored to the interests and needs of the government and its ruling bureaucrats. Certain texts were universally perceived as important, but debates about *which* commentary to adapt, and a philological approach to analyzing the classics and their compilation, created contention over a common canon.

Censorship

The existence of curricula worthy of universal study throughout East Asia co-existed with the other extreme of standardization: the formation of lists of banned and heterodox works. Hints of lèse-majesté or the violation of taboos led to books being banned and burned. Despite occasional censorship campaigns, attempts to ban books also met with considerable resistance. This resistance was perhaps facilitated by technology. Woodblocks, after all, were highly mobile, so printers could forestall their confiscation. But it is also likely due to the "chilling" effect of bans and the practice of self-censorship by authors and printers that there were relatively few cases of book burning.

Despite the reputation it has today as a period of strict censorship, the Qing dynasty was not always harsh. In the famous case of Zeng Jing (1679–1735), a moderate Yongzheng emperor pardoned Zeng for attempting to incite an anti-Manchu rebellion among the Han Chinese. In a long tract arguing for cosmopolitanism, the emperor condemned Zeng's writings, noting that place of origin had nothing to do with one's suitability to rule. He castigated Zeng for being someone who "wrongly conjured the selfish idea of 'this border' and 'that line' . . . [and for] not knowing that this dynasty being Manchurian is the same as the Chinese having native places. After all, [the sage king] Shun was a person from the Eastern tribes and [the sage king] Wen was a person from the Western tribes. Was this any detriment to their sagely virtue?" Zeng's works were banned, but he was released from prison after his imperial reeducation.

Zeng's pardon in his lifetime proved only temporary. The following ruler, the Qianlong emperor (r. 1735–96), declared Zeng's crimes against the Manchu throne unpardonable. Zeng's body was exhumed and beaten in public, a spectacle befitting the ruler who began one of the longest censorship campaigns in Chinese history. There are many reasons why the Qianlong emperor pushed for censorship. Some scholars have argued that he feared Manchu as-similation and interethnic tension. Others have seen his drive to censor as part of the court's attempt to shape intellectual culture through the empire. Regard-less of its causes, the compilation of the *Complete Library of the Four Treasuries* (*Siku Quanshu*) and the resulting censorship campaign have become emblem-atic of Qing despotism.

In brief, the *Four Treasuries* was an encyclopedic project initiated by the Qianlong emperor in the early 1770s. The purpose of the project was to scour the empire in order to collect and reproduce books of literary and philosophi-cal merit. Approximately eleven thousand titles were collected and submitted to court inspectors. Thirty-five hundred of these titles were printed in seven copies each (in movable type!) and stored in official libraries for scholarly use around the empire. The book collection campaign served the purpose of ren-dering the textual landscape of the empire legible to the court. In the process of collecting books to reprint, others were found unacceptable and confis-cated. Approximately three thousand titles were burned, and in many more, taboo words, such as "barbarian," which the emperor deemed offensive to the Manchu elite, were expunged.

Despite the censorship accompanying the *Four Treasuries*, many censored works survived. But the influence of the campaign was felt far beyond China. Regular visitors from Chosŏn Korea learned about Qing censorship, and their reports likely inspired more censorship at the Chosŏn court. Despite this mo-ment of shared censorship, the practice was not new to Korea. During the Ming dynasty Chosŏn sensitivity over perceived insults to the Chosŏn founder led the court to petition the Jiajing emperor to revise the chapter of *The Col-lected Institutions of the Ming* (*Daming huidian*) describing Korea. Factional politics also played a role in determining what was censored. In 1709, the chief councillor of state Ch'oe Sŏkchŏng (1646–1725) became the target of impeach-ment in a lengthy memorial. Yi Kwanmyŏng accused Ch'oe of attempting to outshine the classical commentaries of the Song thinker Zhu Xi (1130–1200), who had written the orthodox commentaries on the classics. Ch'oe's com-mentary on the *Book of Rites* was condemned for subtly changing Zhu Xi's perspective on the classics, and all copies of the text were burned.

Sensitivity toward dynastic founders also inspired selective forgetting in Nguyen Vietnam. The state banned histories from the Le period (1428–1788) that cast doubt on the legitimacy of its origins. But such measures seem to have been exceptional rather than ordinary in Vietnam before the nineteenth century. Philiphê Binh, a Vietnamese priest who spent much of his life in

Lisbon, praised the Portuguese ability to censor printed works before publication. His description of the process illustrates that while he considered it desirable for the state to have a hand in selecting which texts should be printed, this perspective was exceptional for someone from the southern part of Vietnam.

Tokugawa Japan censored works it found potentially damaging to state interests. Beginning in the 1630s, Christian works were almost universally prohibited because of their perceived dangers to the state. The ban remained in effect for most of the Tokugawa period, but there was a loosening in the 1720s after Yoshimune began to promote the study of Western sciences. Other forms of censorship in the Tokugawa period are harder to trace. A large number of ad hoc edicts occasionally banned the circulation of certain works, and authors were occasionally imprisoned. One way around taboos seems to have been through the circulation of manuscripts. A large number of manuscript accounts of foreign places *leaked from government offices into wider circulation. These texts contained sensitive information and, while not explicitly banned, were accessible only to trusted members of a scholarly network.

In sum, banning books was a common tactic of rulers throughout East Asia, although it rarely was entirely successful. Instead, as in much of the world, taboos and government restrictions created a dampening effect. Scholars understood the sorts of books they were supposed to publish, and they kept anything potentially controversial in manuscript to circulate among limited groups of readers.

Archival Compilations

The control of information was typically entwined with summarizing or condensing. When texts were too long, or when space was limited, the ability to condense information efficiently and accurately was critical. Summarizing became important in encyclopedias—many of which were astonishingly long. In fact, the length of some books, even affordable household encyclopedias, could become the object of humor. A 1797 Japanese text complained that "the eighty-two chapters" of the *Japanese Illustrated Universe* (*Sancai tuhui*) were too much for a child. The author decided to summarize the entire text in fifteen pages so that even a three-year-old (*sanzai*, a homophone for "universe" in Japanese) could manage to learn its key points. The humorous illustrations throughout the work's fifteen pages poked fun at the conceit of encyclopedism, while also providing useful points for a positive learning experience.

Summarizing was important not just for popular readers; it was also at the core of government labor. Every Qing office functioned on a much larger scale than any European bureaucracy from the same period. Groups of officials and clerks coordinated and merged vast textual burdens of print, manuscript, and correspondence into succinct summaries for imperial perusal. They developed standard forms for submitting information to the throne that facilitated summarizing a legal document of several hundred pages in a handful of sentences. Information processing was the undertaking of hundreds of officials working in concert and without individual recognition; for an individual to emerge as a moderating node (as Jean-Baptiste Colbert did under Louis XIV in seventeenth-century France) would have been perceived as a fundamental flaw and failure.

One place to begin considering the strengths of the summarizing system of premodern Asia is with the state and its archival burden. Vertically integrated bureaucracies like those in China, Korea, and Japan governed through a series of registers. Registers made important parts of local government visible to the central government and allowed for the formation of appropriate policy. One challenge with trying to centrally legislate empire, however, was the need to keep everything up-to-date and synchronized.

In the early Ming, Zhu Yuanzhang (r. 1368–98), the founder of the dynasty, attempted to keep government offices working by commissioning the compilation and publication of a text containing the regulations of central government offices, entitled *Duties of All Government Offices* (*Zhusi zhizhang*). The compilation guided Ming governance until the 1470s, when officials began complaining that the nearly one-hundred-year-old compilation was out of date.

In the 1490s, the court ordered officials to begin searching through their archives for updated regulations. These updates were submitted to the court and compiled into a new work entitled the *Collected Institutions of the Great Ming* (*Daming huidian*). Completed in 1509, the preface by the Zhengde emperor (r. 1505–21) highlighted the importance of the text as a compilation that brought order to the chaos of contemporary administrative practice. He summarized the need for the *Collected Institutions* as follows:

> [Zhu Yuanzhang ordered] the writing of *Duties of All Government Offices* which recorded the guiding principles. . . . Truly it may be called a [collection] of laws of unprecedented greatness. But if we examine it as a text, then we see that it was made in the middle of the Hongwu reign [of Zhu Yuanzhang]. Matters which were fixed later in the reign, even if the offices were

named in the text, had been altered. The late sagely rulers followed time, and circumstances made changes that both increased and decreased [regulations]. Since every age differs, they did not fall short of the intentions of the sagely ancestor [Taizu]. . . . So it is that over the years there has been much accumulated. Registers and texts have piled up. Some of the separate boards and respective offices are unable to completely know what is within them.

The book that the government printed was a snapshot of the fragments of the archive. The hundred or so pages of *paratext before the work explained its compilation and fostered trust in the hundreds of chapters of archive-derived rules that followed.

While government offices rarely preserved drafts of books created from the archive, surviving compilations provide useful insight into scholarly working methods. The scholar-official Qi Biaojia (1602–45) was keenly interested in compiling a record of the Wanli reign (1563–1620). He began his work by cutting important entries from his father's manuscript notes on the court gazette, a manuscript newspaper circulated to officials throughout the Ming empire to report on court news. He supplemented these notes by making and cutting out his own notes on the Wanli reign. He then arranged all these materials, whatever their origins, in chronological order and pasted them into a series of blank notebooks. The cover of each notebook listed its main concerns and topics, a form of indexing that made the twenty-volume manuscript navigable.

Qi Biaojia's methods of managing information were likely shared by scholars across East Asia. The archives of the preconquest Manchu (which started its central archives around the year 1616) exist in a variety of different states, preserving a rare example of government work. Notes in a local register recording runaway enslaved peoples show that government scribes carefully selected what information to transfer into hierarchically superior registers of state precedent. Those registers, known as the "original Manchu archives" (Manwen yuandang), were subsequently edited into an even more condensed record—The Manchu Veritable Records (Manzhou Shilu)—after being carefully examined by officials in the National History Office.

The selection and use of archival and printed materials for practical matters was common throughout East Asia. In foreign relations, China's neighbors often had to do research into precedent as a matter of course. In 1462, when Zuikei Shūhō was charged with composing letters to the Ming court, he wrote a history of Japanese foreign relations. In 1470, he completed his *Precious*

Record of Benevolent Neighbor States (Zenrin kokuhōki). The text is a tour de force of Chinese and Japanese sources. Shūhō used Ming texts, such as the *History of the Yuan,* and several different Japanese sources to reproduce the documentary exchanges between Japan and China, and Japan and Korea, from 600 to 1400. This work seems a clear antecedent to the anti-Manchu *The Barbarization of Civilization (Ka'i Hentai),* compiled by Hayashi Gahō (1618–88). This work gathered and presented documents relating to the Manchu invasion of China and circulated in manuscript for much of the Tokugawa period. The sources of the documents were (1) letters and requests written from Ming officials to the shogun, (2) translated summaries of news from China based on interviews with Chinese merchants in Nagasaki, and (3) documents such as edicts and letters that were circulating within China and were brought to Japan. Like Zuikei and Qi Biaojia, Hayashi Gahō seamlessly blended the archival and the printed to create a narrative of recent history.

Conclusion: Information Alters Time and Space

Whether we call them early modern or late imperial, the fifteenth to nineteenth centuries in East Asia saw major structural shifts in information practices. Printing grew from its early invention and limited use to play a major role in societies throughout the region. The period witnessed the emergence of many different types of popular compilations. Encyclopedic compilations spread knowledge about states and their place in the world. A concept of the nation was built through print publications that circulated different kinds of information beyond the classical canon and government-sponsored projects. Formerly closed forms of knowledge became shared widely, as commercial publishers poached and recycled information from one another and from the collections they could access.

Across East Asia, an increased volume and variety of texts accompanied significant increases in urbanization, literacy, and travel. This early modern textual archive helped to shape how time and space were conceived and performed, at scales that ranged from the household to the state and the empire and helped to generate new approaches to history and cartography. These texts reflected a new emphasis on completeness and holistic coverage and associated anxieties about any potential lack thereof. A holistic vision of the polity characterized cadastral and cartographic surveys of the land such as those seen in gazetteers, whose form and style tended to convey a sense of the unity of that which was being mapped. This knowledge became part of a shared stock of information and cultural memory; it taught users how to read the state and the empire, and to think of themselves as part of both entities.

Information practices and the early modern transformations they wrought were deeply shaped by the transnational circulation of information. As this essay has illustrated, the region of East Asia shared information practices, starting with a learned language, script, and textual canon, and including the high value placed on scholarship, the collection of books and records, and performance on examinations. Local information cultures within this large geographic area (including China itself) emerged from a negotiation between the local and more distant cultural centers made possible by the circulation of people, manuscripts, and printed books. For every inhabitant in the region, persistent engagement with the foreign and novel, as well as growing confidence in their own places in the world, contributed to the reshaping of identities that both created and unbound ideas of the nation.

But this outline is still limited. Our focus on the coherence of an "East Asian Mediterranean" has excluded interactions within a still larger geographic framework of Inner Asia, such as the Persian-reading astronomers of the Yuan court, the Arabic- and Persian-literate Confucian Muslim scholars of the Qing, and the hybrid Tibetan Mongolian Buddhist scholars of Inner Asia. An Inner Asia–oriented history of East Asia would illustrate how China went from peripheral in the Ming to central in the Qing, as the Qing court became a center for polyglot practices. It would also illustrate how scholars in Japan and Korea grappled with the "barbarization" of Chinese civilization as Manchu rulers transformed Sinitic traditions for their own end. The history given above coexists with the Inner Asian history of early modern East Asia, and scholars are only now beginning to bring these stories together.

Further Reading

Mary Elizabeth Berry, *Japan in Print: Information and Nation in the Early Modern Period*, 2006; Willem Jan Boot, "The Adoption and Adaptation of Neo-Confucianism in Japan: The Role of Fujiwara Seika and Hayashi Razan," PhD dissertation, Leiden University, 1983; Cynthia J. Brokaw and Kai-Wing Chow, eds., *Printing and Book Culture in Late Imperial China*, 2005; Susan Cherniack, "Book Culture and Textual Transmission in Sung China," *Harvard Journal of Asiatic Studies* 54, no. 1 (1994): 5–125; Kai-wing Chow, *Publishing, Culture, and Power in Early Modern China*, 2004; Joseph R. Dennis, *Writing, Publishing, and Reading Local Gazetteers in Imperial China, 1100–1700*, 2015; Hilde De Weerdt, *Information, Territory, and Networks: The Crisis and Maintenance of Empire in Song China*, 2015; George Edson Dutton, *A Vietnamese Moses: Philiphê Bỉnh and the Geographies of Early Modern Catholicism*, 2017;

Benjamin A. Elman, *Civil Examinations and Meritocracy in Late Imperial China*, 2013; Jahyun Kim Haboush and Martina Deuchler, eds., *Culture and the State in Late Chosŏn Korea*, 2002; Matthias Hayek and Annick Horiyuchi, *Listen, Copy, Read: Popular Learning in Early Modern Japan*, 2014; Catherine Jami, *The Emperor's New Mathematics: Western Learning and Imperial Authority during the Kangxi Reign (1662–1722)*, 2012; Daniel Koss, "Political Geography of Empire: Chinese Varieties of Local Government," *Journal of Asian Studies* 76, no. 1 (2017): 159–84; Peter H. Lee, *Sourcebook of Korean Civilization*, vol. 1, *From Early Times to the 16th Century*, 2010; Federico Marcon, *The Knowledge of Nature and the Nature of Knowledge in Early Modern Japan*, 2015; Osamu Oba and Joshua A. Fogel, *Books and Boats: Sino-Japanese Relations and Cultural Transmission in the Eighteenth and Nineteenth Centuries*, 2012; Kiri Paramore, *Japanese Confucianism*, 2016; Kurtis R. Schaeffer, *The Culture of the Book in Tibet*, 2014.

4

Information in Early Modern Europe

Ann Blair

THE PERIOD OF EUROPEAN HISTORY from roughly 1450 to 1789 is now commonly called "early modern" on the notion that various features of "modernity" originated then. An earlier label for the period of "*Renaissance and *Reformation" emphasized the contents and impacts of those movements, whereas the preference for "early modern" that has spread since the 1980s invites attention to a broader array of developments and their interactions. In devoting multiple chapters to the fifteenth to eighteenth centuries in Europe and elsewhere, this volume seeks to highlight the presence and significance of information practices before the term and concept were in use in their current manner. In using the term *modern* we reject abstract definitions of modernity (e.g., as advanced by modernization theory in the 1950s and 1960s); instead we use the term pragmatically to describe developments that endured into the later period called "modern" by convention and convenience. These early modern chapters focus on expanded travel and trade linking long-separate parts of the globe (Ghobrial, chap. 5); the consolidation of political power through bureaucratic and archival practices in city-states, nation-states, and colonial empires (Head, chap. 6); the circulation and impact of news (Slauter, chap. 7); and the parallel and distinct cultures of information in the Islamicate world (Muhanna, chap. 2) and East Asia (Fitzgerald and Nappi, chap. 3). These topics were selected from among many other possible areas of study especially because of the depth of existing scholarship on them.

This chapter, focusing on the chronologically earlier part of the early modern period, roughly 1400–1650, will set the stage for subsequent chapters on European information culture by examining the situation circa 1400 and the invention (around 1450) and rapid spread of printing by metal movable type (or typography). It will consider the transformation of medieval information practices and the rise of new ones in the wake of printing and the information explosion that it fueled and will close by emphasizing a second major contemporaneous development—the improvement of the postal system in western Europe. The confluence of these developments with others that were quite independent of them generated a remarkable spate of changes for which the period is famous: not only Renaissance and reformations, the consolidation of nations and empires, and the globalization of commerce, but also (with consequences for all those processes) new ways of producing, managing, and disseminating information.

The Context of the Early Fifteenth Century

A number of the features of the information landscape that we associate with the early modern and modern periods were already well established in medieval Europe, so that the history of information involves long continuities as well as sudden innovations. A new technology like printing is best understood as the product of its historical context and its impacts as resulting from a whole range of factors, some of them technical, many of them social and cultural. Europe in 1400 featured the technical prerequisites for the invention of printing as well as the conditions for a rapid commercialization of this method of mechanically reproducing texts.

The manuscript culture of late medieval Europe was grounded in centuries of continuous growth, including the Carolingian Renaissance (around 800 CE), noted for the foundation of new schools offering instruction in Latin, and the "twelfth-century Renaissance," which featured the transmission of Aristotelian philosophical works to the Latin West from the Arabic translations circulating in Spain (see Muhanna, chap. 2), the foundation of universities where those and other texts were studied, and the spread of the manufacturing of paper first in Italy and Spain and later north of the Alps (see Grafton, chap. 1). Strong demographic and commercial growth between 1000 and 1300 had made possible the rise of cities as centers of government, commerce, and culture, and of trade routes between them sustained by roads, rivers, and regular fairs. The medieval church was a widely distributed institution featuring multiple branches—secular (priests), regular (following rules in monastic houses), and mendicant (the Dominican and Franciscan orders founded in the thirteenth century). After the Christianization of Scandinavia in the twelfth century and of Lithuania in 1387, it spanned all of western Europe.

Experiences of information in the Middle Ages varied widely by place and social standing. The spoken word (in sermons or proclamations or other texts read aloud) and sounds (like bells and tocsins) were typically accessible to all the inhabitants of villages and towns. Writing was encountered in legal and administrative contexts, in complex mercantile operations, and among the clergy and the educated. Historians have moved away from the basic categories of literate and illiterate to identify kinds of *literacy. "Pragmatic literacy" (as coined by Michael Clanchy) enabled people even of lower social orders to manage basic legal and business affairs that increasingly involved written documents. Those who lacked the requisite skills depended on intermediaries, friends, family members, or experts who could be hired. Mercantile literacy included reckoning and reading followed by writing in the vernacular. A career in any branch of the clergy (including all forms of higher education) theoretically involved literacy in Latin, a sacred language that was also a living language common to the learned across Western Christendom. Critics of the church at the time claimed that many clerics were not properly literate and celebrated the Latin Mass by rote; churchgoers too likely acquired a partial literacy in the components of the Mass through force of habit even without being able to read. By the late Middle Ages there was also a growing audience for and production of vernacular manuscripts in a wide range of *genres, from the literary (including Dante and Boccaccio in Italian, Christine de Pizan in French, and Chaucer in English) to practical books like almanacs and how-to manuals that could convey information by pictorial as well as textual elements. New scripts designed for speed and efficiency as well as the increasing availability and use of paper lowered the production costs of manuscripts and facilitated access to them, in response to and further fueling an increase in readership.

It is fiendishly hard to estimate how many manuscripts were produced or in circulation at the time, given the losses suffered as they were reduced to tatters by use or recycled for the material they were written on (since both *parchment and paper were serviceable in other contexts) and given the paucity and unreliability of records of book ownership. Our principal evidence rests in the details about production, circulation, and use contained in the manuscripts themselves that survive. Arguments from surviving manuscripts are of course complicated by the many factors affecting their survival (including a general correlation of greater rates of loss with the greater passage of time). Nevertheless, the explosion in the number of surviving manuscripts produced in the early fifteenth century leaves no doubt about a surging demand for texts across a variety of genres especially in the Italian and German contexts. In each of these areas the number of surviving manuscripts produced each year rose from about five thousand in 1400 to twenty thousand in 1460. In considering examples of two different motives for publication in this period, I will emphasize how late medieval manuscript culture met demands for both the rapid circulation of short texts and the durable preservation of longer ones. In this context the merits of printing in accomplishing both of these goals were readily apparent; in other words, the new technology was developed in a place and a time where it was put into use right away.

Daniel Hobbins has recently given us insight into the life and writings of Jean Gerson (1363–1429), a major French cleric (chancellor of the University of Paris, bishop then archbishop and cardinal) and a prolific author. Gerson wrote sermons delivered orally then circulated in writing, devotional works, learned treatises, poetry, and, most distinctively, *tractatuli* or short tracts written rapidly and widely disseminated, which offered clearly labeled interventions in current events, such as the Council of Constance (1414–18, which ended the papal schism and declared the Czech church reformer Jan Hus a heretic) and the final phases of the Hundred Years' War (including the rise of Joan of Arc). Gerson wrote in Latin as was the norm for clerics, but also in French in order to reach a wider audience. He often composed in his own hand although few of his autographs survive, and he added features to guide and attract his readers such as a *colophon, unusually placed at the beginning of the text, announcing title and author, and "rubrics" and "little rubrics" indicating the divisions and subdivisions throughout the text to facilitate browsing. In doing so Gerson drew on practices of manuscript organization or *ordinatio* that were first developed in scholastic contexts in the thirteenth century alongside alphabetical finding devices like the first biblical *concordances (ca. 1247), alphabetically ordered dictionaries (like the *Catholicon* of 1286), and indexes of contemporary works (like the *encyclopedic *Speculum maius* of Vincent of Beauvais, composed 1240–60, and its index composed separately by Jean de Hautfuney in 1320–23). In major centers like Paris, scribes also prepared manuscripts for sale without a prior commission, confident of the demand for their products, although Gerson's writings did not fit into the best-selling categories on which they focused (Bibles, chronicles, moral treatises, and romances, many of the latter in the vernacular).

To disseminate his works Gerson took advantage of church gatherings, from regional synods to the massive Council of Constance that attracted as many as eighteen thousand clerics from all over Western Christendom. A great deal of copying took place during the council, resulting for example in some eighty surviving copies of Gerson's tract *On Ecclesiastical Power* made there, which were often transported back to their owners' hometowns. Outside these special events Gerson's works were also disseminated through the networks of the Carthusian and Celestine orders to which Gerson had strong ties, but principally north of the Alps rather than in Italy. The late medieval culture of oral debates and sermons and extensive manuscript copying, combined with the clerical infrastructure of large gatherings and interconnected religious houses, made it possible for someone like Jean Gerson to achieve an immediate impact in current events through wide and rapid diffusion of his short tracts. Gerson did not live to see Gutenberg's invention, but he modeled attitudes and behaviors of authorship that later clerics ambitious to have an immediate impact in the world could adopt even more effectively thanks to printing.

Gerson's methods of publicity owed a great deal to the scribal culture of Italian city-states in which the humanist movement had started to develop already in the fourteenth century, inspired most famously by his own favorite modern author, Francesco Petrarca (Petrarch, 1304–74). Italian contexts also experienced a surge of manuscript production in the fifteenth century, with distinctive humanist emphases. The humanist project involved cultivating classical Latin (as opposed to the scholastic forms of Latin common in clerical and university contexts) and when possible learning Greek in order to appreciate the ancient texts in their original languages. With the patronage of wealthy backers like the Medici who covered the significant expenses involved, humanists searched for manuscripts of ancient texts that had been neglected or forgotten in order to copy them and collect them in libraries. They sent agents to purchase Greek manuscripts before and after the fall of Byzantium in 1453, and they scoured monastic libraries in Europe looking for hidden treasures that had been copied onto parchment centuries earlier. The Council of Constance proved a fruitful base of operations, for example for Poggio Bracciolini (1380–1459), a Tuscan whose skill in humanist Latin landed him employment as papal secretary for some fifty years. In 1416–17, while the council wrestled with appointing a new pope, Poggio was on hiatus and used the time to visit monastic libraries in Switzerland and Germany. There he recovered manuscripts of hitherto lost works by Cicero, Quintilian, Statius, and most spectacularly Lucretius, whose "De rerum natura" was fascinating for its expansive vocabulary and skillful poetry rather than for its shocking Epicurean ideas about the universe, which only a few—such as Niccolò Machiavelli—pursued in detail. Although the copy that Poggio made of Lucretius does not survive, it served as the basis for subsequent manuscript copies. The flurry of copies that resulted marked the first time Lucretius's text had been read since the ninth century, when the manuscript Poggio found had been made.

Humanist manuscripts commissioned by noble patrons were often lavish productions, sometimes made on parchment even though paper was available, typically bearing colorful floral decorations and the patron's coat of arms. They were copied in new scripts that the humanists had devised first by imitating older manuscripts (such as Carolingian minuscule, resulting in our "roman" fonts), then by adding a *cursive slant (which inspired italic fonts) for greater speed. The major collectors of this period amassed significant libraries comprising hundreds of manuscripts. The Florentine collector Niccolò Niccoli (1364–1437), for example, gathered one of the largest collections of his time, with eight hundred manuscripts. After his death these books formed a crucial core of the new library of San Marco founded in 1444 by Cosimo de Medici as the first public library of Florence. Although that institution did not endure past the early modern period, its manuscripts did, while the ideal of forming a vast secular library for the "use of all men of letters of our own age and of subsequent time" was realized in the Vatican Library, founded in 1451 by Pope Nicholas V. Nicholas's plan was to gather the best manuscripts of ancient texts in order to serve as a reference library. His successors invested further in manuscripts and then printed books, in addition to bigger quarters that were beautifully outfitted. With the exception of a few restrictive decades during the Counter-Reformation in the later sixteenth and early seventeenth centuries, the Vatican Library has served as a major resource for scholars down to the present.

Keenly aware of the masses of ancient texts that they would never manage to recover, humanists aimed to preserve for all time all the classical texts that they could find, to spare posterity the trauma of further losses. As a result they soon appreciated how printing could contribute to the preservation and transmission of painstakingly recovered texts. To be sure, some were hostile to the new technology. One scribe of luxury humanist manuscripts, Vespasiano da Bisticci (1421–98), complained about the cheap production values of a book printed in black and white on paper that could never be as durable as a parchment manuscript, nor as beautiful or valuable as the writing of a scribe with an elegant *book hand. Nevertheless his favorite customer, Federico da Montefeltro, Duke of Urbino, also owned many printed books even while he too affected to despise them. Poggio's great find was one of many classical texts printed soon after Gutenberg's invention. The *editio princeps* (or first printed edition) of Lucretius appeared in 1473, at a price that made it accessible to many who could not have afforded a manuscript copy; although only four copies from this first edition survive today, other editions followed, and printing played a powerful role in the survival of vast numbers of texts (recovered from antiquity but also composed at the time) that would otherwise have been lost.

Printing originated in a cultural context in which many were eager to put to use a new technology that could achieve at lower cost and more quickly what manuscript copying was already producing—a wide spectrum of texts both learned and vernacular, designed for rapid impact or for long-term transmission or both.

The Development and Features of Typography

Printing could reproduce a short text fast (to satisfy a Gerson) and ensure the preservation of scholarly texts far into the future (to satisfy a Poggio). Indeed, Gutenberg himself likely printed texts in both of these modes: his famous 42-line Bible took an estimated two years to produce and was surely not the first thing he printed. He no doubt ran his first successful experiment on a short text, such as a twenty-eight-page grammar book by Donatus, or an *indulgence, printed on just one side (in a broadsheet that would be cut into multiple indulgences). Both types of texts could be sold rapidly in large numbers— respectively to students and to the church, which took charge of retail sale of indulgences to penitents. Both were the kind of practical imprint that survives very poorly (at a rate of about 0.003 percent in the case of indulgences). By contrast, when Gutenberg printed a Bible, presumably in order to showcase his new technology and gain respect for it, it survived at an unusually high rate of almost 33 percent; in addition fragments of lost copies also survive. This book was large in size and sacred in content, its early owners were mostly religious institutions, and its later ones were book collectors—all factors that contributed to its high survival rate.

Given that our evidence for early printing largely rests on what has survived, we can be sure that vast numbers of ephemeral imprints have been completely lost. These likely included printed forms to be filled out by hand (such as contracts, receipts, and bills in addition to indulgences that called for the name of the penitent to be written in) and leaflets of many kinds (such as government notices, news, songs, and religious prayers and messages, with or without accompanying images). *Ephemera were the cheapest imprints, accessible to the greatest number of buyers, who in due course reused the paper on which they were printed for many purposes from starting fires to wrapping or wiping things. That reuse has occasionally led them to be found, notably as the endpapers inserted into the binding of later books. Despite its poor survival, cheap print was especially effective in reaching a wide audience rapidly and at low cost. Government proclamations, reports of recent events from far and near (whether reliable or not), and religious exhortations and prophecies were among the major genres of ephemera that kept printers financially afloat and readers in the sway of political and religious trends. In earlier periods similar information was diffused orally (through sermons and town criers, formal meetings and informal gossip) and by manuscript copying. Oral and manuscript media remained essential (and indeed still are), but printing lent a new level of impact to whatever was selected for publication, whether by the official authorities of church and state, or by the private calculus of printers hoping to make a profit. That profit motive and the fear of punishment generally discouraged printers from challenging the authorities under which they operated. But the fragmentation of competing European polities and the trade in printed matter among them also made it possible for ephemera to circulate content that one church or state considered undesirable while others did not (such as Protestant broadsheets).

Gutenberg was still experimenting when he printed his first Bible: he drew on his skills as a goldsmith to create multiple separate sorts for each letter. This method resulted in multiple versions of each letter, which differed slightly and were recycled through the book, as scholars have tracked with the aid of digital imaging. Over time Gutenberg streamlined the production of letter sorts, by forming one perfect punch for each letter, which could be used to shape the matrix in which to cast (using a molten lead alloy) as many identical copies of the same letter as needed. Gutenberg must also have experimented with inks that would stick to the metal but transfer cleanly onto the paper, and with sizing for the paper, treating it with alum to prevent the ink from seeping too deeply into the paper and becoming illegible. Oil-based paints devised a few decades earlier and most famously adopted by the Flemish panel painter Jan van Eyck may have inspired Gutenberg's use of oil-based ink. The screw press that was characteristic of the handpress era, down to 1800, was familiar from wine and oil presses. The idea of imprinting a pattern by woodblock was also familiar from the long history of creating patterned cloths. But the latest assessment is that block books formed by woodblocks containing a mix of image and text did not predate Gutenberg's invention, but rather coincided with the first decades of typography.

Another crucial ingredient was paper, but for commercial not technical reasons since one could print on parchment. Indeed, Gutenberg printed some of his Bibles on *vellum, presumably on commission for wealthy buyers. Imprints on vellum were exceptional, reserved for copies to be presented to special patrons. Paper was expensive enough to account (given the vast quantities necessary) for about half the expense of a print run; using parchment for a whole print run would have been punitively expensive. Finally, printing required more workers and more division of labor than scribing: a compositor to set the type (upside down and backward) and lay it in the bed of the press; another to prepare and apply the ink to the type; a pressman to pull the bar, pressing the blank sheet onto the inked text so that it was transferred onto the page. Large printing houses would run multiple presses at once and would hire specialists to proofread, draw up an index, or make woodblocks for illustrations. Binding was the purview of other experts whom printers or buyers hired to assemble the book from the printed sheets; whether they used a costly material like stamped leather or the less expensive vellum, a bound book was easier to store and more likely to be saved and transmitted than one left unbound in lightly stitched folded sheets.

It is impossible to measure the odds of someone else inventing printing if Gutenberg had not, but I suggest that they were high. Claims of a simultaneous invention by Laurens Janszoon Coster seem grounded only in a sixteenth-century attempt at burnishing the reputation of Coster's hometown of Haarlem, in the Netherlands. But all the elements were readily available, as well as existing demand for what printing could offer, so the idea could plausibly have occurred to someone else around the same time. We now appreciate that printing by both woodblock (xylography) and (more rarely) movable characters (made of wood or porcelain but also metal) was in use centuries earlier in multiple East Asian contexts. Nevertheless, there is no good evidence of a westward transmission of printing from Asia to Europe, although gunpowder and papermaking clearly were transmitted in that way. Xylography and typography involve distinct affordances that become erased in our use of the single term *printing* to denote both of them. The distinctive features of typography include the inflexible nature of the initial decision of how many copies to print. Once each sheet was printed in a given number of copies, the metal sorts used to print it were distributed back into the case from which they would be used to compose the next sheet. To print more copies of a sheet that had already been printed and dismantled would require investing the labor of setting type all over again (although the labor of planning the layout could be reused). On the contrary, a woodblock could be saved once it was carved and reused a long or a short time later to reprint a great number of extra copies. Woodblocks used in European imprints for illustrations and decorative elements were similarly stored, traded, and reused; but the text printed alongside these blocks by metal movable type could not be. By the early eighteenth century a few innovative printers had experimented with the casting of full pages of type that could be stored and extensively reused; stereotype printing was deployed in this early phase in the printing of inexpensive Bibles, before its heyday in the nineteenth century.

While East Asian xylography offered the advantages of print on demand (provided the blocks were stored in good condition, which might entail significant expense), European typography was always a more speculative and risky undertaking, involving high expenditures up front and no way to profit from strong sales beyond the copies that had already been planned without incurring most of the production costs again. For example, Gutenberg raised the number of 42-line Bibles he produced partway through that first edition, evidently for fear of missing out on the opportunities for profits that those extra copies could offer. It meant resetting the pages that had already been printed at the point when he decided to raise the size of the print run; the small differences between the two settings of type on these pages provide the evidence for this decision. The second distinctive feature about the development of typography in Europe is its immediately commercial nature. In East Asia books were for the first five hundred years mainly printed by Buddhist temples, central or local governments, or families—these were commissioned and private printings rather than commercial ones.

On the contrary, in Europe printing was a commercial and capitalist venture from the start. Printers who lacked the necessary funds partnered with *publishers who provided the capital. For example, Gutenberg could not repay the loan taken out to cover his initial expenses and lost his business to his creditor Johann Fust. Variations of that pattern would be repeated many times over, in the initial explosion of interest in the new business and even once the industry had matured. In Italy printers set up in eighty different towns and cities in the fifteenth century; the resulting overproduction led the vast majority of them to fail. By 1500 Italian printing was consolidated in eleven locales, with four cities accounting for 80 percent of the total output for the peninsula. The same was true on the scale of Europe, where a few major centers dominated

the business. Venice, Frankfurt and Cologne, Paris and Lyon, Basel, and Antwerp each had the crucial advantage of being located on a major river and at
the intersection of existing trade routes. Since any local market would soon be
saturated, access to more distant ones was crucial. Partnerships were a common method of sharing in the risk of producing a book and seeking broader
markets. Printers would band together to publish a book, with each member
of the partnership receiving a share of the printed copies proportional to their
investment. Some partnerships were formed among colleagues in one city
(like the three Johanns of early sixteenth-century Basel: Amerbach, Petri, and
Froben). Other partnerships spanned multiple cities, whether based on family
ties or international contracts. The Giunti family, which started printing in
Venice in 1489 and Florence in 1497, involved some thirty family members
down to the 1620s in producing, warehousing, and selling books in dozens of
cities in at least six countries. In addition, learned books especially, being expensive and written in the international language of Latin, were the object of
partnerships where the reciprocity of commercial interests rather than family
ties kept multiple parties faithful to their agreements, even across national and
confessional differences. Finally, book professionals throughout Europe used
the major fairs (Frankfurt being the largest among them, overtaken by Leipzig
after 1632) to trade stock and information with colleagues and competitors
every fall and spring. Despite all these methods of distributing risk, many
printers died with a lot of debt and unsold stock.

The risks inherent in the business could be offset by job printing—the production of small items that would sell quickly (e.g., pamphlets with exciting
claims or news) or that were paid for in advance by church or government.
Some genres were steady sellers and reliable sources of revenue, thanks to
strong buyer demand—notably devotional, liturgical, and pedagogical books.
More generally, whenever the same printer published a second edition of a
work we can presume the first one had sold well. A wise printer would plan
a mix of projects, so that risky ones could be covered by safer ones. A study of
the practice at the university press in seventeenth-century Cambridge revealed
a complex choreography of presses being assigned to short-run pamphlets in
the midst of printing much larger works. For works produced on speculation,
profit depended on the correct choice of print run: print too few and miss out
on profit, print too many and incur uncompensated expenses that could prove
ruinous. A rare case of a book colophon mentioning a print run of three hundred copies gives us one data point for the period of incunabula (i.e., books
printed before 1500). In the sixteenth century print runs usually ranged up to

1,000–1,250 copies, since this was the number of copies of one sheet that could typically be printed in one day (as we know from the exceptional set of archives that survive from the Plantin Moretus shop in Antwerp starting in 1564), but higher print runs were also possible.

A crucial feature of a printed item is that it was never produced alone: from one surviving copy we can deduce that hundreds more were produced at the same time, even if they do not survive. Imprints that were never bound, especially printed forms and short practical works and pamphlets, have often been completely lost; but new finds continue to be made—as lost books are identified from fragments found in the bindings of other books, or appear during house renovations centuries after they were hidden to avoid religious persecution. Overall printing generated quantities of texts on an unprecedented scale: at least twenty-seven thousand editions of incunabula were printed by 1500, followed by more than 320,000 editions in the sixteenth century. The number of printed books that resulted (maybe more than three hundred million, excluding the many ephemera that have been completely lost) dwarfed not only the estimated number of European manuscripts surviving from the sixth to the sixteenth century (1.3 million) but also the number of manuscripts estimated to have been available in 1500 (six to seven million).

Printing was a business but a special one given the intellectual content of the product. Books circulated ideas and connoted the power of the written word. In setting up printing presses in various colonies, Europeans valued them as tools to achieve their various goals of converting Indigenous populations, creating cohesion among the colonists, or representing imperial power, even though they were not very successful commercially. In Mexico the Seville printer Juan Cromberger produced his first books in 1540, with the support of the bishop there, but probably profited more from his monopoly on importing books than from the one on printing them, both granted to him by Spanish royal decree. Printing started in Goa on the west coast of India in 1556 thanks to a press transported from Portugal by the Jesuits. The first press in the British colonies in America was brought over in 1639 to aid the population of one thousand colonists in Boston and the college they had just founded three years before. The production from these presses was not very great but was symbolically important. Conversely printing was forbidden in places where the authorities feared it would foster further resistance, for instance, in the Latin-occupied Greek Levant (such as Crete) where the Roman Church hoped to spread its control in the wake of the fall of Byzantium and banned printing lest it be used to shore up Orthodox Christianity instead. Cracow and Prague were the largest printing centers in eastern Europe, producing books in a range of languages and scripts. The first incunabula and Bible printed in Cyrillic type were published there in 1490–91 and 1517, respectively, as well as many Hebrew imprints for the Jewish communities of Ashkenaz.

More generally European printers needed to cultivate favorable relations with the government under which they operated. Unlike East Asian xylography, which could be practiced almost anywhere without leaving a trace, typography required considerable capital and could not easily be carried out in secret—the press and metal type were so heavy that some printshop floors collapsed under their weight. Portable presses were devised and used clandestinely in special circumstances, as in the production of the Marprelate pamphlets in England in 1588–89, but in most cases the new industry operated in full view of its urban environment and subject to regulations of two kinds: commercial and ideological. Printers themselves set up commercial regulations to protect their ability to recover the great expense of publishing a book by preventing others from printing the same work. On the continent printers would seek a privilege that granted them a monopoly on printing a work for a certain number of years, free from competition within the jurisdiction of the grantor. Privileges issued by monarchs or the pope or the emperor were never automatic—they required the favor of the grantor (which could prove difficult to obtain) and the payment of a fee. In England the Stationers' Company, founded in 1557, operated like a guild and issued licenses to print specific works or kinds of works to members who bid for them. The trade relations that printers and publishers maintained across jurisdictional boundaries also served to regulate behavior; although piracy (which undercut a printer's market) was a real threat, the fact that printers could retaliate against one another and controlled a powerful medium in which to voice their complaints worked against rampant piracy.

The second form of regulation came from outside the industry, as churches and states sought to control the content that was printed. Censorship did not originate with printing. Producers of texts both oral and written (including preachers, teachers, authors, and scribes) had long since been held responsible for content deemed heretical or seditious. The medieval church issued general condemnations of certain positions and persecuted individuals who seemed to espouse them, especially once heresy became a major concern in the thirteenth century. Self-censorship of speech and writing was a natural by-product of the efforts to enforce religious, political, and social norms that were widespread across most medieval and early modern contexts. Printing introduced new players in the production of written texts, and printers were soon required to include their name on all their imprints, so they too could be held responsible; one evasive maneuver was to list a false printer's name and address. Prepublication censorship was common in both Catholic and Protestant contexts, whereby printers had texts approved by the authorities before investing in publishing them, in order to spare themselves the risks of their stock being destroyed or their persons punished. The Catholic Church was unique in forming (in 1559, as part of the Counter-Reformation) a bureaucratic wing of the papacy devoted to postpublication censorship. The Index of Prohibited Books published lists of banned authors and texts, and of specific passages in otherwise allowable texts that Catholics should refrain from reading as dangerous to their faith. Of course a large area of Europe had become Protestant by this point and produced these "bad" books in abundance, beyond the sway of Rome. Depending on their location Catholics could access more or less easily such books through the market, and some—especially experts, such as medical men seeking to keep up with the latest publications—even did so with permission, which the church granted to trusted individuals. Protestant contexts also exercised postpublication censorship. In Tudor and Stuart England, for example, royal authorities removed from circulation books they judged offensive and sometimes staged public burnings of them, occasionally accompanied by the corporal punishment of their authors or distributors (as in the cases of John Stubbs and William Page in 1579, and William Prynne in 1634 and 1637). Public book burnings, complete with many symbolic elements, were designed to display the power of the state or the condemnation of rebels against authority (as in the case of the schismatic Jan Hus or the burning of antiroyalist books at the restoration of Charles II in 1660), but that power did not extend to the contemporary reaction, which could include voices of sympathy for those condemned.

Publishing new ideas could be risky but also supremely successful. The German reformer Martin Luther was especially adept at marshaling the power of the press. His printers at Wittenberg and elsewhere ended up benefiting handsomely from the brisk sales of his works starting with the ninety-five theses of 1517; the books helped to bring about a religious schism that protected their makers from Catholic repression. In other cases, when new ideas did not catch on, printers could pay a heavy price for advancing a cause in which they believed or on which they had wagered; the Lyon printer Etienne Dolet, for example, was executed for heresy in 1546. Authors could hope to keep their identity secret, and some succeeded in doing so; thanks to elaborate ruses, Jonathan Swift avoided being identified as the author of texts that would have been grounds for conviction of *libel. But printers had more limited options—a false imprint was the most common evasive maneuver and not always successful as the authorities could identify printers by the characteristics of their work much as bibliographers do today. As a result, manuscript remained the medium of choice for the distribution of texts that risked legal proceedings against their makers as intolerable on religious, political, or moral grounds. Identifying the culprits was more difficult, and the authorities generally cared less about what circulated in manuscript once printed books were available to cause greater damage.

Impacts of Printing

Contemporaries were struck by the power of printing: the ability to produce in one day what would have taken many men more than a year to write, as multiple contemporaries noted as early as 1470, and the remarkable drop in price that resulted for a text that was printed rather than manuscript (which one contemporary estimated at 80 percent). Printing was the optimal way to produce very many copies of a text, and, given the commercial incentive to produce enough copies to ensure a profit if they sold, the technology favored abundant output. One modern bibliographer, Hugh Amory, astutely observed that as a result most printed books (i.e., individual copies of books) have never been read. A good number were never even purchased but lingered unsold, reused to make new works (as I discuss below), or recycled for the paper. Printing became a new option for publication but was not the medium of choice for making a small number of copies for narrow circulation. In other words, printing never replaced manuscript copying, although the production of manuscripts declined steeply in the fifty years following its height around 1470.

The need for professional scribes dropped significantly, but their activities did not disappear entirely. Most important was probably their continued primacy in producing official documents—charters, treaties, and the like. They also provided models for type design and took on new kinds of work in the printing business; others retooled themselves as teachers of handwriting and authored printed books to showcase their skills and attract students. A few carried on producing manuscripts commercially, in various specific genres such as chamber music parts, which were expensive to print and were needed only in small numbers, and newsletters produced for subscribers that would be customized to meet their interests and could contain news considered unfit to print. Printing also likely encouraged the use of handwriting, since it was no longer associated with the mere copying best delegated to scribes. The Benedictine abbot Johannes Trithemius (1462–1516), drawing on medieval sources, depicted the work of monastic scribes as literally holy, in a way that the mechanical work of compositors and pressmen was not. Nevertheless humanist pedagogues introduced new grounds for handwriting: they advocated taking reading or classroom notes in one's own hand in order to retain them better in memory (indeed this advice has been reiterated recently in response to digital note-taking). The great humanist Desiderius Erasmus (1466–1536) also portrayed autography as an important skill for a gentleman because "a man's handwriting, like his voice, has a special, individual quality." Correspondents were increasingly expected to write letters to family and associates in their own hand, though using a secretary was considered appropriate for writing to social superiors or inferiors and for keeping copies of outgoing correspondence.

The earliest printed books were designed to look and behave like manuscripts—they were *skeuomorphic by design in order to offer buyers a product that would seem familiar and thus desirable. Over the first eighty years or so, by 1530, printers introduced several features that were new at the time but have since become defining elements of a book, such as the title page, page numbering, and paragraphing; these facilitated the use of books by a growing number and a broader range of readers. In order to replicate the role of color in manuscripts to guide the reader's eye to key points in the text, incunabula were printed with blank spaces for initial letters and headings to be filled in by a scribe using red (or sometimes blue) ink. Two-tone printing was possible and used in some cases throughout the handpress era, but since it involved running the sheet through the press twice, to apply the black and red inks separately, it was time-consuming and expensive. Over time printers devised other methods to distinguish the different sections of a text, including the use of blank space and lines (e.g., paragraphing), varying sizes and types of fonts, and the little symbols known as dingbats. Most of the abbreviations common in medieval scripts were gradually dropped (but the suspension of nasals persisted for another century or more, and the ampersand has remained in use until now). Books in romance languages were usually printed in roman or italic font, whereas Germanic languages used versions of Gothic script. If a text shifted between Latin and English or German the font shifted according to this convention; in England blackletter signaled popular (since it was the font of the hornbook from which children first learned to read) or old-fashioned by around 1600, but it continued to be used in some genres like royal proclamations into the eighteenth century. In German Fraktur remained common until the mid-twentieth century.

Printing increased access to the written word for those reading and those writing alike. The earliest imprints were existing texts that circulated in manuscript—liturgical and pedagogical texts in particular. Humanists soon sought to print their recent finds of ancient texts, hoping to gain reputation for themselves and for the recovered ancient author through a learned edition, including translation into Latin as needed for texts in Greek, and often some commentary. But a growing percentage of books were new compositions by authors from many walks of life. In addition to learned authors (e.g., in the clergy, law, medicine, or education) who dominated textual production in the Middle Ages, artisans and merchants had greater access to books as they became cheaper. Although there were medieval autodidacts (e.g., the prolific Islamic medical author Ibn Sīnā, known in Europe as Avicenna, d. 1037), the phenomenon of teaching oneself from books became more feasible. Similarly, publishing a book was within reach of a broader range of writers. While a few craftsmen and artists had composed practical manuals in the manuscript era, their counterparts in the age of print produced large numbers of how-to books and collections of "secrets" that were widely reprinted in Latin and the vernaculars. Many factors were involved in these developments, including the rising status of an elite of artisans who received princely patronage, and efforts to improve schools that originated in both the Reformation and the Counter-Reformation.

Literacy is hard to define (see the different types of literacy mentioned above) and even harder to measure, but the mandate of parish record keeping common among Catholics and Protestants starting in the sixteenth century has been used to track rising rates in the ability to sign documents (rather than leaving simpler marks such as crosses). Literacy rates varied widely by place (with urban rates higher than rural ones), by gender (with male literacy rates usually double those for women), and owing to specific circumstances. For example, unusually high rates of literacy resulted in Sweden by 1700 from its being mandated by the church there as a precondition to marriage; English Quakers and the men of New England reached near universal literacy in the eighteenth century, while these rates were reached more broadly in Europe only around 1900. Overall literacy rates rose in western Europe from the fifteenth to the eighteenth century, from estimated averages of 5–15 percent in 1500 to 50–75 percent in 1750, and the greater availability and lower price of books was both a cause and an effect of that rise.

With more and new readers to address, printing prompted the development of new ways of guiding the reader: title page, errata lists, and pagination. The title page was rarely present in medieval manuscripts; instead bibliographers identify manuscripts by their incipit or first words of the text. The title page played a key role in attracting buyers who in a shop or at a fair faced many options of books to purchase. The title page included identifiers (author, title, printer, place and date of publication) and made alluring claims about the topic of the book or its special features, like "a most abundant index" or a "most correct and enlarged" text. Since the purpose of the title page was above all to prompt a sale, exaggerations and inaccuracies were common. The errata list was another feature new to printed books. Scribes committed errors too, but whereas their errors were unique to each manuscript, typographical errors affected every copy of the print run. Sometimes errors were corrected partway through a print run in a "stop-press correction." This practice resulted in variations among the extant copies within one edition, because printers were typically reluctant to dispose of the sheets containing the error and, as a result, some copies of the book for sale would contain the error while in others it had been corrected (the two different versions that resulted are called "states" within an edition). Occasionally errors were also corrected in the printshop with a manuscript annotation or by pasting a correction slip over the error. But the easier remedy was to include (typically at the back of the book) a list of errors and their corrections. This list of errata was designed to forestall complaints of readers by enjoining them to make the corrections in their copies by hand and to guide those producing future editions of the text. Errata lists occasionally also featured short blurbs in which the author or the printer could take or assign blame for the faults; these shed light on the multiple people involved in book production and the potential for tensions among them.

Errata lists referred to specific passages by page or folio numbers, which were also innovations linked to printing. Uniform numbering of pages was rare in manuscripts. Early printed books, formed by folding each printed sheet into a cluster of pages called a quire, featured signature numbers in the lower right of the first pages in each quire; these were meant to guide the compositor and the binder to ensure the proper assembly of the quires. For the use of readers, incunabula introduced foliation (which appeared on the recto, or front, of every page); then pagination (on both recto and verso, or back of the page) became the norm by 1530. Paratexts (i.e., front matter or back matter) that referred to the text (such as errata lists but also tables of contents and indexes) did so by page or folio numbers, whereas medieval indexes used layout-independent forms of reference such as book and chapter number that could apply to any manuscript. An index tied to a specific edition represented some loss of information since it was not easily transferable to another edition (or to a manuscript copy), but by making the index specific to each edition printers may have hoped to lure buyers for an edition with a "new and improved" index even if they already owned an earlier edition of the text. Indexes were clearly an attraction for readers. Some were drawn up in haste as a short list of the marginal summaries printed in the text; but large informational books typically featured detailed indexes and often multiple ones—for different languages, thematic headings, proper names, "memorable things and words," or for "things of note not contained in the earlier indexes." The first page of the enormous *Nuremberg Chronicle*, a world history published in 1493, advertises the index ("Registrum") of the book, before the text itself, in large Gothic type. Early indexes often featured short explanations of how to use them, that is, by searching alphabetically and following the references provided—a clear sign that this practice was not widely known even among the educated. But by the end of the sixteenth century these explanations were uncommon. Thanks to printing, many more readers had become familiar with the use of indexes than the small numbers of scholars who had access to them in the Middle Ages. Few paratextual elements were truly unique to printed books, but, more consistently than medieval manuscripts, printed books featured more different kinds of paratexts, and longer ones. Tables of contents, dedications (occasionally more than one, with each attached to a different part of the book), prefaces by author or printer or both, commendatory odes, alphabetical indexes, and errata lists were the most common types. These were variously designed by authors and printers to help a book sell by vaunting its merits and the support of respected contemporaries and by offering aids to encourage its reading and use.

More generally printing facilitated the production of longer works. Just as the *codex had proved more efficient in storing text than the papyrus roll, so too the printed page could pack in more words per page than a manuscript. The two-column layout developed in medieval manuscripts remained in continuous use through the early modern period and indeed well beyond, down to the present, for longer texts including the Bible and reference works. But denser typesetting and smaller fonts made possible pages with many more words—a page in Gutenberg's Bible held about 480 words whereas a page of the *Magnum Theatrum Humanae Vitae*, a massive reference work of 1631, held fifteen hundred words, and the whole work spanned more than ten million words in seven volumes. Of course some very large works were composed in the Middle Ages: the encyclopedic *Speculum maius* (Greater mirror) of Vincent of Beauvais topped 4.5 million words in the thirteenth century. But long works rarely circulated in their entirety in the manuscript era: instead users commissioned copies of only the parts that they wanted. Of the *Speculum* we have only two complete manuscript copies and three hundred partial copies, most of which are of the *Speculum historiale* (the most popular of its four parts) and often only subsets of that part. Every manuscript could be tailored to the interests that motivated that particular copy. By contrast a printed book had to be produced in the same form in a large number of copies, so each copy had to include all the parts that would appeal to every subset of its target audience. In the incunabular period the four parts of Vincent's *Speculum* were published singly multiple times, then the whole work was published together in four volumes in 1591 and again in 1624. Printing a long work was of course more expensive than printing a shorter one, but printing greatly reduced the production costs in any case, and the profit margins on expensive books were typically higher because their buyers were wealthier. Since a printed book did well if it appealed to as many readers as possible, genres based on compilation, like collections of recipes or sayings or reference books more generally, typically became larger in each successive edition. The additions or enhancements offered in a new edition would also help it compete against earlier ones, which would remain available as used books even if the print run had sold out initially.

Given its ability to produce more books, larger books, and massively more copies than manuscript copying (books that proved equally durable except insofar as they were less expensive), and given cultural dynamics that produced plenty of supply and demand for texts to print—medieval, ancient, and recently written—printing rapidly generated an unprecedented accumulation of books. Complaints about too many books predate printing, including the biblical lament "of making many books there is no end" (Ecclesiastes 12:12) or the thirteenth-century prologue in which Vincent of Beauvais complained of "the multitude of books, the shortness of time, and the slipperiness of memory" that motivated him to write a compendium of all knowledge. While only a narrow elite of scholars had experienced it in earlier periods, after the first century of printing a broad cross section of the educated articulated a concern about what we would call *"information overload"—the sense that there were too many books for an individual to read and to master. Complaints about an overabundance of books became a well-worn refrain throughout early modern Europe and were used to justify any number of postures: railing about the base commercial motives of printers who produced whatever sold without a care for quality or intellectual merit, mocking the vanity of bookish learning, worrying about the end of civilization from too many people writing (bad) books and no one reading good ones anymore, or on the contrary worrying that authors with new ideas would be discouraged from writing by the mass of what already existed.

These complaints about the consequences of printing were of course made in printed books, which added to the abundance of which they complained while offering various remedies to the overload: advice on how to read well, for example by taking good notes; judgments and reviews of books to aid in selecting them (a prime content of learned periodicals starting in the late seventeenth century); bibliographies to identify existing books (and possibly to deter the unnecessary composition of new ones); and reference works designed to collect the best parts of the best books to spare readers the trouble and expense of making these selections themselves. Printing prompted a new awareness of the need to manage information in and about books and also facilitated the development of new methods for doing so, among them printed questionnaires and lists, images and tables, cutting and pasting from printed books, or using the backs of printed playing cards.

Managing an Information Explosion in Early Modern Europe

The complaints about overabundance that strike a familiar chord today should not obscure an equally widespread attitude in early modern Europe that played a crucial role in causing the explosion of printed books: enthusiasm for *copia, the accumulation of information of all kinds and the abundant writing that would follow. The development and rapid growth of printing coincided with and was fueled by a number of independent cultural movements focused on info-lust or a desire to accumulate information in many forms—texts but also things natural and artificial, including natural specimens or images of them, paintings and sculptures, medals and coins. Renaissance humanists with their focus on classical antiquity recovered and studied not only texts but also methods of architecture (e.g., the dome) and art (sculptures large and small), coins and inscriptions, and other cultural remains. At the same time exploratory travel, most famously to the Americas, but also to Asia far and near, to Africa, and all over Europe, generated a new fascination for collecting plant and animal specimens and the artifacts of cultures distant in space and time. The two movements were linked in that ancient works of history and natural history recently recovered or brought to renewed attention—like those of the Roman encyclopedist and natural historian Pliny the Elder (23–79 CE), the Greek botanist Dioscorides (40–90 CE), and Aristotle on the parts of animals— provided models for the observation and description of fauna, flora, peoples, and places both familiar and newly encountered.

The travelers (merchants and diplomats, missionaries and scholars, soldiers and adventurers) brought back reports of their interactions but also objects that by gift or purchase ended up in collections formed by the wealthy and the great throughout Europe. The trade in collectibles enabled members of local elites to form collections in emulation of the large and famous ones. Some collections were focused on particular kinds of objects. Botanical gardens became de rigueur for the best medical faculties in the late sixteenth century; zoos, being much more expensive, became symbols of power that only the greatest monarchs could maintain. Collections of coins and other remains appealed to antiquarians, who studied them for clues about the past. Sixteenth-century antiquarians surveyed ruins in various Italian cities, in Istanbul and Anatolia (Pierre Gilles and Ogier Ghiselin de Busbecq), the Holy Roman Empire (Conrad Celtis and Conrad Peutinger), England (John Leland and William Camden), and elsewhere; their studies ranged from Egyptian obelisks to Nordic runes and medieval remains, like the Merovingian tomb of Childeric discovered in 1653 during the digging of the foundation of a hospital in Tournai (in today's Belgium). By contrast those with less specialized interests formed *cabinets of curiosities that reveled in a miscellaneous mix of items, natural or human in origin, local or exotic; highlights might include a crocodile or a horn of a unicorn (in fact from a narwhal), a Native American artifact, or a decorative piece beautifully wrought around a gem or a shell. We have a glimpse of these remarkable collections, despite their dispersal in the interim, through the catalogs drawn up at the time, which applied to new objects the methods of recording sacred relics in the later Middle Ages.

Some of these collections resulted in the foundation of museums that still exist today, such as the Uffizi in Florence founded by the Medici family or the Ashmolean in Oxford founded by the wealthy antiquarian Elias Ashmole in 1677. Whereas in the Middle Ages royal and ecclesiastical treasuries were kept out of public view, the owners of cabinets of curiosities typically welcomed visitors (at least with a letter of introduction), as we know from some guest books that have survived. A few images of early collections (printed in books about them) show a room full of items of many kinds in close proximity and little apparent order. Surviving inventories and catalogs (usually manuscript but occasionally printed) show a concern to organize the collections, at least on paper but also in specially labeled drawers or cabinets. In the eighteenth century Hans Sloane (whose massive collection became the seed of the British Museum) and his amanuenses (or secretaries) recorded provenance and date of acquisition and location codes that corresponded to labels on the objects that were attached or sometimes written directly on them. At the Francke Foundation in Halle, Germany, one can visit today the eighteenth-century collection formed for the education of the pupils (many of them orphans) in this pietist Lutheran school. It featured one section of *naturalia* or natural specimens and another of *artificialia*, including not only exotic artifacts (with an unusual emphasis on written media from around the world) but also miniature models of many trades from the time. Teaching from objects was a pedagogical technique advocated already by Jan Amos Comenius (1592–1670), who as a member of the Moravian Brethren and religious refugee had difficulty creating durable institutions. But Comenius's innovative textbook for children with illustrations, *Orbis sensualium pictus* (World of the senses in pictures, 1658), was the object of many translations and reeditions and surely helped to inspire the pedagogically oriented Wunderkammer in Halle. At the other end of the European world, eighteenth-century Harvard created a Philosophy Chamber for its students, including specimens and scientific instruments. There is much to be learned still about the way objects (including everyday items such as clothes, tools, and cooking utensils) were vehicles of information in early modern Europe and can be for historians today, as recent work has begun to explore.

Methods of managing texts have been better studied, thanks to a variety of sources including advice books about reading and writing books, manuscript notes and drafts, and many examples of large printed compilations of information. These kinds of books, which are rarely extant from the Middle Ages, became more common in many early modern fields thanks to the increasing amounts of information available and the opportunities that printing offered for financial and reputational gains from publishing them. Although they were often large and thus expensive books, reference genres included some steady sellers like dictionaries and *florilegia (collections of quotations by classical or religious authorities sorted under thematic headings) in addition to works that appeared only once but then inspired imitations. The large books I offer as examples bring into sharper relief practices that applied to informational genres in smaller sizes and across many areas of compilation, from ancient inscriptions to medical recipes to political treaties. Some of the practices of information management—like alphabetization, chronological order, the use of topical headings, and the morselization of information into discrete units—were already known in the Middle Ages and became more widespread through printing. Other techniques, including making images from life, weighing conflicting sources, and the use of mobile slips to store and sort information either temporarily or for the long term were new or newly emphasized in the early modern period.

Images were of course not new as vehicles of information, but printing and a new emphasis on close observation among natural historians gave them a new prominence. In medieval manuscripts, diagrams and *illuminations were copied along with the text by the scribe or a specialist. We know less about the presence of illustrations in ancient papyrus rolls, but it is plausible to imagine that drawings of plants and animals were copied along with accompanying text from ancient originals onto the parchment of medieval manuscripts. Judging from these manuscripts, even near-contemporaries in antiquity varied in their attitude toward images: many surviving manuscripts of Pliny's *Natural History* have none, while those of Dioscorides typically include an image for each plant described. Just like texts, images were subject to modification in transmission; but unlike with texts, changes introduced in images could not be identified and corrected as easily as textual variants, which could seem suspect on philological grounds. In the Renaissance, natural historians devoted much energy to studying the ancient sources in combination with natural specimens they could observe directly. A new attention to observation and an expansion of travels not only to the New World, but also within the known "old" worlds of Europe and the Near East especially, generated an explosion of new flora and fauna to describe. Whereas in 1550 the most complete enumeration of known plants was a humanist edition of Dioscorides with some five hundred kinds, by 1623 Caspar Bauhin published a massive tome describing six thousand of them. The major authors of Renaissance natural history were keen to integrate direct experience with textual descriptions and commentaries and strove to offer images of plants and animals made "from life." This meant drawing plants and animals where they could be seen live in botanical gardens or displays of exotic animals, or when climbing up mountains or traveling to distant locations; but in some cases images "from life" in fact involved drawing from the more or less reliable reports of others who had traveled. Image making also required decisions about whether to depict features specific to the particular specimen on view (like a wilted leaf or a damaged stem) or to aim for a more abstract representation of the species; those decisions were especially difficult when only one specimen of an otherwise unknown species was available to view.

Printing an image from life was costly, since it involved hiring a draftsman before the usual stages of transferring the image to woodblock and carving the block (each of which was performed by a specialist). Color (essential in many cases, e.g., for identifying plants, birds, or fish) could be described verbally but was not part of a printed image. Printed images could be colored by hand according to directives provided by the makers of the book (available at the printer's in one colored copy to serve as a model) or without such guidance on a simply decorative basis. In either case the addition of color was a considerable extra expense for the buyer, but one that conveyed valuable information if carried out well; of course that work could also be completed in haste and inaccurately, as the Swiss naturalist Conrad Gessner (1516–65) complained of the colored copies of his natural histories that his printer commissioned. The expense of making the original image motivated as much reuse of it as possible. Since the original editions for which the images were made were generally large-format and expensive Latin works, they might not warrant a reedition. Instead the publishers could reuse the images in vernacular translations, or in an abridged "picture book" version focused mainly on the images, or in smaller format editions that would reach a broader market; the latter would require carving new woodblocks to fit the smaller size of book but could rely on the same original drawings. This tactic of selling the most expensive edition first to tap the wealthiest buyers, followed by less expensive editions that would have broader appeal, was favored for illustrated books and other expensive genres.

The value of natural historical works lay in the trustworthiness of their information and in their ability to persuade readers of it. The German botanist Leonhard Fuchs (1501–66) accompanied his massive *History of Plants* (*De historia stirpium*, 1542) with unusual images not only of himself but also of the three men responsible for the abundant images; by showing and naming them he presumably meant to offer evidence to support his claim of images made "from life." The near contemporary Gessner prefaced each of his four volumes of natural history on quadrupeds (1551), reptiles (1554), birds (1555), and fish (1558) with other displays of the trustworthiness of his work. Many Renaissance books (including some of Gessner's earlier works) opened with a list of authorities cited as a bare list of names of authors alphabetically ordered, including even ancient authors whose works did not survive and who were known only secondhand through the citations of others—suggesting that the list was more a show of erudition than a list of sources actually used. By contrast, in each of the volumes of his natural history Gessner included a detailed bibliography of books published, from ancient and medieval times down to the recent books of contemporaries. He concluded with a list of experts whom he had consulted in person or by correspondence. Gessner named them ostensibly in order to thank them, but in so doing he also highlighted how well connected he was to many expert scholars, doctors, and apothecaries, who gave him information and thus lent further credibility to his work.

After naming these sources in the paratext Gessner did not try to cite them at every relevant point within the text. There he occasionally mentioned books and correspondents as sources, but also things he saw himself or learned from personal contact with "an old woman" or anonymous fishermen. Gessner and other early modern naturalists embraced sources of all kinds—including *canonical ancient works but also practical knowledge that they or their correspondents gleaned from experience and from talking to contemporaries even of low social standing. While they were aware of the merits of identifying their sources, their practice of citation was principally designed to make unusual information more convincing or to provide the evidence available in cases where conflicting information from different sources needed to be weighed (leaving the final judgment to the reader). A more systematic culture of citation developed piecemeal starting in the later seventeenth century, and the footnote originated around then too, though it served other purposes than citation alone, as the famously mocking and critical footnotes in Gibbon's *Decline and Fall of the Roman Empire* (1776–89) make clear.

Most early modern compilations were driven by the supply of information from their sources rather than systematic inquiry. Nevertheless Gessner made a concerted effort to treat for every quadruped a series of eight topical sections labeled by a letter of the alphabet: (a) on the names of the species in different languages; (b) on the places where it lives; (c) on its bodily habits (nutrition, reproduction, and death); (d) on its moral habits; (e, f, and g) on the uses of the animal for humans (e.g., for labor, food, or medical remedies); and (h) on philology, focused on the appearance of the species in proverbs, poetry, metaphors, or other literary settings (and this section was further subdivided into eight types also labeled a–h). Gessner's history of quadrupeds spanned 1,096 pages, followed by eight pages of supplements (*paralipomena*) devoted to images of animals for which he could not offer a systematic treatment, and a further nine pages of corrections and additional information (to be inserted according to page and line number). Gessner clearly labored hard to make this work as complete, systematic, and correct as possible, although he also apologized for being too prolix in the philological sections. Interestingly, in the later volumes in the series Gessner abandoned the scheme of answering the same questionnaire for each species and proceeded as other contemporaries did, by generally following a similar outline, but without calling attention to it and thus to places where he lacked answers to all the questions. (On other questionnaires, see Ghobrial, chap. 5.)

Fuchs and Gessner and others like them were attentive to the problems of ordering their vast material. Many Renaissance compilers hoped to find a systematic order that would match the order "of the things themselves." Of course there were conflicting views on what such a perfect order should be. One scholar has counted over two dozen kinds of systematic order in Renaissance encyclopedic works, including the order of Creation, of the Decalogue, of the biblical narrative or the *catechism; various chronological and geographical orders; and hierarchical orders of the disciplines or of the chain of being. In addition, some authors, like the great humanist Desiderius Erasmus in his *Adages* (a vast collection of ancient sayings explained), embraced a miscellaneous order as particularly pleasant owing to the unpredictable variety of the reading experience. The ancient precedent of the "haphazard order" (*ordo fortuitus*) of Aulus Gellius's *Attic Nights*, rediscovered by the humanists, lent miscellaneity a new respectability; this method also avoided the logistical difficulty of physically reordering the material according to a change of plan. By contrast the encyclopedist Theodor Zwinger (1533–88) devised and revised an elaborate hierarchical system for his *Theater of Human Life* (*Theatrum humanae vitae*, in three editions of 1565, 1571, 1586, each of which was enlarged and rearranged), which he touted as teaching ethics by example rather than precept. Despite the complex branching diagrams that extended over multiple pages to lay out the logical structure of his system, it was no better than a random order in the judgment of one contemporary who recommended using the alphabetical indexes instead to access the text.

Whatever the order chosen for the text of a large informational book, one or more alphabetical indexes provided the most predictable kind of access. Erasmus drew up himself, with the help of one or more amanuenses, not only an index of adages by opening words, but also an index according to 257 topics or "loci" that listed relevant adages for each. While the first kind of indexing can be considered fairly mechanical, the second kind involved both expert and personal judgment. But he and others were aware of a basic problem with topical indexing: that the same concept could occur under different keywords or headings. Indexes in the sixteenth century opened with explanatory blurbs for readers who might not be familiar with how to use them. In one of these Zwinger recommended explicitly: "If things do not occur under one heading, look for them under a synonym." Zwinger introduced occasional cross-references in his text, but never systematically, and almost none were offered in his indexes. As Erasmus noted in one of his "index blurbs": "Remember that what pertains to generosity is at the same time considered as pertaining to avarice under the heading 'avarice' and thus in different instances of the same kind." As a result, using indexes in the sixteenth century was "often unpleasant" as Gessner observed and required intelligent reflection and diligent labor in consulting multiple entries and across multiple indexes. In the seventeenth century some encyclopedic works (like Alsted's *Encyclopaedia* of 1630 or the sequel to Zwinger's *Theatrum*) palliated this problem by consolidating separate indexes into a single one and introducing more cross-references.

The problem of heading choice was a concern not only for great compilers like Erasmus, Zwinger, and Gessner in indexing but also for ordinary readers who had been enjoined by their teachers to take notes by excerpting memorable passages from the books they read and storing them for later consultation and retrieval in notebooks. These were called commonplace books because they were organized according to the common "places" (*loci* or *topoi*) of argumentation. Humanist pedagogues offered advice on the selection of headings for these notebooks, and the number of headings considered optimal ranged widely. Erasmus used 257 in his index by places; others recommended only thirty headings. By contrast, Vincent Placcius in 1689 touted a piece of furniture, first described by Thomas Harrison in the 1640s—a "literary closet" that could accommodate up to three thousand separate headings, each with a hook on which to stick relevant note slips; but such a closet was costly, and we know of only two exemplars that were actually built, neither of which survives. There was no attempt to create an equivalent to the controlled vocabulary for subject indexing or book cataloging until the nineteenth century. In these earlier periods, teachers and some printed books no doubt prompted some to imitate their categories in their notes; in particular, the vices and virtues had been traditional topics since the florilegia of the Middle Ages. Overall, though, choice of headings and methods of taking notes more generally were left up to each individual; even Renaissance pedagogues who articulated the "best practices" of the day acknowledged that individuals should modify the general pattern of note-taking to suit their purposes. The grip of humanist pedagogues further loosened over time, and eighteenth-century methods of note-taking were especially varied.

The mobile paper slip became a key tool for the organizing and reorganizing of material according to keywords or alphabetical order. The slip, cut from a sheet of paper before or after it had been written on, was a new tool of information management in the early modern period. Although some have argued that alphabetization in antiquity and the Middle Ages must have been performed with movable slips, there is no firm evidence to support these rational reconstructions. The earliest surviving slips glued into notebooks date (to my knowledge) from the fifteenth century. The cheapness of paper facilitated the practice since to make slips one could write on only one side of a sheet and would waste the verso in order to glue the slips in place. The first explicit advice about the use of slips likely dates to Gessner's 1548 description of his method of indexing. A few years before his works of natural history Gessner had published a universal bibliography of books in learned languages, extant and not, manuscript and printed, totaling about twenty-five thousand items by five thousand authors. He accompanied this *Bibliotheca universalis* (Universal library, 1545) with a topical index to the contents of as many of those books as he could access, the *Pandectae* (1548—the title, by alluding to the Pandects of Roman law, connoting a summary treatment of a large subject). For each topic within the major fields of study Gessner listed all the relevant books in over six hundred pages of such lists. Clearly Gessner spent a lot of time ordering a vast set of textual information and had optimized his working method in the process. Following the section of the *Pandectae* on dictionaries Gessner explained how to make abundant and accurate indexes: cut the material into loose slips that can be stored in bundles or envelopes and rearranged as needed until the proper order is reached, at which point glue the slips into place. This method allowed for fully alphabetized indexes by contrast with medieval and early printed indexes, which were typically sorted only by the first or first two letters of the term being indexed. Partial alphabetization of that kind resulted from listing the items to index on to separate sheets for each first (or first two) letter(s) in the order in which the items occurred in the text. By contrast the use of slips became the norm for alphabetization (or ordering of other kinds) in the early modern period. We have many examples of surviving manuscripts prepared for print, collections of notes, library catalogs, and manuscript indexes that take the form of slips glued into place, most often in alphabetical order. Placcius's note closet remained unique in recommending keeping the slips fully mobile, so they could be moved around indefinitely, and sorted in different ways, or shared with others without jeopardizing the whole collection. In most cases scholars stored their slips in bundles or containers of some kind (pigeonholes, envelopes, or pouches).

Gessner's advice on indexing was not limited to the use of mobile slips, which may well have predated his published mention of them and certainly became standard practice. More unusually Gessner also recommended, as in 1548, cutting and pasting from printed books in order to save the labor of creating slips by copying out the passages to index. Indeed, some of Gessner's surviving notebooks feature short excerpts cut from books printed in Latin or German and glued in place. The excess copies that were inevitably generated by printing presumably played a role in suggesting this practice. Copies of books with no or low commercial value (either because they had been marked up for making a new edition or because they were damaged or left unsold, like our remaindered books) could be cut up for note-taking or indexing purposes, or reused as material in a new publication. Zwinger's *Theatrum* served in this way as the basis for a much expanded *Magnum theatrum vitae humanae* (Great theater of human life, 1631), as described in the preface of that work. Cutting and pasting from print or manuscript materials was efficient in avoiding not only the effort but also the errors that would be involved in making an intermediate copy. The practice was widely used in composing large reference works, including the great *glossary of medieval Latin by Charles Du Cange (1678), Samuel Johnson's *Dictionary of the English Language* (1755), and the *Encyclopedia Britannica* first published in 1768–71, which William Smellie jokingly said he had made with a "pair of scissors." In the eighteenth century a new form of slip came into use for note-taking and (accidentally at first) for cataloging the holdings in a library: printed playing cards featuring blank backs and in some cases space to write on the front as well.

Every society is an information society, as Robert Darnton and others have pointed out, but early modern Europeans became uniquely aware of their information technologies in comparison with earlier periods. Printing was widely perceived as a major innovation. For example. Jean Bodin and Francis Bacon hailed printing along with gunpowder and the compass as crucial recent inventions unknown to Greco-Roman antiquity; a few contemporaries, like Michel de Montaigne and Loys LeRoy, also appreciated that these technologies had originated much earlier in China. In Europe the spread of printing prompted both admiration and complaints, but also new practices and explicit discussions of them—from censorship to methods of compiling. Renaissance compilers took medieval practices of excerpting and ordering to new levels by handling much greater quantities of materials—objects, images, and texts—and experimenting with many ordering principles including miscellaneous order, which was considered especially pleasant. Alphabetical indexes of many kinds served as the main points of access for collections of written information, and their use became so widespread that indexes no longer featured explanatory blurbs after the sixteenth century. Mobile slips, cut from sheets of paper, first recommended for indexing, proved versatile, for example, for note-taking, sorting of many kinds, and cataloging books; for the latter task stiffer playing cards used in the eighteenth century prompted the development of standardized index cards in the nineteenth.

Communication

The impact of information is constrained by the means of its circulation. Essential to the success of printing in the mid-fifteenth century was the mercantile network that made possible the distribution of books far and wide throughout Europe. At just around the same time Europe developed a postal system that could convey letters and messengers at speeds similar to the ancient Roman *cursus publicus* or the medieval Islamic *Barīd*. The crucial element was a network of relay stations with fresh mounts. In the centuries since the decline of the Roman system, merchants' posts had been the most reliable form of mail. Major rulers also kept a staff of messengers to deliver diplomatic messages. But since there was no provision for a change of horses, deliveries on foot were the norm, yielding a maximum speed of sixty to seventy kilometers per day. In the fifteenth century innkeepers started to retain their own couriers, each covering their own portion of well-defined routes. When these inns served as a source of fresh horses and riders more ground could be covered (up to 170 kilometers per day). The Habsburgs' engagement of the Taxis family to provide a standing post service of that kind from Milan to Innsbruck (notably after Maximilian's marriage in 1494 with Bianca Sforza from Milan) set up the backbone of a network that was soon extended throughout the Habsburg territories to include Spain and Flanders and neighboring areas, and onto which the English and French monarchies each grafted their own system of relay riding. Wolfgang Behringer has called the resulting speeds a "communications revolution" within western Europe. In 1505 the Taxis system guaranteed delivery times that in some cases rival those of today's regular mail—for example, from Brussels to Paris in less than two days, to Lyon in four, and to Innsbruck in five and a half, although it took twelve days to Toledo and fifteen to Granada. (These were summer delivery times; winter deliveries took longer.) The mail system allowed for transportation of letters and small packets, not heavy goods, so that Europe was integrated intellectually far more successfully than agriculturally during this period when it continued to suffer from localized famines even when crops were abundant elsewhere.

Letters circulated in truly vast numbers throughout the early modern period. A small fraction of them were printed by senders or recipients, during their lifetimes or after their death. One scholar has estimated that by 1627 forty thousand letters had been printed in Italy alone. Far, far more had been written and sent. Untold numbers of letters have of course been lost, yet large collections also survive. Among the earliest are the letters of the Paston family from the English gentry (1,088 letters between 1422 and 1509); large surviving collections include four thousand letters to and from Erasmus, ten thousand for the French polymath Nicolas-Claude Fabri de Peiresc (1580–1637), and nineteen thousand for Voltaire (1694–1778) in the French Enlightenment. The *Republic of Letters (*respublica litterarum*) described a pan-European community united by "letters" ("litterae") in the sense of learning, but the second meaning (at least in English and French) of letters as epistolary can serve as a reminder of the crucial role of the medium in stoking the friendships and rivalries that existed within this complex community. The terms and ideals of the Republic of Letters and its practices of communicating by letter and printed matter remained remarkably stable throughout the early modern period despite a major shift in its emphasis, between Erasmus and Voltaire, from a humanist focus on classical learning to a focus on the arts and sciences of the "moderns" carried out in the vernacular, especially in French, which had replaced Latin as the dominant language of international communication by around 1700.

The mail enabled the exchange of information over larger distances than correspondents could actually travel. Some of these letters preceded or followed personal travel, but many were also exchanged between people who never met in person, but learned of one another through other people or through printed matter. Conrad Gessner, for example, collected observations in the mountains near his native Zurich, but relied principally on a vast network of correspondents to gather information about natural historical species and books and manuscripts from all over Europe with which he filled his publications. Gessner also applied his habit of cutting up useful information in the letters he received, parts of which can be found pasted into notebooks (with care taken that both the front and the back of the letter can still be read). Conversely Gessner sought to elicit new correspondents through the distribution of his printed books to unknown and distant readers. In his *Historia animalium* on birds (1555), Gessner ended the list of those he thanked for sending him information with a general plea to other readers to join the effort, especially those from "remote regions" like Spain or Scandinavia where he had few contacts. Gessner explained to his readers how to send him something via a local merchant who frequented the major fairs and could there pass on to a merchant from Zurich material to reach him. Gessner promised to answer by the same route in reverse with a countergift if desired; and he had already shown that he used print to publicly thank helpful contacts so a new correspondent could hope for recognition in one of Gessner's future publications as well.

Gessner's advice is a reminder that the Taxis postal system did not eliminate the more informal networks of communication through merchants. Services were never perfect, and anxious correspondents sent duplicate letters through different routes to maximize the chances of success. All these communication channels played a crucial role in circulating information in print and manuscript at speeds, distances, and quantities that had not been experienced before in Europe. The confluence of technical and cultural innovations, from postal service and printing to the discoveries, recoveries, and schisms for which the period is famous, made possible and motivated a desire to collect and consume information across many fields on unprecedented scales and also to discuss the best ways of doing so.

Further Reading

Wolfgang Behringer, "Communications Revolutions: A Historiographical Concept," translated by Richard Deveson, *German History* 24, no. 3 (2006), 333–74; Jean-François Bert and Jérôme Lamy ed., *Les cartes à jouer du savoir. Détournements savants au XVIIIe siècle, Heuristiques* 1 (2023); Ann Blair, "Printing and Humanism in the Work of Conrad Gessner," *Renaissance Quarterly*, 70, no. 1 (2017): 1–43; idem, *Too Much to Know: Managing Scholarly Information before the Modern Age*, 2010; *British Library Treasures in Full: Gutenberg Bible* (online); Eltjo Buringh, *Medieval Manuscript Production in the Latin West*, 2011; John Considine, *Academy Dictionaries*, 2014; James Delbourgo, *Collecting the World: Hans Sloane and the Origins of the British Museum*, 2017; Paul M. Dover, *The Information Revolution in Early Modern Europe*, 2021; Paula Findlen, ed., *Early Modern Things: Objects and Their Histories, 1500–1800*, 2012; Findlen, *Possessing Nature: Museums, Collecting, and Scientific Culture in Early Modern Italy*, 1994; Jonathan Green, Frank McIntyre, and Paul Needham, "The Shape of Incunable Survival and Statistical Estimation of Lost Editions," *Papers of the Bibliographical Society of America* 105, no. 2 (June 2011): 141–75; Daniel Hobbins, *Authorship and Publicity before Print: Jean Gerson and the Transformation of Late Medieval Learning*, 2009; Markus Krajewski, *Paper Machines: About Cards and Catalogs, 1548–1929*, 2002, translated by Peter Krapp, 2011; Sachiko Kusukawa, *Picturing the Book of Nature: Image, Text, and Argument in Sixteenth-Century Human Anatomy and Medical Botany*, 2011; Hannah Marcus, *Forbidden Knowledge: Medicine, Science, and Censorship in Early Modern Italy*, 2020; Joseph P. McDermott and Peter Burke, eds., *The Book Worlds of East Asia and Europe 1450–1850: Connections and*

Comparisons, 2015; David McKitterick, *Print, Manuscript, and the Search for Order 1450–1830,* 2003; Paul Needham, *The Printer and the Pardoner: An Unrecorded Indulgence Printed by William Caxton,* 1986; Andrew Pettegree, *The Book in the Renaissance,* 2010; Aysha Pollnitz, *Princely Education in Early Modern Britain,* 2015; Christoph Reske, "Hat Johannes Gutenberg das Gießeninstrument erfunden? Mikroskopischer Typenvergleich an frühen Drucken," *Gutenberg Jahrbuch,* 2015; Mary Rouse and Richard Rouse, *Authentic Witnesses: Approaches to Medieval Texts and Manuscripts,* 1991; idem, *Manuscripts and Their Makers: Commercial Book Producers in Medieval Paris, 1200–1500,* 2000; Nikolaus Schobesberger et al., "European Postal Networks," in *News Networks in Early Modern Europe,* edited by Joad Raymond and Noah Moxham, 2016, 19–63; Maren Elisabeth Schwab and Anthony Grafton, *The Art of Discovery: Digging into the Past in Renaissance Europe,* 2022; Angus Vine, *Miscellaneous Order: Manuscript Culture and the Early Modern Organization of Knowledge,* 2019; Eric White, *Editio Princeps: A History of the Gutenberg Bible,* 2017.

5

Networks and the Making of a Connected World in the Sixteenth Century

John-Paul A. Ghobrial

One should fear more the nib of a Jesuit's pen than the point of an Arab's sword.

—NICCOLÒ MANUCCI, A VENETIAN MERCHANT IN
THE MUGHAL EMPIRE (1638–1717)

LONG BEFORE MODERN PROPHETS foretold the rise of a "network society" in the twentieth century, information underpinned what historians have often referred to as a "connected world" in the *early modern period. On the heels of the discovery of the Americas, scholars, statesmen, and clerics alike re-imagined their world through the sometimes unpredictable circulation of letters, handwritten news, and printed documents, which connected the newly discovered worlds of the Atlantic to the "old worlds" of the Mediterranean, Africa, and Asia. Although building on old practices, these novel forms of circulation connected unfamiliar societies to each other in surprising and powerful ways.

Consider, for example, two books published in the space of twenty years of one another in the last decades of the sixteenth century, which have been the subject of close study by the French scholar Serge Gruzinski. The first was an Ottoman Turkish work called the *Tarih-i Hind-i garbi*, or *A History of the India of the West,* the earliest manuscripts of which date to 1580. The work is the first ever account of the discovery of the New World written for an Ottoman audience in Istanbul. Although we know almost nothing about the person who wrote it, clues in the text suggest that the Anonymous Chronicler drew primarily on classic Spanish accounts of the New World that had been published in the sixteenth century, alongside several passages lifted directly from Spanish, Italian, and Portuguese news accounts. To access this world of printed information in Istanbul, the Anonymous Chronicler almost certainly relied on the help of a local European merchant or renegade in Istanbul, someone, at least, with a good working knowledge of European and Ottoman languages. Out of this act of collaborative translation, the *Tarih-i Hind-i garbi* presented the exotic wonders of "New India," or the West Indies, to an Ottoman audience. Readers in Istanbul could read firsthand the tales of the Spanish conquest of Mexico, descriptions of the Inka Empire of Peru, and fantastical observations of the great mining center of Potosí, in the Andes, from where American silver was transported into the Ottoman world and further east. In some surviving copies, intricate Ottoman miniatures have been added in an attempt to capture the wild variety of flora and fauna in the Americas, for example, manatees, tapirs, turkeys, bison, jaguars, avocados, and papayas—all wondrous discoveries to an audience in Istanbul.

More than ten thousand kilometers away, around the same time, a book was published in Mexico City called the *Repertorio de los tiempos,* or *Repertory of the Times,* which set out to satisfy the curiosity of readers in New Spain with two chapters focused on the Ottoman Empire. Both chapters reflected on distinctly presentist matters: the first explored "the way in which one deduces from predictions, prognoses, conjectures and natural reasons the fall and the destruction of the monarchy and the empire of the Turks," while the second chapter sought to explain "the origins of the Turkish Empire, and the way in which it grew and in which it achieved the power it wields today." Unlike in the case of the *Tarih-i Hind-i garbi,* we know much more about the man behind this book: one Heinrich Martin, a German migrant from Hamburg whose family settled in Spain during Martin's youth in order to take up work at the center of the thriving print trade. At some point, Martin traveled to the New World and set up a print shop in Mexico City in 1599, where the *Repertory* was published in 1606. Like the *Tarih-i Hind-i garbi,* the *Repertory* was assembled from information, individuals, and texts in motion in the sixteenth century. While Martin was unlikely to have had any Ottoman informants to guide his work, he was able from Mexico City to access some of the most authoritative accounts of life in the Ottoman Empire in his time, many of them written by individuals who had observed the Ottoman Empire directly for themselves.

Mexicans imagining life in Istanbul, Ottomans reflecting on the wonders of Mexico City: taken together, these two works reveal the extent to which, already in the sixteenth century, the circulation of information connected societies separated not only by huge distances but also by profound differences in language, culture, and religion. Information contributed to a certain lived experience of global simultaneity, that is, a consciousness shared by separate societies that they inhabited the same world even if the actual movement of information continued to require weeks or even months to travel around the earth. And yet both works were also intensely "local" in their genealogies: both emerged in very specific contexts—colonial Mexico and the literary milieu of the Ottoman capital—through the somewhat haphazard intersection of a handful of texts and individuals able to read them. The presence of Ottoman histories in Mexico City and Spanish conquest narratives in Istanbul was itself a reflection of recent political, religious, and financial transformations un-leashed by the discovery of the New World and the proliferation of empires in this period. In this way, early modern global historians have argued compel-lingly for the importance of information in the "world making" of the sixteenth century: a first phase of global integration through the circulation of informa-tion that predated by four centuries the phenomena usually conjured up by the term "globalization" for the twentieth century.

This chapter explores the role information played in the making of connect-edness on a global scale. After briefly describing the historical transformations in trade, politics, and religion that defined this period, the chapter focuses on two types of human networks—merchants and missionaries—that contrib-uted in important ways to the flow of information before the advent of modern technologies of communication. These groups drew on the prevalent media of the day—especially handwritten letters and questionnaires—as ways of circu-lating information to communities far beyond their own networks. In the last half of the chapter, I concentrate on a case study—European knowledge of Islam—as a way of understanding the many intellectual, political, and religious consequences of information flow in the age of early modern globalization.

Coming into Focus: Early Modern Globalization

Worldwide integration in the early modern period set the stage for the emer-gence of the first global networks of information. It is impossible to under-stand the way in which information became global in this period without reference to how political, economic, and religious transformations of this period all contributed to the circulation of information. Four central changes deserve mention. First, this was a period during which genuinely global commercial exchange networks emerged for the first time. Of course, long-distance trade had always been an important feature of the ancient and medieval worlds, but it was only in the early modern period that the regular and predictable movement of peoples, commodities, and capital would connect the distant reaches of East and West, the Americas and Asia. Information moved hand in hand with this trade, and indeed the mechanics of long-distance trade networks relied on a wide array of practices that influenced the spread of information, for example, information gathering about local markets, the dissemination of information to business partners through correspondence, and the standardization of new *bookkeeping and accounting practices.

Second, and arising in part from the establishment of global trade flows, this was a period of large-scale migrations of people—the largest of which involved the slave trade—and, with them, increased contact between different languages, cultures, and societies. In such a context, information brokers thrived, especially those who commanded multiple languages or specific chancery skills of use to political powers.

Third, the discovery of new worlds set into motion a period of worldwide biological exchanges. The movement of New World seeds, plants, and foodstuffs, for example, introduced both new challenges and new opportunities into European societies. At the most basic level, questions arose about the identification of biological species that had never been seen before, but there were also more complicated questions that demanded collaboration and information gathering: Which plants could be cultivated in different climates, which plants could be eaten, which could be smoked or made into drinks, which had medicinal properties, and which were, put simply, dangerous? How were they grown, processed, and used by the peoples who had first cultivated them? These questions developed naturally out of a wider set of interests in the interactions among humans, animals, and the natural world.

Finally, this was a period of great religious upheaval as much for Christianity as for Islam. The Protestant and Catholic *Reformations of Europe unleashed a particular interest in the spread of Christianity to the new worlds now firmly planted in the European imagination. Similarly, the emergence of Muslim powers like the Ottoman, the Safavid, and the Mughal Empires witnessed the spread of Islam to new geographies far from the core caliphates of the medieval Middle East. Missionary strategies required close engagement with native and local societies, the collection of information about religious practices and beliefs, and the careful comparison and handling of all this information in a meaningful and organized way.

Trade, migration, biological exchanges, and the spread of religion were all central to the emergence of new global networks of information in the early modern period and underpinned by long-term demographic trends in which the world's population doubled between 1500 and 1800. To be sure, there was much that was old in these new networks. One marker of continuity with the past was the perseverance of the letter as a most important medium of communication that carried on from the medieval period into the early modern. One need only consider S. D. Goitein's classic study of medieval Jewish trading networks to know that letters had always been an important instrument of communication: the Cairo Genizah alone holds some three hundred thousand fragments of letters, written in Hebrew, Arabic, and Aramaic, a testament to a world of trade that stretched across Egypt, Palestine, Lebanon, Syria, Tunisia, Sicily, and as far as India. Similar stories could be told about trade around the Mediterranean, the South China Sea, and the Indian Ocean, each area animated by its own distinct networks of communication in the medieval period. In contrast, early modern networks transcended familiar regional configurations, creating new and sometimes surprising geographies that reflected the preoccupations of political and mercantile actors in this period. Indeed, if early modern global networks were distinct from their medieval predecessors, it was not only in the truly global reach of their networks but more importantly in the extent to which information networks were embedded in the distinct political and financial institutions of this period. The consolidation of power by maritime empires, the profit motives of trading companies, and the expansion of global missionary orders: all depended in critical ways on the scale and reach of information flows.

Of course, there were also imbalances and asymmetries in these information networks. Europeans, for example, played a disproportionate role in the movement of goods, information, and cultures connecting port cities across Asia, the Atlantic, and the Mediterranean world. Once overseas empires were established by the Spanish, the Portuguese, the Dutch, the English, the French, and even the Scandinavian empires, much of the work of global information networks would cater specifically to their needs. Alongside these imperial networks, regional information networks continued to thrive, but it was often Europeans who played the critical role as agents who connected American, Asian, and Middle Eastern information networks not only with Europe but also with each other. This is an important reminder that networks never existed in the ether, simply to be uncovered or connected into, but rather they were fashioned, constructed, subverted, managed, and organized according to the interests and needs of specific actors. In what follows, attention is given therefore to two main sets of actors—merchants and missionaries—and the effects they had on the circulation of information in the early modern period.

The Power of Merchants: Trading Companies and Trading Diasporas

Information was the dark matter that connected the early modern world. Much of this circulation was organized around the preoccupations and interests of merchants whose global careers straddled both the old worlds of the East and the new worlds of the West. In Europe, with the support of patrons normally in positions of authority in the state, several trading companies emerged and competed with one another to establish themselves in markets scattered across the Middle East, Asia, Africa, and the Americas. Although local, regional patterns of trade had always existed in such places as the Indian Ocean, European merchants created new hubs of communication as trading companies sought to consolidate their supply chains in sites far from their home countries. The Dutch East India Company is a case in point. Established in 1602 with its innovative structure of a joint-stock corporation, the company was given a twenty-one-year monopoly on the Dutch spice trade. Key to its success was the development of a vast administrative machinery, which effectively meant the creation of a second headquarters of operations in Batavia, present-day Jakarta. Because much of the company's success in the Indian Ocean relied on its access to intra-Asian trade, the company employed a host of translators, go-betweens, and intermediaries whose main job was to make communication possible between Dutch merchants and their local, Asian counterparts. In port cities like Makassar in eastern Indonesia, entire family dynasties arose to command these roles as translators and interpreters for much of the eighteenth and nineteenth centuries, a reminder of the extent to which information was also a business in the early modern world.

Some scholars have seen in such ventures as the Dutch East India Company the emergence of a "modern business infrastructure," where information networks paved the way for the rise of the stock exchange and institutions like the Royal Exchange in London. That may be the case, but more important in its time was the series of transformations in the handling of information occasioned by the rise of trading companies. Apart from the basic task of gathering information about markets, commodities, and the foreign societies in which they operated, trading companies dealt with a series of challenges related to the management of information. On the micro level of everyday practicalities, they developed systems for dealing with the sheer mass of accumulated information, including filing systems, the organization of documents, and techniques for retrieving information efficiently when needed. How busy merchants were with information management is clear from the archives of the Dutch East India Company, which alone amount to some twenty-five million pages of paperwork scattered today in repositories in Jakarta, Colombo, Chennai, Cape Town, and The Hague.

Alongside official trading companies whose work necessarily carried information across great distances, it was trade diasporas (that is, communities of merchants settled in foreign lands) that were responsible for the intricate ways in which information crossed languages in this period—the Armenian merchants of New Julfa, for example, or the Sephardic merchant networks based around Livorno. Like trading companies, trade diasporas had a structure that combined a central hub with the operation of multiple nodes separated by immense distances, all of which functioned to help circulate merchants, credit, goods, and especially information around the globe. In the case of the Armenian networks studied to such great effect by Sebouh Aslanian, the central hub could be found in New Julfa, a suburb of Isfahan in present-day Iran. But beyond New Julfa, the activities of Armenian merchants were spread across several other nodes in such a range of places as Amsterdam, Venice, Izmir, Madras, Canton, Manila, and even St. Petersburg and Jakarta. These sites were connected by the circulation of personal and business correspondence through a well-developed courier system. The vagaries of weather, warfare, and piracy could all cause significant delays, yet the Armenians remained connected through a regular, stable, and remarkably efficient communication network.

Trade diasporas played key roles in the circulation of information thanks to the specific structures and institutions of trade in the early modern world. In the case of both Armenian and Sephardic merchants, the *commenda* system of trade first devised in the Islamic world centuries before provided the organizing framework for most legal contracts. In this system, a junior partner would begin working in New Julfa with a senior partner, often connected by local family and kin networks, and this collaboration offered the junior partner an opportunity to learn the trade under the supervision of a skilled merchant. Once he had achieved a certain level of expertise, the junior partner could sign a commenda contract, wherein he would undertake to leave New Julfa in order to carry out trade using the capital and investment of the senior partner. At the same time, the senior partner undertook to look after the agent's family while he was away, which acted as an important mechanism to securing trust between the two agents. Importantly, commenda contracts included explicit clauses directing the junior agent to keep his partner informed through regular, detailed, and frequent correspondence. A strict set of expectations governed this sort of business correspondence, and merchants abroad would fall foul of their partners if they did not adhere to such conventions. In one case, for example, in 1711, a merchant was reprimanded by his senior partner because his "letter was without flavor or salt because it contained no news about purchases and expenditures" (Aslanian, 157). A similar case could be made for the array of documents and instruments of trade used in this period: printed bills of exchange, letters of recommendation, broadsides with price descriptions, and advertisements all contributed crucially to early modern trade by circulating information in oral, written, and printed media.

In the case of trade diasporas, these networks played a central role in connecting European trading companies to the Mughal, Ottoman, and Safavid Empires of the East. When a French merchant ship leased to Armenian merchants was taken captive off the coast of India in April 1748, the British privateers who inventoried the ship found that it contained more than seventeen hundred letters intended for Armenian merchants around the world. If we consider that this was only a single ship of the hundreds in motion around the world, we can capture a glimpse of the scale of information networks constructed around trading diasporas. And yet, we should also view such evidence with some caution: merchants typically sent several copies of a single letter by various routes as a way of managing the routine uncertainties of postal communication in this period.

Information was important to merchants, therefore, but it also played a crucial role in the forms that empire took in this period. In part, this is because so much of early modern colonialism was based on the informal partnership of merchants and state authorities. The relationship between information, capitalism, and empire crystallized in important ways in this period. The English East India Company, and its role in establishing British empire in India, provides a good example. Different modes of communication functioned as sinews of power in the expanding world of empires. Merchants carried royal letters that were deployed to build new commercial relationships in the East Indies. Forms of accounting and bookkeeping were developed in coastal trading posts to help the company organize and most efficiently use this information of trade. Even pamphleteers and propagandists used communication and information to protect the monopoly rights of the companies, while the development of new forms of stock keeping and price watching contributed to the idea of a self-regulating and quasi-independent market system. Information was wielded in manuscript and in print, in the work of surveillance, imperial administration, and information gathering by a growing imperial bureaucracy. In this way, entire empires were forged from the work of communication, writing, inscription, record keeping, and correspondence. The British Empire was built on communication—of handwritten letters and printed forms—as much as on trade, governance, and sheer military power.

Jesuit Information Networks, Local and Global

Even more important than merchants in bringing different cultures into contact with one another were the extended networks of missionaries, both Christian and Muslim, that spread into new geographies in this period. In the case of Christianity, this phenomenon was driven mainly by the development of Catholic missionary organizations who aspired to revitalize Catholicism in the wake of the challenges posed by the Protestant Reformation. In this context early modern Catholicism developed an acute sense of the importance of its global mission to the world beyond Europe. The Counter-Reformation Church dispatched Catholic missionaries to the Middle East, Africa, Asia, and the Americas and established sophisticated communication networks to manage the movement of people, funding, relics, sacred objects, and of course information. The main hub of this emerging Catholic network was located at the Vatican in Rome, but new hubs of Catholicism crystallized in other centers, for example, across Germany, in the New World centers of Mexico City and Lima, and as far away as China. Between these centers of gravity, new and unexpected geographies were created through the spread of information between Mexico, Europe, and China.

In his excellent study of the global *Jesuit network, Luke Clossey offers perhaps the best case study for understanding the role of missionary networks in the circulation of information. From the moment of the establishment of the Jesuits' mission to the world, information was seen as a vital element in the mission. The first General Congregation of the Jesuits included clear orders about the importance of establishing a system of epistolary exchanges such that "in every place . . . [the superiors] should know about the things that are being done in other places" (Clossey, 194). This insistence on the acts of writing, reading, and circulating information explains how someone like Niccolò Manucci, a Venetian merchant living in Goa in the late seventeenth century, could warn his readers that the "nib of a Jesuit's pen" was mightier than the "point of an Arab's sword." The tens of thousands of letters that circulated across this global geography are a telling reminder that the work of the missionaries went far beyond the goal of conversion and proselytization to include important consequences for the spread of information.

The Jesuits were a truly global network, whose members were scattered across the world and also moved efficiently from one node to another. Clossey's meticulous research offers an intriguing snapshot of detailed aspects of communication in the Jesuit information network. Of the sample of Jesuits under study, Clossey identified some fifty-three Jesuits who were known to have been active in at least two of three missionary theaters in this period, including in Germany, Mexico, and China. The output of these fifty-three individuals alone comes to some twelve hundred surviving texts, mostly letters. Almost half are written in Latin, and another quarter in Spanish. A fifth survive as copies or summaries, mostly in German. The rest are written in Chinese, Dutch, French, German, Italian, and Portuguese. The physical circulation of these documents is evident from the fact that only a few are preserved today in the Roman archives of the Jesuit order; most of them in fact are scattered about in manuscript collections in Europe and the Americas. Of course, these fifty-three were only a small part of a network that numbered more than fifteen thousand Jesuits scattered across the early modern world over the course of two centuries of the order's existence. And all of these wrote as many letters to other Jesuits as they did to private correspondents, such as relatives and friends. In one three-year period, for example, a missionary based in China by the name of Adam Gerstl wrote some twenty-six letters to his father in Germany.

Surprisingly perhaps, the information that circulated in this vast network was not mainly, or even primarily, about conversion practices. Rather, the letters included a wide array of information, mostly covering current news, but also science, climate, theology, travel, and what we might term today cultural ethnography or anthropology. In addition to this diversity of subjects, the actual practices of letter writing by Jesuits magnified the impact of their individual letters. First, they often sent letters in multiple copies to different correspondents in Europe, encouraging them to forward the letters on to others. In the short term, the writers hoped that their letters would be copied and read aloud to larger audiences, but in the long term the order aimed to print them. Although the earliest books of Jesuit letters were published in Rome in 1552 in Italian, publication also took place in several Catholic centers across Europe—in Germany as well as across Italy, Portugal, Spain, Bohemia, and France. At multiple sites, therefore, popular Jesuit works were being printed in standard print runs of a thousand copies. This geographically wide publication history, combined with the preference for publishing the letters in inexpensive editions, meant that letters rooted in specific, distinct, local networks abroad managed to find a wide reading audience at home in Europe.

Second, the vagaries of communication meant that letters could have long, and often surprising, afterlives in the Jesuit communication network. A copy of the first letter written by Francis Xavier from Goa in the mid-sixteenth century arrived in 1664 in Vilnius, Lithuania, more than a century after Xavier himself had composed it. In another case, a "Chinese narrative from the letter of Father Joannis de Haynin," written in 1669, was still circulating in the Upper German province of Regensburg as late as 1726. The information circulated in these ways was durable. In this context, modern conceptions of communication are ill suited to understanding the attitudes of individuals to the speed and route of communication in the early modern world. There was, for example, a regular and dynamic exchange of letters that connected Jesuits in China to their counterparts in Mexico. Although news over the Pacific could face severe delays, the Jesuits involved in this particular exchange only began to complain when they didn't hear from their counterparts after a period of three years.

Third, information traveled in surprising ways that defied any straightforward descriptions of standardized "routes" of communication. News from China was normally sent first to Jesuits in Mexico before being forwarded on to correspondents in Europe. Even so, there were instances where Mexican Jesuits would write to Europe with requests for news about China, when they seemed unable to receive it directly. Contemporaries had expectations about the spread and speed of information travel, which were vastly different from our own assumptions of near instantaneous communication in the age of *digital technologies. Put simply, the speed and efficiency of information might have been less important in the sixteenth century than the dependability of its arrival and the completeness of its account.

In Clossey's sample, the lion's share of letters focused not on the exchange of "best practices" of conversion but rather on local news and current events from the various outposts in which the Jesuits were scattered. In many ways, this made Jesuit correspondence somewhat distinct from merchants' letters, where current events were reported only inasmuch as they appeared to have an impact on business, trade, and commodities. Within the global geography of Jesuit networks, certain centers came to function as unique clearinghouses for the circulation of news from one region or another. The Jesuits in Mexico, for example, received news directly from Asia, and they would come to play a natural role in the gathering, editing, rewriting, and publishing of information about China for audiences in America as well as Europe. In this way, someone like Juan González de Mendoza (1545–1618), a missionary who never set foot in China, could become a major authority on the Chinese Empire. In 1586, he published his *History of the Most Notable Things, Rites and Customs of the Great Kingdom of China*, which became one of the earliest and standard introductions to the history of China for European audiences. Information flows could turn writers who never traveled into sources of authority distributed across the world.

Beyond current events and news, Jesuit networks also played a central role in the collection, circulation, and dissemination of scientific information. Scattered as they were across the world, they were ideally and uniquely suited to gathering comprehensive information on such things as comets, astronomical data, weather, longitude and latitude, and other aspects of the study of the natural world. For good reason the emergent scientific societies of this period sought to cultivate their connections with the Jesuits. Clossey's study describes how in 1667, Henry Oldenburg, the first secretary of the Royal Society of London, wrote to Robert Hooke of his hope "to procure for the Royal Society a correspondency all over the world by means of missionaries." The Jesuit network was also the target of the interests of the architects of royal power, for example, Jean-Baptiste Colbert, who envisioned that the first expedition of French Jesuits to China should have as its primary goal the collection of astronomical data. Through such processes, Jesuit networks provided the foundation for several types of knowledge formation in this period. Athanasius Kircher, who has been called the "last man who knew everything," proposed making a *Concilium Geographicum*, or Geographical Council, tasked with gathering measurements collected in Jesuit colleges around the world. Even Gottfried Wilhelm Leibniz, who was renowned in his time for his interest in Chinese philosophy and politics, could joke with a friend in 1697 that he relied so much on news obtained from the Jesuits that he had considered putting a sign over his door saying "post office for China" (as reported by Clossey).

Centuries before multinational corporations would dream up taglines like the "world's local bank," the Jesuit information network managed to operate effectively both on a local scale, in specific regions across the world, and on a global one by circulating the information it produced throughout its worldwide network. This global reach was even a recurring theme in the titles of its publications, such as *On the Society of Jesus Fighting in All Parts of the World* (1675), *Catholic Christendom Spread through the Whole World* (1678), and *The Society of Jesus Have Moistened the Whole World with their Sweat* (1701). Titles like these underscored the global frontiers of Jesuit information but also contributed to the feeling of simultaneity and global consciousness that connected people separated otherwise by space, religion, and language.

Letters and Questionnaires: Two Modes of Communication

The physical letter—ink inscribed on a sheet of paper—appears to be under threat of extinction today. But in the early modern period, letters continued to be one of the most critical instruments of communication; it is difficult to exaggerate their ubiquity. If we focus on what might be called with some imprecision "learned letters," something like twenty thousand collections of learned correspondence might have been printed between 1500 and 1800. Even more survive in manuscript. The Oxford-based Cultures of Knowledge project—which has pioneered an ambitious attempt to catalog and document all this correspondence in a single database—has estimated that a million letters survive from this period, perhaps even twice that many. Other anecdotal measures of the scale of letter writing are available in the attitudes toward letter writing expressed in early modern literary culture. The anonymously published *Letters of a Portuguese Nun* in 1669 or Aphra Behn's *Love-Letters between a Nobleman and His Sister* (1684–87), among other examples, speak to the rise of the epistolary novel in the late seventeenth century, itself a reflection of the growing importance of the *genre of letters to early modern Europeans.

The importance of letter writing was obviously not just restricted to Europe, but rather it reflected a practice that connected individuals across Europe, the Middle East, and Asia. Around the globe there were men and women who spent their time scribbling, copying, crossing out, reorganizing, and dispatching letters, while waiting for new ones to arrive to fill their time. As Gagan Sood has shown for eighteenth-century India, European merchants and missionaries existed in a shared world of epistolary exchange, in which similar conventions, practices, and processes united European merchants and missionaries to their Indian counterparts. Evidence for this can be gleaned from the distinct terminology that Sood has identified as present in multiple languages to signify the set of agents who were central to everyday communication: scribes and clerks—who might be referred to alternatively as kātibs, nivisan-dahs, écrivains, escrivãos, writers—and translators, that is, interprètes, linguas, tarjumāns, dubashis, and gumashtahs. Beyond this terminology, epistolary cultures across Islamic Eurasia had much in common, from the general struc-ture of letters to the specific forms of address and opening and closing formu-las, and in the array of topics normally discussed in letters. They also shared similar strategies aimed at restricting the flow of information to all but the intended recipient: techniques of seeking privacy, for example folding, sealing, and in some cases the use of ciphers.

In a global context, one of the challenges facing the spread of information was how to transcend linguistic diversity across different locales. To this end, lingua francas existed in specific regions—a form of Italian in the Ottoman Empire, Portuguese in India—and they helped individuals overcome language barriers. Nonetheless the circulation of information owed much to collabora-tive translation carried out by several individuals working together. Gagan Sood has described, for example, the revealing case of Bernard Picot de la Motte, a French merchant based in Mahe in Malabar in the latter half of the eighteenth century. A native speaker of French, La Motte likely dictated the first draft of his letters in French, then wrote them (or had them translated) into Portuguese for the Indigenous Malabar clerks who were more likely to know Portuguese than French. The clerks then sought out someone who was able to translate the Portuguese into Arabic, the language spoken by La Motte's trading partners in India. In his own records, La Motte preserved all three versions of his letter: the original French draft, the neat copy in the Portuguese lingua franca, and the final Arabic version intended for his recipient. This was the distinct process through which information could transcend language bar-riers in multilingual contexts.

Apart from multilingualism, there were other more mundane challenges to the spread of such information. No matter where they originated across the globe, letters in this period shared a common set of complaints and refrains. The lack of letters was a constant source of worry, even unhappiness; recipients were not writing often enough or in enough detail; handwriting was hasty and difficult to read; important subjects had gone neglected; reminders were made, in vain, that more letters should be sent; and genuine pleasure was expressed at the perfect letter, swift in its arrival and comprehensive in its reporting. It is difficult to know how to read these complaints: a reflection of anxieties about information before the twentieth century or, more likely, a reminder that for most people in this period, information was precious and highly valued, especially when it traveled across great distances.

How far these global networks of information relied on personal contacts is clear from the short, general phrases used to address letters to their recipients. A European merchant in India could tell his associates in Lisbon to write to him simply by name "at the Portuguese factory in Surat," and it was assumed the letter would get to him. Likewise, a correspondent in London could tell his Oxford correspondent: "Sir, send me two lines in reply to [my] letter without fail, and when you send them address them to the printing shop. For when a letter is addressed to that house it will reach me, because everyone there knows me." The global world of information was so personal that even the most basic information—a name and a city—could carry a letter across the world to its intended recipient.

Alongside letters, other instruments of communication played an important role in the making of information networks. Unlike the long traditional genre of the letter, questionnaires appeared as a novel feature of the media landscape of the sixteenth century, as a means of collecting mass information long before the advent of modern research methods. In 1671, for example, while preparing for his travels to the Islamic world, the diamond merchant Jean Chardin received a questionnaire from a savant in Paris called Cabart de Villermont. Known by his friends as a "curieux," or someone with a voracious appetite for information, Villermont had spent his career collecting as much information as he could on the customs, practices, and realities of the East. When he learned of Chardin's intention to travel to Persia, he sent him a questionnaire complete with 107 questions about the East. The subjects of interest ranged wildly across a vast array of topics: mostly about the Dutch and French trade in spices, drugs, and tea, but also about Eastern customs and manners, the state of ports in the Middle East, and the quality of manufactured goods produced there. Through this questionnaire, Villermont hoped to gain certainty on some of the topics he had been discussing with friends in Paris. It would be several years before Chardin finally replied to Villermont's questions, but the questionnaire grew in importance, particularly for those individuals who could not manage to carry out the global travels of merchants and missionaries in this period.

Questionnaires were important not only to individuals like Villermont but also for the aspirations of political and religious elites. In 1580, royal officials in Spain distributed around New Castile a set of printed questionnaires called the *Relaciones Topográficas* (Topographical Accounts), which contained several questions aimed at collecting information about the economic resources of the country. Interestingly, the *Relaciones* included questions on local religious practices, offering invaluable insight into religion in sixteenth-century Spain. Questionnaires had already been deployed in the New World as a form of administration, an innovation that inspired new procedures and practices back in Europe. Questionnaires showed how information could be standardized around the interests of those doing the collecting. In this way, local information could also become the basis for larger, state-led initiatives dealing, for example, with conversion and conquest. Yet for all the effort carried out in the circulation of these questionnaires, in most cases religious officials never actually did anything with the information contained in them.

Nonetheless questionnaires acted as bottom-up modes of communication that played a role in forging new regional identities on the basis of local information gathering. This was the case in the seventeenth and eighteenth centuries when scholars and antiquarians based in *learned societies around Britain began to disseminate questionnaires to various shires, communities, and urban centers in Wales, Scotland, and Ireland. Such ventures had an earlier history, for example, in the "enquiries" that had been circulated from time to time in local parishes during the fifteenth century. But it was only in the sixteenth and seventeenth centuries that these occasional, ad hoc efforts began to be systematized in the form of printed questionnaires. Francis Bacon formulated "heads" or "articles of inquiry" aimed at identifying questions for future study and to structure empirical research in natural history. By the end of the seventeenth century, the printed questionnaire had become a natural method for learned societies in search of antiquities, as in the 1677 publication of *That the Northern Counties which abound in Antiquities and Ancient Gentry, may no longer be bury'd in Silence Information is desired concerning the following Queries as they lye in order.* Questionnaires of this kind contributed to the rediscovery and the development of histories and identities that transcended any single parish or locality in England, Ireland, Scotland, or Wales.

As with the Spanish questionnaires, the circulation of these questionnaires did not always result in direct answers, or any at all. Of four thousand questionnaires sent out by the Dublin Society in the late eighteenth century, for example, responses to just forty are preserved (as studied by Fox). As today, all sorts of factors dissuaded individuals from replying: some people simply ignored circulars, perhaps out of indifference or apathy; others lacked the ability, or sufficient time, to respond to the sorts of detailed questions being asked of them; still others simply found the questionnaires to be "bothersome" and "intrusive" meddling from strangers. Whatever the case, it is striking that questionnaires of this sort continued to be produced well into the nineteenth century and, indeed, would become a familiar tool in the arsenal of modern social science researchers presaging such things as the founding of Mass Observation in Britain in the 1930s. That individuals remained so optimistic about the promise of these questionnaires is evidence of the faith placed in such modes of communication, even if their ambitions were not always realized.

The Case of European Knowledge of Islam

Not only were the information networks of this period important for the discovery of new, unknown worlds, but they also contributed to profound changes in the understanding of societies about which much was already known. This final section examines how European knowledge of the Islamic world was transformed in the early modern period. Before the sixteenth century, knowledge of Islam in western Europe stemmed mainly from a handful of texts that circulated primarily among European theologians and scholars working in Latin. These works were mostly of a polemical and ideological nature: even works that appeared to be straightforward—for example, European translations of the Quran or accounts written by medieval travelers who had witnessed Islamic societies firsthand—were intended to serve an anti-Islamic purpose. In such a world, Shakespeare could write in *Henry VI, Part I*: "Was Mahomet inspired with a dove? / Thou with an eagle art inspired then," a reference to a medieval trope according to which the Prophet placed corn in his ear to attract a dove, as a sign of revelation from the Holy Spirit. By the end of this period, such a polemic may have persisted in its appeal to some people, but it competed with a range of new evidence about the Islamic world that was circulating in Europe.

This new information drew, in the first instance, from the emergent networks of diplomacy and trade that connected Europe to the Ottoman Empire. Starting in the 1530s, European powers agreed to a set of treaties, or capitulations, with the Ottoman sultan, which paved the way for the establishment of permanent European embassies and consuls in the Ottoman Empire. First the French in 1535, then the English in 1579 and the Dutch in 1612: one by one, new communities of Europeans were established in Istanbul, Smyrna, Aleppo, Cairo, and further afield in Basra and Isfahan. By the end of the eighteenth century, Istanbul had become one of the few places in the world where all the major European powers—both Catholic and Protestant—encountered one another, a virtual clearinghouse of information exchanged between the representatives of Austria, Russia, Sweden, Sardinia, Denmark, Prussia, Spain, and, by 1830, even the United States. European embassies and consulates in the Ottoman Empire became critical hubs of information where the daily business of trade and diplomacy brought together individuals from a wide range of social and cultural backgrounds. In 1687, the English embassy alone counted among its staff several Turkish scribes, Italian doctors, local Eastern Christian translators, English merchants, the family and household of the English ambassador, the English secretaries of the Levant Company (one of whom was married to the daughter of a local Greek notable), and Turkish janissaries guarding the doors, not to mention the countless travelers, scholars, and missionaries who stopped at the embassy during their travels to and from the East. In this way, European embassies became dynamic hubs of information, rumor, and gossip that circulated orally, in the first instance, but with important consequences for handwritten and printed news in the wider world. Indeed the business of diplomacy in the Ottoman Empire required European ambassadors to spend much of their time writing and reporting local matters to their correspondents and superiors at home.

Information first obtained from the official and private correspondence of European diplomats in turn fueled the news diet of European readers with reports about the contemporary Islamic world. News of the deposition of the Ottoman sultan Mehmed IV in 1687 is a case in point. A contemporary of Louis XIV, Mehmed IV was the longest reigning sultan in Ottoman history until November 1687, when he was deposed in a series of events that were covered in some detail in both English and French printed news. Both the *London Gazette* and the *Mercure Galant*, for example, recounted how Mehmed's obsession with hunting had created so many costs for the Ottoman court—and during a period of extended warfare with Europe—that the janissaries would no longer accept his presence as ruler. An earlier generation of scholarship might have seen in such stories a symptom of European orientalism—that is, exotic and fanciful imaginations about the Orient—but in this particular case, many of the printed news reports had a genealogy that stretched back to actual letters first written in Istanbul as the events of the deposition were unfolding. In the case of the *London Gazette*, most of the reports that ended up in print in London repurposed a set of intelligence dispatches that had first been compiled by a secretary working in the English embassy named Thomas Coke. His letters, in turn, drew on oral rumors and reports that he had gathered personally from Ottoman and Greek informants working in the Ottoman palace. In this way, oral information that circulated originally in Turkish was reported by

Coke in English in letters and became front-page news in the printed gazettes of England and France. In this way, networks of information exchange operated on a small-scale level across many localities in the Ottoman Empire and even in the "border zones" along the Ottoman-Habsburg frontiers, thereby carrying political intelligence and diplomatic news directly and effectively to the Ottoman imperial capital.

Political news represented only a small part of the information that Europeans sought about the Islamic world in this period. Even landlocked scholars who never set foot in the Ottoman Empire might turn to trading and diplomatic networks for information about a wide range of things. Nicolas-Claude Fabri de Peiresc (1580–1637) offers an excellent example. Peiresc was a man of insatiable curiosity, a *polymath, philologist, and cat lover ("I really like that kind of animal") whose interests stretched across a remarkable variety of objects—manuscripts, printed books, coins, fossils, gems, pottery, mummies—and subjects ranging from the rhythms of the tides to the movements of Jupiter to the contemporary practices of Samaritans, Copts, and Muslims, to name just a few. His wonder about the world around him, particularly about the East, is reflected today in the more than seventy thousand pages of correspondence by which someone in the South of France became so well informed on the Islamic world. His particular asset was his connections to Mediterranean merchants: the familiar factors of Marseille but also those faceless agents further afield whom Peiresc could identify only by their handwriting. Moreover, individuals like Peiresc acted as important sources of information to the work of orientalists, university scholars with interests in Arabic, Persian, Turkish, and Syriac. Oriental studies was one field of study that developed in dramatic ways on the back of new information networks. Consider, for example, the career of Edward Pococke, who spent six years as a chaplain at the Levant Company factory in Aleppo. He devoted this period of his life to studying Arabic, learning about the Islamic tradition, and working with local Arab scholars. When he returned to England, Pococke kept up a regular correspondence with one Darwish Ahmed, a scholar based in Aleppo, who kept Pococke supplied with the latest works to excite the interests of Muslim scholars in Aleppo. Some of Pococke's seminal publications are indebted to the networks of trade and diplomacy that supplied him with manuscripts and information from the Ottoman Empire.

Trade, diplomacy, scholarship—sometimes these impulses intersected in a single person with important effects on the circulation of information. The appointment of Charles Marie François Olier, the marquis de Nointel, as

French ambassador to the Ottoman Empire in 1669 was one such case. While his official work in Istanbul focused on the everyday business of diplomacy and trade, he had also been approached by the Jansenist scholars of Port-Royal in hopes that he could collect information of use to them in their ongoing debates with Protestants. The specific matter concerned the doctrine of transubstantiation, and Nointel was asked to learn as much as he could about the practices of the Eastern churches in this regard. From September 1673, therefore, Nointel made a tour of the Ottoman Empire that lasted over seventeen months. During this period, he met with priests, bishops, and patriarchs of the various Eastern Christian communities living in Chios, the Cyclades, Palestine, and Egypt. In these encounters, he directed a series of questions at his interlocutors about their beliefs and practices, requesting detailed written answers. The confessions of faith produced out of these encounters functioned much like the questionnaires discussed above, and these texts were duly sent back to France, where they eventually became part of great polemical projects like Antoine Arnauld's *Perpetuité de la foi* (The perpetuity of the faith, 1669–79). In this way, not only did diplomatic information networks provide material to Europe in the form of dispatches and letters, but Europeans like Nointel participated in the creation of specific documents and forms of record keeping about the Ottoman world. It is not an exaggeration to say that the frontiers of knowledge about the Christian and Muslim East developed in ways that were a direct representation of European preoccupations.

In a very practical sense, information moved in the form of the manuscripts, antiquities, coins, and objects that Europeans carried with them from the Ottoman Empire back to Europe. Acquisitions were made during trade missions by the Dutch, English, and French trading companies, but specific missions were also sponsored by powerful political figures like Louis XIV's minister Jean-Baptiste Colbert, who funded several missions to collect manuscripts in the East. In England, Archbishop Laud insisted that every Levant Company ship returning from the Middle East should carry with it at least one Arabic or Persian manuscript. The movements of all these materials created new problems of their own, and they should not be taken as a sign that Europeans always understood the information they obtained. One anecdote tells of the discovery by the archbishop of Paris during an Easter procession in 1709 that the luxurious fabric that had been used to wrap the bier carried in the procession was not simply an expensive cloth obtained from the East but rather a flag bearing the Islamic credo "There is no God but God." With abundant information came new opportunities for misunderstanding.

Information obtained through personal relationships had a transformative impact on literary cultures in Europe. The case of the discovery of the *One Thousand and One Nights* is revealing in this regard. The French orientalist and scholar Antoine Galland had traveled to the Ottoman Empire in the 1670s as one of a small number of people tasked with the collection of manuscripts, antiquities, and coins. During this journey, Galland developed an interest in the popular tales that he found circulating in the mouths of storytellers but also in Arabic manuscripts. Years later the personal relationships he had forged in the Ottoman Empire contributed to one of the greatest literary events of the eighteenth century. In 1709, a young Syrian merchant named Hanna Diyāb through a set of peculiar circumstances found himself in Paris and face-to-face with Galland, who, at the time, was working furiously to complete a French translation of the fantastic tales of *One Thousand and One Nights*. Galland was convinced that there were in fact 1,001 stories corresponding to each of the nights, but despite his best efforts, he could come up with only a few hundred based on the manuscripts he had obtained thus far. When he heard of Hanna's presence in Paris, therefore, Galland sought him out and asked him whether he knew of any tales that he could add to his collection. The two men, Hanna and Galland, met together at Galland's home for several weeks, during which time Hanna recounted stories to him while Galland scribbled them down hastily. (Hanna told the stories in Arabic, and Galland wrote them out in French.) Today, *Nights* specialists refer to the stories that Hanna told Galland as the "orphan tales," a reference to the fact that, curiously, there is no known manuscript tradition in Arabic that corresponds to any of the stories that Hanna told to Galland. In other words, oral improvisation and information lay at the roots of the first Western telling of the *One Thousand and One Nights*. It is especially striking that some of the most popular stories from the book—such as "Aladdin and the Lamp" and "Ali Baba and the Forty Thieves"—can be traced back only to the stories that Hanna shared with Galland in Paris.

Yet Europeans' exposure to more information about Islam did not always mean that contemporaries knew how to read, understand, and interpret that information. One should not overestimate the relationship between the mobility of information in this period and the extent to which it was intelligible to contemporaries. The growing array of information, manuscripts, and texts in foreign languages created its own set of problems for Europeans tasked with having to understand and make sense of them. For example, the growing presence of Arabic, Persian, and Turkish manuscripts in manuscript libraries in Europe necessitated the assistance of Middle Eastern Christian and Muslim translators who took up posts in these libraries to make this information intelligible to European orientalists. Purposeful use of the new information circulating about Islam in this period required a particular form of expertise, not simply in the strict sense of record keeping but also in all the related practices of copying, translating, cataloging, and, perhaps most importantly, determining the authenticity of information. As in other areas of *information overload in this period, the possession of information about Islam opened a host of new problems: Who would read and translate these works? How might they be copied, organized, and managed? Who could authenticate and date these documents? Above all, who could identify the salient information in them while discarding what was ephemeral, unlikely, and not useful?

Beyond these circles of scholars, merchants, and missionaries, information about the Islamic world was also accessible to a wider and more diverse segment of European society. Among a broader public, perceptions of Islam more often involved an encounter with stories and information rather than direct contact with Ottoman subjects. "Stories of the East" circulated in a wide range of oral, scribal, and printed media, from songs about the Turks sung in taverns to cheap print sold by itinerant chapmen. This information came in all shapes and sizes to suit the diverse interests of readers. Most readers in Europe learned about Islam in the pages of newsletters, broadsides, cheap print, and novels; these sources give us a firsthand glimpse of how Europeans knew what they knew about the Ottoman world. Consider, for example, a story that circulated in Paris: the curious tale of a man called Padre Ottomano, as revealed in a book published in 1665 by a Maltese knight who claimed to have knowledge of the "true history" of the "Reverend Father Dominique Ottoman." As the knight told the story, Dominique Ottoman was an Ottoman prince who had been captured by corsairs and imprisoned in Malta, where he converted to Christianity and ultimately became a Dominican friar (hence the "Padre"). This man now traveled from one European court to another on a mission to raise money so that he might lead a crusade against the Ottomans and, thereby, restore himself as a new Christian sultan of the Ottoman Empire. Looking at such stories today, we might immediately dismiss them as little more than the imaginative musings of Grub Street hacks. But for seventeenth-century readers who were inundated with fanciful tales, the boundaries between fact and fiction were rarely so clear. As for Padre Ottomano, there was indeed a man living in seventeenth-century Italy who called himself Dominique Ottoman and claimed to be the son of the Ottoman sultan. His identity was a subject of great debate that kept European writers arguing well into the eighteenth century.

The abundance of information, therefore, did not always lead in a teleological way to increased certainties of knowledge about the Islamic world. If scholarly orientalists were able to challenge old misrepresentations of Islam, they did so mainly because they had access to more, and more diverse, information about the Islamic world. But this is not to say that such information produced more tolerant, ecumenical people: Ludovico Marracci, who drew extensively on new sources to write his Latin translation of the Quran, did so with the clear goal of better refuting Islamic theology. The establishment of a regular presence of diplomats, merchants, and travelers to the Islamic world meant that entirely new, and neglected, realms of information became available to Europeans for the first time. Their knowledge of Muslims was no longer limited to core texts but drew on direct experience of their politics, and also of their families, social practices, and dining habits, which formed the basis for real ethnographic study. As Alexander Bevilacqua has shown, the consequence was that European scholars of the seventeenth and eighteenth centuries made remarkable efforts to understand Islam on its own terms, unclouded by the polemical biases of their time. As Barthelemy d'Herbelot wrote in the introduction to his *Bibliothèque Orientale* (Oriental library), "The reader shall judge whether the Orientals are as barbarous and as ignorant as public opinion would suggest." It was the connected world of this period that made it even imaginable for d'Herbelot to offer this possibility to his readers.

Conclusion

Information was crucially important to the "world making" of the early modern period. This was a period when the coalescence of religious, political, and financial networks brought people into contact with one another across huge expanses of space. Animated by such modes of communication as correspondence and questionnaires, information could move efficiently across both space and language barriers. We are right to see in these interactions the first stirrings of a global network of information. But two caveats require mention. First, while these networks were global, they also remained intensely local, personal, and rooted in close interactions between a circumscribed set of individuals. At the heart of early modern global flows of information, therefore, we find not strangers reaching out to one another but systems of communication developed out of familiar relationships.

Second, in these cross-cultural and cross-confessional networks that spanned the whole globe, information took circuitous and unpredictable routes. Even if there were obvious nodes—Rome, New Julfa, Batavia, London, Istanbul—there was also an emergent multipolarity in this world where several nodes further afield also projected themselves onto the world stage. In this polycentric world of information, those who commanded unique linguistic skills—multiple languages, writing abilities, forms of oral and written communication—would thrive most. If vagaries and uncertainties existed in these information networks, they represented nonetheless a first phase in the globalization of information that would, by the twentieth century, become truly global in its aspirations and its mechanics.

Further Reading

Sebouh David Aslanian, *From the Indian Ocean to the Mediterranean: The Global Trade Networks of Armenian Merchants from New Julfa*, 2011; idem, "'The Salt in a Merchant's Letter': The Culture of Julfan Correspondence in the Indian Ocean and the Mediterranean," *Journal of World History* 19, no. 2 (2008): 127–88; Francisco Bethencourt and Florike Egmond, eds., *Correspondence and Cultural Exchange in Europe, 1400–1700*, 2007; Alexander Bevilacqua, *The Republic of Arabic Letters: Islam and the European Enlightenment*, 2018; Michael Carhart, *Leibniz Discovers Asia: Social Networking in the Republic of Letters*, 2019; Luke Clossey, *Salvation and Globalization in the Early Jesuit Missions*, 2008; Filippo de Vivo, "Microhistories of Long-Distance Information: Space, Movement and Agency in the Early Modern News," in John-Paul A. Ghobrial, ed., "Global History and Microhistory," *Past and Present* supplement 14 (2019): 179–214; Paula Findlen, ed., *Athanasius Kircher, the Last Man Who Knew Everything*, 2004; idem, *Empires of Knowledge: Scientific Networks in the Early Modern World*, 2018; Adam Fox, "Printed Questionnaires, Research Networks, and the Discovery of the British Isles, 1650–1800," *Historical Journal* 53, no. 3 (2010): 593–621; John-Paul A. Ghobrial, *The Whispers of Cities: Information Flows in Istanbul, London and Paris in the Age of William Trumbull*, 2013; Serge Gruzinski, *What Time Is It There? America and Islam at the Dawn of Modern Times*, 2008, translated by Jean Birrell, 2010; Peter N. Miller, *Peiresc's Mediterranean World*, 2015; Simon Mills, *A Commerce of Knowledge: Trade, Religion, and Scholarship between England and the Ottoman Empire, 1600–1760*, 2020; Miles Ogborn, *Indian Ink: Script and Print in the Making of the English East India Company*, 2007; Robyn Radway, "Vernacular Diplomacy: The Culture of Sixteenth-Century Peace Keeping Strategies in the Ottoman-Habsburg Borderlands," *Archivum Ottomanicum* 34 (2017): 193–204; idem, *Portraits of Empires: Habsburg Albums from the German House in Ottoman Constantinople*, 2023; Gagan Sood, "'Correspondence Is Equal to Half a Meeting': The Composition and Comprehension of Letters in Eighteenth-Century Islamic Eurasia," *Journal of the Economic and Social History of the Orient* 50, nos. 2–3 (2007): 172–214; Elizabeth Yale, *Sociable Knowledge: Natural History and the Nation in Early Modern Britain*, 2016.

6

Records, Secretaries, and the European Information State, circa 1400–1700

Randolph C. Head

Informatio enim incipit a sensu. At universum negotium desinit in Opera; atque quemadmodum illud principium, ita hoc finis rei est.

For information commences with the senses. But the whole business terminates in works, and as the former is the beginning, so the latter is the end of the matter.

—FRANCIS BACON, *NOVUM ORGANUM* 2:XLIV

INFORMATION OCCURS UBIQUITOUSLY in human societies whenever human senses perceive phenomena and treat them as data; perceived data, in turn, informs the creation of knowledge by individuals and shapes how they respond to their world. Information is thus at one level an ephemeral process transacted in a moment: when a worshipper hears the bell announcing services, when a storyteller's listeners absorb elements that shape their consciousness, and in innumerable other ways. As human interactions and the political systems that frame them intensify, more and more informational moments also result in durably recorded traces, or records, which can be saved and conveyed through time. In consequence, the term *information* generally comprises both the (potential) *content* of such traces and also the underlying *processes* by which people became informed. Whereas information theory since Claude Shannon's pathbreaking work concentrates primarily on processes of communicating information and their reliability, semantic information as discussed by historians emphasizes the content that is transmitted. Notably, recorded information plays a disproportionate role in all historical thinking. Only records enable us to reconstruct any sense of how the world informed human minds at specific times and places. Written records play a core role in such reconstruction, although information could always also take place through images, by performances (possibly based on recorded scripts), and in various other ways. A focus on written records, in turn, privileges literate societies—such as late medieval and *early modern Europe—and literate individuals within them, while also drawing our attention to the institutions that enabled the creation and preservation of written records.

Western Europe experienced major developments in its management of recorded information from the fifteenth to early eighteenth centuries. Shifting cultural contexts and new media technologies not only changed the scope of information but also changed the relationship between the world, institutions, and records in consequential ways. This chapter probes society-wide transformations by focusing on one exemplary site where information practices intensified after 1400: the writing offices and archives of political domains. Such offices, not coincidentally, were also a focal point for the expansion of European states' knowledge about their own territories and subjects and about the complex world beyond Europe. Growing state knowledge paralleled expanded erudition in the *Republic of Letters and burgeoning scientific knowledge about the heavens and nature that emerged over the same period. Various learned knowledge management techniques, first from the Scholastic learning of medieval universities, then from humanist pedagogy and from scientific analysis, provided vital resources for the growth of the information states analyzed below. Such information states operated through and thus become visible in their accumulated records, in part; indeed, new ways of organizing such records helped give intelligible form to the abstract concept of a state. After delving into how European states transformed their information systems between the 1400s and the 1700s, this chapter also briefly considers noninscribed information such as ceremony and architecture, reflects on the limits on early modern state information, and concludes by asking how changes in the media, organization, and cultural contexts of information may have been connected with changes in cognition and reasoning.

Frameworks for Formal Information
in Europe after circa 1400

Information's role in transmitting knowledge always depends on larger frameworks of meaning, which help make information intelligible or simply recognizable as informative in the first place. Information becomes trustworthy and knowledge develops in coherent ways when the actors involved share languages and effective channels for communication. Equally, failed or distorted communication can lead to misinformation or disinformation, or can block information processes altogether. Understanding the expansion and intensification of written information systems that characterized early modern European states therefore begins by considering the larger communicative environment and the assumptions that educated Europeans brought to it.

In premodern Europe, well-developed cultural ideas lay behind the way various actors understood information and its value. In particular, theology and law provided ways to assess the value and reliability of political information from various sources. Most broadly, Europeans understood a single Creator as the ultimate guarantor of meaning, and they valued sources of information in part by their association with a divine order. In the words of Baldassarre Bonifacio in his *De Archivis* of 1632, "Through order, [God] gave form to formless things. Deservedly, order is called the soul of the world." Roman law and its reinvention in high medieval Europe (ca. 1000–1300 CE) provided a second powerful way to assess information. Indeed, the language of neo-Roman law suffuses both early modern and modern knowledge terminology: information itself, along with *fact, evidence, testimony, and data, were all originally legal terms, honed by the endless work of courts seeking to weigh the reliability of conflicting human statements. Legal practices, notably those developed by the Roman Church's inquisitions, provided powerful tools for gathering and deploying information. Additionally, God's demand for justice required rulers to be "fully informed" before adjudicating disputes, which encouraged their systematic collection, use, and preservation of evidence. Theological and legal discourses profoundly shaped the information orders developing in European political chancelleries.

Medieval ways of framing information, always contested and fluid, began to change systematically after about 1400. Both new social contexts and improved media tools enabled new approaches. Paper and then printing greatly reduced the cost of reproducing texts and images, enabling more people to access more recorded information in more ways (see chapter 4). Intensifying commerce across the Mediterranean and around the globe stimulated communication and reporting, while also providing the resources that allowed officials, scholars, and merchants to produce and preserve records (Ghobrial, chap. 5). As record keeping expanded, the sites where records were gathered, preserved, and organized took on new importance. After 1400, we see rulers across Europe shifting their record keeping from strongboxes full of charters to writing offices that managed archives filled with letters, reports, and deliberations. These archives became an important new site for producing information of value to rulers.

Information Media and Tools:
Continuities and Sites of Change

Edward Higgs defines "information states" as polities that rely on the "generalized and *structured collection of information . . . the creation of routine administrative records, and of databases, paper and electronic." In such states, accumulated written records played a growing role in the circulation of information. The analysis of their growth in early modern Europe here will follow two paths. The first looks at the media used for recording and regenerating information—whose basic forms remained remarkably stable from the fifteenth to eighteenth centuries, but whose deployment became both more intensive and more extensive. The second considers the architecture of state information systems, which evolved in ways that connected the world beyond chancellery offices to the operations of a new imagined actor, the European bureaucratic state. Both rely on a second important theoretical concept, namely the "information order." Understanding the connections between the "state's intelligence and social communication," as Christopher Bayly notes, requires us to look at "the generators of knowledge, the institutions of information collection and diffusion and the discourses to which they give rise." Equally, analyzing the evolving architecture of state information systems helps us further explore both the potential and the limitations of what James C. Scott characterized as "seeing like a state," that is, relying on the information gathered in reports, offices, and archives, especially after the sixteenth century.

Becoming informed through the use of records inherently means responding to signs and symbols that convey meaning; such signs, in turn, depend on durable physical media that allow them to be transmissible between persons and between eras. The basic medial equipment that European rulers used to build bureaucratic states changed only slowly from the late Middle Ages to the eighteenth century. Letters from the Roman alphabet and Roman or Arabic numerals were inscribed in Latin or a *vernacular language onto either parchment or paper surfaces. Images and maps, while rare, conformed to contemporary *canons of visual representation. Nontextual objects of various kinds played a decreasing role in political record keeping as the period went on, despite their continuing importance in ceremonial and performative contexts.

At the next level of organization, too, media technologies changed relatively slowly from 1400 to 1700. Inscribed leaves either could circulate independently—as letters, charters, reports, and so on—or could be gathered into folded quires and books, or into bundles wrapped or strung together or placed in a box or sack. Many domains built chests and armoires to house larger accumulations of paper and parchment, leading to various schemes to organize the resulting spaces. For use in chancelleries' daily routine, the book reigned supreme throughout this period. Books offered a powerful suite of organizational technologies that had emerged from Europe's universities in the twelfth century. As they created *concordances, Summae, and other tools of learning, Scholastic intellectuals learned how to use pagination, page layout (mise-en-page), indexing, alphabetization, and similar tools to make vast amounts of data accessible. Like their colleagues in the thirteenth-century Inquisition, who collected thousands of testimonies in books tracking suspected heretics in southern France and elsewhere, chancellery secretaries working for Europe's princes and cities found these Scholastic tools effective and economical as they sought to gain control of their informational treasures.

The same suite of tools supported the erudite humanism that emerged outside European universities after 1350, and humanist scholarship developed further innovations in reference and organization as chancelleries grew. Since early modern administrative secretaries typically had some university education, the flow of techniques between scholarship and secretaryship is not surprising. Just as humanists routinized and disseminated methods for excerpting key texts as *commonplaces, urban and princely secretaries refined their ability to capture key points in *protocols and finding aids: both practices contributed to the parcelization of data that underlay later developments in both erudition and bureaucracy. European scholars also pioneered schemes to use glued slips, cards, book wheels, or tricky cabinets to disaggregate and organize many separate texts. Chancelleries were slower to turn to card files and long relied on book-form registers connected to masses of loose records in either chronological or topical order. Still, the shared experience of too much to know, and the shared challenge of finding the right information among thousands of paper leaves, connected scholars and secretaries.

Information Architecture in Political
Chancelleries, 1400–1700

The records accumulated by political authorities serve to illustrate how records from the past became information for the future during this era. To be sure, most political life both before and after the transformations discussed here took place beyond the sphere of written records. Still, the scope of written records grew explosively after 1400 (depending on region), which changed how records informed rulers in the course of governance. The case studies below trace three distinct modes of using written records. First, documents could serve as performative objects bearing signs with emotional and social meaning. Charters and other documents could be displayed in court ceremonies, promenaded in processions, and take center stage when urban citizens swore loyalty to their communes. Second, documents could preserve information about either occasional or systematic inquiry and action on the part of political authorities: from the charters recording specific deeds to Inquisition registers recording testimonies to the vast information-collecting efforts that the Spanish crown undertook in the sixteenth century, chancelleries preserved records about specific circumstances that could be accessed in the future. Finally, records became tools of administration, oriented to the needs and actions of the state. Such use of records, while taking account of particulars, also transformed political life by framing resources or burdens as parts of a systemic whole, as in tax rolls, military census records, or land cadasters; or by framing the flow of information as part of state processes, as in the document registries discussed below. Importantly, the aggregation of information that took place in early statistics prioritized knowledge gained by combining records, rather than by what was found in any one record. All these approaches already existed in Europe before 1400 (or in any polity with institutionalized administration), but the balance among them shifted, ultimately justifying our description of some European polities as information states by the later 1600s.

The Medieval Background

The societies that emerged after the collapse of the Western Roman Empire remained literate throughout the following period. Christianity's reliance on canonical texts ensured clerical *literacy, and political life also produced formal records for certain occasions, though far less often than under the Roman bureaucracy. Written documents' roles expanded again during the High and later Middle Ages, ranging from memorials of specific grants or transactions (such as charters and *notary records) to treaties, settlements, and verdicts, to statutes and ceremonial records. Both those claiming political authority and those subject to it made and kept records with increasing frequency after 1000 CE, which they deployed in multiple ways. The later developments discussed here rested on this rich and complex foundation.

A large proportion of surviving political records from before 1400 purported to transmit authentic memories of an authoritative *action*: the general term for such documents is *charter* or *instrument*. In form and words, charters served as evidence of an act or deed—in itself performative and oral—that they preserved "for perpetual memory." Charters were treated as material objects of value and rested in rulers' treasuries among money, jewels, and other evidential objects such as swords, flags, or even clods of earth. At the same time, a charter's evidence could be reproduced in other documents; indeed, the text of many a medieval charter survives today only as an entry in a register or a cartulary. Charters typically demonstrated their authenticity through tangible signs such as signatures, witness lists, seals, or notary signets (although many of the earliest European charters are in fact inauthentic). The status of a document's possessor could also lend a document credence, especially after Roman-law rules of evidence were reintroduced after the eleventh century.

This view of records—as traces proving past actions—was the focal point for earlier research but has recently been supplemented by studies of documents' use in multiple communicative contexts, both at the time of their creation and later. As Geoffrey Koziol shows, in the mid-ninth century, a document's material and textual features reveal only part of what was significant during the political act of its creation. In one case Koziol analyzes, the most important feature was which persons did *not* appear among the parties named in the document's text, since such absence communicated a powerful statement about ruptured alliances. Peter Brun's study of the charters that Emperor Sigismund issued after 1415 to his regional allies in Switzerland shows that Sigismund gave his urban supporters charters that had no content at all: they simply confirmed, without details, whatever privileges each town might already possess. The point of such charters was not to inform anyone about past actions, Brun concludes, but rather to demonstrate that Sigismund was empowered to grant imperial privileges. Notably, when he appealed to local aristocrats, Sigismund relied on ceremonial feasts instead of charters, since these nobles made little use of written evidence.

Close study of how documents could be deployed after their production shows similar results: the performative context of displaying a document was separate from, and often just as important as, the words it contained. Ron Makleff, for example, traces how documents belonging to Liège and several other cities defeated during a rebellion in 1408 were handed over to the victorious bishop. The bishop's agents cataloged the trove and destroyed some records, while returning others with physical marks of cancellation, all as part of a theater of authority. For Lucerne, Jeannette Rauschert has reconstructed how city fathers repeatedly changed the text of their *Geschworener Brief*, the allegedly ancient contract that bound the citizens and validated their law. Careful research can sometimes retrieve the information communicated during such documentary performances, but much is lost, even though performative contexts were vital to establishing documents' meaning at the time.

Multiple factors led to an explosion in political record making and record keeping across Europe in the fourteenth and fifteenth centuries. Increasing formalism in the law, the growing influence of administrative specialists, and the expansion of mercantile record keeping all contributed to the habit of making written records, accelerated by the appearance of paper as a durable and inexpensive medium. Law courts influenced by Roman law greatly expanded their use of written procedures, while customary-law courts increasingly wrote down their traditions and eventually codified their statutes. Political and ecclesiastical administrators turned to written reports, notes, instructions, and memoranda in more and more situations, while merchants began keeping more detailed contracts, inventories, and letters as they conducted their business. Political functionaries responded to the resulting masses of documents with new ways of authenticating and preserving them. The resulting accumulations of original documents, copies, registers, summaries, finding tools, and more became a source of anxiety for those responsible for managing it all. Secretaries wrote about "swimming in a world of paper" with "many lovely parchment charters trodden under foot and crumpled up," evoking tropes of being overwhelmed that emerged across multiple intellectual spheres in this period.

While the sheer volume of records produced after 1400 was impressive, extensive record production also transformed the relationships between human communities and their records, as suggested by Simon Teuscher. Making or using a record remained a political act, always conditioned by the immediate context's contention. In the fifteenth century, however, these contexts shifted in ways that increased the salience of other documents and their texts at the expense of performances and communities. Teuscher illustrates this change on a local scale in an early sixteenth-century dispute between a Swiss village, Dürnten, and its bailiff from the city of Zurich. During a boundary dispute, the bailiff, Jürg Berger, sought a copy of the bylaws (*Weistum*) that the Dürnten villagers had accumulated in a book. The villagers, however, refused his request to use the Weistum unless a delegation of villagers could accompany their statutes: in their view, only the community's presence ensured proper reading of the bylaws' words. In the end, Berger did get his copy, which he placed on a shelf next to copies of other villages' bylaws in a compact corpus of documents. In place of a community, texts came to rest among other texts, right down to the present.

This development paralleled contemporary changes in legal process, as adjudication by expert judges relying on written evidence displaced face-to-face confrontations before a community. Texts surged in importance relative to performances, which allowed documents to be viewed as sources of information by themselves apart from their original interpretive community. This shift only accelerated as energetic scribes produced whole new *genres of documents on paper, which increasingly piled up in offices, storerooms, and attics. By the late fourteenth century, we see systematic efforts across Europe to organize such materials. As Gérard de Montaigu put it in the first systematic inventory to the French royal treasury of documents, created in the 1370s, he organized the repository "so that it would be possible to find at once and promptly whatever letter was sought by a particular person." Management of political and legal information increased in intensity and sophistication during the late Middle Ages and continued to evolve after 1500, although it remained focused on recovering evidence about particular persons and properties. More and more political actors—rulers, councils, and bureaucrats—expected to become informed by consulting documents that were provided by their archives, which thus became vital parts of Europe's evolving political information order.

The Architecture of Political Record Keeping after 1400

We take it for granted that formal governance today takes place through offices that rely on written records (or *digital resources), which may ultimately be conserved in a public archive. In contrast, a large part of early modern governance, especially in smaller political units, took place through face-to-face interactions and performative events that did not necessarily find their way into council protocols or charters. Even in Europe's great courts, interactions between kings and their most important subjects remained personal, neither relying on nor producing many documents. High medieval royal families and towns did have documentary treasures, often kept with other treasures such as money and gems. Sometimes these traveled along with itinerant kings, at risk of capture as happened when King Philip II of France lost most of his records to the English at the 1194 Battle of Fréteval. Generally, though, nobles and towns preserved their most precious charters in safe places such as the sacristy of a cathedral or in a family monastery. Ecclesiastical institutions, which combined Christian respect for the power of words with reliance on gifts from the powerful for their survival, also preserved ancient document collections. Few clear distinctions existed among various sites for accumulated records, which largely lacked dedicated keepers.

Efforts to organize records after 1400 generally proceeded through a series of differentiations, as originally small and unordered bodies of documents (such as chests and sacks) grew and split into increasingly large and systematically organized bodies, gathered in bundles or boxes or copied into books. As the distinctions between different kinds of records became more stable, new principles for arranging and describing them also developed, eventually producing sophisticated registries that could track the documentary trail of important matters over years and decades. According to Robert-Henri Bautier's influential periodization, many state-like actors from about 1400 to 1800 sought to create documentary *arsenals* that they could use to maintain control over their subjects and to fend off threats from other domains. As German archivist Georg Aebbtlin put it in 1669, a properly ordered archive allowed "documents to be drawn just like weapons, so that the interests of a lordship can be battled for, defended, stiffened, preserved and maintained." In consequence, the ability to respond to specific conflicts about particular lands or rights remained at the forefront of *archival thinking well into the eighteenth century. Only slowly did officials across Europe begin to use accumulated records to understand their states as a whole, introducing new practices of collection and analysis that are generally associated with the beginning of statistics (that is, the science of the state).

The short studies that follow illustrate how early modern European rulers and their bureaucrats understood accumulated records, which helps us see how they thought these could inform their decisions and actions. Our cases include systematic efforts to manage information by means of books in Portugal and in Austria, and to organize archival spaces in France and Switzerland. Later examples will include the comprehensive information gathering undertaken in late sixteenth-century Spain, followed by the development of state information management tools such as censuses, land cadasters, and administrative registries across Europe.

Organization and Access: Case Studies and Contrasts

As written communication burgeoned across the fifteenth and sixteenth centuries, so did the benefits of organizing the growing masses of material that writing produced: strong positive feedback loops drove the rapid proliferation not only of writing itself, but also of the registering, indexing, and sorting that followed. Two exemplary projects to compile information in books just after 1500, from different parts of Europe, show how willing Europe's most successful rulers were to invest in their record-keeping priorities. In Lisbon, the thriving Portuguese state began creating carefully organized and materially splendid register books after 1460 that reproduced in accessible form a large number of older privileges that the Crown had given out. In Innsbruck, an administrative and financial center for the Austrian Habsburgs, the elevation of a new ruler in 1523 spurred the creation of paper copybooks to systematically record correspondence between the ruler, the regional administration, and the territories it supervised. Both projects drew directly on well-established media technologies in book form, including layout, pagination, and indexing with page references to help searchers quickly find what they sought.

Like most European crowns, the kings of Portugal issued charters to individuals, towns, and noble families as part of their exercise of power. By the mid-fifteenth century, the royal chancellery had accumulated voluminous records about such issuances, mostly on parchment quires that provided a date and a summary for each issued privilege. The passage of time rendered these primitive registers increasingly hard to read, however. In 1460, responding to complaints from the kingdom's estates, the royal chancellery launched an ambitious program to select grants of privilege "suitable for perpetual memory" for copying into new, high-quality parchment books. A generation later, with the accession of Manuel I, who could draw on revenue from Portugal's growing overseas empire, this initiative grew into a carefully articulated series of copybooks known as the *Leitura Nova*, the "new reading." Using fine parchment and calligraphy, and embellishing the volumes with *illuminated frontispieces that celebrated royal power, the royal chancellery between 1505 and the 1550s compiled over sixty volumes of privileges organized by region, type, or category of recipient. These splendid volumes helped the Crown manage its relations with Portugal's powerful patrimonial nobility and towns while displaying the king's wealth and knowledge in material form. Yet these refined chancellery products were backward looking as information tools. They preserved traces of royal acts with meticulous notarial authentication, but the project's design did not include alphabetical indexes, and its sketchy entries gave only scant details about long-past actions. In short, the project's focus on materially reproducing authentic acts limited its value as a source of broader information.

In Innsbruck, Habsburg administrators faced rather different challenges. As rulers over a composite monarchy that stretched from Spain to the Netherlands to Hungary, the Habsburgs relied on regional administrators to manage conflicts and revenue flows, while family members (including Emperor Charles V, his brother Ferdinand, and royal mothers, sisters, and wives) traveled to the places that most needed their attention. Rather than jockeying with a tightly knit aristocracy, the Habsburgs needed to stay informed about developments in territories with divergent needs. A series of volumes produced in Innsbruck after 1523 reflected these circumstances in the way it captured the correspondence among king, administrators, and subjects in book form. At the system's heart lay two chronologically organized series of copybooks whose names reveal their purpose: one, filling a volume every year or so, was entitled "To the princely Highness," the other "From the princely Highness"; additional series recorded the princely chancellery's correspondence with regional agents and the courts. In the first series, every letter from the Innsbruck chancellery to its itinerant prince was copied before sending; in the second, every incoming letter from the prince was copied before going to the relevant officers. The books used mise-en-page tools such as marginal keywords and highlighting to enable searching, while alphabetical indexing made key terms in each copied letter accessible. In contrast to the Portuguese *Leitura Nova*, therefore, which continued to privilege acts, the Innsbruck copybooks privileged communications about particulars: names, actions, events, and conflicts made accessible for an audience of future administrators.

The similarities and differences between these two projects to organize records are instructive. In the first place, both projects selected and copied records into books, in the process silencing material and performative aspects of the originals. Both projects also changed records' contexts by locating copies or abstracts side by side with copies of other documents that had not originally been placed there. This increased the salience of intertextual relations among records by assimilating them within a shared environment. Both, finally, drew extensively on the technologies of the book that scholars had perfected in the Middle Ages to manage large amounts of textual data.

Their two projects' differences are equally telling. The *Leitura Nova* and its fifteenth-century predecessor kept a sharp focus on acts by Portugal's kings and invested heavily in capturing such acts in honorable and authenticated form. The volumes' audience consisted of the Crown and aristocracy, mediated by the notaries in the royal chancellery. In Innsbruck, royal commands and administrative responses were also central but were represented as an ongoing conversation, copied into alphabetically indexed registers that covered all sorts of matters. Its audience consisted of Habsburg regional agents who sought to be informed about the domains they were charged to oversee and about the wishes of their prince. Rather than acts, the Innsbruck copybooks therefore focused on commands and reports, while incorporating far more systematic browsing tools and indexing than the *Leitura Nova*—all in paper copybooks that were relentlessly utilitarian in appearance. Ultimately, both projects, which absorbed substantial labor over many decades, illustrate just how important access to records was becoming for European rulers.

Selecting and copying records into books created powerful reference tools for those who could afford to create and sustain them. The explosive increase in stored documents, however, led many chancelleries after about 1450 to begin organizing the actual records within their storage spaces instead, thus avoiding the labor of recopying them. In place of the haphazard chests and sacks of medieval collections, chancellery staff dreamed about defining a place for every document that would make it easy to find. Organizers' ideas about how records could inform future users shaped their organizational schemes, which thus provide evidence about the information order at the time. Notably, almost all early modern archival plans concentrated on content, or pertinence, as a key locational principle: secretaries wanted to group documents according to what they were *about*, in contrast to the modern archival principle of provenance, which organizes records based on their role in the creator's operations. By focusing on content, early modern archiving derived order from the world outside the chancellery, rather than from the institution itself.

Two cases illustrate the ways premodern chancelleries organized separate documents. Further investigation would reveal a wide variety of intermediate and intersecting approaches, however, emphasizing how variable and creative the organizing work of early modern chancellery staff could be. The first case, from Paris in the 1360s, shows that many tools for organizing archival spaces were already available at that time. When Gérard de Montaigu became warden of the French royal charters, the *Trésor des Chartes*, in 1370, he found in the storeroom of the Sainte Chapelle "an ocean of letters and registers confused as by a storm." As he worked on the collection over the next eighteen months, ease of finding was a central concern. Older organizing schemes already shaped the *Trésor*—in this case, a system of boxes dedicated to specific regions such as Delphinatus, Flandria, Navarre and labeled with two letters, which apparently confused users. Montaigu preserved the topical boxes but chose to number them, because of the "infallible continuity of numbers." He also created an inventory, consisting of an alphabetized register that included various subtopics. As he observed, "there is no name of a prince nor sobriquet for a country or city that does not begin with some letter of the alphabet, and it is thus impossible to fail to find the one you want whenever you look." Topically focused boxes linked to an alphabetical inventory created an effective way to move from a particular name or place to a specific document, and variations on this approach can be found all across Europe.

Many early modern archivists chose a different path, however, and created systematic architectures of storage spaces that reflected their understanding of the world. This approach, defined by Peter Rück as ideal-topographical organization, started with topically defined units of accumulation (usually boxes or bundles) but added a systematic dimension by arranging the resulting masses according to a coherent worldview. An illuminating example comes from mid-seventeenth-century Zurich, where city secretary Johann Heinrich Waser undertook a complete reorganization of the city's repositories and finding tools in 1646. As in Montaigu's *Trésor*, subject-oriented boxes remained the basic organizational unit in Zurich. In his overview of the city's information resources, the *Index archivorum generalis* (Comprehensive Index of the Archives), Waser sketched the major divisions among the city's documents, from the courts to the finance office, before turning to 475 core boxes of material under his direct authority. Action was urgent, since Waser, like his predecessor Montaigu, had found rooms and boxes with "everything overfilled."

When Waser was done, his boxes were arranged in careful order, with boxes arranged in storage and mapped onto the pages of the *Index archivorum generalis* according to an identical sequence. The first two boxes contained documents pertaining to the Holy Roman emperor and corresponded to the first two pages of the inventory, the third (surprisingly!) to the "Turkish" emperors in Constantinople. European monarchs from France and England to Poland found their places in boxes and pages 5 through 17, while lesser principalities and towns occupied the following boxes and pages through 45. A new series started with the papacy and cardinals (box 46) and continued with bishops, abbots and abbesses, and so forth. Waser's boxes and inventory thus tracked first the worldly and then the spiritual hierarchy of western Europe from top to bottom. To find material about a particular actor, a user did not rely on alphabetization, but only on the actor's rank in the hierarchies mapped onto the pages of Waser's *Index*. Eventually, to enable searching by specific names or places, Waser also laid out an alphabetical *Index specialis*, which allowed "matters that are connected [to] come together even if they are located in different boxes."

Critical similarities as well as important differences connect Montaigu's 1370 inventory and Waser's 1646 *Index generalis*. Each was a sophisticated finding tool created during the physical reorganization of an archive. Each archive relied on boxes as a key organizational unit, with each box or group dedicated to a single topic, often a domain or office. As a direct consequence, other features of documents—their material form, the context of their creation, and their genre—were subordinated in the finding system. A charter issued by the pope and a dossier about relations with the pope both belonged in Waser's box 1, for example. The logic by which these boxes were placed in their archives' space was very different, however. Montaigu placed his numbered boxes so that they would fill his armoires efficiently, although he sought to keep related material in the same general section. To allow users to find the right box, he depended on alphabetical indexes to topics more specific than the box titles. Waser started by organizing the boxes themselves into a systematic architecture, following the strategy that Rück identified as "mirroring relationships between the archival and the state organism" so that "the mental and material orders should match." This allowed Waser to defer the laborious work of indexing in favor of a summary index that was sufficient for most searches (although users' interest in particulars ultimately made an alphabetical register necessary, too). Alphabetical indexing and mapping according to the order of the world each solved the problem of too much material to recopy, but in very different ways. Still, each approach prioritized the content, not the administrative function or provenance, of the documents involved.

Fully Informed: Grand Schemes and Limited Practices in Sixteenth-Century Spain

Although traces of authentic actions remained a core concern for most involved, early modern chancelleries also sought to collect and control ever more information about multiple topics. The growing primacy of informing rulers becomes particularly visible in several projects launched by King Philip II of

Spain during his long reign from 1556 to 1598. The earliest evidence of Philip's approach appears in a memorial that his humanist adviser Juan Páez de Castro submitted to the then crown prince in 1555. Páez proposed that Philip establish a new knowledge center with three major chambers: the first would contain a library of books, the second would collect maps and scientific instruments useful in geography and seafaring, and the third would include crucial charters from the pope or pertaining to the royal family, but also reports from agents in the Indies and across Europe. After ascending the throne, Philip created several institutions that embodied this plan, including the royal archive in Simancas outside Valladolid and the royal library at his monastery-palace at El Escorial. At these and additional sites, the founding documents called for the creation of guides in book form that would help in finding information. At each site, as well, a "libro de hystoria" was ordained, whose purpose was to provide narrative highlights from the assembled materials.

In parallel with these collecting institutions, Philip and his agents also ordered enormous data-gathering projects across his realms in Iberia and around the world. A key figure, along with Páez de Castro, was Juan de Ovando, who first inspected, then led the Council of the Indies after 1567. During his inspection, many complaints arose about the council's ignorance, its susceptibility to corruption, and the spiritual harm to the Crown that abuse of the Indigenous peoples was causing. A powerful faction inspired by Bartolomé de las Casas complained that little was known about the Americas, and such information as did arrive was distorted by the self-interest of those who sent it. Ovando proposed that henceforth the council should follow a scheme much like Castro's, including a new codification of the laws, a new cosmographer-chronicler to collect information, and the creation of a new book of descriptions, constantly updated, to guide the council in its decision making. Whereas in the past, the council "had not had, and could not have information (*noticia*) about the Indies' affairs and those of each province, upon which governance can and must rest," henceforth "it is necessary that they have full information (*entera noticia*) of such affairs."

In response to Ovando's urging, the Spanish state turned to a familiar information tool, namely interrogatory questionnaires. Standardized questions already played an important role in Inquisition procedures, and Ovando had served as an Inquisitor before presiding over the Council of the Indies. The council's interrogatories ultimately reached many parts of the Spanish government in the Americas in printed form in 1577 and 1584; over two hundred responses trickled back to Spain, which are known as the *Relaciones Geográficas*

(Geographical Accounts). A similar approach to gathering reports from parishes across Spain produced the parallel *Relaciones Topográficas* (Topographical Accounts) after 1574. Drawing on the humanist discipline of chorography (geographical description), the lists of questions asked for information about physical features, animals and plants, recent history, religious life, and Indigenous languages.

These initiatives in Spain display three important features: a desire to be comprehensively informed, the systematic establishment and organization of repositories, and broad questioning of royal agents to gain knowledge about local circumstances around the empire. The entire initiative, notably, served a king who notoriously so disliked face-to-face interaction and ceremonial events, preferring to manage affairs on paper, that he gained the epithet *rey papelero*, the paper king. Philip's initiatives produced results: the archive at Simancas and library at El Escorial were built and quickly filled, among other things with the reports arriving in response to royal interrogatories. Surprisingly, however, these enterprises had little impact on what the Spanish crown knew in the succeeding decades, or on how it made decisions. By the 1620s, when inspected by a royal commission, the archive in Simancas had become moribund, with much material disordered or lost. The *Relaciones Geográficas* and *Relaciones Topográficas*, meanwhile, were packed up and rarely accessed. Particularly surprising from a modern perspective is the absence of compilation of the data that came in. For example, the council asked local authorities to estimate the number of Hispanic and Indigenous people in each district—which local administrators loudly complained they had no means to do—but there is no evidence that the results were compiled to create statistics about the overall population. Indeed, the absence of statistical handling is typical for this period, as will be discussed below. Gathering information and creating sites to preserve it, though necessary for the operation of an information state, were not sufficient to bring it into being.

While the technical challenges involved in registering, copying, or indexing the rivers of paper flowing into Philip's chancelleries contributed to the meager results of his initiatives, early modern archival practice was also simply not oriented toward producing statistics (in the sense of calculated conclusions about the state as a whole). Behind even the most sophisticated early modern organization and indexing lay the assumption that archivists were there to reveal particulars about the world on demand—"to find at once and promptly whatever letter was sought by a particular person," as Montaigu had put it in the 1370s. Similar assumptions shaped approaches to organizing records, which continued to rely on pertinence—that is, records' connection to the outside world—as the natural approach to large accumulations of documents. Only when the administrative state itself became the primary frame of reference did it become urgent to categorize and use stored records primarily in relation to that state and its operations.

From Collection to Knowledge: The Riddle of the Emerging Bureaucratic Information State

An enormous amount of research shows that bureaucratic states with effective information management capabilities did evolve from the fifteenth to the eighteenth centuries, however unevenly, but the causes for this development remain controversial. Phenomena ranging from the rise of the bourgeoisie to intergenerational dynamics among elites have been proposed as the key driver, as have mechanical printing, colonial expansion, and climate change. Rather than adding to possible causes, the following section will focus on shifts in the relationships among political actors, stored records, and processes of information, with particular attention to the mundane techniques of gathering, organizing, and using written records that were employed to inform rulers and their agents. As the history of the largely fruitless Spanish *Relaciones* of the late sixteenth century shows, the mere gathering of reports was not enough. Despite commands from the highest level that every administrative officer should respond to a detailed list of specific questions, the Spanish *Relaciones* never became information in operative terms because the people with access to them did not frame them as comprehensive data about an imaginary but increasingly salient actor, the state.

Large-scale efforts to gather data were nothing new in the sixteenth century: we need only point to the English Domesday Book, completed in 1086, which described land tenancies in some thirteen thousand places. Enumerations of population became common in Italian cities by the late fourteenth century, and amazingly detailed tax rolls survive from towns as modest as Zurich (1467) and as prosperous as Florence (1427). The key point in defining information states is therefore not simply the accumulation of large amounts of recorded information, but rather how such records were understood and how they could be used. The discussion here will begin with two illustrative examples before reviewing more systematic approaches to collected data, such as the creation of censuses and cadastral maps. The final section on archival registry will argue that changes in archival practice reveal an intensification of information use and the consequent emergence of information states after 1600.

A first illustration of the challenges that early modern rulers faced in synthesizing information from a broad range of records comes from the France of Louis XIV. Fiscal oversight is one logical place to look for such synthesis: not only did the quantum nature of money make it easy to consolidate multiple records into sums or debits, but the maturation of double-entry *bookkeeping after 1500 also provided a clear method for transforming fiscal transactions into actionable information. Yet as Jacob Soll demonstrates for France, applying accounting tools to the monarchy's finances became possible only in the later seventeenth century. Despite many earlier demands for better accounting, Jean-Baptiste Colbert was the first to provide his king, Louis XIV, with compact budget documents for each year. These pocket ledgers (*abrégés*) started in 1669 and showed Louis the state's receipts and expenditures in major categories with year-to-year comparisons. The books were richly illuminated and compact enough that Louis could carry them in his sleeve for ready reference. In these short volumes, the finances of France as an ongoing fiscal-military enterprise became visible as a whole: the books thus represented France as single actor, the state—embodied, famously, in its king—that received income and incurred expenses.

In another corner of Europe a few years later, the Swiss city of Lucerne in 1698 illustrates another key shift in perspectives. In Lucerne, decades of poor order among the city's records (which covered the city, its rural territory, and its partners in the Swiss Confederation) finally provoked the construction of a dedicated repository in 1698, along with a reorganization of the documents by the city's chancellor, Johann Karl Balthasar. Balthasar found the records haphazardly arranged in a typical content-oriented system. He responded with two radical changes. The first was to separate out many older records that were rarely used, thus creating a true archive in the sense of papers withdrawn from routine use. The second was to completely reorganize how documents were ordered within the archival space. Instead of mirroring people and places in the external world, Balthasar's new organization rested on categories of state action, such as legal disputes, commerce, or cloisters. This switch—from nouns to verbs, so to speak—aligned the material with the evolving needs of Lucerne's rulers, who increasingly saw themselves as presiding over a state. Balthasar's reorganization project is revealing in another way. The new system revolved around a detailed index to the entire body of material, but this index was never completed, since local crises apparently drew the chancellor away from the project even before his death in 1703. A report commissioned a generation later showed that the entire archive was nearly unusable without an index. The sheer drudgery of information management in tediously copied parchment and paper books should never be ignored, and it lies behind many archival failures in the early modern period.

Information State Practices before the Nineteenth Century: Census, Cadaster, Registry

Studies of how comprehensive record collection projects like the Spanish *Relaciones* were *used* are still rare. Some research discusses censuses and cadastral maps, which became transformative genres of informational record in the eighteenth century. Comparing the evolution of census taking and cadaster making is useful because the first also invited quantification, and thus shared features with fiscal bookkeeping, whereas cadastral mapping, while equally valuable to the state, produced largely relational and visual rather than quantified knowledge. Other studies consider the appearance of educational tracks for state service, for example in the *Kameralwissenschaft* (Science of state service) that appeared at German universities after 1727, or the establishment of a chair in diplomatics whose graduates had a monopoly on validating archival records in Coimbra, Portugal, late in the eighteenth century. Such education was critical for fiscal management, which encouraged numeracy and quantification among the men who were trained in this way, but also required familiarity in reading and interpreting older records. Even less attention has been paid to the registry systems for tracking administrative processes that developed after 1500 in intimate connection with developing state machinery. Further research from the perspective of the history of information is still needed to understand the deep shifts in knowledge, practice, and culture that accompanied the emergence of both modern states and modern informational consciousness in Europe.

Counting the inhabitants of a territory or social group is an old and widely distributed practice around the globe, as the Roman etymology of the word *census* suggests. Control over citizens and knowing who owed revenue or military service were typical reasons to enumerate individuals both in Mediterranean antiquity and in European societies as they emerged in later periods. Most premodern enumerations did not include everyone, but only those households owing taxes or service, omitting the indigent and exempt. In Europe after the *Reformation, both the Catholic and the Protestant authorities began ordering local clerics to register births, marriages, and deaths, which transferred earlier concerns about controlling citizenship into the spiritual sphere. European authorities were willing to invest in extensive data collection for such ends, but little evidence suggests that early modern authorities used the resulting material to synthesize new information about the population as a whole. Inquisitors might use parish registers to help track down dissidents, and tax rolls could be used to distribute taxes within a community (often long after the data was obsolete), but even the simple totaling of population from such sources was rarely undertaken until the eighteenth century. Indeed, quantification itself has a history that begins surprisingly late in Europe; as Daniel Headrick notes, only in the *Enlightenment did Europeans come to the conclusion that "numbers could be used to analyze something other than money, such as population, health and illness, nature, or even divine Providence."

Some of the earliest efforts to use the data that states and other public actors were collecting took place in England, where private authors such as John Graunt (1620–74) and William Petty (1623–87) began compiling information about deaths published by London's parish clerks to understand the city's population. Petty coined the phrase "political arithmetic" to describe such calculations, which he attempted to apply to land values, manufacturing, navigation, agriculture, and other areas of public life as well. By the late seventeenth century, the powerful incentives driving England's (and Europe's) fiscal-military states made state officials ever more interested in participating in such arithmetic and the synthesized information it could provide. Although this interest appeared under different names in each major kingdom—political arithmetic, political economy, Kameralwissenschaft—the forces driving it and the resources available for understanding populations and their characteristics were similar. The transition from record keeping that gathered information about individuals or families to censuses that sought to comprehend entire populations was complete only after 1800.

Another area in which statistical approaches emerged was the creation of cadasters, that is, systematic land maps showing the possessor of each parcel, forest, meadow, and so forth. In contrast to conventional topographic maps, which visually represent a terrain and its human geography, cadasters visually represent ownership as meticulously as possible, with topographical features playing a secondary role. Cadasters, not surprisingly, are closely linked to both tax collection and judicial disputes over landownership, including the great disentangling of communal and individual rights over land that took place across Europe in the eighteenth and nineteenth centuries. Some land maps (usually not to scale and not comprehensive) had been created by landholders from Italy to the Netherlands in the late fifteenth and sixteenth centuries for their own use in tax collection. Other early efforts to visually represent land-holding came from areas with strong communal traditions, such as the polder authorities, who maintained the dikes in the Netherlands. Only in the seventeenth century, however, did public authorities begin making comprehensive cadastral maps; as Roger Kain and Elizabeth Baigent conclude, these quickly became "a highly contentious instrument for the extension and consolidation of power, not just of the propertied individual, but of the nation-state and the capitalist system that underlies it."

The long-term enterprise to create systematic cadasters in the German principality of Hesse is described by Karin Gottschalk. Tax collection was a primary driver of the Hesse project. When traditional revenues failed to cover costs during the Thirty Years' War, a direct tax on real property, the *Kontribution*, had been introduced, which was made permanent after the war. The tax was levied on the basis of long-past statements of wealth, however, which led to a widespread perception of unfairness. After several failed starts, Hessian officials began creating a comprehensive cadaster in 1736, which was completed only in 1791—demonstrating just how many obstacles such projects faced. Tensions between central agents and local officials interested in preserving the status quo slowed progress, as did evolving survey technology and differing goals that divided the stakeholders in the process; as Gottschalk notes, "questions about which data [*Informationen*] should be collected and processed by which agents and at what accuracy kept being raised anew and answered differently."

The government's initial questionnaires for gathering data proved to be so unreliable that by 1750, the program ground to a halt after central commissions agreed with local complaints about the inconsistency of assessments. Meanwhile, the central authorities kept raising their expectations for the uniformity of results, causing repeated cycles of remapping and reregistration. When local maps and property lists were finalized, another problem immediately arose: with three copies—one held locally, one in the district's center, and one at the landgrave's court—keeping versions synchronized as properties changed hands proved to be impossible. Land gained new owners, or boundary stones were (often illegally) moved, but the registers were not updated. Even if the local version was up-to-date, moreover, reproducing the changes in the district and central copies was entirely beyond the capacity of this early modern administration. Nevertheless, central officers pursued ever-expanding expectations about the accuracy and amount of detail the newly created maps and land registers should include.

As the problem of synchronization shows, coordinating large bodies of data raised considerable challenges for record keeping. Gathering systematic reports was relatively easy by the sixteenth century, though the responses to the *Relaciones* and the struggles over measurement in Hesse show that even collecting faced resistance. Rendering the collected data useful, and learning to see in them not just individual places and people, but also features of a new actor, the state, required greater effort, both technical and conceptual. This transformation clearly affected every part of European political culture, from intellectuals' debates over sovereignty to local communities' efforts to find a modus vivendi with increasingly obtrusive rulers and their book-toting bureaucrats.

In addition to supervising large data-gathering projects like censuses and cadasters, seventeenth- and eighteenth-century chancelleries also increased their ability to manage documents consistently, and thus to track matters of interest out in the world. A general term for this development is registry (from the German term *Registratur*), with three key features: (1) new administrative structures dedicated to managing documents and the information in them, with the documents (2) organized in ways that privileged the internal processes of the state involved and (3) intentionally held accessible to support decision making by rulers and their agents. Registry focused record keepers' attention on making and executing decisions within a political apparatus, rather than on circumstances beyond. In a registry, the outside world became raw material for state action, rather than providing the framework that shaped the internal architecture of the archives.

An early form of registry appeared in the book-form protocols that European cities began creating in the High Middle Ages. Items in such protocols were entered chronologically, which tended to dissociate people and conflicts from their circumstances and reduce them to one item on a list. Registers and protocol books in various political units grew in volume and became more specialized in their content over the sixteenth century, adding more and more *metadata that oriented individual records to contexts defined by offices, councils, or other state institutions. Such registers reveal that their creators were beginning to understand the state—an abstract entity, in principle— as the actor whose existence linked records over time. Registry further expanded this perspective by organizing records, in the first instance, by their relation to state processes rather than in relation to the world. The most intensive form of registry emerged in the north German and Netherlandish transaction-file registry (*Sachaktenregistratur*) after 1700, but related practices can be found in every city, lordship, and monarchy in western Europe.

Such systems have received relatively little scholarly attention, and the way that the sophisticated transaction-file registries of nineteenth-century Prussia and its neighbors developed still needs considerable study. Comparing the starting point and the end point of this process is nevertheless useful for tracking a fundamental shift in what political information meant. To simplify, for many early modern secretaries and archivists (and, by extension, scholars, merchants, and princes), information involved a process of communication from world to political actors, which took place when traces of a past action or situation (increasingly in writing) informed a political actor in the present. Records, when viewed from this perspective, consisted primarily of signs about the world. Logically enough, secretaries and archivists therefore preserved and organized records according to the action or circumstance they pertained to (pertinence, in archival science). They also developed sophisticated ways to articulate archival space and used the powerful technologies of the book to enable later users to find records according to the persons or places involved. This approach did not go away in the eighteenth century, to be sure, and persists in commonsense notions of archiving today. However, this orientation was supplemented and eventually superseded in state repositories by a different conception of information that derived from, and also shaped, new ways of organizing and accessing records. A symptomatic example of this new view appeared in the Lucerne reorganization of 1698: here, not the world, but the actions of a state provided the primary framework for accessing records.

As collected records across Europe expanded in volume and became differentiated into more categories, specialized agents emerged who could mediate between the user and the records. A key step in some German states, notably Brandenburg-Prussia, took place late in the seventeenth century, when a dedicated office, the Registratur, began supervising this mediation. When fully developed in the nineteenth century, this office stood between the world and the state apparatus, but also between the chancellery that gathered information and guided the deliberation of the ruler and his councils, on the one hand, and the archive (now meaning the corpus of closed cases) on the other. Incoming correspondence was all directed to the Registratur, where each item triggered the creation of a transaction file that was placed into a preexisting system of categories. Whether a petition from a subject, a query from a lower court about how to handle a case, or a bill for river dredging, each incoming message went into the same system. The Registratur added relevant past documents to the file and routed it to the appropriate officers and councils for deliberation. The authority's decision and the final communication of the outcome entered the same transaction file in the registry, all documented according to a complex tracking system.

In such a system, the term "information" gained a second, novel meaning: rather than being the process by which the world informed rulers, information became the raw material that entered the registry. Divided into categories and circulated in *coded documents, information in a registry became a thing, a substance to be processed by the state. The work of the state, from this perspective, consisted of identifying the right information and the right office to analyze it, leading to a decision (another piece of information) that could then be sent out into the world. The subject's petition was denied, the court was instructed how to sentence the defendant, and the dredger's bill was either paid or returned for further proof of work completed. Events and actions in the world were still vital to an administration that operated in this mode: "the whole business terminates in works," as Francis Bacon (himself an administrator) proclaimed. But for the offices involved—and specifically for their management of records—the world was approached through bundles of information that could be stored, moved, divided, categorized, and otherwise processed to reach a decision. At every step, the organization of records revolved around their place in an administrative process, carried out not by a fully informed lord but by the state itself. As the most famous eighteenth-century Prussian king, Frederick II, put it, he was simply the first servant of the state.

The archival principle that (slowly) captured this new orientation—in which documents are organized by and for the institutional actor that produces or collects them—is provenance or *respect des fonds*. Provenance rests on the following argument: because state records are meaningful primarily in the context of the actions of a state and its agents, only preservation in the order created by the state's offices can preserve their intelligibility. If removed from their transactional context, their meaning will be corrupted or lost. Therefore, the shift from pertinence to provenance in archival theory is one marker of shift from public records as evidence about the world itself to records as evidence about administrative processes by which a state deals with the world.

Beyond Texts in Political Information Processes

While writing played a central role in the transmission of political information in Europe from at least the thirteenth century, other ways to communicate information remained important. Research has begun exploring many of these ways, such as ritual forms that recapitulated important informational moments and architectural and other monumental self-representations erected by rulers and communities. Moreover, we must not imagine that the sphere of dusty records tediously scrutinized by withered clerks was separate from alternate spheres of public performance or celebration. Political information flowed through various channels by means of different media in ways that ensured no sharp boundaries existed between written, oral, and sensory information. In addition, European political actors were perfectly capable of self-conscious reflection about how they became informed, and to combine or distinguish different informational channels when it suited them. The world of political paperwork provides only one perspective on a more complex world.

Francis Bacon's epigram cited above offers one way to approach the wider universe of nontextual informational processes. Information commences with the senses, he claimed, and ends with works, that is, with human action. Recent historical research on the senses—hearing, smell, even touch—makes it clear that each could provide a channel, given appropriate media, for signs to move from the world into human minds. A first challenge in considering such forms of information lies in the ephemerality of much sensory experience: smells and sounds are difficult to record directly and largely lack a shared language for preserving traces of them. Sight—the sense most at work in reading written records—can be evanescent, too, but the marks that provoke it are not, since writing preserves traces of language in a durable visual medium, making them seemingly easy to recover or reperform. It is this ease enabled by writing, as much as the durability of paper and parchment per se, that lies behind the way that written material predominates in most historical research and analysis. However, visual images can be analyzed according to the grammar of iconology and iconography, and ceremonies too have their own structures and rhetorical dimensions. Discussions of visual and ceremonial communication and how they can create recorded traces therefore offer rich potential for information history.

Information and Truth in Early Modern Europe

So far, this essay has not addressed questions of truth in political information—that is, whether the insights that early modern European rulers and their growing staffs of officers derived from the information available to them corresponded to conditions in the larger world. This is because actors became informed through reading official records whether or not the records were authentic, accurate, or manipulated. In reality, however, chancellors, secretaries, and princes were acutely aware of how unreliable records could be: erroneous, incomplete, or actively forged to misrepresent the truth. To assess the reliability of records, these agents first turned to their religious and legal frameworks to assess whether what they read was trustworthy, and to sharpen their ability to discern misinformation. The oaths that accompanied much record making threatened eternal sanction for false statements, while a large body of legal literature reaching well back into the Middle Ages addressed problematic evidence by establishing criteria for trusting some records and dismissing others.

In addition to assessing records' truth, any work with durable informational traces has to confront the many possibilities that existed for loss and silencing. Loss was possible in multiple ways, even within the paradigm that described charters as authentic traces of authorized actions, and only grew in importance as the scope of recorded information expanded. In the first place, recording anything in textual form necessarily left out much about the record it claimed to describe. Such omission was inevitable, and indeed necessary: records concentrated on what seemed important to the actors involved while parsing out everything from the weather on the day a charter was issued to what the king had for breakfast. Omissions could also be entirely intentional, like the missing witnesses that were so important in the charters analyzed by Koziol (discussed above). In a context where the absence of certain words or people could convey meaning just as much as their presence, omission was both effective and largely invisible to later readers. Such processes of omission and silencing, inherent in the recording of information, also enabled the exercise of power in part by blotting out knowledge about much of life—notably, the life of those excluded from power by their race, gender, religious difference, or other forms of subalternity, as trenchantly analyzed by Michel-Rolph Trouillot.

Loss could take place later as well. Beyond the traditional archival terrors of fire, flood, and hungry vermin, documents could fade or be stolen, altered, or simply misplaced. Another cycle of loss began at the moment of rereading, especially when this took place long after the material had been written down. Changes in language or legal expectations could make what had been clear at one time cryptic or incomprehensible later. The Swiss villagers' assumption that someone from the village had to be present to understand their statutes shows considerable hermeneutic sophistication on their part: they recognized that without their contribution, an outsider might simply fail to comprehend the intention of a village bylaw or a description of its boundaries.

Beyond issues of truth and silencing, the commodification of information implicit in the early modern developments raised further challenges to the reliability and accessibility of records and the information processes they enabled. Most obvious are the various forms of concealment or censorship of documents and their texts that early modern states were happy to undertake. Denying particular parties access to the archives was routine (whether they requested a specific document known to exist or sought to search for records about some issue). At least formally, archives and chancellery papers were closed to anyone not authorized by the ruler, and secretaries' oaths of service contained detailed stipulations about not reading, copying, or otherwise circulating anything without explicit orders from above. A notorious example appears in the Venetian archives' policy of appointing only illiterates as service personnel in the Archivio Segreto—though as Filippo de Vivo shows, such prohibitions had become little more than a formalized pretense by the seventeenth century. In Spain, access to material in Simancas required an authorization signed personally by the king, while litigants seeking information about events in the Indies were generally turned away, and some documents were kept in chests to which even the archivists lacked a key. Like political information in other media, the history of misinformation and disinformation is an open topic waiting for more research. From spies and codes to the material fate of records during wars, floods, and fires, political information was never a passive and fixed quantity.

As information became increasingly packaged and commodified, financial incentives to hide or reveal it grew, leading to veritable information markets. In Venice, the detailed reports filed by the city's ambassadors across Europe and in the Ottoman sphere became desirable commodities owing to the trust that readers developed in the legates' perspicuity. As de Vivo shows, transcripts of these *Relazioni* were available for sale in the city and beyond, despite repeated prohibitions, giving rise to an entire economy of political knowledge emanating from the Venetian chancellery. Print provided another avenue for both welcome and unwelcome divulgence of political records from Europe's chancelleries. By the early seventeenth century, much political literature— especially the more polemical sort—included an appendix of "genuine" documents to support the author's points. Erudite scholars (who often worked in the chancelleries and administrations) jumped on board, so that by midcentury thousands of pages of documents could be consulted by learned readers. Even petty oligarchs in political backwaters joined the game: in 1622, amid invasions, political murders, and the plague, one local faction in the Swiss Grisons added twenty-nine documents from between 1289 and 1570 (translated into contemporary German) to a print manifesto protesting an Austrian military occupation. Naturally, the ability of various parties to publish documents favoring their arguments encouraged authorities with opposing views to censor such books, which in turn encouraged curious buyers to seek them out and savvy printers to churn out new editions. A complex overlap developed in the print world between political and commercial interests, and between affairs of state and public rhetoric, which supplemented the older world of face-to-face and manuscript circulation of information.

Ultimately, it follows from the fraught nature of human communication that political information in early modern Europe—and in any society—remained dynamic and unstable in both process and content. The manifest significance of changing information practices for any society has been highlighted by recent research in media and memory studies and finds considerable resonance in recent investigations into early modern humanist practices such as making *commonplace notebooks. At the intersection of these trends, a few scholars have suggested that the changing ways that European intellectuals and secretaries coped with the flood of "too much to know" had consequences not only for politics and erudition, but also for the cognitive structures of European readers. Following in the footsteps of Marshall McLuhan, Alberto Cevolini and Markus Krajewski each analyze the evolution of card-filing systems, as found first in bibliographical and encyclopedic projects and eventually in libraries and archives. Cevolini claims that card files brought about a "radical transformation to the relationship between memory and time" by parcelizing knowledge in ways that fundamentally changed how intellectuals found, managed, and circulated texts. Ann Blair has also explored how the development of reference books since the Middle Ages drove the trend toward packaging information in discrete parcels—whether as index entries, index cards, or *encyclopedia entries—while at the same time creating networks of linkages among them. The consideration of how such techniques found entry into secretarial and political contexts has begun generating exciting new research. We need to investigate thoroughly what was taking place in chancelleries as well as in scholars' studies before we can understand the implications of new excerpting and organizing practices for thought and society.

Conclusion

Close examination of official record keeping in post-medieval Europe suggests that unraveling the shifting cultural foundations from the practical architecture of information orders as they existed in different contexts can reveal new perspectives on multiple developments. Behind European cultures of record keeping lay the contentious ways Europeans understood the human political order with its spiritual and legal foundations, as well as the channels of communication at different scales that crisscrossed European societies. Correspondingly, behind European information architectures lay the media technologies by which political communication was transacted and embodied and the durable traces of such communication that accumulated in the hands of various political actors in rapidly increasing volumes after the fourteenth century.

Turning first to the symbiosis between political communication and the evolving political order in western Europe after 1400, the evidence presented above offers fresh perspectives on a very old question, namely the transformation of Europe from a patchwork of domains into a system of increasingly national states. Comparing the way various polities organized their records helps us understand not only what kings and chancellors could know, but also how they understood the political landscape on which they operated. Two broad organizational principles predominated through most of the early modern period. The first was that a repository's organization should privilege key actors outside the repository in the political world, such as emperors, kings, popes, and so on. The second was that the most important purpose of accumulated records was to memorialize the authentic actions of particular actors in the form of proofs that could be "drawn like weapons" in later contention. Even as archivists differentiated more genres of documents and accumulated more informational records, these priorities—in concord with medieval understandings of political order—continued to predominate in archives large and small. Meanwhile, the book technologies developed by medieval *scholasticism provided powerful tools for implementing rulers' and their officers' understanding of how records could and should be used.

By the sixteenth century, motivated in part by critical perspectives from humanism but also by the capacities of Scholastic media tools and by Europeans' confrontation with Asia and the Americas, chancelleries across Europe began collecting information in larger amounts than they ever had before. Agents at every level received commandments to send more reports to central offices: parish priests had to record baptisms, marriages, and deaths; citizens had to declare their wealth for taxation; and in Spain, the Crown circulated extensive questionnaires throughout its new empire in search of information. Meanwhile, the growing effectiveness of archival tools created new possibilities for information tracking and management. Although the media that were used (paper, writing, boxes, strings) and the available media technologies (alphabetization, registers, topographic and chronological articulation of storage spaces) changed very slowly if at all, the simple fact of accumulation in ordered spaces by increasingly professional staff created new opportunities for use and action.

Most importantly, as seen in initiatives for systematic censuses and cadasters, and even more through the development of registry techniques that categorized and managed documents in relation to their place in a state's decision-making processes, the growing mounds of paperwork accumulating across Europe made a new actor legible and intelligible, namely the abstract state itself. Combining old conceptions of office with a proliferation of specialized officers (often to the anger of traditional noble elites), this state became visible through its paperwork practices in resonance with emerging theoretical discussions of sovereignty (Bodin), unitary state power (Hobbes), and state service (German Kameralwissenschaft). Like these theories, the practices emerging in chancelleries and the capabilities for deploying information offered by registries did not at first directly challenge older regimes of kinship-based princely dominion and documents viewed as proofs of privilege. What they did do was to add a new layer of reified information, whose practical successes and ideological implications eventually transformed Europe's political information orders.

Further Reading

C. A. Bayly, *Empire and Information: Intelligence Gathering and Social Communication in India, 1780–1870*, 1996; Ann Blair, *Too Much to Know: Managing Scholarly Information before the Modern Age*, 2010; Arndt Brendecke, *The Empirical Empire: Spanish Colonial Rule and the Politics of Knowledge*, 2009, translation by Jeremiah Riemer, 2016; Peter Brun, *Schrift und politisches Handeln: Eine "zugeschriebene" Geschichte des Aargaus 1415–1425*, 2006; Alberto Cevolini, *Forgetting Machines: Knowledge Management Evolution in Early Modern Europe*, 2016; M. H.-François Delaborde, "Les Inventaires du Trésor des Chartes Dressés par Gérard de Montaigu," in *Notices et Extraits des Manuscrits de la Bibliothèque Nationale et autres Bibliothèques*, vol. 36, pt. 2, 1900; Filippo de Vivo, *Information and Communication in Venice: Rethinking Early Modern Politics*, 2007; Matthew Eddy, *Media and the Mind: Art, Science, and Notebooks as Paper Machines, 1700–1830*, 2023; Markus Friedrich, *The Birth of the Archive: A History of Knowledge*, 2013, translated by John-Noël Dillon, 2018; Karin Gottschalk, "Wissen über Land und Leute: Administrative Praktiken und Staatsbildungsprozesse im 18. Jahrhundert," in *Das Wissen des Staates: Geschichte, Theorie und Praxis*, edited by Peter Collin and Thomas Horstmanneds, 2004; Randolph Head, *Making Archives in Early Modern Europe: Proof, Information, and Political Record-Keeping, 1400–1700*, 2019; Edward Higgs, *The*

Information State in England: The Central Collection of Information on Citizens since 1500, 2004; Roger Kain and Elizabeth Baigent, *The Cadastral Map in the Service of the State: A History of Property Mapping*, 1984; Geoffrey Koziol, *The Politics of Memory and Identity in Carolingian Royal Diplomas: The West Frankish Kingdom (840–987)*, 2012; Markus Krajewski, *Paper Machines: About Cards and Catalogs, 1548–1929*, 2002, translated by Peter Krapp, 2011; Ron Makleff, "Sovereignty and Silence: The Creation of a Myth of Archival Destruction, Liège, 1408," *Archival Journal* (2017); Marshall McLuhan, *The Gutenberg Galaxy: The Making of Typographic Man*, 1962; José Luis Rodríguez de Diego, *Memoria Escrita de la Monarquía Hispánica: Felipe II y Simancas*, 2018; Peter Rück, "Die Ordnung der herzoglich savoyischen Archive unter Amadeus VIII (1398–1451)," *Archivalische Zeitschrift* 67 (1971): 11–101; Andrea Rusnock, *Vital Accounts: Quantifying Health and Population in Eighteenth-Century England and France*, 2002; James C. Scott, *Seeing Like a State: How Certain Schemes to Improve the Human Condition Have Failed*, 1998; Jacob Soll, *The Information Master: Jean-Baptiste Colbert's Secret State Intelligence System*, 2009; Simon Teuscher, *Lords' Rights and Peasant Stories: Writing and the Formation of Tradition in the Later Middle Ages*, 2007, translated by Philip Grace, 2012; Michel-Rolph Trouillot, *Silencing the Past: Power and the Production of History*, 1995; Cornelia Vismann, *Files: Law and Media Technology*, 2000, translated by Geoffrey Winthrop-Young, 2008; Geoffrey Yeo, *Records, Information and Data: Exploring the Role of Record-Keeping in an Information Culture*, 2018; Cornel Zwierlein, ed., *The Dark Side of Knowledge: Histories of Ignorance, 1400 to 1800*, 2016.

7

Periodicals and the Commercialization of Information in the Early Modern Era

Will Slauter

THIS CHAPTER EMPHASIZES two long-term changes: the commercialization of timely information and the proliferation of periodical publications. The two phenomena were linked, and together they had profound effects on the information cultures that developed in many parts of the world in the seventeenth and eighteenth centuries. There are earlier examples of treating information as a commercial product and of publishing at somewhat regular intervals; calendars and almanacs, for example, had long been produced annually. But beginning in the seventeenth century, commercialization and periodicity combined to create new forms of publication that were to have remarkable futures. These included newspapers, magazines, and learned journals as well as specialized periodicals covering commerce, urban health, and criminal justice. The story was not the same in Spain or Russia as it was in the British Isles or North America, not to mention South Asia, the Middle East, or the islands of the Caribbean. But the overall pattern is unmistakable: by around 1800, a growing number of periodicals containing reports of recent developments—in politics, commerce, science, literature, and other areas of inquiry—were transforming the information landscape.

Periodicals are open-ended publications (with no end date announced) issued at regular intervals (daily, weekly, monthly, and so on) and with a stable title or other recognizable features, such as a consistent format or numbering.

There is nothing natural about publishing information on a regular schedule, and to the extent that we can speak of the rise of periodicals it was a process that involved experimentation, adaptation to local circumstances, a fair amount of risk, and quite a bit of failure. But over time periodicals became the medium of choice for the rapid exchange and discussion of information in many domains. The success of periodicals did not result from the inherent advantages or affordances of periodicity so much as from the strategies and conventions developed over time by writers, printers, government officials, advertisers, and readers. Individuals and groups devised formats and modes of distribution that they exploited to achieve various goals.

By commercialization I mean simply the process of turning something into a product that can be sold. Of course, information of various sorts was exchanged among individuals without any expectation of a monetary transaction, and the business of selling information should not be conflated with the broader cultural experiences of information in any given time and place. But there is little doubt that contemporaries in the seventeenth and eighteenth centuries perceived a process that can be referred to as the commercialization of timely information. By the 1620s, when the Thirty Years' War (1618–48) increased demand for foreign news and the ongoing expansion of postal networks facilitated the more regular delivery of this news across Europe, the English playwright Ben Jonson could mock the greed of printers and the gullibility of readers caught up in the incipient news cycles of his day. The title of one of Jonson's plays—*The Staple of News* (first performed in 1625)—evoked the sense that news had become a commodity that flowed into and out of the merchant's emporium or staple. Some contemporaries indeed used the term *commodity* to describe the way reports of recent events were being sold for a profit. Samuel Butler, another English writer of the seventeenth century, defined a newsmonger as "a retailer of rumor" who "deals in a perishable commodity, that will not keep. . . . True or false is all one to him; for novelty being the grace of both, a truth goes stale as soon as a lie." It was the timeliness of news that made it a viable commercial product, which in turn raised questions of authenticity and trustworthiness.

News and other sorts of information were sold in various forms, including books, pamphlets, and broadsides, but it was the open-ended nature of periodicals that troubled critics most. Periodicals created an appetite among readers, a forum for ongoing discussion, and an obligation to fill the available space even in the absence of verifiable reports. While critics worried about the financial and political interests that shaped accounts, authorities weighed the benefits and risks of setting up official periodicals or tolerating unofficial ones. It was periodicity combined with commercialization that created the first news cycles, for better and for worse.

And yet periodicity did not affect just the world of political and military news; it also structured information about commerce, literature, and scientific endeavor. In the late seventeenth century, the editors of the first scientific and literary journals highlighted the advantages of publishing timely reports at regular intervals. During the eighteenth century, writers in many places celebrated the role of journals in spreading *enlightenment and facilitating discussion of economic, social, and philosophical questions. By the end of the century, faith in the newspaper as a democratic medium was expressed by leaders on both sides of the Atlantic. Individuals highlighted the capacity of newspapers to foster an informed citizenry by relaying information cheaply and quickly over vast distances. These ideals were not always realized, but their expression became commonplace. Information in the form of reference books, maps, and single-sheet broadsides remained important, but regular and timely access to newspapers and other periodicals was increasingly seen as vital to understanding the world and effecting change within it.

Even in areas where printing presses did not exist, the proliferation of periodicals could still be felt. Periodicals traveled alongside letters in the post, reaching readers in far-flung places. And periodicals did not have to be printed. Manuscript newsletters were also periodicals that made timely information available in exchange for money. The audience for newsletters was more restricted, but they were a semipublic form of correspondence that continued to matter long after the creation of the first printed newspapers. For example, by the late eighteenth century, a number of printed gazettes and journals circulated in the Italian peninsula and in France, but the manuscript accounts known as *avvisi* and *nouvelles à la main* continued to attract subscribers because they provided information that could not be printed for reasons of censorship. Even in Britain, where prepublication censorship effectively ended in 1695, handwritten newsletters remained crucial for certain kinds of information—such as parliamentary proceedings—well into the eighteenth century. Newsletters also thrived in places without a printed newspaper, such as Iceland before the 1790s and many areas of Latin America during the wars of independence in the early nineteenth century. In India, there were no printed newspapers until the 1780s, and none in Indigenous languages until the 1820s. But the English-language and *vernacular Indian press built on a rich information ecosystem that included newsletters known as *akhbarat*, which were produced by professional news writers on behalf of rulers who paid for regular updates from other regions. These were the Indian counterparts to the newsletters in multiple languages that circulated through the expanding postal networks of Europe.

Without a functioning postal system, the collection and distribution of timely information in periodical form would have been next to impossible. Printed periodicals, like manuscript newsletters, were embedded in correspondence networks because their editors relied on information that arrived in the mail to fill their columns. The *publishers then used the post to distribute their final product to subscribers. Postal schedules enabled weekly publication in many places and semiweekly or triweekly publication in some places. Daily publication was reserved to a few cities where the concentration of customers and sufficient local sources of information made it viable. Working in tandem and traveling together in the mail, letters and periodicals connected people and facilitated the circulation of information of all sorts. The way periodicals and correspondence reinforced each other enabled information to travel faster and farther than before and encouraged the development of what Brendan Dooley has called "contemporaneity"—the sense among individuals in different places that they were living through a shared present, paying attention to the same events.

In reality, communication over vast distances was unpredictable and often frustrating. But the fact that people were expecting more regular updates was an important development. The quantity and variety of information that was publicly available was not everywhere the same, and within a given society access to information depended on one's location, social status, gender, race, professional affiliations, degree of *literacy, and other factors. But by 1800 individuals in many places sought out timely information and looked for ways to manage that information to advance their goals in the present. These were not information societies in the sense that the production of information was the primary economic activity—far from it. But these were societies in which information was increasingly seen as an important factor in political, economic, intellectual, and social life.

Recent scholarship has emphasized the benefits of studying the interaction of oral, written, and printed media as well as the need to avoid the reification of "print culture" and teleological narratives of the rise of the newspaper. The chronology of printing and the types of periodicals produced varied by place. Moreover, the fact that a newspaper or journal existed somewhere does not tell us how people at the time used it in relation to other sources of information at their disposal. In many places and fields of inquiry, printed periodicals could not compete for freshness or level of detail with what individuals could learn through conversation and private letters. Information came in many forms, and the emphasis here on periodicals does not mean that other modes of communication were not important to people at the time.

But if we take a long view of the history of information—rather than trying to understand all the ways information mattered in a given context—then one fruitful way to think about the *early modern period is to highlight the growth in the number and variety of publications that were delivered at regular intervals and devoted to information about recent occurrences. This process began with the creation of the business press in the sixteenth century and entered a new phase with the development of printed newspapers and scientific journals during the seventeenth century. This chapter covers these early developments before turning to the eighteenth century, which witnessed major changes in the scale, density, and perceived significance of periodicals as media of enlightenment and revolution.

The Publicity of Commerce and Urban Health

It is nearly impossible to sell information independently of its representation in words, figures, or illustrations. Information can be shared without any financial transaction, but it cannot be sold unless it is embedded in some material object—such as a handwritten newsletter or a printed pamphlet—or part of some service—such as a subscription reading room where the information is displayed. Information is nonrivalrous (one person's enjoyment does not diminish the quantity available for others) and only partly excludable (publishers can charge for access, but information permeates most borders). In the case of a printed ballad or a newspaper, for example, some people purchased copies while others learned the information by listening to the ballad sung on the street or by perusing the newspaper in a *coffeehouse. Still, the availability of this information to the public generally depended on its appearance in publications that were produced in order to be sold.

Specialists of the history of news, including C. John Sommerville, Joad Raymond, and Andrew Pettegree, have pointed out that periodicals were not the most obvious or efficient way of commercializing news. When an event occurred that seemed likely to interest paying customers, it often made more sense to issue a broadside or pamphlet, both of which could be produced quickly, cheaply, and anonymously. Periodicals required a production schedule in a fixed location—which made them easier for the authorities to monitor—and a continuous supply of copy. Events of public concern do not normally occur on a predictable schedule, though news publishers have long been attracted to events that are announced in advance, such as ceremonies, trials, and public executions. Ongoing events such as wars and treaty negotiations also lent themselves to publishing in installments, and some periodicals engaged in speculative commentary while awaiting confirmation of what actually happened. But many writers and publishers censored their comments in order to avoid trouble with the local authorities. Independent of the question of censorship, periodical publication required that there was something to print and that it arrived in time to go to press. In the case of reporting foreign news, this problem was overcome gradually as a result of the creation of more regular and reliable mail services after 1600. The fact that the first weekly newspapers developed only in the early seventeenth century, about 150 years after the invention of printing, is due in large part to the expansion of private and public postal networks.

A specialized business press developed even earlier. Indeed, the first printed periodicals devoted to timely information focused on commerce rather than politics or diplomacy. Merchants and brokers needed reliable sources of information about market conditions, such as the prices of goods and the movement of ships. Such information had long been exchanged in private letters, and much of it had been closely guarded since knowledge of market conditions could be a serious advantage in trade. But beginning in the mid-sixteenth century, as John McCusker has shown, merchants in important trading centers in the Italian peninsula and northern Europe adopted a new approach. They recognized that publicizing certain kinds of information on a regular basis was mutually beneficial. The result was the creation of commodity price currents, which were single-sheet publications listing the prices at which goods were trading, and exchange rate currents, which itemized the rates at which foreign bills were being exchanged locally. Though specialized, these business papers were to provide a model for subsequent newspapers and journals.

The earliest surviving printed price currents are from the 1580s in Frankfurt, Amsterdam, and Venice, but there is evidence that they existed in Antwerp as early as 1540 and probably even earlier in Italy. Exchange rate currents soon followed. Florence had one by 1598, though it seems likely that the French city of Lyon, whose international trading fair also served as a major money market, had one as early as the 1550s. By the early seventeenth century, many trading centers had either commodity price currents or exchange rate currents or both. Amsterdam had a price current by 1585, Hamburg probably by 1592, and London from at least 1600. Eventually they existed in ports on the Mediterranean and the Atlantic, such as Lisbon, Bordeaux, and Cádiz. This chronology makes sense. The Italian cities were the center of trade in the fourteenth and fifteenth centuries. In the mid- to late sixteenth century, Antwerp was the most important hub of commercial news, but by the early seventeenth century Amsterdam had taken over. In 1617, the English diplomat James Howell was able to refer to Amsterdam as the "Great Staple of News," using the same term that Jonson would for his satire of news culture a few years later. The Amsterdam price currents were available not only in Dutch but also in English, French, and Italian, making them useful to merchants across Europe. During the Dutch Golden Age, the prices at Amsterdam served as a benchmark; though a broker might have fresher information or find a way to buy lower or sell higher, the published weekly prices remained an important international reference.

The sale of commercial information at regular intervals represented a conscious effort to use publicity to promote certain interests. In Amsterdam, for example, members of the *guild that ran the *beurs* or exchange envisioned the publication of an officially sanctioned price current as a means of attracting more buyers and sellers to Amsterdam. The municipal authorities also recognized that carefully managing the flow of information could help boost the local economy. Individual merchants and brokers also benefited from access to a trusted source that other traders were also using. The adoption of such benchmarks lowered the cost of gathering information and reduced risk. Finally, these business newspapers were profitable ventures in themselves—profitable enough, in fact, to lead members of the exchange to outbid each other to have the privilege of being the official *courantier*. Such privileges constituted an official monopoly on a whole category of information for which merchants were willing to pay. The brokers' guild that ran the exchange had an interest in making sure the information was accurate and reserved the right to cancel the privilege and assign it to a more trustworthy *courantier*.

Over time, London surpassed Amsterdam as the single most important hub of commercial information, and its business press took off. In seventeenth-century England, as in the Low Countries, business periodicals were treated as official monopolies governed by privileges. In addition to price currents, there were bills of entry, which provided a digest of the goods entered in the custom house books, and marine lists, which detailed arriving and departing ships. These were all published as periodicals protected by letters patent. In the 1690s, the creation of the Bank of England and the growth in joint-stock companies spawned a new kind of business paper: the stock-exchange current. This was not protected by patent, and there was competition in this field at times—such as in the years leading up to the South Sea Bubble of 1720—but in most decades merchants and brokers gravitated toward a single source, John Castaing's *Course of the Exchange* (see figure 7.1).

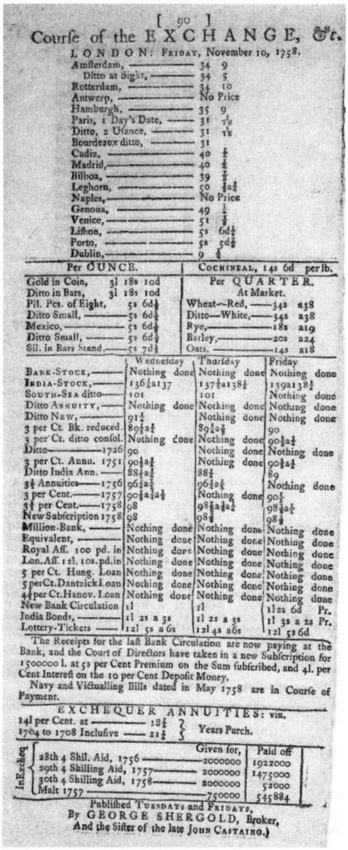
[90]

Course of the EXCHANGE, &c.

LONDON: FRIDAY, November 10, 1758.

Amsterdam,	34 9
Ditto at Sight,	34 5
Rotterdam,	34 10
Antwerp,	No Price
Hamburgh,	35 9
Paris, 1 Day's Date,	31 5/16
Ditto, 2 Usance,	31 1/16
Bourdeaux ditto,	31
Cadiz,	40 ¼
Madrid,	40 ¼
Bilboa,	39 ⅞
Leghorn,	50 ⅞a¾
Naples,	No Price
Genoua,	49 ¼
Venice,	51 ⅞
Lisbon,	5s 6d¼
Porto,	5s 5d⅞
Dublin,	9 ⅛

Per OUNCE.		Cochineal, 14s 6d per lb.	
Gold in Coin,	3l 18s 10d	Per QUARTER. At Market.	
Ditto in Bars,	3l 18s 10d		
Pil. Pcs. of Eight,	5s 6d⅛	Wheat—Red,	34s a38
Ditto Small,	5s 6d¼	Ditto—White,	34s a38
Mexico,	5s 6d⅛	Rye,	18s a19
Ditto Small,	5s 6d⅛	Barley,	20s a24
Sil. in Bars Stand.	5s 7d¼	Oats,	14s a18

	Wednesday	Thursday	Friday
Bank-Stock,	Nothing done	Nothing done	Nothing done
India-Stock,	136¾a137	137½a138¼	139a138½
South-Sea ditto	101	101	Nothing done
Ditto Annuity,	Nothing done	Nothing done	Nothing done
Ditto New,	91¼	Nothing done	Nothing done
3 per Ct. Bk. reduced.	89½a¼	89¾a⅞	90
3 per Ct. ditto consol.	Nothing done	Nothing done	90⅛a¼
Ditto 1726	90	Nothing done	Nothing done
3 per Ct. Annu. 1751	90⅛a¼	Nothing done	90⅛a¼
Ditto India Ann.	88½a¼	88¼	89
3½ Annuities 1756	96¼a⅜	96¼a⅜	Nothing done
3 per Cent. 1757	90⅛a¼a⅛	Nothing done	90¼
3½ per Cent. 1758	98	98⅛a⅜a½	98⅜a½
New Subscription 1758	98	98⅜	98⅜
Million-Bank,	Nothing done	Nothing done	Nothing done
Equivalent,	Nothing done	Nothing done	Nothing done
Royal Ass. 100 pd. in	Nothing done	Nothing done	Nothing done
Lon. Ass. 12l. 10s. pd. in	Nothing done	Nothing done	Nothing done
5 per Ct. Hung. Loan	Nothing done	Nothing done	Nothing done
5 per Ct. Dantzick Loan	Nothing done	Nothing done	Nothing done
4½ per Ct. Hanov. Loan	Nothing done	Nothing done	Nothing done
New Bank Circulation	1l	1l	1l 2s 6d Pr.
India Bonds,	1l 2s a 3s	1l 2s a 3s	1l 3s a 2s Pr.
Lottery-Tickets	12l 5s a 6s	12l 4s a6s	12l 5s 6d

The Receipts for the last Bank Circulation are now paying at the Bank, and the Court of Directors have taken in a new Subscription for 1500000 l. at 5s per Cent Premium on the Sum subscribed, and 4l. per Cent Interest on the 10 per Cent Deposit Money.

Navy and Victualling Bills dated in May 1758 are in Course of Payment.

EXCHEQUER ANNUITIES: viz.

14l per Cent. at	18¼	Years Purch.
1704 to 1708 Inclusive	21¼	

In Excheq		Given for,	Paid off
	28th 4 Shil. Aid, 1756	2000000	1922000
	29th 4 Shilling Aid, 1757	2000000	1475000
	30th 4 Shilling Aid, 1758	2000000	52000
	Malt 1757	750000	545884

Published Tuesdays and Fridays,
By GEORGE SHERGOLD, Broker,
And the Sister of the late John Castaing.)

FIGURE 7.1. A copy of the twice-weekly London *Course of the Exchange* from 1758. Lewis Walpole Library, Yale University.

Price currents offer a good example of how publishing a periodical by subscription helped overcome a paradox identified by the economist Kenneth Arrow. Most people want to know what they are buying before they commit to paying. But Arrow pointed out that when it comes to information, if customers are allowed to see the product—or enough of it to ascertain its value to them—then their incentive to purchase that information is reduced. Periodicals sold by subscription provided a solution for cases in which individuals wanted timely access to information of a certain kind. Merchants and brokers wanted the latest prices, whatever they might be, and they were willing to pay an annual fee to receive them from a trusted source. They might not use the price current every week, but it was better to have access just in case. Meanwhile, for the publisher, selling by subscription meant having dedicated customers in known locations; that made it easier to know how many copies to produce and where to deliver them. These factors provided an incentive for the ongoing collection and distribution of certain kinds of information.

Another area where regular updates of numerical data underpinned a long-standing periodical was what we would now call vital statistics. A telling example, though specific to London, is the "bills of mortality." These provided weekly updates on the number of christenings and burials (especially plague burials) in each parish of London, Westminster, and nearby districts. The collection of this information was of interest to the English monarchy and the City of London, but details leaked out in manuscript copies from the late sixteenth century, and starting in 1603 (a plague year) printed copies were sold to the public through annual subscription and one-off street sales. By the following decade, the Worshipful Company of Parish Clerks had a royal charter recognizing its duty to deliver weekly reports to the authorities and the exclusive right to sell bills of mortality to the public. The clerk of each parish tallied the christenings and burials in his district and relied on individuals known as searchers, usually elderly women supported by the parish, to determine the cause of death of each victim. These weekly tallies were given to a central clerk who aggregated the data and prepared the bills for the printer (see figure 7.2).

It may be surprising that the bills of mortality were sold to the public instead of being reserved for government use, but in fact many government documents and services (judicial or archival) were available for sale in premodern Europe. Crucially in this case the timely collection of the information depended on the decentralized and commercial nature of the operation. Beyond their sense of duty, the parish clerks had a financial incentive: in exchange for making timely reports to government they had the exclusive right to sell the printed bills in their respective parishes. The City of London and the king also saw the advantages of publishing an official record rather than letting rumors and misinformation take over, especially during epidemics. Those who read the bills or heard their contents being discussed were able to track the progress of the epidemic; the listing of individual parishes made it possible to see at a glance which areas were affected. Contemporary letters and diaries reveal that people paid most attention to the increase or decrease in burials from one week to the next, a telling example of how periodicity could structure the way people made sense of events. As with price currents, knowing the latest figures—whatever they were—was valuable to people and it influenced their decisions. Wealthy individuals who had the luxury of being able to leave London during the plague used the bills to know when to depart and when it was safe to return. London was unusual in having this weekly publication available in print from the early seventeenth century, but variants later existed in other places, including the French city of Rouen, where merchants and municipal leaders had an interest in managing information about epidemics, thereby counteracting rumors affecting trade with their city.

London 35	Bur.	Plag.	From the 15 of August to the 22.	Bur.	Plag.	1665	Bur.	Plag.
St Alban Woodstreet—	11	8	St George Botolphlane—			St Martin Ludgate—	4	4
Alhallows Barking	13	11	St Gregory by St Pauls—	9	5	St Martin Orgars—	8	6
Alhallows Breadstreet—	1	1	St Hellen—	11	11	St Martin Outwitch—	1	
Alhallows Great—	6	5	St James Dukes place—	7	5	St Martin Vintrey—	17	17
Alhallows Honylane—			St James Garlickhithe—	3	1	St Matthew Fridaystreet—	1	
Alhallows Lesse—	3	2	St John Baptist—	7	4	St Maudlin Milkstreet—	2	2
Alhallows Lumbardstreet	6	4	St John Evangelist—			St Maudlin Oldfishstreet—	8	4
Alhallows Staining	7	5	St John Zachary—	1	1	St Michael Bassishaw—	12	11
Alhallows the Wall—	23	11	St Katharine Coleman—	5	1	St Michael Cornhil—	2	
St Alphage—	18	10	St Katharine Creechurch	7	4	St Michael Crookedlane	7	4
St Andrew Hubbard—	1		St Lawrence Jewry—	2		St Michael Queenhithe—	7	6
St Andrew Undershaft—	14	9	St Lawrence Pountney—	6	5	St Michael Quern—	1	
St Andrew Wardrobe—	21	16	St Leonard Eastcheap—	1	1	St Michael Royal—	2	1
St Ann Aldersgate—	18	11	St Leonard Fosterlane—	17	13	St Michael Woodstreet—	2	1
St Ann Blackfryers—	22	17	St Magnus Parish—	2	2	St Mildred Breadstreet—	2	1
St Antholins Parish—			St Margaret Lothbury—	2	1	St Mildred Poultrey —	4	3
St Austins Parish—			St Margaret Moses—	1		St Nicholas Acons—		
St BartholomewExchange	2	2	St MargaretNewfishstreet	1		St Nicholas Coleabby—	1	
St Bennet Fynck—	2	2	St Margaret Patrons—	1		St Nicholas Olaves—	3	1
St Bennet Gracechurch—			St Mary Abchurch—	1		St Olave Hartstreet—	7	4
St Bennet Paulswharf—	16	8	St Mary Aldermanbury—	11	5	St Olave Jewry—	1	
St Bennet Sherehog—			St Mary Aldermary —	2	1	St Olave Silverstreet—	23	15
St Botolph Billingsgate—	2		St Mary le Bow—	6	6	St Pancras Soperlane—		
Chrifts Church—	27	22	St Mary Bothaw—	1	1	St Peter Cheap—	1	1
St Christophers—	1		St Mary Colechurch—			St Peter Cornhil—	7	6
St Clement Eastcheap—	2	2	St Mary Hill—	2	1	St Peter Paulswharf—	5	2
St Dionis Backchurch—	2	1	St Mary Mounthaw—	1		St Peter Poor—	3	2
St Dunstan East—	7	2	St Mary Sommerset—	6	5	St Steven Colemanstreet	15	11
St Edmund Lumbardstr.	2	2	St Mary Stayning—	1		St Steven Walbrook—		
St Ethelborough—	13	7	St Mary Woolchurch—	1		St Swithin—	2	2
St Faith—	6	6	St Mary Woolnoth—	1	1	St Thomas Apostle—	8	7
St Foster—	13	11	St Martin Iremongerlane			Trinity Parish—	5	3
St Gabriel Fenchurch—	1							

Christned in the 97 Parishes within the Walls— 34   Buried— 538   Plague— 366

St Andrew Holborn —	232	220	St Botolph Aldgate—	238	212	Saviours Southwark—	160	120
St Bartholomew Great—	58	50	St Botolph Bishopsgate—	288	236	S. Sepulchres Parish—	403	274
St Bartholomew Lesse—	19	15	St Dunstan West—	36	29	St Thomas Southwark—	24	21
St Bridget—	147	119	St George Southwark—	80	60	Trinity Minories—	8	5
Bridewel Precinct—	7	5	St Giles Cripplegate—	847	572	At the Pesthouse—	9	9
St Botolph Aldersgate—	70	61	St Olave Southwark—	235	131			

Christned in the 16 Parishes without the Walls— 61   Buried, and at the Pesthouse—2861   Plague—2139

St Giles in the fields—	204	175	Lambeth Parish—	13	9	St Mary Islington—	50	45
Hackney Parish—	12	8	St Leonard Shoreditch—	252	168	St Mary Whitechappel—	319	270
St James Clerkenwel—	172	172	St Magdalen Bermondsey	57	36	Rotherith Parish—	7	2
St Kath. near the Tower	40	34	St Mary Newington—	74	52	Stepney Parish—	371	273

Christned in the 12 out Parishes in Middlesex and Surry— 49   Buried— 1571   Plague— 1244

St Clement Danes—	94	78	St Martin in the fields—	255	193	St Margaret Westminster	220	191
St Paul Covent Garden—	18	16	St Mary Savoy—	11	10	whereof at the Pesthouse—		13

Christned in the 5 Parishes in the City and Liberties of Westminster— 27   Buried— 598   Plague— 488

FIGURE 7.2. London bill of mortality for the week of August 15–22, 1665. The Wellcome Collection (CC BY).

News through the Post

The first periodicals reporting political and military news were handwritten newsletters that began to circulate in the sixteenth century. In Italian the news-letters were called *avvisi*, and the individuals who produced them were known as *reportistas* or *novellistas*; in French, the *nouvelles à la main* were put out by *nouvellistes*; in English the compilers of newsletters were known as "intelligenc-ers," a name that was subsequently adopted in the titles of printed newspapers such as the *Publick Intelligencer* (1655–60). Similarly, in German the term

Zeitung was used for both printed relations and handwritten newsletters. The most well-known of the latter are the *Fuggerzeitungen* (Fugger newsletters) associated with the Fugger banking family and preserved by the Austrian National Library. Over the course of several decades beginning in the 1560s, the brothers Octavian Secundus Fugger and Philipp Eduard Fugger received and collected thousands of letters compiled by professional news writers and other individuals based in cities across Europe. The collection, which has recently been digitized and indexed, offers an exceptional window into how information circulated in sixteenth- and seventeenth-century Europe.

In general, the compilers of newsletters worked for clients who paid them to receive regular updates of news from other places (local news spread orally). Some had numerous subscribers and hired clerks to make copies. Others worked alone in fly-by-night operations. But by around 1620 they could be found in many cities and courts of Europe. The newsletters were largely tolerated because they met the information needs of well-connected people. Indeed, the sources of information included reports leaked by diplomats and spies as well as rumors gathered locally and newsletters from other cities. In that sense, we can speak of networks of newsletters, rather than just one-to-one relationships between intelligencers and their customers. The newsletters fed into each other and later became crucial sources for printed newspapers.

In the early seventeenth century, individuals began to reproduce newsletters in print for sale to a larger clientele. The first may have been Johann Carolus of Strasbourg, a city that was at the crossroads of European trading and postal networks. In 1605, Carolus began to produce a printed version of his existing manuscript newsletter. Thanks to a privilege from the municipal council, he was the only person in Strasbourg who had the right to put out such a publication. Printers elsewhere, including Basel, Frankfurt, Berlin, and Hamburg, soon followed Carolus's lead. But they faced competition from officials of the imperial post, who were uniquely positioned to collect intelligence and exploit their free use of the mails to distribute their periodicals to customers. The weekly publications that they produced were known as *Postzeitungen*, the first of many titles to announce the essential link between news and postal transmission. The *Frankfurter Postzeitung* (Frankfurt postal newspaper), for example, was founded in 1615 by the local imperial postmaster. In other places *Zeitungen* were the initiatives of printers or merchants, such as Johann Meyer in Hamburg, who used his connections in business to create a manuscript news service and then switched to print with the *Wöchentliche Zeitung* (Weekly newspaper). This paper had a rather exceptional circulation of about fifteen hundred copies owing to Hamburg's importance as a trading center. Most of the early news periodicals had print runs in the low- to mid-hundreds, but this could still be enough to turn a profit.

Meyer's experience also shows how periodical publishing involved struggles for control of a given territory. Pettegree has explained how the Hamburg city council sought to appease local booksellers, who also wanted to profit from demand for news. The city council decided that Meyer could sell his paper directly to customers for the first three days of the week, after which point local booksellers would have their turn. But in the 1630s a new imperial postmaster declared that he had a monopoly on news in Hamburg and tried to drive first Meyer, and then his widow, Ilsabe, out of business. Ultimately the city council gave the postmaster exclusive use of the title *Postzeitung* but denied that he had a monopoly on printed news in Hamburg, allowing Ilsabe Meyer to compete directly with him.

Like Carolus and Meyer, the publishers of news often sought privileges in order to protect their investments against competition. A privilege could be a valuable monopoly for the publisher as well as an instrument of control for the authorities, but enforcement depended on a number of factors. In the Dutch Republic, for example, the close proximity of cities, each with its own privileges, meant that an individual who was excluded from issuing a newspaper in one place might succeed in obtaining a privilege in another. Moreover, the privilege to print news in one city did not automatically come with the right to stop the importation of publications from other cities. Postal policy was a separate lever that authorities could use to manage the flow of information, as the example of France discussed later reveals.

By 1618 or so, Amsterdam had a regular newspaper or *courante*. This term and related ones in several languages, including *coranto* and *currant*, evoked the idea of messengers (couriers) and the mail they carried, not to mention the idea of being up-to-date or *au courant*. By the 1640s, Amsterdam had nine different corantos, though according to an agreement between city officials and the publishers they had to appear on designated days of the week so as to avoid ruinous competition. Because of its importance as a trading center and the relative openness of its government—it is no coincidence that merchants were at the center of municipal politics—Amsterdam had a thriving information culture that included the production of quality maps, polemical pamphlets, and the business press already mentioned. But in order for regular news periodicals to succeed, there had to be an ongoing story to capture the attention of readers and make them willing to subscribe. Apart from the Thirty Years'

War, which boosted demand for news across Europe, the story that caught the attention of Amsterdamers, as Michiel van Groesen has shown, was the fledgling colony of Dutch Brazil. The struggle between the Dutch and Portuguese for control of Brazil was framed as part of a broader conflict between Protestants and Catholics, but it also had major financial stakes for the Dutch West India Company and individual merchants. It was the perfect recipe for a thriving news culture that supported the sale of corantos as well as news maps—a popular visual medium—and polemical pamphlets. The Dutch West India Company and city leaders were initially able to manage the flow of news from Brazil, but over time this became more difficult, especially after soldiers and colonists returned to Amsterdam and shared their firsthand observations of life in Brazil.

As news periodicals cropped up in various places, from the Dutch Republic and the Habsburg Netherlands to the German lands and the Italian peninsula, it was common for the local authorities to govern these publications through privileges. The princes or city councils that granted such privileges sometimes gave explicit instructions about what topics should be avoided and what tone should be taken. Some of them required each issue to be submitted to a censor. From the standpoint of political or religious authorities, ongoing periodicals were easier to monitor than one-off publications like broadsides and pamphlets, many of which were anonymous and sold on the street. Periodicity also encouraged self-censorship. In exchange for a monopoly in their geographic territories, most publishers could be counted on to avoid certain subjects; it was generally understood that domestic politics was off limits and that reports should be presented in a neutral tone without editorial commentary. The need to attract subscribers and advertisers similarly led publishers to avoid topics that might alienate them. Periodicals made the sale of timely information viable, but they also required catering to political patrons and customers.

In more centralized states, such as France and Spain, monarchies established official gazettes. The French *Gazette* dates to 1631 and the Madrid *Gaceta* to 1661. In England the idea of an official newspaper was proposed as early as 1620, when two "intelligencers" with experience producing handwritten newsletters petitioned the king for a privilege. They argued that the creation of an official printed periodical would enable the monarchy to counteract rumors and better control the flow of news. But King James I (r. 1603–25) was not ready for this idea. Instead, he appointed a censor to authorize news publications by a few members of the London Stationers' Company, which had a monopoly on printing and bookselling in England. The stationers knew that they were on a tight leash with respect to political news. During the English Civil War (1642–51), publishers enjoyed greater freedom, though Parliament still monitored the press and called writers and printers to account for the occasional article. During the 1640s the publication of news became truly regular, with several competing periodicals appearing each week. The idea of an official newspaper became more of a reality in England during the 1650s under the Protectorate of Oliver Cromwell, when only two news periodicals (one covering Parliament and the other foreign news) were authorized. But a true state-run newspaper did not exist in England until 1665, when the *London Gazette* was created.

The example of the *London Gazette* illustrates how secret and public intelligence were intertwined during this period. The secretaries of state, who oversaw diplomacy and espionage, were also given responsibility for the gazette. The post office was central to all three. Postal officials were expected to monitor correspondence and report details that might be of interest to government. In exchange they received copies of the *London Gazette* to sell to local customers, thereby facilitating the spread of the official version of events. The undersecretaries of state who supervised the *London Gazette* also ran subscription newsletter services for a more restricted clientele. By sharing fresh news with these elites, they received other information in return, plus the profit from the sale of the newsletters.

This connection between secret and public intelligence existed elsewhere in Europe, including France, Spain, the Habsburg lands, and later, Russia. The official gazettes tended to include edited selections from the diplomatic correspondence of the realm. They provided a means of counteracting rumors and promoting a particular image of the monarchy. It was also hoped that they would provide readers with enough information to reduce demand for unofficial publications. In France, for example, the monarchy adjusted its policies over time in an effort to limit the creation of rival sources of information. After printers in the provinces began to pirate the official *Gazette* in the early eighteenth century, the monarchy responded by setting up official franchises. Printers in various towns were licensed to issue local reprints of the *Gazette*, thereby giving the printers a source of profit while encouraging wider dissemination of the official news.

The need for some kind of information policy had long been evident to rulers, as early privileges for printing and postal monopolies make clear. Princes and city councils often worried about how to manage the production and circulation of information. By the late eighteenth century, the question of what kinds of information should be made available to the public was the subject of debate among writers and government officials in several countries. Periodicals received special attention because they offered a regular channel of communication with subjects but also posed the danger of encouraging ongoing criticism of institutions or policies.

Beyond Newspapers: Scientific and Literary Journals

In the German lands, a complex patchwork of political jurisdictions combined with high literacy led to a vibrant periodical press. As Jeremy Popkin has explained, by the end of the seventeenth century, newspapers had become common enough to be the subject of the first book-length celebration of the medium, Kaspar von Stieler's *The Pleasure and Utility of Newspapers* (1695). Stieler had worked as a court secretary, where his responsibilities included reading gazettes and diplomatic dispatches. He championed newspaper reading not only for statesmen and merchants, but also for landowners, clergy, teachers, soldiers, artisans, and literate women. Stieler thought all people had a natural curiosity to follow events. He remarked on the way individuals hurried to the printing shop or post office, impatient to learn the latest developments. But unlike most writers before him, Stieler saw periodical news as a positive development for people of various walks of life. To understand the world, he claimed, it wasn't enough to read history. One also needed newspapers to be well informed about the present.

The sense that periodicals enabled people to be up to date was not limited to the realm of politics and trade. The late seventeenth century saw the first scientific and literary journals, and their creators also highlighted the advantages of timely reports of new books and recent discoveries. The French *Journal des Savants* (Journal of the learned), created in 1665, announced that it would appear once a week "because things would become too dated if we waited a month or a year to talk about them." Some of the journal's prospective subscribers had also made it known that they would prefer short weekly installments to a copious annual volume that would lack "la grâce de la nouveauté" (the charm of novelty). Receiving each week's issue would be a pleasant diversion and would enable people to tune in to the latest conversations among the *curieux* of Europe. Still, like many subsequent journals, the *Journal des Savants* had continuous pagination so the weekly numbers could be bound into annual volumes with indexes to help readers locate information. Periodicals were a flexible *genre: they promoted the exchange of what was new while enabling readers to take stock of the accumulation of knowledge that each year was sure to bring. The destiny of many information-rich periodicals was thus to serve as a kind of reference book. For the same reason, political gazettes often had continuous pagination as well. Surviving collections of periodicals reveal that some readers indeed gathered individual numbers into bound volumes, made annotations in the margins (called *marginalia), and even created their own indexes to facilitate subsequent consultation, sometimes quite self-consciously turning newspapers and journals into material for the writing of history.

Interest in what was novel and timely and the desire to foster more regular communication of knowledge encouraged the creation of learned journals. By the time Pierre Bayle began to edit the *Nouvelles de la République des Lettres* (News of the Republic of Letters) in 1684, he anticipated the objection that there were already too many journals. Why start another? In response, Bayle insisted that journals could complement each other by covering different subjects and even by providing different reviews of the same book. Over the next century, learned journals were set up in many places, often in connection with academies or *learned societies, from London and Paris to Copenhagen and Stockholm, Berlin, Saint Petersburg, and Philadelphia.

Learned journals emphasized the benefits of timeliness and periodicity, and like other periodicals they were embedded in correspondence networks. Journals were often consciously envisioned as a public form of correspondence that enabled collaboration and debate among geographically dispersed individuals. Beginning with the *Philosophical Transactions of the Royal Society* in 1665, learned societies used their journals not just to communicate their proceedings, but also to create a forum for further observations and criticism of published reports. General-interest magazines and journals, which developed in parallel to learned journals, also encouraged reader submissions. The *Mercure Galant* (Courtly mercury), which began publication in 1672 and became the *Mercure de France* (French mercury) in 1724, contained literary and cultural news, court gossip, discussion of etiquette and fashion, obituaries, and other material. As an early example of a society journal, it was to inspire many European magazines during the eighteenth century. The *Gentleman's Magazine*, established in London in 1731, was the first monthly miscellany to use the word *magazine* in its title. Its many imitators in Britain and abroad published a mix of essays, poetry, book reviews, and information of various kinds, from mortality figures and observations on the weather to reports of inventions and short digests of political news.

We should not assume a sharp distinction between the kinds of information of interest to members of the *Republic of Letters and those of interest to the mercantile and political elite. These worlds overlapped. In England, as Miles Ogborn has pointed out, many of the virtuosi who orbited around the Royal Society owned stocks in overseas trading companies. They frequented the same coffeehouses as merchants; they read price currents as well as foreign gazettes and learned journals. The development of political arithmetic—the systematic study of economic and demographic data—depended on the networks of the Royal Society and its counterparts in other countries. But it is hard to imagine early scholars of population change such as John Graunt and William Petty being able to treat numbers of births and deaths as data *series* if these numbers hadn't first been collected and published in a weekly *serial*, namely the bills of mortality. A fellow of the Royal Society named John Houghton was also an apothecary and dealer of colonial imports such as tea, coffee, and chocolate; his shop was very close to the Royal Exchange. Much like the Royal Society itself, Houghton used print to disseminate useful information. The title of his weekly periodical, *A Collection for the Improvement of Husbandry and Trade* (1692–1703), indicated that his goal was to provide readers with information that was useful to them (such as explaining how the Bank of England worked) while actively promoting agricultural improvements and the growth of trade.

A clever use of correspondence to facilitate the exchange of information was developed by John Dunton and his associates on the *Athenian Mercury*, which appeared twice a week in London from 1690 to 1697. Dunton's journal was nominally produced by the Athenian Society, which consisted of Dunton and a few friends in a coffeehouse answering letters from readers. Women and men alike were encouraged to ask the Athenian Society questions on a range of subjects, from religion and family life to history, economics, and science. In 1693, Dunton also launched the first journal explicitly aimed at women, the *Ladies' Mercury*, but it only lasted four weeks. Yet the success of the *Athenian Mercury* confirmed readers' curiosity about everyday phenomena and their desire to interact through the medium of a periodical.

Although most subsequent journals did not imitate the question-and-answer format developed by the *Athenian Mercury*, reader submissions remained central. The *Spectator* (1711–12), produced in London by Joseph Addison and Richard Steele, encouraged readers to send in queries and observations. Addison and Steele printed some of these and used others as the basis for their own essays on social, economic, and cultural topics. The *Spectator* spawned numerous reprintings in bound volumes and imitations in French, German, Dutch, Swedish, Russian, and other languages. Such essay-based periodicals could be seen as privileging comment and informed opinion rather than information per se, but it should be remembered that readers turned to them not only for essays, poems, and book reviews, but also for numerical information such as the prices of goods, estimates of state budgets, the relative size of European armies and navies, and casualty figures in a century of almost incessant warfare.

A good example of the connections between correspondence networks, periodical publishing, and information exchange can be seen in a newspaper genre that flourished in France in the second half of the eighteenth century known as the *affiches*. (They are called *affiches* because they usually appeared with some variation of the title *annonces, affiches, et avis*, but they should not be confused with posters, which are also called *affiches* in French.) Because the official *Gazette de France* had a monopoly on political news, the affiches largely eschewed politics. But as Elizabeth Andrews Bond has shown, these periodicals were crucial vectors for the exchange of practical information and should be seen as counterparts to loftier enlightenment projects such as Diderot and D'Alembert's *Encyclopédie* (Encyclopedia) (1751–72). In addition to official notices, advertisements, and market news, the affiches gave significant space to correspondence. Readers were encouraged to make queries or contribute observations on practical issues of health, nutrition, agriculture, manufacturing, architecture, astronomy, and botany, among other subjects. Most of the contributors were anonymous, and they represented a range of backgrounds, though scientists and doctors wrote more than clergymen, lawyers, or artists (see figure 7.3).

The affiches appeared in many provincial towns, and it is not surprising that one was also set up in the increasingly prosperous sugar colony of Saint Domingue in the 1760s. The affiches catered mainly to local subscribers and advertisers, but they were embedded in wider correspondence networks, and the way publications in different regions reprinted each other's articles allowed the information provided by readers to circulate. The affiches therefore had something in common with other vectors of enlightenment, such as provincial academies, learned journals, and *encyclopedias: they embodied the ideal that knowledge could be known and that its circulation was beneficial to society. The affiches are also a good example of how correspondence and printed periodicals reinforced each other, enabling individuals to share information and discuss its reliability and significance. Readers of the affiches

FIGURE 7.3. A page from the weekly *Affiches* published in Toulouse with notices advertising property, books, and a young clergyman seeking employment as a tutor. Bibliothèque municipale de Toulouse.

debated the efficacy of various medical remedies, agricultural techniques, and methods for repairing things.

The affiches were different from question-and-answer journals such as the *Athenian Mercury* or essay-based journals like the *Spectator*, but all three types of periodical catered to the intellectual curiosity of readers and created new habits of information exchange. Editors and readers exploited key features of periodicals—their regular interval of publication and their dependence on the post—to engage in an ongoing quest for beneficial and reliable information. The role of periodicals in the spread of enlightenment can be traced back to the first scientific journals of the seventeenth century through to the essay contests that appeared in the journals of learned academies and general-interest monthlies such as the *Berlinische Monatsschrift* (Berlin monthly), which published Immanuel Kant's essay "What Is Enlightenment?" in 1784. As Kant admitted in a letter to Johann Gottlieb Fichte in 1797, "My choice of the journal *Berliner Blätter* (Berlin pages) [which succeeded the *Monatsschrift*] for my recent essays will make sense to you and to my other philosophizing friends . . . for in that paper I can get my work published and evaluated most quickly, since, like a political newspaper, it comes out almost as promptly as the mail allows" (Maliks, 4). The affiches were more focused on commerce than the periodicals Kant contributed to, but their editors believed that economic progress depended on the timely circulation of information of all sorts, not just the prices of goods and the arrival of ships.

The Rise of Advertising

Advertising was crucial to the survival of many kinds of periodicals, not just trade-oriented ones like the affiches. By the end of the eighteenth century, advertising was viewed by publishers as essential to the profitability of most newspapers and quite a few journals. The process began in the Dutch Republic, where the weekly corantos of the 1620s already contained advertisements. Most of the early advertisements were for books sold by local printers and booksellers, but by the 1650s they included notices for goods and services paid for by private individuals and public money (such as notices for wanted criminals or information about market days). In France, Théophraste Renaudot, whose Paris-based *Gazette* had a monopoly on political news starting in the 1630s, also had an advertising business protected by privilege, the *bureau d'adresse*, which facilitated communication between employers and job seekers and between buyers and sellers of goods. Notices were posted at the office and printed in a periodical that was separate from the *Gazette*. The *Gazette* itself rarely included advertisements, but unofficial gazettes and journals, which were tolerated beginning in the late eighteenth century (more on this later), sometimes contained ads for luxury products, property, and employment.

The rise of advertising was particularly noticeable in Britain and its American colonies. In the 1650s, some English news periodicals contained ads, but the real growth came after 1695, when parliamentary legislation governing the printing trades was allowed to lapse, putting an end to prepublication censorship and the monopoly of the Stationers' Company. The extent to which 1695 marked a turning point in book publishing remains a matter of debate (big London booksellers continued to dominate), but it was clearly a boon for the periodical press. As newspapers and journals proliferated after 1695, publishers turned to advertising as an important source of revenue in addition to subscriptions. Even for essay-based journals like the *Spectator*, paid notices were a crucial source of profits. Although the *Spectator* had a print run of about three thousand copies a day, Joseph Addison suggested that the readership was twenty times that number, since copies were consulted in coffeehouses and shared among friends. As Pettegree has suggested, the multiplier of twenty readers per copy also represented a bit of salesmanship on the part of Addison, who no doubt had advertisers in mind when he boasted about the *Spectator*'s reach. The *City Mercury*, a paper that contained only advertisements, gave a similar figure of twenty readers per copy back in the 1690s, and clearly the goal was to attract further paid notices.

The printer of the *New York Gazette* in 1769 referred to advertisements as "the Life of a Paper," a claim that would have been confirmed by his counterparts on both sides of the Atlantic. By the mid-eighteenth century, the daily and triweekly London newspapers devoted between one-third and three-quarters of their space to ads. Newspapers in English towns outside London were published weekly, but they were similarly reliant on advertisements as the main source of profits. By the 1760s, a type of newspaper that for lack of a better term might be called the "commercial advertiser" dominated English-language journalism on both sides of the Atlantic. Its mix of news paragraphs, essays, letters to the printer, accounts of trials, excerpts from books and pamphlets, and shipping news made it harder for separate essay-based journals to survive after midcentury. The daily, triweekly, and weekly commercial advertisers became the primary means of selling timely information and an important venue for political debate.

Many English-language papers had the word *advertiser* in their title, though it should be remembered that advertisement, news, and information were related terms at the time. In Samuel Johnson's English *Dictionary* (1755), the verb *to advertise* was defined as "to inform another; to give intelligence." *Advertiser*, meanwhile, referred both to "he that gives intelligence or information" and to "the paper in which advertisements are published." Paid advertisements became crucial to most English-language newspapers, which were not protected by privileges (as many gazettes on the continent still were during the eighteenth century) and which catered largely to the mercantile and political elite. Even the European gazettes, however, tended to contain at least a few ads—often for luxury goods and property—and in the Netherlands and Germany, advertising was very present in the newspapers of the period. The German *Intelligenzblätter* (intelligencers), which existed in roughly two hundred cities by the end of the eighteenth century, were advertising-based newspapers.

An Expanding Network

The eighteenth century witnessed tremendous growth in the periodical press, but there were important differences by country and region. In England, the lapse of press licensing in 1695 was the result of disagreements among members of Parliament about how best to regulate the press. At the time it was assumed that some sort of legislation was forthcoming, and many bills were proposed over the next fifteen years. But developments in state finance such as the creation of the Bank of England and the national debt, coupled with an increasingly interventionist foreign policy under William III (r. 1689–1702) and his successors, created a situation in which the circulation of timely information about trade, finance, and diplomacy became crucial. In hindsight it is clear that the lapse of licensing in 1695 enabled the growth of the newspaper press, but it also affected literary and scientific periodicals. It was now possible for private commercial ventures to compete with officially sanctioned publications such as the *London Gazette* and the *Philosophical Transactions of the Royal Society*.

In addition to ending prepublication censorship, the lapse of licensing in 1695 cancelled the Stationers' Company's monopoly and the restriction that presses had to be located in London. Soon printers began to set up in provincial towns, and most of them started a newspaper. By 1750 there were over forty provincial newspapers, and by 1800 there were over seventy. In addition to reports collected locally and reader submissions, the provincial papers reproduced material from London periodicals, and, over time, their counterparts in other towns. Copying enabled news and commentary to spread. Although Britain enacted its first *copyright statute in 1710, the law did not explicitly protect writings in newspapers and periodicals. Moreover, the business and culture of news publishing that developed in Britain and its American colonies worked against the very idea of literary property for time-sensitive information and commentary on recent events. Newspapers actively relied on each other, and news collection was a casual affair. Most newspapers did not have paid reporters. In addition to material produced by the printer or editor, they relied on reader submissions, the occasional letter from a correspondent in another city or country, and articles copied from other publications. The main expenses were paper, printing labor, and government taxation in the form of stamp and advertising duties; together these dwarfed the occasional amounts spent paying a writer or collector of news. Copying was common, and it was generally viewed in positive terms as a means of spreading information and facilitating commentary.

Britain, like the Netherlands, enjoyed a relatively open information culture. Reports of political decisions, fiscal policy, and the progress of wars were laid before the reading public and vigorously debated in clubs and coffeehouses. Such an information culture reflected the interconnected nature of business and government. In the Netherlands, merchants and trading companies had long enjoyed influence in politics. In Britain, the parliamentary system and the mechanisms of state finance that developed in the late seventeenth and early eighteenth centuries made the regular circulation of information increasingly important. Reports of trade and finance were not just of interest to merchants and brokers; they were essential to the political fortunes of the state in an age of imperial rivalry and warfare on an entirely new scale. Investment in the national debt by individuals and the large trading companies meant that financial news was inherently political and political news had financial stakes. It seems inconceivable that the British monarchy could have borrowed the money it needed to finance the increasingly costly wars of the eighteenth century without allowing its activities to be publicized and scrutinized by those who were loaning money to the state.

And yet certain activities remained closed to public scrutiny longer than others. By the 1720s, British writers were developing arguments about the role of newspapers in monitoring the actions of politicians and sounding the alarm against corruption and abuse of power. But coverage of Parliament was for many decades restricted to manuscript accounts and veiled and somewhat speculative reports, such as Samuel Johnson's imaginative accounts of proceedings "in the Senate of Lilliput," which appeared in the *Gentleman's Magazine* in the early 1740s. In the early 1770s, actions by John Wilkes and several printers finally led both Houses of Parliament to accept regular newspaper coverage of proceedings. By this time some members of Parliament argued that the public had a right to be informed of proceedings, but others complained that printed accounts distorted their words, a problem exacerbated by the way newspapers spun accounts to serve political ends. Still, open coverage of Parliament in the 1770s was a turning point as important as the end of press licensing in 1695. The statements of government ministers and members of Parliament were henceforth reported, scrutinized, and criticized in the press. Gazettes and journals in other cities and countries copied and translated from London newspapers, allowing debates in Westminster to reverberate throughout Europe and North America, sometimes with effects that the speakers could never have imagined.

The Seven Years' War (1756–63) was a watershed for the periodical press across Europe and the Atlantic World. In France, the government adopted a new policy in the late 1750s whereby gazettes and journals printed outside France were admitted into the French royal post on favorable terms. The monarchy realized that a two-tiered information system, with an official channel represented by the *Gazette de France* and an unofficial one represented by the foreign gazettes, provided a means of monitoring criticism while allowing elites to have access to information they wanted. Rather than relying on pre-publication censorship, the monarchy kept these foreign gazettes within bounds by threatening to deny them access to the French post, which would have cut them off from most of their subscribers. The result of this policy was a much richer variety of information coming into France from Amsterdam, Leiden, The Hague, the free cities of Hamburg and Altona, the Prussian enclave of Cleves, the Duchy of Zweibrücken, and other communication hubs. The international French-language gazettes had a reputation for providing reliable information. Between 1760 and 1789 about sixty of them were produced outside of France aimed primarily at a French audience. In addition, a number of European cities saw the creation of French-language gazettes and scientific and literary journals for the local population. These include Berlin, Cologne, Vienna, Warsaw, Copenhagen, Stockholm, and St. Petersburg, not to mention the French colonies of Saint Domingue (which had a newspaper from 1764), Martinique (1766), Grenada (1779), Guadeloupe (1785), and Francophone areas in British Canada (Quebec City had a bilingual gazette from 1764).

The growth was even more spectacular in the German lands. By the end of the eighteenth century, there were perhaps two hundred newspapers in Germany, most of them serving an average of between five hundred and one thousand subscribers, although some had much higher figures. The best-selling newspaper in the world around 1800 was the *Hamburgischer Unpartheyischer Correspondent* (Hamburg impartial correspondent), which printed an estimated thirty-six thousand copies per issue. But there was much more to the German periodical press than newspapers. Scholars estimate that as many as three thousand new journals were created in the second half of the eighteenth century. Many of them were short-lived, and print runs varied from a few hundred copies to a couple thousand. There were journals covering literature, theater, economics, and various branches of science, but the most common were general-interest periodicals containing a mix of practical information, news of scientific discoveries, historical essays, medical advice, and literary pieces. These journals were like miniature encyclopedias delivered in regular installments. Rolf Engelsing has referred to a "reading revolution" in eighteenth-century Germany, a term that he used to describe a general shift from "intensive reading" of a small number of books to "extensive reading" of a wide range of printed sources. Though the thesis is debatable—many readers read both extensively and intensively—it is clear that many contemporaries discussed what they perceived to be an "addiction" or "mania" for reading; they worried about how new reading habits affected individuals and society as a whole.

In the Italian peninsula, Milan and Florence joined Venice as the most important information centers. The Florence-based *Notizie del Mondo* (News of the world) achieved the relatively high circulation of seventeen hundred at a time when most Italian papers were selling only a few hundred copies. By translating reports from English, French, and German sources, gazettes and journals in the Italian peninsula kept elites fairly well informed despite the existence of censorship in many regions. As in the German lands, political fragmentation meant that press policies varied. In Lombardy and Tuscany, the struggle between the ruling Habsburg family and the church for control of culture led to a freer atmosphere than in Rome, where the *Diario ordinario di Roma* (Journal of Rome) was the official voice of the papal government. In some places, such as Naples, governments saw periodicals as a means of building consensus rather than a force of opposition that needed to be suppressed.

This point holds for other areas of Europe as well. Many periodicals were linked to government initiatives. The development of the press and the cultivation of public opinion was often promoted by authorities, rather than always developing in opposition to the state. In many places, the printing trades were not as tightly controlled as the official decrees might make us think. Frederick the Great of Prussia (r. 1740–86) approved more than forty decrees regulating the press during his forty-six-year reign, but enforcement was uneven, and many authors were affiliated with the regime in some way, making it hard to distinguish between official and unofficial publications. In Russia, the Muscovite rulers repeatedly modified their policies with respect to newspapers in an effort to maximize the benefits for local and imperial administration. Under Catherine the Great (r. 1762–96), there was an expansion of the periodical press that included essay journals on the model of the *Spectator* as well as the creation of official newspapers in Moscow, St. Petersburg, and the provincial capitals.

According to some writers at the time, the circulation of periodicals helped to foster a cosmopolitan public. In 1764, Cesare Beccaria published an essay on the role of periodicals in the Italian journal *Il Caffè* (The coffeehouse). He claimed that gazettes and journals "make us citizens of Europe; they produce a continuous commerce among the different nations and destroy that diffidence and contempt with which isolated nations look on foreign ones. Everything in Europe tends to become closer and more similar, and there is a stronger tendency towards equality than in the past" (Barker and Burrows, 209). Beccaria saw periodicals as promoting social and political harmony, but many of his contemporaries expressed a more pessimistic view. The words *journaliste* and *gazzettiere* often had negative connotations, and the diaries and letters of the period contain plenty of remarks about the unreliable and suspect nature of reports circulating in the periodical press. But such remarks constitute further evidence of engagement with timely information and the mutually reinforcing nature of periodicals and correspondence.

During the American Revolutionary War, the London press became the primary source of information for newspapers and journals across Europe. The American politician John Adams, who spent several years on diplomatic mission in Paris, described the London press as "an engine, by which everything is scattered all over the world" (September 8, 1783). He noted that an article inserted in a London newspaper was bound to be reprinted in other countries. As Adams observed, the key to understanding how information could be manipulated was the way newspapers and gazettes copied and translated from each other, enabling false and exaggerated reports to spread. "Stock jobbers are not the only people, who employ a set of scribblers to invent and publish falsehoods for their peculiar purposes," Adams wrote. "British and French, as well as other politicians, entertain these fabricators of paragraphs, who are stationed about in the various cities of Europe, and take up each other's productions in such a manner, that no sooner does a paragraph appear in a French, Dutch or English paper, but it is immediately seized on, and reprinted in all the others" (June 24, 1783). Adams lamented that some of these dubious paragraphs were being reprinted in American newspapers. Periodicals were interdependent, and they were open to anonymous submissions, for better and for worse.

Informing Revolution

The French Revolution was another major turning point for the periodical press, leading to an explosion of newspapers in Paris and the French provinces and a corresponding decline of the international French-language gazettes. Between the storming of the Bastille in 1789 and Napoleon's coup d'état in 1799, more than two thousand different newspapers appeared in France. The French Revolutionary and Napoleonic Wars also led to the tightening of press controls in countries across Europe and the Atlantic World; these reactions revealed the extent to which newspapers and periodicals were seen as channels for the spread of revolutionary ideas. In 1793, as he tracked the news from his home city of Montreal, a young writer named Henri-Antoine Mézière explained, "The French Revolution has electrified the Canadians and enlightened them more about their natural rights in a year than a century of reading would have been able to do. . . . Every day, they assemble in the towns in small groups, tell each other about the latest news received, rejoice with each other when the news is favorable to the French and grieve (but not desperately) when it is unfavorable" (Taylor, 105–6). But for Mézière, newspapers and correspondence were not only a means of learning about distant events. They enabled the spread of revolutionary consciousness. An anonymous piece in the *Montreal Gazette* that Jordan E. Taylor plausibly attributes to Mézière dismissed the importance of writings by Locke and Voltaire and stressed how international commerce led to "reciprocal communications" through the press that enabled the "genius of information" to awaken people to the fundamental "rights of man."

Mézière was not alone in highlighting the connection between information circulation and democratic revolution. Thomas Jefferson famously declared in 1787 that if given the choice between government without newspapers and newspapers without government he would choose the latter. But the quote should not be taken out of context. Jefferson was describing the potential of newspapers to create an informed citizenry essential to a functioning democracy. For him, this could work only if everyone had access to newspapers and was able to read them. In 1792, the US Congress put its full support behind this idea by creating a new postal system that encouraged the circulation of newspapers (which were charged a very low postage rate) and subsidized the process of news gathering itself (printers were allowed to exchange their newspapers free through the mail, thereby treating news as a shared resource). By 1800, there were over 230 newspapers in the United States, including more than twenty dailies, compared to a total of approximately thirty-five newspapers in 1783.

On the other side of the Atlantic, amid debates over press regulations in revolutionary France, the deputy J.P.F. Duplantin made explicit why periodicals were the democratic medium par excellence: they enabled ideas to spread quickly among a large and dispersed population. According to Duplantin, "separate writings" such as books were slower to produce and less affordable. Citizens needed the "rapid and secure communication that only periodicals can offer, to circulate opinion and enlightenment from the center to the periphery and to bring them constantly together from each point to the opposing extremes, just as in the biological world the fluids necessary for life carry the essentials of survival to all parts of the human and vegetable body" (Barker and Burrows, 189). Then as now, circulation was the most common metaphor for the movement of information, and it was the fact that periodicals were faster to produce and cheaper than books that made them seem like the ideal medium. Periodicity also encouraged ongoing discussion. The openness to reader contributions was not inherent to periodical publishing, but its development makes perfect sense given the strong links between postal correspondence and periodicals.

The remarks by writers and political leaders quoted above represent idealized views of newspapers and their role in democratic societies. But it is important not to assume too sharp a distinction between political news and other kinds of information that appeared in periodicals and circulated through the post. Philosophical debates took place in journals; newspapers and magazines contained summaries and excerpts from books. News, science, literature, and practical information mingled in the pages of periodicals. The Dutch patriot movement, constitutional changes in Poland, Thomas Paine's *Common Sense*, the American Declaration of Independence, the debates in the French National Assembly and the colonial assemblies of Saint Domingue and Martinique—all this and more was printed in local periodicals, which traveled outward to be copied and translated into other periodicals, acquiring new meanings for readers in new contexts.

A 2017 forum in the online journal *Age of Revolutions* entitled "(In)forming Revolution" provides a sample of how specialists of the late eighteenth and early nineteenth centuries have recently been studying the role of information in varied and sophisticated ways. Examining not only Europe and North America but also the Caribbean, South America, Eastern Europe, Japan, and

China, the contributors to this forum explore the agents and media of information as well as the different ways individuals collected, exchanged, manipulated, and recorded information. They note the role played by newspapers and other periodicals, but they also stress the importance of oral and written communication, not only for places where printing was nonexistent but also in cases where the speed of events made other modes of communication paramount.

Many places in the Americas and the Caribbean lacked locally printed periodicals, but publications sent by mail were available to those who could afford the postage and subscriptions. In colonial Venezuela, as Cristina Soriano has shown, between 1770 and 1810 roughly one in five postmortem inventories of private libraries included newspapers and other periodicals, with some elites owning lengthy runs of periodicals in Spanish, French, and English that had been printed on one side or the other of the Atlantic. Official gazettes appeared in colonial Mexico (1722), Peru (1743), and Guatemala (1729–31, revived 1794). At the end of the eighteenth century, journals such as the Lima-based *Mercurio peruano* (Peruvian mercury) (1791–94) offered a forum for discussion of economics, politics, and science.

But in most places the freshest information spread orally or through manuscript newsletters. Several of the islands in the French Antilles had presses with officially sanctioned newspapers, but reports of the French and Haitian revolutions mostly spread by word of mouth. The momentous nature of events combined with delays in receiving verified reports allowed speculation and rumor to thrive. Cuba had an official newspaper in Havana starting in 1790, and the authorities tried to stop the spread of reports about slave insurrections on neighboring islands, but the news still arrived via sailors and French refugees from Saint Domingue. In India, the English-language and vernacular Indian press built on what C. A. Bayly referred to as the "information order" of the Mughal Empire, which included manuscript newsletters, running spies, and newsmongers in the bazaars who provided grist for the rumor mill. These modes of communication provided a base on which the vernacular Indian press would build in the mid- to late nineteenth century.

Conclusion

This chapter has highlighted the commercialization of timely information in periodical form as an important development of the early modern period. Clearly, any history of the age of enlightenment and revolutions would be incomplete without also considering information that was not perceived as time sensitive—from dictionaries and encyclopedias to recipe books and instruction manuals, not to mention government surveys and scholarly investigations. Much information was never published, either because it was held secret or because it was more effectively transmitted orally. In addition, timeliness is a relative concept. Information about medical remedies or the latest farming techniques had a sense of urgency for people suffering from illness or in need of a good harvest; such information may have been entirely new to them even if it was not to others. Periodicals contained a lot of practical information of these sorts, and some encyclopedias were published as serials, with subscribers receiving installments that they could later bind into volumes. As noted above, many journals had continuous pagination so that each new issue—fresh in itself—could be preserved and consulted for years to come. The editors of magazines and reviews often described their compilations as materials for future historians.

So not all information published in periodicals was time sensitive, and periodicals were not the only source of information. Print did not reduce the importance of writing or conversation. Periodicals did not eliminate the value of other kinds of informational works—maps, charts, and reference books are obvious counterexamples to any such claim. Even in places where printed newspapers gained prominence at a relatively early date, such as the Low Countries, the German lands, and England, they did not reduce the importance of receiving information through private letters. Indeed, correspondence was the lifeblood of the periodical press. Without it, most newspapers and journals could never have existed. They simply would not have had a reliable means of obtaining information to include in their periodicals. Political newspapers, scientific journals, literary reviews, and price currents—all depended on what came in the mail. Many periodicals invited readers to submit queries or information; they relied extensively on such unpaid submissions. In some places, printers doubled as postmasters; in others, postal officials acted as wholesaling agents for periodicals. Printed publications traveled through the post alongside letters, and many people enclosed them in their correspondence, sometimes commenting on the authenticity or significance of the information they contained. The proliferation of periodicals and the commercialization of timely information went hand in glove, and together they were central to the information cultures that developed in many places during this period. The process was neither inevitable nor linear, but it transformed the way people shared, analyzed, and commented on information about the world around them.

Further Reading

Adams Papers Digital Edition; Kenneth J. Arrow, *The Rate and Direction of Inventive Activity*, 1962; Bryan Banks, ed., "(In)forming Revolution: Information Networks in the Age of Revolutions," *Age of Revolutions* (online journal), 2017; Hannah Barker and Simon Burrows, eds., *Press, Politics and the Public Sphere in Europe and North America*, 2002; Christopher A. Bayly, *Empire and Information*, 1996; Elizabeth Andrews Bond, *The Writing Public*, 2021; Samuel Butler, *Characters and Passages from Notebooks*, edited by A. R. Waller, 1908; Robert Darnton and Daniel Roche, eds., *Revolution in Print*, 1989; Brendan Dooley, ed., *The Dissemination of News and the Emergence of Contemporaneity in Early Modern Europe*, 2010; Brendan Dooley and Sabrina A. Baron, eds., *The Politics of Information in Early Modern Europe*, 2001; Ada Ferrer, *Freedom's Mirror*, 2014; Richard R. John and Jonathan Silberstein-Loeb, eds., *Making News*, 2015; Reidar Maliks, *Kant's Politics in Context*, 2014; John McCusker, "The Demise of Distance: The Business Press and the Origins of the Information Revolution in the Early Modern Atlantic World," *American Historical Review* 110, no. 2 (2005): 295–321; Miles Ogborn, *Indian Ink*, 2007; Andrew Pettegree, *The Invention of News*, 2014; Jeremy Popkin, "New Perspectives on the Early Modern European Press," in *News and Politics in Early Modern Europe*, edited by Joop W. Koopmans, 2005; Joad Raymond and Noah Moxham, eds., *News Networks in Early Modern Europe*, 2016; Will Slauter, "The Paragraph as Information Technology: How News Traveled in the Eighteenth-Century Atlantic World," *Annales HSS* [English edition] 67, no. 2 (2012): 253–78; idem, *Who Owns the News?*, 2019; C. John Sommerville, *The News Revolution in England*, 1996; Cristina Soriano, *Tides of Revolution*, 2018; Jordan E. Taylor, *Misinformation Nation*, 2022; Michiel van Groesen, *Amsterdam's Atlantic*, 2016.

8

Documents, Empire, and Capitalism in the Nineteenth Century

Craig Robertson

IN 1859, SARAH REMOND, a thirty-five-year-old "freed person of color," arrived in London with a US passport. In the two years she spent in London Remond delivered more than forty-five antislavery lectures as she studied for a degree at Bedford College for Ladies. Neither of these activities attracted the attention of newspapers in the United States. The press paid attention to Remond only once a US official in London refused to recognize her passport.

The controversy around the issuance and rejection of Remond's passport that I outline below brings to the foreground important aspects of the debate generated by the belief that governments and organizations needed to collect a large range of information that could be easily circulated, at times on a global scale. Concerns included the reliability of information, the conditions necessary for the production of accurate information, who controlled the production of information, and whom information was used to control. The struggle to use, and make sense of, documents amid these issues and in response to significant changes in scale provides the contours of the history of information addressed in this chapter.

To start with a controversy over a passport is a deliberate decision intended to emphasize that many of the anxieties that states and organizations had about information in this period came from the belief that it was necessary to know more about individuals combined with a heightened concern about the effectiveness of the documents used to circulate information. In this context the function of passports was beginning to change. Reflecting a dominant existing perception of a passport as a letter of introduction, the *New York Times* approvingly reprinted Remond's letter of complaint and endorsed her right to have a passport before commenting that the official "seems to have been instructed to take his cue from the face of the bearer rather than from that of the document." Someone's face and appearance (and documents) could be seen, and represented as information, in very different ways. The notary public in the United States who prepared Remond's passport application described her hair, complexion, and face as "dark"; in contrast the official in London described her as "dark mullato with wooly hair and negro features." Seeing her as "Black" identified Remond as someone who prior to the Fourteenth Amendment could not be a US citizen and therefore was not entitled to a passport.

So how did Remond come to have a US passport? In a world of few documents and limited administrative reach, the State Department still had to trust the honesty of local officials and applicants to provide the information required to issue a passport. Department memos noted an expectation that a person applying for a passport would state if they were a "person of color." Remond's passport application did not mention her race but it identified her as a citizen of Salem, Massachusetts, where she lived. Her application took the form of a handwritten affidavit, not the recently introduced preprinted application form; it would be several more decades before the State Department started returning applications that did not use the form. When it arrived in Washington, DC, one of the twenty-eight officials and clerks who made up the State Department would have read it; some of those clerks and officials had "passports" listed as one of their designated responsibilities. These duties likely included signing a passport in the name of the secretary of state. This practice became a necessity in the 1850s when the department issued forty thousand passports, which totaled twice the number issued in the previous five decades.

In an era when passports were not required, but with the number of passports increasing and the definition of citizenship becoming even more contested, the State Department, along with its officials abroad, sought to establish the passport as a certificate of citizenship. This was a work in progress in 1859. In arguing that Remond should be able to carry a passport, the *New York Times* saw no necessary connection between the document and citizenship. Because it did not see a passport as an identification document, it presented a passport in its traditional role as a letter requesting protection and, therefore, something a woman traveling alone definitely needed. The *New York Times*'s stance could also be a case of playing dumb in support of abolitionism.

In the middle of the nineteenth century, while uncommon, it was definitely not unusual for a Black person to apply for and receive a passport. Beginning in the 1830s, the abolitionist movement had strategically used US passport applications to further its cause. These applications attempted to exploit not only a lax federal administrative structure, but also loose passport laws and differences between federal and state citizenship laws. Remond (coming from a family steeped in abolitionism) deliberately sought to manipulate the still-developing relationship between information and documents, particularly the understanding of documents as "objective" evidence of *"facts" such as citizenship. This faith in official documentation was particularly prone to manipulation with documents used to constitute an ever-expanding administrative space.

The controversy around Remond's passport highlights a still-developing relationship between information and documents, between authority and evidence, which is the focus of this chapter. The nineteenth century saw the aspirations to collect information according to an increasingly pervasive faith in centralized standards and practices paired with a lack of administrative reach. This lack manifested itself in the need to rely on information generated by the work of people who often had at best an ambiguous relationship to a centralized authority, be it a government or a large business concern. As the Remond incident illustrates, this could easily mean that an individual's opinion or action could subvert or trump the authority of a document as a record or evidence. This could be done intentionally or through a failure to understand the logic of the procedures used to produce official documents.

In response to problems of scale, people acting in the name of institutions created documents to collect, collate, and circulate information. These documents needed to be easily stored and retrieved, but more importantly they had to be able to move information across territories and into different social and cultural contexts. The intention was that the circulation of documents would contribute to the work of governing or "managing" (the profession of management emerged out of larger US business enterprises at the end of the nineteenth century). However, this goal involved a struggle over the status of documented information that illustrated not only an attempt to establish a new set of relationships between information and people, but also a historically specific understanding of information as instrumental. In this period, neither the form of information presented in documents nor the authority of documents was a given. A focus on the details of forms, structures, and systems that mediated people's interactions with information makes this apparent. Or put another way, this chapter explores a period when the people that institutions empowered to organize the production and circulation of information acted with little or no knowledge of the previous attempts to articulate paper and information in the name of control discussed in previous chapters. Therefore, in some cases, they reinvented the proverbial wheel in the form of previously used classification techniques and filing systems, while in other cases they invented new technologies and systems to record and store documented information.

This discussion begins with an examination of documents that governments introduced to manage and control the movement of people. Then the broader structures introduced to support these documents are analyzed by widening the focus to consider the articulation of an ideal relationship between documents and information in the extension and maintenance of empires and an examination of how that relationship played out in practice. The final section of the chapter moves away from empire and government as a site of organization to a more localized effort to produce and organize relatively large amounts of information: the nineteenth-century reorganization of capitalism on a corporate scale.

Global Mobility

The example of Sarah Remond illustrates the informality of state practices when it came to collecting and presenting the information used to identify individuals in the middle of the nineteenth century. This would change as the long century wound its way to an end in 1914. The outbreak of World War I is often presented as the end of an era of freedom of movement in the Western world, signaled in part by the emergence of a global passport regime. However, the impetus and groundwork for the standardization of official identification practices emerged in a nineteenth-century world increasingly on the move.

An expanding industrial economy (within a developing international state system) provided the context for the movement of people. Readily available ideas to make sense of this changing world included the rights of individuals, national identity, and the free movement of goods, money, and people. Racism often mediated the contradictions between these liberal ideas and governing practices; this was definitely the case when it came to the establishment of a global system of migrant identification between the 1880s and 1910s.

In the decades after Remond's encounter in London, migration around the world increased dramatically. In the middle of the nineteenth century the annual number of migrants totaled fewer than half a million people. By the late 1890s, this had increased to 1.5 million people, and in the first decade of the twentieth century it doubled to more than three million migrants a year (as the arguments in this chapter about record keeping make clear, such numbers should be taken as a rough approximation). Much of this migration involved a transatlantic journey; however, a considerable number of migrants came from East Asia and South Asia (and there were large circulations of people within those regions). Racism directed at Chinese and Indian migrants produced many of the principles and techniques central to the development of modern border control, particularly the use of documents to create stable *individual* identities increasingly articulated to *nation*-states. Managing mobility and difference was central to the work of empires, which functioned both as political orders grounded in difference and as systems that depended on mobility, whether of slaves, indentured or free workers, soldiers and police, or administrators.

The attempt to manage the movement of particular people centered on documents that used standardized categories to present the information governments believed necessary to identify a person. However, officials at borders greeted the introduction of such documents with indifference at best. To function as identity documents to police migration the papers presented to officials had to be recognizable as official and authentic, and be accurately and easily linked to the bearer. Officials assigned to ports of entry did not trust the papers to do any of these things. Instead they continued to believe that as they were the people on the spot, their own face-to-face judgment was all that was necessary to verify identity.

Identifying Chinese and Indian Migrants

In 1882, the federal government halted the migration of Chinese laborers to the United States. Documents were issued to Chinese exempt from exclusion. These included merchants and their families, college students, travelers, and laborers already resident in the United States; women could enter only if married to a man in one of the exempt categories. The complicated set of documents used to manage the exemptions from the act was the first of its kind at US borders. However, officials trusted neither the "Chinamen" who presented the documents, nor the absent official they did not know whose signature authorized the document. Therefore, customs officers charged with enforcing the act tended to prioritize evidence from what was present: the body and appearance of the person who presented the document. The bodies of Chinese who claimed to be merchants were read to provide evidence of labor: calluses, sunburnt legs or arms, the size and shape of fingers, clothing, and demeanor were all accepted as proof that the applicant was a laborer pretending to be a merchant. The legal system was less certain about the use of this evidence. Chinese denied entry did enjoy some success in using courts to overturn decisions. However, most reversals occurred because of the presentation of other proof; judges upheld personal appearance as an acceptable criterion equal in value to documents.

Similar identification practices were followed at seaports in the South African colonies. In the early twentieth century the estimated forty thousand Indians in the southwest Indian Ocean area were quickly perceived as a threat to local trade and culture and became subject to immigration bans and restrictions. In the Cape Colony, Indian boys under eighteen years old whose fathers already lived in the Cape constituted an exempt category from such bans. As the historian Uma Dhupelia-Mesthrie shows, officials favored visual evidence centered on the applicant's body to verify a claim under this exemption. There were efforts to make this reading of bodies produce more "objective" evidence that the applicant was less than eighteen years old and related to the person who presented himself as his father; officials introduced formal medical exams centered on teeth, genitals, and body hair, along with x-rays (similar techniques and technologies were used at other borders around the world). When papers were used to assess the identity of a boy, they tended to be statements that officials had taken from interviews with resident Indians who claimed to be related to the applicant. Although Cape officials introduced a requirement for documents issued by Indian authorities, they tended to ignore the document when an Indian boy presented it upon arrival in Cape Town.

Significant changes to the US enforcement of Chinese exclusion changed the role of documents in border control. As the historian Adam McKeown argues, this first attempt to systematically manage a range of identities through documents produced a template that would be used to manage the movement of Chinese migrants (and other targeted populations) around the world. The shift away from personal appearance toward a faith in documents occurred partly in response to the number of Chinese who claimed exemption through familial relationships. This increased faith in documents occurred during a period in which the US government began to adopt increasingly more rigorous administrative structures and methods.

In the 1890s, the arrival of a Chinese person generated a handful of pages that as a "file" offered little if any assessment of the evidence used to approve or deny entry. Officials did not use standardized forms or a standardized set of questions. However, by the end of the 1920s, the arrival of a Chinese person generated a case file that usually contained a single-spaced typed manuscript of around thirty pages and a multipage explanation of the decision to admit or exclude an individual. Standardized forms and an improved indexing system indicate that officials created files in anticipation of future use. These files were prepared on the assumption that someone with no previous knowledge of a case could read it and understand it. Cross-referencing and the production of monthly reports in triplicate illustrated a new understanding of accountability and predictability intended to prevent individual discretion from affecting cases.

Equally significant were attempts to better control the work of US officials who issued documents in China. This involved the standardization of methods of investigation and the introduction of comprehensive filing systems to improve communication among officials. The former was relatively successful; the latter proved harder to maintain. In both cases the increased use of documents sought to relocate US officials and Chinese into a centralized administrative network where procedures would produce reliable identification. The local knowledge previously used to verify identities was now considered unreliable. In this scenario, local Chinese were considered "interested parties," in contrast to the administratively neutral US government officials whose endeavors to enforce the act apparently did not come with any "interest."

Therefore, in practice the identity of "merchant" originated in the criteria outlined in Chinese exclusion law and policy, not the social networks within which Chinese lived. Policy directed officials not to use evidence and witnesses provided by Chinese. The application centered on an interview. In recording his impressions on a standardized form, the US official determined the applicant's fate. These impressions became "objective" owing to the belief that the categories in standardized forms would discipline officials to ignore other information outside the document, especially personal bias. This paper-based procedure was intended to produce a fixed identity constituted by information comprehensible to multiple officials and institutions, regardless of their location. The claim to objectivity through procedure masked the political and racist worldview that created Chinese exclusion.

The increased use of documents did not decrease the problems associated with policing migration. Problems arose from both the failure and the success of documentary systems. In the newly created Union of South Africa, corruption scandals in 1915 revealed officials who worked with Indian agents to exploit the system (or lack of system) for profit. These officials removed or destroyed existing documents and provided Indian immigration brokers with blank forms to create false identities. If thumbprints were required, some officials ensured they were deliberately smudged to make them ineffective or had them added to fraudulent documents after arrival. The subsequent reforms in record keeping, salaries, and fingerprint detection, along with the standardizing of rules across departments, did result in more efficient identification of migrants at seaports. However, as the historian Andrew MacDonald shows, an unintended consequence of the success of the reforms was to shift the site of illegal entry to land borders. A market in fake identity permits developed along South Africa's eastern frontier with Mozambique and Swaziland. Networks of local officials on either side of the border colluded with Indian merchant houses of the coastal West, syndicates from Madeira, and "tropical" African migrants to move permits, people, and money across the region.

While corruption occurred among US officials, the main impediment to enforcing Chinese exclusion came from the successful attempt to limit the information used to verify identity to categories outlined in law and policy. The reality that the documentary system produced the identity used to manage the movement of Chinese resulted in the creation of "paper families." These "families" came into existence when on his return to China a man exempt from exclusion through US citizenship sold his status as a "father" to men who could then enter the United States as the child of a citizen. Frequently the "children" received coaching to prepare them for their arrival in the United States, in addition to fraudulent papers.

In response, officials doubled down on their reliance on documents. They closely read documents to find inconsistencies between statements and comments from a "son" with those already recorded in the files of other "family" members. A system developed in which inspectors were usually able to cross-check an applicant's answers with those provided in previous interviews with people identified as family members, even if those interviews had taken place several years earlier and at another immigration office. In a typical case, twelve additional files would be pulled for comparison. However, despite these attempts at verification, in 1950 it was estimated that nearly one-quarter of Chinese in the United States had illegally entered as "paper children."

Travelers and Passports

At the same time governments sought to use documents to better police the movement of migrants, passport laws were removed or simply lay dormant in most European states; South American countries introduced constitutions that granted citizens and foreigners a right to travel without passports. This changed with the outbreak of World War I, when emergency wartime passport laws were introduced to secure borders. In the 1920s, under the guidance of the League of Nations, these temporary passport laws became a permanent system used to manage the movement of individuals through a system of nation-states.

In a society that had frequently relied on local reputation to identify someone, the idea that a government could replace respectability with an impersonal document seemed preposterous. Therefore, some people viewed a required passport not as a privilege, but as a symbol of eroding trust between citizens and their government. The request for supporting documents in an application over and above someone's statement underscored this. To demand information in the form of official documents instead of accepting a person's word was understood not as evidence of identity but as evidence a government did not trust you, that government officials considered you dishonest and untrustworthy.

This criticism of passports came from a particular part of the population, those who could afford to travel for leisure. This was a group whose class and race meant in most cases they had not been placed in a position where documents had been required to prove their identity. Although the origin of the passport as a required document to systematically manage people's mobility is attributed to regulations introduced during the French Revolution, most people who traveled through Europe for leisure did not encounter a demand for passports. In the nineteenth century, the European states that followed the French model used passports (along with permits and registration systems) to control mobility, criminality, and military desertion. This practice arose particularly as paupers and vagabonds became the target of regulations introduced in response to the perceived danger of unemployment and the fear of revolution in the 1830s and 1840s. However, by the middle of the century, passports largely ceased to play a role in the policing of mobility.

Therefore, required passports introduced a wider population to the world of identification documents. The anxiety and concerns this created are captured in the reaction to the use of photographs on passports, which was part of the so-called passport nuisance. From an official point of view, a photograph promised to erase bias from the identification process. Prior to photographs most passports contained a written physical description usually in the form of a list to which people added single-word descriptions, for example, Face: Oval; Nose: Roman. Officials came to see this as too subjective. Some applicants immediately considered this representation of identity to be unnecessary and inappropriate. The belief that a physical description presented an affront to a person spoke to the lingering idea of the passport as a letter. This association conveyed a very different understanding of identity and a person's relationship to information. From this point of view identity was not a thing to be reduced to a handful of categories generated by administrative procedure. Rejecting such an approach, an English novelist ignored the list of descriptors and completed his passport application describing himself as "of melancholic appearance."

However, when photographs supplemented a written description on a passport a photographer had to follow a set of guidelines to produce an image that officials considered objective evidence. These included photographing the subject in natural light looking straight at the camera in front of a light background. This photographic style, borrowed from criminal identification, sought to eliminate context to bring to the foreground information that could be seen as neutral or objective. This version of photographic accuracy clashed with the understanding of photographic truth shared by most applicants. Borrowed from portrait painting, this "truth" depended on a dark background with a three-quarter pose often including the whole body, not just the face. The clashing of these two different styles resulted in claims that a passport photograph in its similarity to a rogues' gallery image misrepresented a person as a criminal.

The idea that someone did not look like their passport photograph captured the anxiety at the core of the resistance to passports that emerged in small pockets in the early twentieth century. For critics of the passport a fundamental misidentification existed at the very core of this purported identity document. It appeared the government had created an identity separate from a person's sense of self; an honest, trustworthy person had become an object of inquiry.

Concerned citizens considered the government was telling people who they were. In fact this was precisely what was happening. Well-to-do-travelers were encountering the consequences of faith in the purportedly objective information that officials used to identify migrants. Instead of using information from existing social networks, states chose to use administrative procedures to reduce personal identity to the minimum information necessary to know and recognize an individual for the purposes of governing. Therefore, accuracy and reliability created an identity that individuals had to measure up to when they presented a passport.

Governing Empires

The difficulties officials encountered using documents to manage the movement of migrants is one example of the problems associated with using paperwork to govern over distance. With its investment in extending markets, developing forms of government, and promoting specific ideas of progress and civilization, empire involved an intensification of the problems that distance created for rule within states. In addition, empire in the nineteenth century experienced both continuity and change. The century saw the fragmentation of the Ottoman and Chinese Empires and the decline in imperial power of Spain, Portugal, and the Netherlands along with the rise of Japan and the United States. Britain, France, Germany (after unification in 1871), and Italy became the major European imperial powers. The end of the nineteenth century also saw the beginnings of a marked increase in struggle against empire that would intensify throughout the twentieth century. At the same time, the exploitative economic possibilities that drove empire increased as the use of the steamship and steam locomotive made it easier to move goods over long distances (aided by the opening of the Suez Canal). Along with the telegraph these technological developments also increased the speed at which information could travel.

In this context, despite the problems it generated, the systematic collection of documentary information became a key part of how governments responded to the ambitions and uncertainties that nineteenth-century empire raised. As we have seen in the attempts to identify migrants, the introduction of documents did not guarantee control. However, this did not lessen the desire to ground government in the use of documents to name, constitute, and know people and things. This mode of governing produced information that was "local" in the sense it was about specific people and places and "local" in the sense that it was collected and classified in a specific place by specific people. However, if it was to be used to make sense of events and to determine actions, local information had to be mediated through the worldview of the officials located in an empire's administrative center.

Attempts to establish the reliable participation of officials from the imperial power or local community became a critical part of administrative practices. The role of local information and colonial intermediaries emphasizes that the colony and the "metropole" need to be considered together, not isolated as two discrete entities. Increasingly historians have come to view empires as structures always in process, not static units. From this perspective, whether subordinate agents actually ran the show, or whether the pervasiveness of "investigative modalities" limited the role of local workers, is a subject of debate among historians. Aspects of that debate are evident in the following discussion. However, the focus remains on the changing role and status of information in the administration of empires (and reflecting the historiographical bias toward the dominant empire of the period, it centers on the British Empire). To look at imperial documents from this point of view is to recognize their role in a system of control, not simply as a means to transmit information; it emphasizes the centrality of information to the maintenance of imperial rule in colonies. However, while it is important to recognize that empire was conceived through a desire for order, this aspiration did not result in total control; failure and improvisation marked the administration of empire.

Changing Local Information Practices

Imperial governing involved claims to authority that depended on articulating localities and local knowledge to the centralized authority of the empire. In the late 1840s, the Dutch government introduced a policy to manage schooling in the Dutch Indies (present-day Indonesia) that made clear the status of the local in the production and circulation of knowledge. The policy sought to have Dutch parents send their sons to be educated in the Netherlands. Dutch Indies schools that were run on European principles could educate Dutch children, but colonial officials believed a child's education would be more successful if it took place in the Netherlands, where students would receive an authentic Dutch education. In addition, officials expressed confidence that anything the children learned about the Dutch Indies would be presented within a framework that recognized the superiority of European-based knowledge. The policy resulted in a series of protests from the Dutch population who had decided to stay in the colony. They viewed it as a challenge to their status as full Dutch citizens and a bid to intervene in their familial relationships.

The use of paperwork and specific documents provided a more common mechanism to relocate local information production and transmission within the dominant ideas of imperial powers. However, in contrast to the Dutch policy, this attempt to articulate local knowledge occurred in a documentary network that connected colonial territories and imperial centers. Procedure and documents were assumed to provide a structure to bring "native" ways of knowing fully into the imperial project. The use of paper involved challenges to existing knowledge practices such as storage and memory. This resulted in an instrumental mode of information that became critical to governing an empire. Officials privileged information produced through procedures instead of knowledge based in the expertise and experience of a "knower."

Nineteenth-century encounters with local cultures that did not use paper make explicit the importance of the materiality of paper to changes in administrative authority. Paper enabled the movement of information across space rather than the transmission of knowledge over time; it was less dependent on the presence and singular expertise of authoritative figures. This becomes apparent in the colonization of New Zealand in the nineteenth century.

Maori cultural authority depended on embodied knowledge embedded within rituals. Knowledge was stored in a range of objects. Made by skilled experts from wood, bone, or *pounamu* (jade), these objects while durable were relatively scarce. Because the knowledge contained in the objects required expertise and rank to be accessed, this system ensured the reproduction of traditional authority and protected *tapu* knowledge.

The paper that the British used to facilitate communication in New Zealand and within the empire offered a new mode of storing information to Maori communities. In the far south of New Zealand, Kāi Tahu Whānui (the primary Indigenous community in the region) used whatever paper became available to create new archives of information. Unlike in British society, the look of paper did not affect its authority and status in Maori culture. Instead, Kāi Tahu were attracted by paper as a new disembodied and therefore more portable way to store knowledge.

As the historian Tony Ballantyne argues, the experiences of Kāi Tahu suggest the arrival of paper in New Zealand transformed Maori cultural practices and political traditions. Print undeniably diluted traditional power, but it did ensure that elements of old knowledge would survive the violence and ruptures of colonialism. Kāi Tahu did not abandon traditional cultural frameworks such as *whakapapa* (genealogy). Letter writing, diaries, minutes from meetings, and whakapapa books gave these frameworks a new archival form. Paper also facilitated engagement with European colonizers. Literate Maori attempted to navigate the paper world that supported the colonial order, and they used paper as a key medium to fight against the inequities of colonial rule.

Another example from the British Empire illustrates how intentional attempts to train people to work with information within the developing paper world of empire challenged existing conceptions of memory and knowledge. As the historian Bhavani Raman shows, from the mid-eighteenth century the presence of missionary schools offered an alternative role for memory in education that initiated a new function for written language in colonial India.

In southern India, existing Tamil *tinnai* (verandah) schools used texts to cultivate memory as a mode of learning. Memorization was taught as a skill to discipline the mind and senses. Regarded in this way, memory training assisted in the development of students' capacity to understand and comprehend their social world. In contrast, schools run by missionaries came to emphasize memorization as a way to teach the more practical skills of writing and reading. Brought back to England, a version of this technique known as the "monitorial system" became popular as an effective way to teach reading and writing to poor children in the first half of the nineteenth century; Quaker networks spread it to North America.

In the Tamil region this technique helped reorient schools toward lessons that would give their upper-caste students the skills required to work in the offices of mission stations and the East India Company. This alternative school model introduced an Anglo *vernacular that prized and restricted English to upper classes. Transcription and dictation became common as schools became places to learn to read and write rather than sites to hone intellectual prowess. The source of lessons became prose, not poetry, as the focus of education turned to mastering the written language, not the spoken language. In textbooks and lessons the teaching of grammar was frequently subsumed under lessons that treated reading and writing as clerical skills.

Establishing the Authority of Documents

Missionary education fits in a wider structure that became the source of a legitimation crisis for British rule in India. Beginning in 1600, the East India Company had governed India through a royal charter that gave it a monopoly over British trade with India in return for customs revenue. At the turn of the nineteenth century, the East India Company introduced administrative reforms intended to make its records transparent and uniform. These changes were a product of parliamentary pressure following scandals and allegations of nepotism triggered by articles of impeachment against Warren Hastings, the first governor-general of Bengal. Hastings was acquitted, but in a trial that lasted seven years, the role of the East India Company in an expanding British Empire became a focus of public debates and political intervention.

The faith that written procedures would provide the transparency and uniformity needed to check abuses of power changed the administrative model the company used in India. This structure continued to depend on local offices overseen by a British collector. However, the documents produced in these offices now had to satisfy the evidentiary requirements of British courts whether they were intended for the British Parliament, company directors, shareholders in London, or colonial subjects. The assumption was that if these standards were followed any interested party would easily understand the information in the documents. Specific forms of attestation became critical to a document's status as transparent and self-evident and, therefore, not subject to local bias. This emphasis on procedures to verify company documents in India gave new status to acts of signing, stamping, and registering, in contrast to traditional practices that depended on the collective validation of people the community identified as respectable.

As in other instances, the attempt to create authority through new verification practices provided the means to challenge or manipulate that authority. The East India Company reforms instituted an administrative structure in which a British collector and judges supervised caste notables, village accountants, native revenue officers, and judicial men. The documents created to record transactions at this local level became subject to fraud based in the signatures and stamps used to verify documents. This fraud contributed to a system that proved to be wasteful and costly. However, instead of changing the conditions in which documents were produced, the official solution reduced documentary requirements for local workers. Company supervision continued, but minor local officials no longer had to maintain detailed records. This decreased the potential for fraud, but it also made supervision more difficult, with the result that abuses of power continued. Raman argues that although these changes did little to prevent abuse of power they did enhance the authority of documents. Put simply, fraud and corruption were no longer a problem of paperwork. Instead, they were attributed to "native duplicity." The response to this was to bring paperwork in as the solution rather than categorize it as the problem: complaints generated written documents and petitions.

Presenting Information

The early nineteenth-century debates over corruption in India also revealed the British Colonial Office lacked basic information, such as a list of the civil and military officials who held appointments throughout the empire. Although the Colonial Office was relatively small in size, a lack of staff to compile such lists was not the cause of its absence; the information necessary to make these lists did not exist in London. The knowledge that did arrive in London from its colonies usually took the form of correspondence. The lack of uniform content across these letters hindered any endeavor to control or envision the empire as a whole, or to make individual colonies legible as discrete entities. The historian Zoë Laidlaw argues that in the first half of the nineteenth century the desire to know the empire and colonies in this way saw the beginnings of a transition away from correspondence to more uniform and numerical-based reports.

An attempt to standardize annual reports from colonial officials produced documents that became known as "Blue Books." Separated from correspondence, these annual returns came to provide numerical information on revenue and expenditure, population, exports, and details of explorations. However, once in London, Blue Books were not used in any comprehensive way. The Colonial Office did not produce a digest of contents or publish information from the reports, nor did it circulate information from the Blue Books to other government bodies; it still lacked the administrative capacity and desire to use the reports for comparative analysis. While Blue Books remained largely unread, officials in London did read the descriptive report that a governor had to compile. Governors were reminded that they had to write these reports, not delegate them to junior officials, as was expected to be the case with the Blue Book.

The importance given to a descriptive report and the status of its author underscored the type of information the Colonial Office continued to value. This information took the form of the written words of people in positions of authority. The Colonial Office remained more comfortable dealing with correspondence from networks established via personal connections between senior London-based officials and administrators and other Englishmen known to the office.

The reliance on personal-based information ended in the late 1830s when an abrupt change in Colonial Office leadership resulted in a renewed effort to create a collection of information less dependent on specific individuals. A desire for transparent information that could be more easily examined reoriented the Colonial Office to the type of information found in Blue Books rather than in the reports that accompanied them. The new leadership sought greater centralization and control of information from the colonies with the belief that it would enable collation and comparison.

The use of numerical information to understand colonies and the empire existed alongside the recognition that this information was frequently inaccurate. Notably, officials circulated Robert Montgomery Martin's *Statistics of the Colonies of the British Empire* even though they knew it contained errors. The origin of the errors seemed to be evenly shared between Martin's transcriptions and the Blue Books he based his volume on. However, Martin's novel use of classifying, recording, and mapping made the book an attractive resource. For example, he included a tabular index and a statistical chart with a foldout sheet that used thirty categories to describe every British colony.

The use of numbers to describe the empire and the uniform presentation that statistical charts and tables offered were part of a shift away from a personal mode of information based in narrative and description. More and more the latter was viewed as a form of information that did not travel well. It was also information that did not enable comparison at a time when governing on a large scale was increasingly seen to require comparative thinking. This was the beginning of a mode of colonial governance and policy implementation that depended on structures of collection and categories of analysis based on an understanding that information should be transparent and therefore easily understood outside of the context in which it was produced.

Compiling Local Information: *Gazetteer and Census

In India, the change to prioritize numerical information picked up momentum in the second half of the nineteenth century when the British government took over colonial rule of India from the East India Company. This was a period during which concerns about security and the loyalty of the population began to replace revenue collection as the driving force behind the gathering of information. The Great Rebellion of 1857 was the catalyst for this. The focus on loyalty brought with it an investment in understanding people and culture to help explain the behavior of specific groups. As the historian Nicholas Dirks contends, British authorities increasingly believed that if they improved their knowledge of the social organization of India it would be easier to maintain social order; numbers could be analyzed and compared to suggest reasons for unrest. Specifically, this information could be directed toward military recruitment, policing, land settlement, and legal policy.

Reflecting the rise of comparative thinking in government, officials believed that if they could take local information and make comparisons across common categories "India" would reveal itself and become an object that could be governed more effectively. Various compendiums, notably manuals and gazetteers, became more important than collections of local information and texts. The key was a format that lent itself to consultation, not reading. Narrative descriptions and explanations were reduced in favor of numerical tables in the belief they allowed information to be more easily digested and compared. However, at the local level, reports and manuals still tended to mix discursive accounts with statistics.

In 1869, W. W. Hunter was appointed director-general of statistics to the government of India; eight years later he became director-general of gazetteers. The existence of these positions represented an attempt to centralize and systematize the collection of information. The goal was to create a single statistical account at the provincial level and then consolidate these provincial gazetteers into a single volume. Hunter was not tasked with collecting information but with coordinating information. His appointment as director-general of gazetteers occurred after he had produced the twenty-volume *Statistical Account of Bengal*. Other provincial gazetteer projects began to be published after 1881.

Hunter's early forays into statistical volumes drew heavily from an all-India census, which took place in 1871 and 1872 (the 1857 rebellion derailed an earlier census). This census built on methods used in previous tabulations. However, earlier efforts to enumerate people in specific territories had been part of the East India Company's goal to enhance revenue collection. The innovation in the early 1870s census came in the attempt to generate uniform procedures, standards, and categories for enumeration within the logic of a census.

Although the subsequent census in 1881 is viewed as much more successful, in both instances problems of definition and categorization thwarted the effort to compare and contrast information collected across India. Difficulties began with the choice of caste as the main organizational category. While this made sense within the orientalist ideas of hierarchy and race shared by British colonizers, it proved impossible to implement with any consensus in a census (as well as in gazetteers). Problems included the definition of specific castes and the consistent spelling of caste names. How to rank castes proved to be particularly fraught especially when officials chose to use the varna principle to determine ranks. Between 1871 and 1881 the number of castes identified in the census increased from 3,208 to 19,044, even though officials had decided to include only castes with more than one hundred thousand people. In 1891, occupation replaced caste as the main organizing category. However, with similar definitional issues and an intensification of ethnological interest in India, caste returned in 1901. Prior to the 1911 census, caste associations formed to petition to have their caste recognized and to contest their position in the official hierarchy; these petitions weighed in at 120 pounds. With the 1911 census it was decided to collect caste information but not classify castes by status.

In Egypt the nineteenth-century development of a census and the collection of vital statistics came directly from a military-based response to security needs and the need to maintain power. Although part of the Ottoman Empire, Egypt's somewhat independent governor, Mehmed Ali, sought to create a modern army to give him more power in his relationship with Istanbul. While he was not from a leading Istanbul household, Egyptian pressure had led to Ali (an Albanian military leader) being appointed in 1805 to restore Ottoman authority after Napoleon's unsuccessful occupation of Egypt. Ali's efforts to create an army of loyal Egyptian soldiers relied on the introduction of a medical and public health administration that provided the foundation for a system to update figures for the numbers of births and deaths and, in 1848, a national census.

The precensus attempts to monitor and police the population in the interests of conscription had centered on the bodies of potential soldiers. Officials rounded up peasants with ropes around their necks or tattooed peasants to make it easier to identify deserters. A registration system was introduced as another attempt to manage the local population. The registers recorded a person's name, physical description, village, and province. It was supplemented with a "passport" issued to people who moved from their home village.

Official concern about the health of soldiers accompanied these fears about desertion. The effort to limit the effect of disease similarly boosted the authority of experts, documents, and record keeping. A new medical school, founded in the late 1820s, trained doctors for the army. Graduating doctors also became involved in public hygiene programs that depended on the systematic collection of information. They worked on smallpox vaccination, enforced quarantine regulations, and established systems to help the police in murder cases. Trained midwives became instrumental in these programs and in the creation and implementation of a system to record births.

According to the historian Khaled Fahmy, the change to systematic record keeping had legal consequences unique within the Ottoman Empire. A legal system centered on public law was created separate from sharia courts and a focus on private law. This began as a system to target elite households. Drawing from the techniques applied to the military and public health, it introduced a documentary system to identify individuals that was distinct from the traditional system that relied on witnesses embedded in social networks. The public law system used to identify people outside of specific social relations introduced a category previously unknown in Egypt's legal system: the individual as an autonomous, isolated person.

Ali's actions in Egypt and the Ottoman Empire in the 1830s (including taking over the Sudan and Syria and his threatening gestures to Istanbul) caused the sultan to grant his family hereditary right to govern Egypt. The fraught relationship with Egypt and increasing economic subordination to European powers contributed to the belief in Istanbul that, as the Ottoman Empire fragmented and decreased in power, its stabilization required the centralization of power and the downplaying, or ignoring, of intermediaries. The resulting changes occurred as part of the Tanzimat ("Reorganization," 1839–71). This included a transformation of the sultan's scribal corps into something closer to a civil service or bureaucracy. A restructured Ministry of Foreign Affairs embraced specialization with a range of offices including the Translation Office, Foreign Correspondence Office, Free Military Press Office, and the Bureau of Nationality. Although consular and diplomatic services were also reorganized, the creation of empire-wide infrastructure often proved too challenging.

"Ethnographic" Information

The movement to numerical and statistical information evident in the census in India and Egypt did not signal the abandonment of the collection of more descriptive information. The ethnographical interest that saw caste maintain its organizational status in the Indian census produced a large body of written literature. For its advocates such literature was essential to interpreting the numbers presented in the census and gazetteers. This investment in what was becoming known as "anthropology" became important to the governing of a number of empires in the last quarter of the nineteenth century. French rule of Algeria provides one example.

From the 1880s, a series of administrative changes increased political ties between the colony of Algeria and France. Algeria had never been regarded as a colony for French settlement. It had been claimed from Ottoman North Africa in the 1830s in the context of domestic politics and power struggles with European states, not from any direct imperial drive. Following the fall of the Second Empire in 1870, French rule of Algeria became linked to the redefinition of empire within a republic, not a monarchy. At the same time that the secular Third Republic increasingly viewed Algerian Islam as a threat, the settler population (including not only French citizens, but also Italian, Maltese, Spanish, and Jewish settler groups) sought to claim Algeria as its own. In this context French officials sought information about Muslim groups with the goal of controlling them. The information took the form of systematically organized narratives. These publications provided the framework the French used to understand Algeria.

The published reports and books comprised narratives, analyses, and descriptions drawn from personal interactions. The historian George Trumbull argues that these interactions were interpreted as typical, that informants became archetypes, and that the authenticity of firsthand observation created "facts" that gave these descriptions the force of truth. Administrators with local language ability became critical to documenting events and social groups. Travelers and scholars also contributed to this literature. However, through logistical aid, its influence on publishing, and the work of colonial societies, the colonial state exerted a critical role in these nonstate publications.

Administrators persisted in writing books and reports as a sideline to their official work into the early twentieth century. They continued to base their expertise in participant observation and a belief in the authority of long-term studies' ability to synthesize and analyze information to make it useful for government. The systematic narrative writing about culture these efforts produced fits into the category of "ethnography." It was an implicit rejection of what administrators viewed as the superficial and limited expertise that questionnaires relied on and that the French authorities had begun to use in the mid-1890s. Surveys were introduced to complement field reports from administrators. Authorities sought statistical information, general descriptions, and photographs of each Sufi order. Questionnaires were produced to guide the collection of information, often completed by officials who lacked the networks of Indigenous informants and language skills of administrators. However, despite the concerns this raised for the colonial administrators steeped in claims to "participant observation," the survey provided the substance of an 1897 report the governor-general commissioned.

Capitalism and Information

The development of modern industrial enterprises provides another site from which to consider the specific relationship between paper, information, and decision-making processes that emerged in the nineteenth century. As with empire and government these new conditions tended to encourage more impersonal modes of information. However, this should not be read as a before-and-after narrative in which preindustrial financial dealings were solely personal, in contrast to the impersonal information industrial economics used to focus on productive investment and that determined credit decisions. Elements of the personal and impersonal existed in both periods.

Credit Networks

To loan money a lender has to decide if a borrower can be trusted. This depends on information. If the borrower is not part of a network of personal ties, another source of information is required, which introduces an impersonal element into the transaction. The relatively limited territory in which most financial dealings took place prior to the nineteenth century has fostered the belief that only personal knowledge underwrote the lending of money. However, from the middle of the eighteenth century, Parisian notaries were the main players in the city's long-term credit market. They functioned as intermediaries who mobilized capital. As the economic historians Philip Hoffman, Gilles Postel-Vinay, and Jean-Laurent Rosenthal argue, *notaries were at the center of a mode of borrowing that mixed the personal and impersonal. While the loans depended on a notary's personal knowledge of borrowers and lenders, the lack of a preexisting relationship between the borrower and lender lent the transaction an impersonal element.

In Paris notaries had begun as legal experts who could draw up papers covering a range of transactions involving property and other assets. However, because the law required them to keep copies of the documents they created, notaries maintained a detailed collection of information about their clients' wealth. It was this information that allowed them to arrange loans between their clients. Notaries could offer information that was more precise than public opinion. Lenders wanted the service of notaries on the assumption that they had evidence of the legitimacy of collateral being offered, for example knowing that the property being put up was not already mortgaged to other creditors.

At the turn of the nineteenth century, Parisian notaries annually brokered new loans for private borrowers and new debt for the state equivalent to the annual earnings of 750,000 day laborers. However, legal and administrative reforms soon made relevant information easier for lenders to access. A system that required real estate transactions and liens to be registered made public the information that used to be the preserve of notaries, which contributed to the rise of other intermediaries like banks. In the early 1840s, new legislation restricted the role of notaries in credit markets.

Credit Reporting

In the United States a challenge to the question of who to trust as a buyer or seller of goods occurred as nationally organized circuits of exchange and finance emerged in the first half of the nineteenth century. Strangers had always been part of local business interactions, but a more nationally focused market increased the potential opportunities to transact with strangers, which exposed the drawbacks of an understanding of trust limited to locally generated reputations. As the media historian Josh Lauer shows, the response to trading in a national market was an attempt to systematically collect local knowledge so it could be nationally circulated as information about an organization or individual's creditworthiness. By the 1920s, this provided the basis for a viable market in information bought and sold within business and financial communities.

In 1841, the businessman Lewis Tappan started a centralized subscription-based service to report on the creditworthiness of firms. In an era without financial statements and annual reports Tappan relied on local correspondents (usually unpaid lawyers) to supply information. In reporting on this new phenomenon, newspapers labeled credit reporters "spies" or "private detectives." Articles played up the acquisition of local knowledge as the collection of gossip from a businessman's family, friends, and domestic staff. As one early critic put it, for all intents and purposes credit reporting was "an organized system of espionage." The extent to which it was either systematic or espionage is debatable, but what is not up for debate is the fact that in the United States the history of documentary surveillance begins in the private sector, not in the actions of the federal government.

In the 1860s, the main commercial credit-reporting companies began to make significant changes in a bid to make their product more useful and appealing to existing and potential customers. Full-time credit reporters were hired to replace local correspondents, and a ratings system replaced descriptive entries. For credit companies a more abstract conception of creditworthiness not only solved the problem of understanding narrative reports, but also made it easier to present large amounts of information. A coded reference book published in 1868 contained information on 350,000 firms; an 1886 edition listed one million firms.

At the same time, organizations emerged to collect information on consumers. They also used alphanumeric *codes to signify relative creditworthiness. This information centered on establishing a person's character rather than listing income and property. Lauer argues that the creation of consumer credit reporting introduced the idea of a "financial identity," an impersonal, disembodied identity that could affect a person's social interactions.

The ongoing struggle to get information from merchants, the time and labor needed to produce reports, and an inability to stop subscribers sharing information with nonsubscribers combined to make consumer credit reporting a difficult way to make money. In an attempt to become a viable industry, consumer credit agencies sought to "modernize" their operations. In line with turn-of-the-century paperwork initiatives this meant standardization of application forms and record-keeping practices, as well as elaborate systems to code, update, and communicate information. Index cards became critical to organizing and storing the information used to identify creditworthiness. These new technologies and techniques in commercial paperwork had emerged to manage the increased volume of information generated when capitalism entered its corporate phase.

Corporate Management and Office Work

Modern industrial enterprises signaled a new alternative to businesses personally run by owners. This occurred when the scale of individual businesses increased. As part of the reaction to this change in scale a new set of organizational structures and techniques (at least new to business) became increasingly pervasive in the second half of the nineteenth century as "managers" arrived to oversee large-scale enterprises, eventually bringing with them the profession of "management." The United States became a global reference point for these developments; in 1913 the United States accounted for 36 percent of the world's industrial output, followed by Germany (16 percent) and Great Britain (14 percent).

The new business enterprises tended to take on a corporate form as production facilities were organized in response to technological changes and as manufacturing enterprises moved into purchasing and distribution through mergers and (what would now be called) vertical integration. The organizational structure had two main characteristics: distinct operating units and a hierarchy of full-time salaried executives to manage the units.

This structure was quickly presented as necessary to exploit the economies of scale and scope enabled by the deployment of changes in production, distribution, transportation, and communication. These changes increased the volume of economic activities to a point where the "visible hand" (of management) replaced the "invisible hand" (of the market); administrative coordination became more efficient and profitable than market coordination. This resulted in a demand for information on a scale not previously encountered in manufacturing and finance.

The new administrative structure placed operating decisions in the hands of managers; hence some historians have taken to calling these changes "managerial capitalism" instead of corporate capitalism or industrial capitalism. In the United States, management as a profession developed from the 1880s as engineers began to occupy many of the new management positions. The new profession advocated the gathering, handling, analyzing, and circulating of information as a way to better control production. The "machine" with its ideas of harmony and order became central to the idea of business as a managerial problem. This explicitly carried the assumption that all problems had technical solutions. The technocratic approach of early management provided the context for mechanical engineer Frederick Taylor's writings on factory management and equipment standardization, as well as his decision to emphasize the rationalization of labor when he promoted his program of scientific management.

However, while the techniques that belonged to management, especially Taylor's form of scientific management, are usually associated with the corporation and the factory, they did not need modern forms of capitalism to develop. The historian Caitlin Rosenthal shows that techniques akin to scientific management existed among American and West Indian slaveholders. On plantations there were hierarchies similar to the multidivisional form of the corporation, a standardization of accounts enabled a form of separation of ownership and management, and, most significantly, there was a commitment to the productivity analysis attributed to scientific management. In the case of the latter the regularity of picking records shows that regimented procedures for measurement of work existed on plantations and that this information when collected was recorded systematically. Plantation owners and scientific management proponents shared a mechanistic view of human labor underwritten by the belief that careful observation would reveal laws that could be used to extract the maximum amount of labor from workers; the information on the picking ability of individual slaves was put to work to determine how to improve the productivity of slaves and therefore the plantation.

In the last quarter of the nineteenth century the new discourse of "efficiency" became central to the articulation of these techniques and to ideas of productivity within industrial capitalism. While establishing maximum capacity and productivity for specific tasks and then using that as a baseline to assess individual workers remained the key, these ideas were articulated as part of a wider set of temporal anxieties. "Saving time" would become one of the major concerns of twentieth-century society as efficiency emerged as the goal not only of modern business but also of the economy and society in general.

However, efficiency was not only about reducing the time it took to complete a task. Efficiency in business also involved knowing what needed to be produced and when. As the business historian JoAnne Yates argues in *Control through Communication*, individual memory was replaced with "organizational memory." This went beyond monetary transactions and correspondence with distant places to facilitate the emergence of written internal communication. Planning became critical as day-to-day business increasingly viewed predicting the future as the path to profit. Information related to production, sales, finance, and accounting had to be coordinated to ensure that corporate capitalism fulfilled its promise to increase production and profit. Managers believed that information would provide the certainty that modern business required.

The quest for predictability transformed record keeping into an analytic exercise, not a descriptive one; this was part of a broader social turn to prediction as a path to certainty (or better managing uncertainty) that included crop estimates and weather forecasting. Cost accounting provides an important example of the rethinking of information and planning within finance. This new technique allowed management to compare and evaluate internal operations. By recording and classifying the costs associated with each aspect of production, cost accounting presented specific information intended to give management the ability to control and modify the production process.

While information became critical to realizing efficiency, the logics of efficiency also structured the production of information and, therefore, changed the way people encountered information. Similar in approach to managing labor, the aim was to break information apart into the smallest functional detail. The key was to do this in such a way that information could still be coordinated, that managers would not lose sight of the big picture.

As Yates shows, the application of principles of standardization to the production and circulation of information led to the increased use of standardized forms and the emergence of the memo. These documents arrived with the promise that impersonality would foster efficiency and enable control of large organizations. The memo eliminated wordy formalities associated with writing conventions to create an impersonal mode of writing centered on information as an easily identifiable unit.

The index card was another important information technology in this period. Tabulated information increasingly appeared on index cards that were stored in drawers and cabinets invented for library catalog cards. Cards were celebrated as part of a broader fetishizing of speed and a more specific desire for easy access to information. They became the home for information on sales, production statistics, and central accounts. The tables on cards became more complex as different techniques and technologies were used to make it easier to see specific information: notches, different colored metal tabs, and punched holes. The index card became the symbol of system. In the first decade of the twentieth century, *System: The Magazine of Business* began publishing in the United States. Almost every other page of the early volumes of *System* carried an illustration of an index card ruled to create a table to store information; on the rare occasion it was not a card it was a drawing of a ledger page. To apply "system" to shipping or insurance businesses, police records, a dentist's office, or a real estate office was to use specifically formatted cards. In the early decades of the twentieth century, as the volume of information increased in finance and insurance, another card would become increasingly important— the punch card, credited to Herman Hollerith, and celebrated for its use in processing the information collected in the 1890 US census.

The information work associated with these new technologies and techniques brought women into the office as clerical workers. In the United States in 1880 about 5 percent of clerical workers were women; in 1930, almost half of clerical workers were women. In the same period the number of employed adults who worked in offices increased from one in forty to one in twelve. A similar pattern occurred in offices throughout the Western world.

An articulation of cultural, social, and economic beliefs contributed to employers' conviction that women provided a competent and affordable supply of labor for new forms of office work. A belief in an innate feminine dexterity, exhibited in knitting and piano playing, aligned with the new technology and new specialization of work. This belief naturalized as feminine the tasks associated with paper and new office machines. When equipment like the typewriter, billing machines, and filing cabinets was exported from the United States, it arrived in countries gendered as something women should operate.

A woman was paid less than a man based on the assumption that she was not a household's primary income earner. The belief that work constituted a temporary phase in a woman's life between school and marriage resulted in women leaving or being fired upon marriage: a practice known as the "marriage bar." The extent to which employers actively used the marriage bar is unclear, but enforced or not, it successfully underwrote the association of women with jobs that required limited training and skill and little opportunity for advancement. Nonetheless, women wanted to be clerical workers. Newspapers and popular culture represented clerical work as one of the best employment options for women regardless of class: better working conditions than in a factory, the potential for better pay than teaching, and a job that allowed a woman to use her education.

Therefore, gender was critical to legitimating and naturalizing the introduction of a particular form of work in the office. In the modern office, men held positions that involved responsibility while women did routine work to assist men. This assistance took the form of working with information. This information and work fitted in the reorganization of capitalism instituted in response to increased production. Through a new mode of manual labor women recorded, produced, and circulated information. This created a more functional relationship to information in which feminine clerical work did not involve skills associated with knowledge of the business.

Conclusion

Throughout the nineteenth century the creation of order became one of the primary roles of information. The employment of women as clerical workers and the emergence of management as a profession occurred as part of the dramatic increase in the speed and volume of production known as the Industrial Revolution. This response constituted an attempt to create order by controlling production at this new scale. Through the influence of a group of men trained as engineers this became an effort to manage a distinct form of capitalism more efficiently. In the development, expansion, and contraction of empires, information also became critical to dreams of total order. Priority was given to information that could be used to know populations and individuals. It was assumed such information would make government more effective. This was information that would make populations and territories "legible." Colonial rulers became increasingly aware of the need for the information they collected to accurately represent "reality" and to be understood as such far from the colonial territory.

These aspirations to order were not benign. Government and business brought specific worldviews to their understandings of how to order the world. Corporations understood order through a set of technocratic ideas. In practice these ideas generated a specific form of control and power through making labor and information visible. Governments, in the creation and maintenance of empires, colonies, and national borders, used information to legitimate hierarchies based on race, religion, class, gender, and sexuality.

A specific conception of information served these aspirations to order. Framed by the scale of empire and corporations this was information that when compiled would stand in for the memory of individuals. This understanding of information suggests what would in the twentieth century be labeled a bureaucratic mode of information and organization, that is, a perception of information that enabled organizations to work beyond the capacities of individuals. Acknowledging the limitations of personal memory in the context of the scalar dynamics of the nineteenth century, the information governments and businesses sought became something that could be comprehended by anyone who read it. Information became distinct from knowledge through this claim to perspectival neutrality. This was not simply a turn to quantitative information, to statistics. It is better understood as information with an instrumental bias. Conceptualized in this way, information became something that could be processed, possessed, and exchanged. To be circulated information had to be less dependent on context. In the nineteenth century, this created an increased sensitivity to the role of documents as the sole source of context and therefore authority. Whether it took the form of an index card, a passport, or gazetteer page, paper was intended to support information so it could be read as self-evident. Paper as an object facilitated an understanding of information as a thing that existed separately from the person who created it. If paper was to fulfill this function the collection and production of information had to be centralized and made as uniform as possible. The goal was a manner of information production that privileged procedure over people. To that end, policies, technologies, and techniques were introduced to limit the discretion of the people who produced documents and those who read them. An important aspect of the nineteenth-century history of information was the attempt to forge a relationship between documents and information so that documents had the authority to make individuals known to the state or to represent their character to businesses, to allow for comparative thinking, and ultimately to make information understandable so it could be used for planning.

Further Reading

Tony Ballantyne, *Webs of Empire*, 2013; Christopher Bayly, *Empire and Information*, 1996; Antoinette Burton and Tony Ballantyne, *Empires and the Reach of the Global 1870–1945*, 2012; Bernard Cohn, *Colonialism and Its Forms of Knowledge*, 1996; Uma Dhupelia-Mesthrie, "False Fathers and False Sons: Immigration Officials in Cape Town, Documents and Verifying Minor Sons from India in the First Half of the Twentieth Century," *Kronos* 40, no. 1 (2014): 99–132; Nicholas Dirks, *Castes of Mind*, 2001; Khaled Fahmy, "Birth of the 'Secular' Individual: Medical and Legal Methods of Identification in Nineteenth-Century Egypt," in *Registration and Recognition: Documenting the Person in World History*, edited by Keith Breckenridge and Simon Szreter, 2012; Delphine Gardey, "Culture of Gender, Culture of Technology: The Gendering of Things in France's Office Spaces between 1890 and 1930," in *Cultures of Technology*, edited by Novotny Helga, 2006; Philip Hoffman, Gilles Postel-Vinay, and Jean-Laurent Rosenthal, "Information and Economic History: How the Credit Market in Old Regime Paris Forces Us to Rethink the Transition to Capitalism," *American Historical Review* 104, no. 1 (1999): 69–94; Zoë Laidlaw, *Colonial Connections 1815–45*, 2002; Estelle Lau, *Paper Families*, 2007; Josh Lauer, *Creditworthy*, 2017; Andrew MacDonald, "Forging the Frontiers: Travellers and Documents on the South Africa–Mozambique Border, 1890s–1940s," *Kronos* 40, no. 4 (2014): 154–77; Adam McKeown, *Melancholy Order*, 2011; Bhavani Raman, *Document Raj*, 2012; Craig Robertson, *The Passport in America*, 2010; Caitlin Rosenthal, *Accounting for Slavery*, 2018; Radhika Singh, "Passport, Ticket, and India-Rubber Stamp: The Problem of the Pauper Pilgrim in Colonial India c. 1882–1925," in *The Limits of British Colonial Control in South Asia: Spaces of Disorder in the Indian Ocean*, edited by Ashwini Tambe and Harald Fischer-Tine, 2008; George R. Trumbull IV, *An Empire of Facts*, 2009; Joanne Yates, *Control through Communication*, 1989.

9

Nineteenth-Century Media Technologies

Lisa Gitelman & Thomas S. Mullaney

TWO CONCEPTS EMERGED in the nineteenth century that were to prove essential to our present-day understanding of information. These were the concepts "media" and "technology." While it is commonplace today to apply the terms *media* (or *medium*) and *technology* anachronistically to earlier developments—such as in reference to Gutenberg's printing press—neither concept was available in its present configuration until the late nineteenth century, and putting the two together as we have in our chapter title would have been unimaginable until quite recently. Only after media technologies emerged explicitly as such would information take on its present characteristics as the relatively abstract entity it is, the alienable "content" that can move across contexts and that comes in discrete chunks like *bits or packets. In what follows we will offer a highly selective history of nineteenth-century media and the ways that communication technologies like telegraphy and photography helped to underwrite information as a matter of interest and concern to historical actors around the globe. As they joined existing and evolving methods of communication, telegraphy, photography, and other in-novations helped broadly to imply that *-graphy* (from the Greek *graphos* for writing) was relevant to information. Since the concept of information itself would remain emergent, however (as explored in subsequent chapters of this volume), we begin with a brief acknowledgment of the abstract terrain on which the concepts of media and technology would come to achieve their relevant force.

According to the literary scholar John Guillory, the concept of media that emerged in the nineteenth century had been wanted for some time, existing as a kind of gap in the Anglophone intellectual tradition as thinkers grappled with the characteristics of human communication as such. Whereas *media* and *medium* had long referred to intervening or intermediary entities—such as "filtering media" used to clarify solutions, or the "medium of gears" used to transmit motion within mechanical devices—the terms eventually came to refer to technical forms of communication: telegraphs, telephones, phonographs, and so on. Likewise, according to the historian Leo Marx, "technology" in its current sense arrived belatedly. Once used to designate a kind of knowledge—the useful or mechanic arts—the term eventually came to denote the cumulative accomplishment of that knowledge, redolent with assumptions about progress and the historical efficacy of innovation and industrial development. "Technology" thus became a dangerously sloppy concept in Marx's telling, the term too easily reified, its referent granted a seeming autonomy that would belie the complexity of actual objects and processes of modernization. The coincident latency of both concepts—their oddly belated necessity—ended as the keywords *media* and *technology* were adapted in relation to the social and cultural formations that they would come to designate. Crucial in the first instance was the proliferation of new technologies of communication, and crucial in the second were whole sociotechnical systems—like railroads—unprecedented in scale and complexity.

While telegraphs and other technical means of communication proved essential for the emergence of the media concept, the ground had already been softened by the philosophical tradition that Guillory explores. Thinkers within this tradition had variously come to appreciate writing as (what would eventually be called) a medium. Celebrations of letterpress printing by Francis Bacon and others, for instance, acknowledged print as a medium for writing. The growing familiarity of printed texts made nonprinted writing newly recognizable as manuscript. At the same time, Bacon and his contemporaries reckoned with the world's diverse writing systems in ways that helped to affirm writing as (what would eventually be called) a medium for thought. The so-called real character of Chinese was instructive in this regard. Chinese characters were "real" to European observers because they were thought to refer directly to ideas and entities themselves rather than referring first to the sounds of speech. It was a gross mischaracterization of Chinese if also an inspiration for John Wilkins's *cryptographic *Essay toward a Real Character and a Philosophical Language* (1668). In short, writing came to beg the concept of media, on the one hand as a sort of back-formation in light of printing, and on the other hand in speculative inquiries addressed to diverse writing systems. Thus it should come as no surprise that writing—broadly in the form of *-graphy*—would play a starring role in the conception of the media technologies that became essential to the developing notion of information in and after the nineteenth century. These media technologies were apprehended within and against structures and practices that they helped partly to reconstruct as and in terms of writing.

The first two -graphies warranting our attention in this context are telegraphy and photography. Etymologically these imply distance writing (tele-) and light writing (photo-). If both were somehow (like) writing, the former emphasizes a transmission function (writing *at a* distance), while the latter by contrast emphasizes a storage function (writing *with* light), telegraphs writing across space (like writing a letter and mailing it away) and photographs writing across time (like taking some notes to consult in the future). Both telegraphy and photography emerged in the late 1830s to become subjects of intense interest, celebrated in the decades that followed while also absorbing the attentions of inventors and entrepreneurs. Too easily reified then as now— telegraphy consolidated singularly as "the telegraph," for instance—neither ever existed in a stable form, as a single technical device or process. Each was instead an area of specialized inquiry and the site of ongoing aspiration and development, productive of variation at almost every turn—technical improvements, specialized applications, and new political economies—amid changing sociocultural landscapes around the world. Our account cannot encompass all of this variation. Instead, and in the interests of pursuing media technologies as groundwork for the emergent information concept, we focus first on telegraphy and photography as open questions of use. What functions were telegraphy and photography intended and then embraced to fulfill and in what contexts? How did the situations in which they were developed and deployed help to indicate the ways their functions were reimagined? Later we broach similar questions about additional media technologies that arrived on the scene beginning in the 1870s.

Telegraphy

Electronic communication was the subject of intense inquiry and experimentation starting in the 1830s. The electromagnetic telegraphs developed in Europe and the United States were understood to be improvements on earlier optical systems like the French *télégraphe* of Claude Chappe, which relied on visible signals passed laboriously along a line-of-sight chain of towers constructed for that purpose. Electromagnetic telegraphs by contrast promised communication over greater distances at unprecedented speeds, using that most modern if still mysterious power, electricity. British inventors William Cooke and Charles Wheatstone had railroad safety in mind when they patented their telegraph as an "Improvement in Giving Signals and Sounding Alarms in Distant Places" (1837), while an American inventor, Samuel Morse, was known for asserting that his telegraph would revolutionize the relay of "intelligence," a contemporary word for news used in a way that presaged "information." The devices and systems developed by these and other experimenters in the mid-nineteenth century all involved coded communication, so while the distance writing of telegraphy offered a novel encounter with transmission— instantaneously across wires—it also required a self-conscious encounter with *semiotics, as the *binary off/on of an electrical circuit was variously enrolled to produce a sequence of symbols within an invented system of signs that referred to linguistic equivalents. The improved *Morse code that was eventually adopted as an international standard in 1865 used sequences of dots and dashes to represent alphabetic characters and numerals 0 to 9.

As distance writing, electromagnetic telegraphy made a virtue of inscription. To that end, many telegraph-receiving devices produced printouts—the most desirable of these printing messages decoded into alphabetic characters—and specialized telegraphs were eventually adapted to print out market information on ticker tape. But by 1860 sending and receiving by sound had become a common telegraphic practice wherein skilled telegraph operators tapped out messages to each other and listened for the sequence and rhythm of clicks made by the receiving device. A message written out on paper by a customer was encoded on the fly, transmitted across the line, and decoded by an operator at the other end who had internalized the code sufficiently to translate dots and dashes also on the fly, writing out the corresponding words for delivery by messenger to the telegram's addressee. Thus the virtue of inscription morphed to imply the virtues of skilled labor across an extensive network infrastructure, and soon additional virtues of automaticity and efficiency took hold as institutions like the British Post Office and the monopolistic Western Union corporation helped to inspire innovations in multiplex telegraphy— sending more than one message at a time across a single wire—and other improvements. Though the word *information* was still seldom used in telegraphic practice, electromagnetic telegraphy represented a decisive, even a revolutionary step in the ongoing reconceptualization of communication. As the media theorist James Carey explains, the age-old identity of communication and transportation was at an end, since messages—effectively dematerialized as electronic signals—could finally be sent without being physically carried.

Telegraphy had many applications and effects. In the United States, where the first working telegraph line was completed in 1844, uptake by competitive private interests was swift and diverse. Two early ventures are especially suggestive in light of the future for information that lay ahead: the Associated Press, a wire service for New York newspapers, was founded in 1846, and the Chicago Board of Trade, an exchange for commodity futures, was founded in 1848. News agencies like the Associated Press would provide telegraphic reports to subscribing newspapers, helping to quicken the pace of the news cycle while intervening in the already intricate geographies of newsprint. Like the contemporary practice of reprinting snippets from other publications, printing telegraphic reports in metropolitan dailies helped to affirm the status of news as alienable content and abstract commodity, what the linguist Geoffrey Nunberg called the "morselized substance" of an informative press. Meanwhile financial exchanges like the Chicago Board of Trade would provide subscribing members with simultaneous access to telegraphic market data, helping to create a single market out of previously disconnected locales. As Carey elaborates, one result would be the displacement of speculation into the temporal dimension. Speculation had forever been a question of geography—guessing which local market would garner a better price, for instance—but now new financial markets arose in which the buying and selling of commodities like wheat was abstracted into the buying and selling of derivatives. These were financial instruments like wheat futures, which represented agreements to buy or sell a certain amount of wheat of a certain quality at a certain date in the future for a certain price. Investors effectively bet on prices across time, trading in futures rather than in bushels of wheat. Telegraphic market data was thus a new and abstract commodity that enabled further abstractions of the kind that enable finance capitalism.

The new technology fostered its own forms of anxiety as well. The shock of near-instantaneous communication—the very feature of telegraphy that proved its greatest asset to speculators, among others—was also, for some, the greatest cause for concern. In an era when mechanization and advanced industrialization were simultaneously objects of awe and terror, late nineteenth- and early twentieth-century society increasingly drew analogies between telegraphy and the human nervous system, imagining the world as an organism in which signals were transmitted at tremendous speeds from the "brain" (understood, in the West, as Western metropoles such as London and New York) to the "organs" and "limbs" (extra-urban outposts and non-Western peripheries). As an organism, it was thought, this increasingly global system might be susceptible to the same kinds of human ailments as those that featured increasingly in discussions of the industrial era: "panic" and "hysteria." For those who took part directly in the new technology, for example, new medical conditions were coined—such as "telegrapher's palsy" (involving the cramping of the hand as part of a nervous condition), a pathology of the industrial age that took its place in medical treatises alongside other neologisms such as "railway spine" and "traumatic neurasthenia."

Quickly adopted by railroads, newsmen, and brokers, telegraphy became essential for armies and empires. The 1860s in particular witnessed the accelerated expansion of modern colonialism and with it a rapid development of the global telegraphic network. In 1864, cables were laid in the Persian Gulf that, when connected to the existing landline system, put India into direct telegraphic connection with Europe. In 1870, a further rapid expansion saw cables laid from Suez to Aden and Bombay, and from Madras to Penang, Singapore, and Batavia. During this period, indeed, the expansion and maintenance of Western empire came to depend on telegraphy, just as the spread and governance of telegraphy relied on Western empire. From the Indian Mutinies of 1857–58, through the Anglo-Egyptian War of 1882, into the period of the Boer War (1899–1902), and beyond, the British Empire in particular increasingly depended on the communicative speed afforded by the new and growing network. In addition, the great cartographic enterprises of British and European empire—so pivotal to the modern imperial project—relied increasingly on techniques of trigonometric surveying that themselves relied on telegraphy (among other emergent and preexisting technologies) to carry out. Arguably no part of the British imperial map was of greater importance than India, where a full three-quarters of all British imperial subjects lived. It also served as a vital transmission node in the overland telegraphic link between Britain and the Far East. One gets a sense of the importance of this area by the speed with which telegraph cable was laid down. In February 1855, the "Electric Telegraph Department in India" opened; two short years later, India was home to just over forty-five hundred miles of telegraphic cable. Throughout the early history of this new communication technology, telegraphy and modern colonialism depended on one another in a tight-knit relationship.

Telegraphy's primary function, however, remained business. By 1865 telegraphy was a globalizing force, subject of the world's first multilateral organization—the International Telegraph Union—and of feverish investment and construction. Initial attempts at laying a transatlantic cable had failed, but by 1866 there were two in operation, and cables had crossed the Mediterranean, the Persian Gulf, and the Red Sea to connect Europe with Ottoman Turkey, Persia (Iran), and India. This was just a beginning. In the decades that followed a web of terrestrial and undersea cables established a global infrastructure for communication. Governments played a role—especially by granting concessions to cable companies—but the prime movers behind the construction and exploitation of this architecture were international cartels. Corporations capitalized largely in the West competed together to carve up global connectivity as effectively as the European imperial powers were carving up African territory into colonies. News agencies—the Associated Press, Reuters, Havas—internationalized, and multinational enterprise enjoyed an expanding marketplace. A similar global architecture and a similar global liberalism persist today, as fiber-optic cables for *internet transmissions follow many of the same routes as the original telegraph lines and are largely the purview of multinational corporations that operate in the contexts of multilateral associations for the adjudication of international standards.

While often viewed through the lens of its material infrastructure—submarine cables, gutta percha, transmission poles, and so forth—telegraphy was in equal measure a linguistic and semiotic infrastructure. At telegraphy's inception, the entrepreneurial Samuel Morse referred to the new invention as "the American telegraph" and, even more intimately, "my telegraph." Even as Morse eagerly promoted the technology in Russia, western and southern Europe, the Ottoman Empire, Japan, Egypt, and parts of the African continent, the telegraph code on which it was based remained fundamentally connected to the Latin alphabet and the English language—that is, to the fabric of Morse's linguistic world. With the short "dot," the long "dash," and code sequences ranging primarily from one to four units in length, the code was originally designed to accommodate thirty discrete units: just sufficient to encompass the twenty-six English letters, with four code spaces remaining. Essential symbols—such as Arabic numerals and a select few punctuation marks—could then be relegated to the less efficient realm of five-unit code sequences (later expanded to the even less efficient six-unit sequences in "Continental Morse").

While the code was ideally suited to handle English, the same could not be said for other languages—even alphabetic ones. With its thirty letters, German bumped up against the limits of the code's capacity, while French and its multiplicity of accented letters spilled out beyond it. Nevertheless, such Anglocentrism was further reinforced by the International Telegraphic Union in its original list of signifiers permitted for telegraphic transmission. At the ITU conference in Vienna in 1868, the collection of acceptable symbols was confined to the twenty-six unaccented letters of the English language, the ten Arabic numerals, and a small group of sixteen symbols (being the period, comma, semicolon, colon, question mark, exclamation point, apostrophe, cross, hyphen, e-acute [é], fraction bar, equal sign, left parenthesis, right parenthesis, ampersand, and guillemet or quotation mark). The expansion of telegraphy's authorized list of transmittable symbols was an extremely conservative and slow affair, moreover. It was not until 1875, for example, that the St. Petersburg conference of the ITU finally expanded the original list of twenty-six letters to include a twenty-seventh: the accented "e" (é), now no longer sequestered to the specialized list of "signes de ponctuation et autres" (punctuation marks and other signs). The conference further stipulated that, for those using Morse code, it would now be possible to transmit six other special, accented symbols: Ä, Á, Å, Ñ, Ö, and Ü. It was not until the London conference of 1903, almost two decades later, that this supplemental list of accented letters was granted admission into the "standard" semiotic repertoire.

The history of Chinese telegraphy is particularly illustrative of the limits of Morse, and the challenges faced when extending this code to writing systems that it was not originally designed to handle. In 1871, the growing network of telegraphic communication reached the shores of the Qing Empire, with a single line opened between Shanghai and Hong Kong in April of that year. Carried out by two foreign companies—the Great Northern Telegraph Company of Denmark and the Eastern Extension A&C Telegraph Company of the United Kingdom—the installation of this line marked the initial step in the construction of an empire- and then nationwide communications web, woven one filament at a time. A line was installed between Saigon and Hong Kong in June 1871, another between Shanghai and Nagasaki in August, and a third between Nagasaki and Vladivostok in November. In the ensuing years, this network expanded to encompass Xiamen (Amoy), Tianjin, Fuzhou, and other cities throughout the empire. Chinese authorities and companies would steadily gain ownership of this web and expand it to a total length of approximately sixty-two thousand miles by the middle of the Republican period (1911–49).

With the entrance of China and the Chinese language into international telegraphy, a vexing question emerged: as the globalization of telegraphy

brought Morse code into contact with scripts it had not been originally designed to handle, would the inclusion of new languages, scripts, alphabets,
and syllabaries prompt a radical reimagination of telegraphy itself, or would
they be absorbed and subordinated to the logic and syntax of existing approaches? How would Morse code, dependent as it was on alphabets for its
functioning, possibly be able to handle Chinese script, which is entirely nonalphabetic? What is Morse code *without letters*?

What ensued was not a reimagination of the modes or syntax of telegraphic
transmission. Instead, the Chinese telegraph code of 1871—invented by two
foreigners—left the global information infrastructure of Morse code unal-
tered, while placing Chinese script in a position of structurally embedded
inequality. Developed by a Danish professor of astronomy named H.C.F.C.
Schjellerup and formalized by a French harbormaster in Shanghai, Septime
Auguste Viguier, the *code of 1871 encompassed a group of approximately
sixty-eight hundred common-usage Chinese characters. These characters were
organized according to the leading Chinese dictionary of the age, the *Kangxi
Dictionary*, and then assigned a series of distinct, four-digit numerical codes
running from 0001 to 9999. Approximately three thousand blank spaces were
left at the end of the code book, and a few blank spaces left within each radical
class, so that individual operators could include otherwise infrequently used
characters essential for their work. To transmit a Chinese telegram using this
system, the telegrapher began by looking up a character in the code book,
finding its four-digit cipher, and then transmitting this cipher using standard
Morse signals.

The code designed by Schjellerup and Viguier thus involved a fundamentally different telegraphic transmission *protocol for Chinese script than for
alphabetic and syllabic scripts. The 1871 code was premised on an additional
or double mediation of Chinese: a first layer mediating between Chinese characters and Arabic numerals, and a second layer mediating between Arabic
numerals and the long and short pulses of telegraphic transmission. By contrast, the transmission of English, French, German, Russian, and other languages involved only one layer of mediation—from letters or syllables directly
to the machine code of dots and dashes. In order for Chinese to enter the
machine code of telegraphy, then, Chinese script would first need to pass
through an additional (foreign) semiotic layer—in this case, that of Arabic
numerals, but also conceivably the letters of the Latin alphabet.

Because of its reliance on numerical transmission, this telegraph code
had immense implications for China's starting position within the global

telegraphic infrastructure, due to the history of the international telegraphic community prior to 1871. From an early moment within the history of telegraphy, a pressing issue facing cable companies and governments was the rapid spread of *coded languages and ciphers. These systems of encryption were geared toward protecting the content of the message and toward reducing the cost of transmission by creating short codes and ciphers that stood in for longer sequences and even entire sentences. While a boon for individuals and companies, these codes and ciphers threatened to erode the profits of telegraph companies and were quickly subjected to higher tariffs and certain limitations on usage (for example, it was stipulated that telegram addresses had to be transmitted "in the clear" and not in code).

The moment that the Chinese language entered into the international telegraph system, then, it immediately fell under the rubric of a "numbered language" and was subject to the entire body of laws that had been developed to confront encryption. From 1871 onward, that is, there was de facto no such thing as a "plain language" in the case of Chinese transmission. Telegraph companies with vested financial interests in the Qing—particularly the Danish company Great Northern and the British company Eastern Extension Australia and China Telegraph Company—focused on compensating for the disadvantaged position of Chinese script by establishing preferential transmission rates. They also advocated special status for the Chinese number code, securing agreements as early as 1893 such that the price of Chinese transmissions would be assessed differently than conventional "numbered language" transmissions. Domestically, various Chinese regimes also promulgated preferential pricing systems. Circa 1933, for example, a regulation was passed that exempted customers from paying the cost of encipherment and decipherment, deferring it instead to the telegraph offices themselves. Even with such makeshift exemptions, however, the Chinese telegraph code was not on equal footing with codes for other languages.

Photography

Whether because it is less explicitly semiotic or because it is less inherently transmissive, the medium of photography may seem at a greater remove from the history of information than telegraphy. Yet from its initial public acclaim in 1839, photography emerged entangled with reigning notions of the real, becoming instrumental within changeable regimes of truth and habits of sociality in ways that would provide key contexts for the recognition of information as such and that remain profoundly relevant today. The earliest observers of daguerreotypes (named after Louis Daguerre in France) were staggered by their precision, the way they reproduced the minutest particulars of a scene. And like observers of the first calotypes (from the Greek for "beautiful impression") or Talbotypes (named by William Henry Fox Talbot in Britain), they were amazed at the nonhuman agency involved, as sunlight itself seemed to be the artist responsible for these images. "Heliography" was one early term for photography, as experimenters developed multiple techniques and processes, and as the new medium became widely enjoyed. The precision and automaticity, or light-activated quality, of photographic images helped to lend them a seeming objectivity as representations of the real. Photographs were assumed to capture the world as it really was. Some early processes (daguerreotypes, ambrotypes, and tintypes, for example) resulted in one-of-a-kind images, the seeming usurpation of one-of-a-kind paintings or drawings. Later techniques involved developing negatives that could then be used to produce as many identical images as desired, a seeming usurpation of xylography (wood-block printing) and engravings that would help to suture the presumptive objectivity of the photographic image to the effects of its infinite *reproducibility.

Unlike telegraphy, photography would become fully domesticated, part of the way that everyday people could see and be seen in new ways. As photographic images turned into consumer goods, landscape "views" and portraits quickly became dominant photographic *genres, tangible, discrete, and finite slices of time to be saved and shared. Home or amateur photography—photographs that consumers could take themselves and have developed—would arrive only in the late 1880s and thanks to Eastman Kodak, which advertised, "You push the button, we do the rest." Also in the late 1880s, halftone technology enabled the incorporation of photographic images into printed materials, aiding in the proliferation of illustrated newspapers and magazines, a stimulus to both an explosive growth of advertising and the nascent practices of photojournalism.

Although early processes were cumbersome, involving dangerous chemicals and intricate manipulations, photography spread quickly around the world, taken up in an ever-widening field of practice. Metropolitan "galleries" and itinerant portraitists traded in showing people to themselves, newly fixed by the camera. Showing people their "others" also clearly had appeal. The acquisitive logic of "taking" pictures seems to have jibed immediately with the logics of imperial conquest and administration, as photography became a new means of knowing colonial sites and subjects. Taken in 1839, a photograph of

Muḥammad ʿAlī's palace at Raʾs al Tin in Alexandria is believed to be the first photograph taken in the Middle East. Five years later the Frenchman Jules Richard brought photography with him when he traveled to Persia, where he taught French and English, and ultimately converted to Islam. Other practitioners of photography in Persia included those from Austria and Italy, such as Luigi Montabone and the Neapolitan colonel Luigi Pesce, first dispatched to the region as commander in chief of the Persian infantry. By the end of 1848, the first calotype business in Calcutta was open, helping to popularize the method across India. In short order, increasing numbers of British and European photographers turned their lenses on India, and other regions of the world were no less well attended. Americans took photography with them to the Mexican-American War (1846–48), for instance, and soon there were photographic images of the conflict in the Crimea (1853–56).

Colonial subjects would eventually take up cameras themselves. In Persia, for example, Naṣr al-Dīn Shāh became well known for his photography and helped lay the groundwork for the introduction of photography into the curriculum of Dar al-Funun College circa 1860. By the 1890s, professional Chinese-run photography studios could be found in China. Meanwhile in Burma, photography studios such as F. Beato Ltd. and Johannes & Co. Mandalay began to employ Burmese staff members, such as Maung Pot Chit and Maung Win. The increasing number of native-born practitioners raised the possibility of decolonizing photography in Asia, Africa, the Middle East, and elsewhere. Students who excelled at Dar al-Funun were sometimes afforded the opportunity to study abroad, where they deepened their aesthetic and technical understandings of the new medium. Photographic societies eventually opened in Bengal, Madras, Calcutta, and elsewhere, their membership and leadership populated by many local Indian photographers. Photography also began to be celebrated at the highest rungs of the state. In Persia, cameras were given as gifts to the shah's cherished courtiers, and, with newly designed cameras, court photographers sometimes accompanied the shah on travels. In China, rulers eventually began to incorporate photography into their repertoire of official gifts, as a means both of generating publicity abroad and of cementing personal ties with the heads of foreign states and delegations.

At the same time, non-Western photography retained its close relationship with its colonial origins. Cameras continued to be produced abroad, serviced by European and American companies. Photographic societies were in many cases dominated by foreigners, and Europeans and Americans in many ways matched the output of local journals and manuals with their own treatises on photography, such as George Ewing's *Handbook of Photography for Amateurs in India*, published in 1895. The customers for photography also remained, in large part, Europeans and Americans. This had a profound and enduring influence on the choice of photographic subject matter. Orientalist themes persisted, with one paradoxical result that the realism of photography—its claims to objectively reproduce the real—became marked in association with the exotic. Nowhere was this more true, perhaps, than in pornography, which became a lucrative if typically clandestine form of photography, promising to reveal the harem and other titillating secrets to the male gaze.

Less clandestine links between photography and exotic subjects were legion, endemic for instance within the Western vogue for stereoscopes and the accompanying stereograph views, which offered a means of vicarious travel. Stereoscope photography involved the production of two images, one for each eye, which when viewed appropriately created a three-dimensional effect. Throughout the second half of the nineteenth century and well into the twentieth, European and American companies competed to supply their well-to-do consumers with sets of stereographs and the stereoscopes with which to view them. A parlor diversion, the consumption of these mass-produced diptychs purported to show the world beyond the parlor as it really was. The alien and exotic were domesticated—tourist sites, modern marvels, distant climes— and realism enhanced as much by the gimmick of the 3D effect as by assumptions about the objectivity of the photographic image over and against other forms of imagery.

In general the photographic view was a popular genre that helped to inscribe the natural and human-made wonders of the world as such, creating a visual iconography for collective recognition. Obviously, the spatial terrain of one's individual or collective life was not photographed evenly or with consistent intensity. Certain sites of life became nonplaces: quotidian, forbidden, or in-between zones that, for a variety of reasons, were rarely if ever incorporated into photographic documentation. Meanwhile, other sites of life came to be photographed incessantly, creating an ever-thickening *palimpsest of commemoration and remembrance, so much so that the visual representation of places might seem to eclipse the very places themselves. Certain sites and landmarks were visually consumed as never before. The Holy Land and Niagara Falls, for instance, began to lose their identity as preexisting sites that were then captured in photographic form. Rather, it was the incessant act of capturing sites like these photographically that began to create or reshape them as known and knowable sights. Photography helped to prepare travelers (actual or armchair) with visual cues, expectations, and itineraries that they might re-create in their lived experience. This was not completely without precedent, of course, since images of other kinds had circulated in similar ways. Prior to the advent of photography Chinese travelers had long employed famous works of poetry and landscape painting to prefigure particular parts of the empire, such that when they themselves arrived, they were in many ways sojourning inside a poem or painting, as much as in geographic space itself.

Just as the genre of the view helped create visual iconography for collective recognition, so the genre of the portrait eventually came to structure or crystallize certain elements of lived experience and to affirm the self as a specifically photographic subject. The "events" of a person's life might increasingly be defined as those moments worthy of, or particularly amenable to, being captured in photographic form. By the same token, photography equally helped to shape the formation of "nonevents": those moments that, for any number of reasons, tend not to be photographed. Photography helped quietly to transform and to forge a new aesthetic grammar through which to signpost a lifetime and to knit kinship, becoming a vital technique of commemoration and remembrance. Events and nonevents varied from place to place, of course, shaped by longer-standing cultural norms that predated or that arose in conjunction with the adoption of photography. In turn-of-the-century Burma, for instance, cameras were used to record not only wedding ceremonies—the kind of life event that would be photographed across many cultures—but also a person's acquisition of particularly fine new clothing or dress. Dour, unsmiling portraits were the cultural norm in America during the nineteenth century, taken frequently against painted backgrounds. Children were held still for the camera, tightly clasped on laps or from behind curtains, but many were also photographed dead and laid out in their coffins.

The self as a photographic subject was produced both by the cultural conventions of photographic representation—by poses and occasions, for instance—and by conventions related to the collection and circulation of photographs as objects. Albums were adapted to preserve photographs as keepsakes, and photographic portraits became important mementos to be shared and given to loved ones. Increasingly mobile populations required a growing traffic in photographs, as dislocations associated with migration, immigration, or military service, for instance, induced individuals to send or exchange pictures of themselves. Portrait photography became in this sense a social medium for the circulation of self-presentations—today we'd say "profiles"—in the production and maintenance of associations among friends and family members as well as aspirational associations among strangers. A token of remembrance, the photographic portrait was thus also a unit of transaction productive of social relations and social capital, a fact made manifest by the enormous numbers of photographs sent through the mails as well as by the eventual emergence of celebrity photographs, which were sold in the tens of thousands as souvenirs by theatrical stars, platform lecturers, and other notables. A midcentury vogue for the so-called *carte de visite* affirmed the photograph as a transactional form. The carte de visite was a portrait printed on a small card and intended, like visiting cards, to be given to and exchanged with others. Immensely popular in America and Europe for a decade or so, the carte de visite became a collectible, a way of making and maintaining social connections.

The ostensible objectivity of photography—the medium's reality effect—was thus an intricate and ongoing project that depended on the emergence of conventional subjects for photographic images as well as conventional practices for producing and then proliferating and using photographic prints. More than simply a visual medium, photography was a collection of materials, processes, norms, and associations. The "truth" of photography was and remains complex, as cameras were used to frame and select certain things and not others, and as images were developed—and potentially cropped, edited, tinted, or otherwise manipulated—often for specific ends. The doctoring of photographic plates and negatives was one of the most important and historically widespread modes of intervening in the space between exposure and final image. Through careful, well-timed alterations of standard development and printing sequences, it became possible for photographers to transmute their work in sometimes subtle, sometimes vibrant ways. Photographic prints in the Palace Museum collection in Beijing, for instance, are known to have been retouched so as to present a wrinkle-free Empress Dowager. In portraits of Yu Xunling, a Qing dynasty bannerman, meanwhile, the young man's face was carefully hand painted, and elsewhere techniques of retouching employed brushstrokes, tonalities, and shading designed intentionally to mimic those of traditional Chinese brush painting. Nor were darkroom manipulations always an act of homage or the benign mystifications of power. Hoaxers like the American William H. Mumler perpetrated fraud, embarking on a practice known as "spirit photography," in which double exposures and other tricks were used photographically to suggest the presence of ghosts, fodder for spiritualists and a means of fooling and fleecing the recently bereaved.

For all of this, photography achieved and retained its authority as a means of representing the real. It stabilized into a taken-for-granted element within a whole repertoire of techniques and practices for visual representation and became enrolled within a widening web of truth regimes, both bureaucratic and scientific (and pseudoscientific). "Rogues' galleries" and later mug shots helped to tie photography to policing and made photographs an early form of biometric registration, a means of collecting data about people for the purposes of categorizing them. In Britain the eugenicist Francis Galton employed a technique of composite photography, superimposing images of multiple subjects, in an attempt to identify types. In France Alphonse Bertillon concocted a whole system for analyzing criminality in which mug shots were supplemented by anthropometric measurements, while Cesare Lombroso did something similar in Italy. Both Etienne-Jules Marey and Eadweard Muybridge adapted serial photography to study animal locomotion. Anthropologists, art and architectural historians, epigraphers, naturalists, astronomers: for these and for many others photography became a form of evidence, a way to document and thus to compare and distinguish, to argue and persuade.

Telephony and Recorded Sound

The dissemination of telegraphy and photography that occurred with such power and rapidity in the nineteenth century was of course but one element amid a confluence of changes that can be broadly if weakly described as modernization. However uneven and chaotic experiences of this process must have been, it became (and remains) commonplace to understand modernity in relation to technological progress. Where telegraphs and photographic technologies were concerned, progress clearly entailed an encounter or reencounter with reigning assumptions about communication, the very substance of communication— be it linguistic or visual, instantaneous or not, inscribed and by whatever means—as well as its functions and effects. These encounters or reencounters, we have been suggesting, formed some of the groundwork on which the concept of information would achieve its ultimate and enduring force. Myriad other developments—in business methods and journalism, for instance—have a bearing, but we will conclude this chapter selectively in reference to two new media technologies of the late 1870s, telephony and recorded sound.

Developed as a form of "acoustic telegraphy," telephony was an offshoot of the earlier electromagnetic communication, losing its -*graphy* as direct voice transmission across wires was hailed as a breakthrough. Alexander Graham Bell captured public attention when he demonstrated a telephone at the US Centennial Exposition in 1876, but telephone devices and telephonic transmission were the subjects of such intense experimentation in Europe and the United States that numerous experimenters might legitimately be given credit for "the telephone," and many played a role in making it practical. Nor did this technology ever fully stabilize; active research and development would continue throughout the next century. With the telegraph companies as their model, capitalization by Bell Telephone Company and others was swift, and telephone networking became an arena for monopolistic or oligopolistic exertions as well as regulatory schemes. (It should be noted that Claude Shannon's 1948 mathematical conception of communication—the basis of contemporary information theory—was an outgrowth of signal-processing research conducted at Bell Labs.) In keeping with its telegraphic origins, telephony was conceived first as a business technology and only later succeeded more broadly as a form of networked sociality. The new telephone infrastructure articulated localities, connecting private businesses and homes to the outside world, and then interurban and rural-to-urban lines integrated localities with one another.

The American inventor Thomas Edison was experimenting with telephony in order to invent around Bell's patents when he stumbled across sound recording. (Scientists had successfully inscribed sound waves before, but now inscription would be the prelude to auditory reproduction of the sounds inscribed.) The crude recording device Edison made and named "the phonograph" was soon given public demonstrations and hailed around the world. It was a proof-of-concept moment and with Bell's 1876 prototype seemed indeed the presentation of modern wonders. Only after a decade or more would the makers of phonographs, related "graphophones," and gramophones identify and exploit markets for the technology. Like telephony, sound recording felt primarily like a business technology at first, a way of taking dictation without a stenographer or a pencil. (*Phonograph* was an adaptation from *phonography*, a form of *shorthand reporting.) Besides the recording and reproduction of business letters, Edison imagined a world of talking clocks and talking dolls as well as the preservation of dying words, important speeches, and famous voices. Only later would prerecorded sounds be exploited as a new commodity form: canned performances of music or recitation for the enjoyment of listeners equipped with a machine for playback. By the late 1890s and into the new century, phonograph and gramophone records had become the content objects of a new global culture industry, akin to and contemporary with other developing culture industries, like movies, an outgrowth of Auguste and Louis Lumière's *cinematograph* and related innovations.

The uptake of telephony in the non-Western world commenced in the late 1870s and early 1880s. As in Meiji Japan, which imported its first telephone in 1877, there was little choice for non-Western modernizing elites but to build new telephone communications infrastructures with foreign-bought or financed components, such as Western Electric switchboard equipment in Japan in 1889. In part reflective of dominant approaches to telephone infrastructure, but also of Japan's experience as the target of fierce western European colonial intrusion (in the form of Commodore Perry's infamous Black Ships), Japanese officials viewed telecommunications as a matter of vital national security. This view resulted in the state's subsidization of the industry, and eventually, the formation of a state monopoly over telecommunications. Over time, moreover, the Meiji state undertook an aggressive domestication policy, with the goal of producing as much of its telecommunications infrastructure as possible through homegrown means. One major outgrowth of this policy was the formation of Nippon Telegraph and Telephone Company, as well as a network of smaller, support-level firms that acted as the beneficiaries of NTT's sizable R&D budget.

As in other parts of the world, the construction of telephone infrastructures in non-Western locales often mapped onto preexisting cartographic and transportation frameworks. In the case of India, for example, where British colonial officials installed the first telephone in 1881, telephone lines were laid down along established routes of information—notably those already stretching from Bengal northward toward Peshawar, via Lucknow and Delhi—which had been in existence during the Mughal Empire (1526–1857).

The history and experience of telephony in the non-Western world was shaped by other preexisting technosocial, geopolitical, and sociocultural frameworks as well. India's comparatively slow uptake of telephony, for instance, was in no small part attributable to the way in which telephony was conceptualized by British imperialists at home in the UK. Viewing the telephone as a device well suited for intrahouse communication, but perhaps for little else, the British Post Office announced as late as 1879 that it had no plans in place for the installation of telephone communications as part of its broader, long-distance telegraph branch. Such attitudes were reflected in the sluggish uptake of the technology in the UK, where the number of telephones rose from just 45,000 circa 1890 to only 818,000 by 1915. By comparison, the number of telephones in the United States is estimated to have risen from around three thousand in 1876, to approximately twenty million by the end of the 1920s. Circa 1910, moreover, the United States is estimated to account for a full

67 percent of all telephones in use globally at that time. British telephone use paled by comparison.

Long-standing ideas about the telephone in Great Britain had repercussions for the levels of growth (or, more accurately, the lack of growth) of telephone infrastructure in British India. From the time of its introduction to British India in 1881, telephony grew at a similarly slow rate: from an estimated fifty-six state-owned telephones in 1882, to just around twelve thousand in 1924, just over forty years later. Also telling is the fact that automatic switching systems, in use as early as 1892 in the United States in some places, 1901 in Canada, and 1908 in Germany, were not introduced to Bombay—one of India's most important metropoles—until 1923. As late as 1923, moreover, there were no public call facilities in the whole of India (rising to only seven by 1932).

The telephone lines that the British did build were in turn shaped by still other geopolitical frameworks. In particular, investment in telephone infrastructure in British India was skewed dramatically toward northern India, propelled by threats of Russian incursion during the so-called Great Game. For those telephone lines that were installed, then, construction efforts were concentrated in cities and military cantonments in north India and the North West Frontier Province (NWFP). Incidentally, the choice of where British Indian officials decided to build, and not to build, telephone infrastructure laid the groundwork, some have argued, for a long-standing *"digital divide" in India today, with north India enjoying a far more advanced information infrastructure than the south.

Sociocultural frameworks also shaped the uptake and transformation of telephony elsewhere in the non-Western world, as illustrated in the case of Japanese switchboard operation. Specifically, the categorization of telephone switchboard operation as a form of "women's work," as it came to be viewed early on in the United States and elsewhere in the West, was not an association that came naturally in Japan. To the contrary, many in Japan regarded it as inappropriate that young women, often from middle-class families, should work not only outside of the home, but also in a profession that placed them in regular contact with strangers of both sexes, sometimes even at night. What is more, the physical location of one of the main switchboard exchanges circa 1890, in Tatsunokuchi, was itself considered a place of ill-repute frequented by gamblers and thieves. Over time, however, the gendered conceptualization of switchboard work in Japan began to sync with more common global tropes, with young women—who cost less to employ—steadily being presented as better suited to the work than young men thanks to their "inherent" gentleness, patience, and politeness. By the year 1905, male telephone operators effectively ceased to exist, with men taking on supervisory positions only.

The same kinds of sociocultural frameworks were significant for the development of recorded sound as a popular medium. Women's voices proved challenging to record well and so became a standard against which the fidelity of recordings might be judged. At the same time, as home phonographs and gramophones started to become popular amusement devices in the mid-1890s, prerecorded music intervened in social norms that separated public and domestic life. Like the contemporary player pianos that "read" music off a perforated paper roll, commercial phonograph and gramophone records upset long-standing associations between the middle-class home and amateur music making as a sacralized and sacralizing womanly accomplishment that was productive of domesticity and helped to distinguish it from public life. Records and piano rolls brought professionally produced music home, where previously public sounds—suggestive of the music hall, bandstand, opera, or vaudeville house—might now be enjoyed in private. Phonograph and gramophone companies plugged opera at home as a kind of touchstone, although more lowbrow fare clearly predominated. The after-dinner sing-along was doomed, observers warned, and sheet music *publishers saw their revenues plunge.

Commercial recording was a global endeavor from the outset, as American and European record companies sent representatives around the world to obtain recordings and as they developed outlets abroad. The British Gramophone Company recorded widely and established subsidiaries in India in 1901, Russia in 1902, and Persia in 1906. A few years later record labels were established in Lebanon, Argentina, and elsewhere, while record-pressing plants were operating in China and Japan. Operations remained transnational at multiple levels. The Lebanese Baidaphone label, for instance, had its records manufactured in Berlin from masters produced in Beirut. The Argentine Discos Nacional label pressed its own records to supply domestic markets, but it arranged to issue its tango recordings in Europe under European labels as well. Meanwhile so-called foreign records were profitable within the United States, as companies like Columbia supplied immigrant audiences and niche markets. In short, the success of sound recording as a popular medium meant the circulation and consumption of culture and cultural differences in the form of mass-produced musical recordings. Records remained brief—most were only about two minutes long—so this wasn't the capture and dissemination of preexisting musical forms as much as it was the creation of new popular musics, plural, selectively representative, and transformative of existing performance traditions.

Largely forgotten amid the success of recorded music as an industrial commodity form were the initial shocks of the late 1870s, when the -graphy of phonographs had amazed listeners worldwide with the possibility—as yet imperfectly realized—of capturing sounds for later reproduction. If seventeenth-century European savants had the "realness" of Chinese script (supposing a direct—that is, nonphonetic—reference to ideas and things), here finally was reality of a different sort. Sound waves delicately inscribed onto a recording surface could be reproduced at will. It was as if some new, futuristic form of written quotation could suddenly speak itself, or as if a new form of musical notation could be made automatically to play itself aloud. Novelty wore off quickly. Sound recording became a familiar idea, and then phonographs and gramophones became commonplace. Only lawyers and judges and policy makers would continue to puzzle the -graphy of sound recording, as musical *copyright remained an open question into the twentieth century and as the publishers of sheet music argued that the new delicately inscribed recordings (and perforated piano rolls) were infringements of their printed scores.

Some nineteenth-century encounters with the -graphy of media technologies prompted explicit questions about writing and written communication: among those who wrestled to adapt telegraphic signals to different writing systems, for instance, or those puzzled by the nonauthored character of phonographically recorded speech. Other encounters prompted implicit adjustments to assumptions about human communication, its character and extent. More than any one technology or one medium, however, it was the proliferation of so many new processes and then habits of communication that would prove particularly salient to the history of information. As the multiplicity of forms came to be understood in common—as media technologies—the very obvious differences among them helped to encourage an abstracted sense of the communicative functions they seemed to share. In light of so many and such diverse options for messaging, so many new ways of meaning and knowing, content itself appeared alienable, the abstract substance available to be communicated: information.

Further Reading

Erik Baark, *Lightning Wires: The Telegraph and China's Technological Modernization, 1860–1890,* 1997; James Carey, *Communication as Culture: Essays on Media and Society,* 1989; Deep Kanta Lahiri Choudhury, "Of Codes and Coda: Meaning in Telegraph Messages, circa 1850–1920," *Historical Social Research/Historische Sozialforschung* 35, no. 1 (2010): 127–39; idem, "Sinews of Panic and the Nerves of Empire: The Imagined State's Entanglement with Information Panic, India c. 1880–1912," *Modern Asian Studies* 38, no. 4 (2004): 965–1002; John Guillory, "Genesis of the Media Concept," *Critical Inquiry* 36, no. 2 (Winter 2010): 321–63; Leo Marx, "Technology: The Emergence of a Hazardous Concept," *Social Research* 64 (Fall 1997): 965–88; Thomas Mullaney, *The Chinese Typewriter: A History*, 2017; idem, "Semiotic Sovereignty: The 1871 Chinese Telegraph Code in Global Historical Perspective," in *Science and Technology in Modern China, 1880s–1940s*, edited by Jing Tsu and Benjamin Elman, 2014; Geoffrey Nunberg, "Farewell to the Information Age," in *The Future of the Book*, edited by Geoffrey Nunberg, 1996; Dwayne R. Winseck and Robert M. Pike, *Communication and Empire: Media, Markets, and Globalization, 1860–1930*, 2007; Kerim Yasar, *Electrified Voices: How the Telephone, Phonograph, and Radio Shaped Modern Japan, 1868–1945*, 2018.

10

Networking

INFORMATION CIRCLES THE
MODERN WORLD

Jeremy Adelman

IN THE EARLY 1890S, American newspapers went into a frenzy with reports about Spanish atrocities in Cuba. In selling the news they cleared the ground for America's first overseas war, which itself became a great story business. William Randolph Hearst was locked in combat with his former mentor, Joseph Pulitzer; they dueled to out-sensationalize each other with appalling stories of distant wrongdoings. Until then, Hearst's pride and joy, the *New York Journal*, had been a struggling money pit. On December 12, 1895, he broke new ground with a headline: "SPANIARDS INHUMAN CRUELTY." Based on eye-witness reports, the article described how Spanish troops were mowing down innocent civilians, including children. Hearst even sponsored a rescue operation of the damsel in distress Evangelina Cisneros, locked in a Cuban jail, as a story to plaster on the front pages. He sent his fellow Ivy Leaguer and illustrator Frederic Remington to get some images of humanitarian desperation. Remington, a racist boor, used to dip his Yale football jersey in slaughterhouse blood before a big game. Now, he was in Havana's Hotel Inglaterra, a beehive of reporters hustling for an angle. But Remington grew bored hanging around the lobby and cabled his boss, "there is no trouble here." Months later, the boiler room of the USS *Maine* blew up, and the chest beaters finally found their pretext. (Hearst, though, was livid because Pulitzer's *New York World* got the scoop first; not to be outdone, Hearst's headline the next day blared: "THE WHOLE COUNTRY THRILLS WITH WAR FEVER.") During the

Spanish-American War, sales of Pulitzer's *World* and Hearst's *Journal* soared to one million each.

Fast forward to the 1960s, when journalists and illustrators again teamed up over atrocity news. This time, the tables had turned. During the Vietnam War, Saigon hotels also had their sweaty lobbies. But by then the media business had become professionalized; it was emerging as independent of official truth peddlers and able to hold them accountable. The press was more deserving than ever of the moniker "fourth estate" by which it was presented as an autonomous field of authority that could question the claims of the three traditional estates, for example in Britain's Parliament, the Commons, the Lords, and the clergy. The Associated Press had a hyperactive bureau in Saigon committed to reporting the truth about a war that defied Yankee heroism. The German photographer Horst Faas turned it into a new-style media hub. He'd figured out how to send photographs instantly by wire to editorial offices in North America and Europe using cylindrical wire photo drums. On February 1, 1968, the seasoned photojournalist Eddie Adams came in, deposited a roll of thirty-five-millimeter film taken on the streets of Saigon, turned around, and went back out. Faas took the roll and retreated to the darkroom. He picked out a few samples from the contact sheets, including the image in figure 10.1, the execution of a Viet Cong assassin, Nguyên Vã Lém, and cabled it to New York. By then, news consumers were becoming accustomed to horror filling the pages of their newspapers and magazines. This image was more: it was evidence of how reporters were truth tellers, pulling back the veil of official claims about soldierly sacrifice and distant do-gooding.

For the century in which print media created and then dominated how strangers learned about faraway places, information became news, a business, then a very good business, a staple of conversation in dining rooms and dentists' lounges, and a matter of boardroom and government fretting. Distant events got packaged for sale; by circulating information and making it a commodity, the news business played a vital role in collapsing expanses between the world's parts, turning readers into remote yet instant spectators long before our globalization.

This essay is about two entangled stories: how news became *the* news and in so doing became a big business, and how mass circulating information went global. It starts with the laying of telegraphic cables and the making of the first kind of cable news. It ends when television—what Marshall McLuhan would famously call "hot" media—challenged dailies and weekly news magazines as the main sources of global news information and representation. It stresses three factors: first, technological shifts; second, business structures that managed and

FIGURE 10.1. *Saigon Execution* by Eddie Adams, 1968. AP Photos/Eddie Adams.

controlled supply chains through hierarchies and networks; and third, the practices of reportage and information gathering as investigative reporters and self-described "photojournalists" managed news. The essay ends with the break of the 1960s. For along with the rise of McLuhan's hot, screen-based media and the blurring of news and entertainment, another line got crossed. Up until the late 1960s, journalists as information brokers largely self-identified as reporters of objective truths. By 1970, a split was opening between a professionalization of the fourth estate, symbolized above all by the reporting on the Vietnam War, and the emergence of activist reportage, which argued that journalists were not just information brokers but ethically and politically committed to social change and justice. One might argue that our contemporary truth wars in the media can be traced back to this split. A new age was upon us in the business of packaging global information as news.

Making News Global

Before 1800, most of the printed news business concerned itself with the information of commercial value (see chapter 7). Print costs were relatively high, transportation was slow and expensive, and readership circles were small. The demand for news focused on information about markets near and far, from the price of cotton in New York to insurance rates for shipping to Canton, mainly for merchant classes who sought out more information to assess risks and opportunities of their bills of exchange and, after the Napoleonic Wars, investments in public bonds. Articles read more like opinion pieces and long-form essays than like reportage. Still, the commercial press was important for the functioning of capital and commodity markets—and for starting the process of making information about distant parts into circulating news.

In the 1820s, it could take over four months for the news from London to reach India and then New South Wales, two to three months to reach Buenos Aires or Cape Town. Even before the advent of the telegraph and cabling, transmission times of information were declining thanks to organizational changes in information business. Indeed, news, especially commercial and coveted financial news, became a business, so that the maritime journal *Lloyd's List* went from being published twice a week to six days a week in 1837, and new economic newspapers and magazines began to flourish, stoking demand for relevant news. The British Admiralty took over the running of ocean mail packets. American packet boats muscled into the Royal Mail business, cutting round trips between New York and Liverpool to five weeks. This was called "steamship news" for a reason.

It was in the middle of the nineteenth century that the marketplace for information about the world surged. Some of this had to do with expanding supply, linked to technological shifts. Some of it was tied to demand, especially as investors with access to pools of money in European capital markets wanted to know more about distant ventures in River Plate mining or Indian railways. But in both supply and demand for news, national government policy played a crucial role in creating markets for global information. Most important was the rise of the idea of "press freedom"—to join the other freedoms in trade and labor. *Libel laws underwent profound changes, which immunized writers and reporters from prosecution by the powerful. Information flows were also considered private goods, even if in some cases governments owned or controlled some of the land cables. The British government advocated "free trade in cables" in part to protect the British advantage as the first movers in the news business; it charged that no one could lay cables and discriminate against other national (read: British) competitors.

Government policies were also crucial in technical diffusion. Long-distance and underwater cables expanded the reach and rapidity of information gathering. Poles went up to raise the lines above ground; new coating techniques employing colonial Malaysian latex and Bengali hemp allowed cables to be laid underwater. A cable linking Dover to Calais was laid in 1851; after that, lines stretched all over the planet to link commercial and political entrepôts. The period between dispatch and receipt of news from London shrank from one month to two days to New York, from 145 days to three to Bombay, from ninety-seven days to three to Buenos Aires. From 1865 to 1903, the global reach of cables went from 4,400 kilometers to 406,000 kilometers. Wartime spending and subsidies for strategic capacities spurred the placement of even more cables where private investors steered clear of laying down infrastructure.

Along with a revolution in transportation and communication, there was also a change in printing technologies. Here there was not one big disruptive breakthrough, but a cluster of innovations. Woodblocks gave way to casting metal type. By the late 1860s (as a response to the cotton shortage of the US Civil War), newspapers were adapting wood pulp as a source of paper. The effect, eventually, was to reduce dramatically the cost of paper, creating the prospects for large rolls of printable sheets and thus unimaginable economies of scale for *publishers who sought to render information about the day's or week's events into immediately legible "news." Approximately four thousand copies could be produced, without interruption, by printing on rolls of paper up to 3.5 miles in length. By 1860, printing on rolls had become a standard practice. Many of the first daily outlets self-identified as *news*papers. The *Daily Telegraph* (named to capture the edge of the new technology) launched in 1855; within three years it could boast unprecedented print runs of three hundred thousand. Prices dropped sharply, down to one penny (or sou or cent) per issue (with the halfpenny paper, like the *Mercury Leader* and the *Daily Mail*, to follow in the 1890s).

Once stamped sheets gave way to rolls, tinkerers tackled typesetting. This lagged a bit, until by 1890, printers had devised a system known as linotype, which eventually became an industry standard, though many newspapers retained their own techniques—which gave printers and typesetters important control over production and often made them into vanguards of the modern labor movement. Still, there was no denying the effect of mechanical casts. By 1900, the Wicks Rotary Typecaster could lay sixty thousand characters an hour.

There was also booming demand for information made into news. Thanks to the spread of basic public education, from the United States to Japan, *literacy rose, and with it the spread of mass readership and a middle-class cult of being seen to be a reader. Investors wanted to know about what was happening to their stocks in western Canadian railways or Peruvian guano. There were also geostrategic forces at work. The outbreak of the Mexican-American War in 1846 created a surge in demand for news from the front. Tensions between Britain and Russia over the Dardanelles in 1851 produced a news frenzy. Getting information was crucial to drumming up public support and for winning wars. Then, when underwater cables got laid to Sebastopol, good reporting became invaluable intelligence. Russian commanders grumbled during the Crimean War that they learned more about the movements of their troops from the *Times* than from their own horse-powered information chains. (Little did they know that British and French commanders were also poring over the news to figure out what was going on.) Crimea was the first war fought with little or no censorship and a burgeoning press—which eventually brought the first photographs of war's lethal results back home. The 1854 *Times*—even the very name of the paper denoted the immediacy of the reporting—became the most influential newspaper in the world thanks in part to its wartime reportage, though it was the *Daily Telegraph* that pioneered sensational headlines, stop-the-press columns, and the all-important filler stories. The result: buoyed by the rising rates of literacy and by the declining costs of print production, news became a global commodity to join the flow of rubber, wheat, and tea. News became not just the way in which information got packaged and distant events represented; news made information an industrial product. It was not a coincidence that the new journalism was tied so intimately to the new imperialism.

Making Global News

By the century's end, any self-respecting city was wired in and boasted any number of telegraph offices. Many of them were manned by a new actor on the stage: the telegraph company, and out of their network sprang information brokers and "agencies." Among the enterprises that grew in the wake of the cables was the news business—which went global as it went mass. Managing information as news brought some industrial-age organizations—and indeed a new business model for managing global flows of information, cartels of national monopolies. It started in Paris, with Charles Havas's agency (later Agence France-Presse or AFP). On the heels of the Dover-Calais cable, Julius de Reuter created his news agency in London (Reuter's Telegram Company, later Reuters). Bernhard Wolff carried the model to Germany. Reuters became among the first truly multinational corporations with agents and "bureaus" scattered all over the planet. The Americans' Associated Press or the AP joined the club a bit later. It was not mere coincidence that these networked firms reflected the imperial molds from which they had sprung. They partitioned the planet like their ruling classes. Reuters made a grab for Asia. AP, in the shadow of the Monroe Doctrine, wanted the Western Hemisphere. Havas mopped up the Middle East. Wielding such market power, the cartel struck pricing deals with equally concentrated telegraph companies; lower, exclusive cable rates helped lock down their edge over other sources of global news, though Australians, Canadians, Japanese, and Russians responded with agencies of their own to rival the informal empires of the cartel. The Japanese Foreign Ministry opened bureaus in Shanghai and New York; later, the Kokusai and Tōhō News Agencies were pre–First World War ventures to feed reports to China to frame East Asian "news" in a common esprit against non-"Orientals." It didn't work. After the Russo-Japanese War, Japanese, Russian, Chinese, and British reporters were crawling all over Manchuria digging up stories of imperial entanglements and encounters. As with so many other facets of the world economy at this stage, the business side of news circulation was a picture of oligopoly and upstart competition.

National news agencies generally operated below the middle-sized agencies. Their activity was strictly domestic. Before 1860, only five news agencies existed: the "Big Three" (Reuters, Havas, and Wolff), the New York Associated Press (the AP's forerunner), and the Torino-based Agenzia Telegrafica Stefani. Between 1860 and 1870, a dozen more were established, and between 1870 and 1900 that number doubled again. Below the national organizations were smaller, regional ones. In the United States, for example, the Western Associated Press and the Southern Associated Press relied on the New York Associated Press for reports.

The result was less a frenzy of competition than an elaborate hierarchy. The Big Three supplied national agencies with world news in return for a subscription fee and national news; those agencies in turn bundled the news for regional agencies and local outlets. This interdependence suited both the national press and global agencies that exercised a monopoly on world news, leaving them free to secure fees from cable companies and to commission news from a network of low-cost reporters.

Here is an example of the multilayered system. The French agency, Havas, took the Latin regions of Europe, including Spain and Italy. With the laying of the South Atlantic cable in 1874 from Carcavelos, Portugal, to Pernambuco, Brazil, Havas also took South America and its existing regional webwork of cables and information production. It opened nine offices around South America and enlisted local subscribers for its global news service, which published daily telegrams about news in Eurasia. It was expensive for outlets to pay the monopoly agency and cable company rates. With the advent of the expanded "duplex" system and later the 1894 "fat cables," which allowed some competition, clients got a bit of a reprieve. Still, they were fed hundreds of words a day from Havas in part because the agency commanded a wider network of information gatherers and was able to negotiate cut-rate transmission contracts to keep its edge over any competition. Buenos Aires's *La Nación* (The nation) boasted a special section of Havas's selection of world news called "Telegrams, Telegraphs, or Telegraphic Bulletin" to connect Argentine readers to the wider world. The daily also sprinkled cable news throughout the rest of the paper to fill in the empty sections, creating something of a random collage of world and South American happenings. From a reader's perspective, it felt as if *La Nación* was the source; behind the datelines, however, was an elaborate supply chain managed by a single firm and its network.

The result was a thickening web of contracts and cables that linked sources to readers through daily newspapers and the first glossy magazines. In spite of the sprawl, there was in fact a high degree of uniformity of sources on which outlets drew, especially when it came to news beyond local sources. So, while social, technological, and legal revolutions gave more people more access to higher-quality, instant, and differentiated information, these changes encouraged the rise of a global media cartel.

Picturing the World

The last piece of the puzzle in making information news was the advent of another industrial by-product: photography (see chapter 9). Mixing light and chemicals to create images of the world that could be transported and reprinted at no extra cost required several separate steps. Photojournalism, traditionally dated to the 1842 launch of the *Illustrated London News*, did not imply direct reproduction of photographs. Before 1870, photographs appeared in mass-circulation periodicals translated into wood engravings and line drawings. Most photographs were made in studios, or if shot in the field, required elaborate setups for long exposures and for plates to dry. Reproduction on cheap sheets of paper was impossible. But George Eastman's 1888 "Kodak" was a simple handheld box capable of taking multiple exposures on paper negatives. Kodak made capturing the everyday life of strangers and strange lands possible—and the goal. It became a global booster of its own. The firm sponsored Hiram Bingham's Yale Peruvian Expedition, equipping it with the tools to showcase its marvels. In return, Bingham was quick to advertise the camera in his visual exposés of Machu Picchu and other finds in *Harper's Weekly* and *National Geographic*—which put on a full spread of over two hundred images in 1913. Kodak returned the favor with Peruvian panoramas in its promotional sales.

Journalists, like the Danish American Jacob Riis, immediately saw the potential. He tinkered with flashes to shoot nocturnal portraits of New York's squalor. In 1889, *Scribner's Magazine* published a montage called "How the Other Half Lives"—which shocked the city's bourgeois readers. It also became a model publication of the Gilded Age; soon, many booming metropolises had their own Jacob Riis to add photographic news to the print narrative. Black-and-whites got easier to print in 1897, when it became possible to reproduce photographs on the cheaper paper of newspapers; the photo was no longer exclusive to higher-quality paper magazines—just in time for the spasm of war in South Africa, the Philippines, Cuba, and China. The 1898 war brought the power of photography to the newsrooms of New York's cut-throat newspaper rivals. When the war began, it became the first war in which photographers would use their new mobile devices to capture living images of the conflict for readers back home. Jimmy Hare, the Brooklyn-based photographer, was dispatched by *Collier's* to shoot the new war after the sinking of the USS *Maine*. Within days, he was in Havana and would establish a reputation for his willingness to expose himself to gunfire to get his shot. When one American soldier remarked that he wouldn't tempt shooters if he didn't have to, Hare replied, "neither would I, but you can't get real pictures unless you take some risk!" And there was a page in *Collier's Weekly*, April 2, 1898 (figure 10.2), a collage of Hare's photos of "liberated" Matanzas, which linked the work of American liberators to the rescue of colonial peoples from the "concentration camps" created by the Spanish military.

The 1898 war anticipated how photography got used to document expansion and catastrophe during the Boer War (1899–1902) and the Russo-Japanese War (1904–5), so images would become instruments in the contest over public opinion in war and moral entanglement with strangers.

Between 1850 and 1900 the news industry changed dramatically. It made news valuable; increasingly, packaged information provided a platform to get the attention of readers—something that advertisers coveted. "Agents" sprung up to place ads in papers and magazines, which yielded publishers' revenue streams and padded profit margins. This in turn led to a frenzy to control local market shares, less to monopolize news than to grab and to monopolize readers' attention in order to parcel and sell it to advertisers and specialized agencies. If

FIGURE 10.2. Jimmy Hare's photos of Matanzas, Cuba. *Collier's Weekly*, April 2, 1898.

in 1800, merchant presses were mainly weekly affairs dominated by dense columns of prices and text-heavy essays or letters, by 1900, the modern newspaper
and literary and increasingly glossy magazine dominated the market.

By 1900, news making was also a profession. It created the modern journalist and the idea of the itinerant reporter working a beat—like policemen—to
get the story. The drive to report "the truth" meant going to the scene. Stringers, often attached to the news agencies and their web of offices, were information gatherers on the spot. Major metropolitan newspapers dipped into their
books to dispatch foreign correspondents to hot spots. By 1900, photographers
were leaping onto trams and ships when they heard rumors or received cables
about happenings, rushing to be the men on the spot to get the shot. Later, the
Toronto Star hired a former ambulance driver with writerly ambitions to report
back on how the peace was being settled in Europe after 1918. His name was
Ernest Hemingway; his reporting for the *Star* influenced his gritty prose.

Newspapers and magazines became in effect bricolages of local social
news with wider political reporting. The layout and eventually the creation of
special sections for wives and children—and even dedicated "Sunday Editions" for working families without the means to afford the dailies but who
aspired to belong to the reading class—formed some long-lasting patterns.
They were public scrapbooks made up of editorials and letters, clippings and
wire service notices. At the high-end papers with their own writers and
photographers, editors had more control over content and stories, though for
budget reasons they deployed in-house staff more for local news; beyond, they
relied on the wire services. For publishers on meager budgets, editing mainly
comprised selecting pieces and letters, and framing the bylines. Beyond the
local variations and social news, newspapers and magazines bore a certain
resemblance to one another. And they all ran ads.

This did not make them identical. Though they depended on the informal
empires of the wire services for the stories from distant places, the bricolages
could be assembled with similar content put to diverse local purposes. For
instance, before becoming a nonviolent activist, Mahatma Gandhi cut his
teeth as an editor in South Africa. His newspaper, *Indian Opinion*, started in
Durban in 1898. Aiming to provide an alternative outlet to the white supremacy of empire and appealing to readers of the raj's diaspora, *Indian Opinion*
provided a pastiche of world news from the wire services, patches from
Ruskin, Tolstoy, and Thoreau, and long editorial ruminations on the idea of
India seen from afar. Indeed, the drafts of Gandhi's famous pamphlet *Hind
Swaraj* (Indian home rule) (1909) first appeared as editorials in *Indian Opinion*,

albeit surrounded by columns about upheavals of the Boxer Rebellion in China and meltdowns on Wall Street. When Gandhi finally returned to India in 1914, he regarded the printing press and the newspaper as indispensable arsenals in his nonviolent campaigns to give his readers a sense of location in a wider, new world.

The result was a global reporting regime that looked something like an hourglass. It was squat and decentralized at two ends: reporters and readers were scattered and particularized. Connecting them was a narrow, concentrated neck where government regulators, private cartels, and advertisers managed the flow of news information from sources to consumers. Private enterprise, which owned about 90 percent of the world's telegraph lines, dominated the capital-intensive nature of cables; naturally, they concentrated on routes that generated high traffic and returns on investment. Where there was competition between lines, managers rushed to consolidate. For instance, the Eastern Extension Telegraph Company absorbed several smaller entities in 1872–73. For the rest of the century, this firm alone handled around one-half the world's cable traffic. In the middle of this bottleneck, connecting the wash of newspapers, advertisers, and readers, were the news agency intermediaries. The agencies bargained and bundled their way to control over the circulation of global news. With such control over circulation, they bargained with cable operators to lower charges in a way that individual newspapers could not and then charged news outlets for "subscriptions" to their information services. In the biggest of all news markets in 1900 (the United States alone sold half of the world's newspapers), the Associated Press was sending fifty thousand words per day to twenty-three hundred newspapers around the country. It was in this fashion that the Big Three cartel (AFP, Reuters, and the AP) became the world's principal supplier of news, even as the number of publications dependent on it proliferated. The effect was to standardize the information they procured and packaged between distant corners of the world.

Eventually, even the outlet side of the news market succumbed to concentration along with the rest of the industrial sector. One method was syndication, mergers of local papers into chains. Another was sprawling behemoths opening up competitor papers and using bargain deals with news agencies to drive down the cost of newspapers—and to drive incumbents out of business. In England in 1910, for example, three "newspaper barons" (Lord Northcliffe, George Cadbury, and C. A. Pearson) published papers that accounted for one-third of all morning circulation and four-fifths of all evening circulation. In Germany, by contrast, a large market was extremely segmented and scattered, perhaps reflecting the deeply regional commitments of readers; most papers were one-man or one-family shows with short print runs of one thousand. Late to the industrial revolution and to urbanization that fueled the newspaper business, Japan's market was very small, and its 250 papers in 1910 looked more like the German model on a smaller scale.

In effect, by the outbreak of the Great War, the market for news had exploded worldwide. With it came standardized content and consolidated ownership. This trend, despite the folklore of American competition, was more acute in the United States than in Europe. Britain's degree of standardization and consolidation stood in the middle.

Brave New World

After 1910, the basic elements of the production and circulation of print news were set and spread. Every city on the planet had its daily, often many dailies. Newsstands and delivery services were hallmarks of urban life everywhere. One of the challenges for the next five decades was spreading print news into the countryside, where markets were more dispersed, literacy rates much lower, and the consumer base poorer. But even villages soon had print news outlets, even if they did not exactly mimic big-city papers. In Shaanxi Province in north China (where Mao Tse-tung would finally end the Long March in October 1935), rural papers and newsletters did not mirror the vibrant Shanghai press, which looked a lot more like London's. More often, provincial papers were organs to recite official proclamations and documents. The provincial governments set up newspaper reading rooms in towns and villages to ensure that their version of the news spread. But there were limits to the circulation of news via print. In some ways, big cities like Shanghai and Beijing were more connected to Paris than to outposts in the Ordos Desert. In early May 1919, when students at the University of Peking received news of humiliating terms conceded by the peace negotiators in Paris—news they got from the wire services connecting Europe and Asia—they rose up against what they saw as a supine government and foreign delegations in the capital. People in Shaanxi learned of the uprising only once students straggled home from Beijing to study for their exams. Word of mouth conveyed the news across the provincial hinterlands. Despite the power of the press, isolation was still a watchword in much of the world; rumor and oral forms of communication remained a resilient form of diffusion. To the extent that newspapers reached into hinterlands, they looked less and less like the "Western" press, while *Shenbao* in Shanghai and *Dagongbao* in Tianjin resembled their cousins in San Francisco or Lima. In more impenetrable markets, radio would soon become a competitor, especially with the arrival of the portable transistor radio in the 1950s.

The basic technologies from 1900 lasted for over a half century. It would not be until the 1960s that new devices disrupted mechanical typesetting. Since 1890, words and lines had been arranged by keyboard to assemble the "hot metal" casts that stamped pages and sheets. Though the days of the old artisanal composer were over, skilled machine operators could control the pace of production. Their days became numbered with the advent of "cold type" systems, or phototypesetting, in the 1960s—by which time the newspaper business was feeling the pressures from other media, especially the television. We will get to that story shortly.

Continuity in basic production, telegraphic diffusion, and retail advertising also meant basic continuity in the business structure. The Big Three remained the paramount purveyors of global news, with secondary regional and national agencies functioning for subglobal news markets. The hourglass remained more or less intact. If it faced major threats it was from states that wanted to control the news business, to harness public opinion making to rulers' ambitions.

One of the perils of the hourglass structure of the news business was its vulnerability to pressures by governments, especially autocrats. In some authoritarian regimes, like the Soviet Union, and later China, "official" news agencies came into being. They seized private firms and turned them into government monopolies over the flow of news. Occasionally, they inherited an official agency but clamped down on any autonomy. During the Cold War, TASS (Russian News Agency) controlled the networks of information flowing into the Soviet Union and its satellite states. Created in 1902 by the Ministry of Finance as a telegraph agency, TASS was Russia's answer to the Big Three. When the Bolshevik Revolution broke out, the leadership immediately saw the importance of information control, seized the agency, and turned it into the mouthpiece of the Communist Party. Thereafter, TASS controlled information flowing in and out of the country, with a lock on the nearly four thousand newspapers across the USSR and in command of a vast network of bureaus around the world—which, not surprisingly, often doubled as intelligence agencies for the Soviet state. Alexander Ivanonich Alexeyev, a seasoned diplomat and intelligence officer, was sent to Cuba in early 1959; he could get a visa only as a TASS reporter—and it was under that aegis that he negotiated the alliance between Moscow and Havana, leading to the broken ties with Washington. It was more challenging for TASS to control the flow beyond the

Soviet borders, as newspapers like *Le Monde* (The world) and the *New York Times* or highbrow magazines like *Der Spiegel* (The mirror) and the *Economist* had permanent stringers dispatching stories. Nevertheless, these writers had to be cautious about their reporting, lest they face deportation.

Monopolizing the news business and putting it into the state was one strategy; ruling by fear and controlling vital inputs, like paper supply and advertising revenue, provided more indirect tools for control. The Nazis in Germany, Franco in Spain, and the Fascists in Italy put the screws on private news purveyors to report pro-regime news through direct censorship. In 1933–34, the Nazis merged Wolff and the Telegraphic Union to create the Deutsches Nachrichtenbüro (DNB) to be a concentrated news distributor and collector of information for the regime. The private press, in effect, subsidized official intelligence through subscriptions to DNB services. Sometimes, the control could take a more indirect form: when Juan Domingo Perón came to power, he managed Argentine paper supplies and prices, favoring papers that lavished praise on him, and taking away advertising and cheap paper sources from those that did not.

The relationship between the press and the state could also take cozier forms; some would say mutually opportunistic. Perhaps the most notorious was the comfortable relationship—"tribal friendship" in the words of Joe Alsop, the ubiquitous columnist for the *Saturday Evening Post* and later *New York Herald Tribune*—between influential editors of the *Washington Post* and the politicos of the American capital. Over dry martinis, Cold War elites of the government and fourth estate reenacted ancien régime *salons and catered to each other's news-making needs; insider reporters would get their scoops while politicians and policy makers could manage the message behind the scenes. What was known as "the Georgetown Set" had similar counterparts in Ottawa, Delhi, London, and elsewhere—albeit without the breezy confidence born of American hegemony. Whether controlled or cozy, the relationship between news makers and global elites would start to fracture in the 1960s and break wide open in the 1970s.

In the meantime, changes occurred more in the practices of news making than in the business organization or technology that these involved. One was the turn to increasing professionalization of journalists and editors who shared a common drive to be information purveyors first and opinion makers second. While newspapers like Gandhi's *Indian Opinion* or the National Association for the Advancement of Colored People's *Crisis* (est. 1910) had more explicit ideological purposes, the large, mass-circulation papers imagined themselves as news outlets, even if their selection of what to report and how to frame the news could tilt to extremes. Mass circulation meant that, increasingly, writers could make a living as reporters. Reporters, accordingly, became public figures. They also designed regimes of professional certification and gatekeeping. Not unlike experts concerned with universal weights and measures, sanitation, meteorology, money, and law, journalists formed their own nineteenth-century International Press Congress (IPC), which called on editors and reporters from around the world to convene and adhere to common standards of ethics and freedoms.

As was so often the case, professionalization expanded through higher education. In 1899, the fifth IPC in Lisbon called for the creation of schools of journalism. The University of Missouri and the École Supérieure de Journalisme lay claim to being the first. University degrees in journalism, by the 1950s, were becoming a prized certificate to secure jobs in top-echelon papers in the United States. It was none other than Joseph Pulitzer, who dreamed of journalistic training—despite his own lack of it, and his affection for sensationalism—that got the ball rolling with a gift to Columbia University to create a graduate school of journalism. It opened in 1912. London University launched its small journalism school in 1919, though for the most part, British reporters learned on the job. In France the École Supérieure de Journalisme de Lille was founded in 1924. The model took longer to catch on elsewhere in Europe and in Latin America. For the most part, training relied on older, artisanal models and personalized networks of recruitment, socialization, and promotion. But even here, higher education was a training ground—if there was no formal journalism school, the proliferating papers and magazines of student life incubated graduating reporters. Then came news guilds (unions for journalists) and reporter associations to monitor ethical behavior and to safeguard professional integrity. By 1950, under Cold War pressures and as the strife over decolonization worsened, journalists founded the International Press Institute to defend principles of freedom for reporters, effectively replacing the old nineteenth-century congress as journalists became more than just witnesses; they were becoming targets. The degree of professionalism should not, however, be pressed too far. Journalism and the news business—bereft of technical expertise and dependent on basic savvy and narrative skills—never went as far as lawyers' or accountants' guilds in governing credentials and professional access. The barriers to exit and entry for aspiring news makers were simply too low. In the end, associations could not bare much tooth in the realpolitik of reporting.

If there was a major disruption, it came less from the men and women with pens than those who wielded cameras. News of the world increasingly took illustrated form as the camera turned the consumption of news into a "being there" moment. News consumers were invited to be spectators. Action photography had to wait for two decisive innovations. The first was getting beyond the constraints of plates and paper to photos that could be made and reproduced more easily. In 1889, George Rochester and Thomas Edison invented a thin, portable, sensitized film made from cellulose acetate that could be used in still or motion picture photography. It was not until 1925 that German engineers developed the portable Leica, a camera capable of swapping out canisters of rolled film. A person behind the lens could cock and repeat up to thirty-six shots a roll before having to switch films.

It is hard to exaggerate the Leica effect. Photographers, now a subspecies of reporter, were spared the "reload" problem; they could replace canisters in seconds, stash the exposed film in a bag or pocket, continue shooting, and save the "developing" for later. In turn, the chassis got lighter and more discrete and became a better instrument for "shooting" the action. Thus began a journalistic scramble to exotic parts and distant wars in search of late-breaking stories and exotic landscapes. No one took this path to greater heights than the Hungarian-born Robert Capa, the celebrity photojournalist and iconic war photographer who followed the frontiers of global conflict. Unlike those who shot previous war photography, which was too slow and cumbersome to enable them to be part of the action, Capa could get close, perilously close. When he jumped off the landing vessel at Normandy in 1944 to shoot the first moments of D-Day, he sent his rolls immediately back to London for developing so he could follow the action for *Life* magazine. He didn't have to worry about the darkroom, or about setting up his gear. He shot like the GIs around him, to record how "the next mortar shell fell between the barbed wire and the sea, and every piece of shrapnel found a man's body. The Irish priest and the Jewish doctor were the first to stand on the 'Easy Red' beach. I shot the picture. The next shell fell even closer. I didn't dare take my eyes off the finder of my Contax and frantically shot frame after frame. Half a minute later, my camera jammed—my roll was finished. I reached in my bag for a new roll, and my wet, shaking hands ruined the roll before I could insert it in my camera" (*Slightly Out of Focus*, 1947). Pictures blurred and out of focus, Capa could shoot alongside the soldiers, oftentimes not bothering with the viewfinder. Like the shooters around him, Capa was shooting the air.

The emergence of action photography coincided with, and provided fodder for, a new *genre of magazine. The German *Berliner Illustrierte Zeitung* (Berlin illustrated newspaper) was the only German magazine that ever approached American-scale circulation. With almost two million in circulation on the eve of the Nazi takeover in 1933, *BIZ* had experimented with the use of feature photographs since the 1890s and pioneered the photo-essay to convey the news. Indeed, the photo became the news: glamour shots, aerials, stop-action sports, behind-the-scenes images—the camera gave reader-viewer-consumers the full range of perspectives, from intimate insider to outsider in the skies. In 1931, Willi Ruge rolled out *I Photograph Myself during a Parachute Jump*, turning the photographer from the spectator to the subject. *BIZ* was so influential that Joseph Goebbels seized it and made it part of his Propaganda Ministry. During the war, one of its most celebrated photographers, Eric Borchert, was embedded in General Erwin Rommel's North Africa campaign. The French *Vu* pushed the genre even further with innovative layouts and double-page spreads. An American magazine entrepreneur, Henry Luce, watched European innovators closely. The founder of *Fortune* and later *House and Home* and *Sports Illustrated*, he bought a struggling weekly called *Life* with the idea of making it the first outlet especially dedicated to print photojournalism. It would be in *Life* that Capa, and many more to follow, would exhibit their portraits of history. Luce also hired the talented Margaret Bourke-White, who had been among the first western photographers to shoot photos of Soviet industry in 1930. *Life's* first issue was full of her dramatic wide-angle shots of the Fort Peck Dam. The February 15, 1937, issue of the magazine carried her portraits of despairing Black flood victims standing forlorn below a placard reading "World's Highest Standard of Living." A decade later, she and the French photographer Henri Cartier-Bresson would use their cameras to chronicle the epic of Indian independence and the human toll of the refugee crisis that followed its wake, all in *Life*.

By the 1950s, the age of print news, a mixture of text and graphic reportage from around the world, was at its zenith. Henry Luce's *Time* magazine, with separate editions niched for different markets, was tailor made for the age of the organization man. Its slogan, "Take Time—It's Brief," aimed at the busy executive who wanted to get the world's news compressed into an hour's read, often digesting the news by flipping through the graphics and reading the captions. In some cases, the textual narratives were being compressed into standardized three-line diminutive text under the graphic spread. Its "People of the Year" marketed celebrity as news. It became the world's largest circulating world news magazine. At its peak, it had tens of millions of weekly readers; it sat on newsstands in Spanish and brought world news to Asia through the Hong Kong–based *Time Asia*. A reader-viewer of *Time, Life,* or *Paris Match* could be excused for confusing the graphic ads with graphic news—and often enough the photographers who took both came from the same studios.

There was a conceit to the glory days of news making: it was that reporters, photographers, editors, and publicists could have it all. They could make news and make money at the same time. And not just at the same time: news making made money, and money could help turn distant, costly information into news. It relied on a virtual monopoly over the means to circulate information about distant happenings.

But, as I have argued, that monopoly was also vulnerable to manipulation and control. Thus, the fourth estate needed to burnish its commitment to objective reportage in order to sustain the impression that the news business could have it all ways. Despite the surface breeze with which news appeared to circulate, there was enormous pressure on the points at which state control and journalistic autonomy found themselves at odds.

Consider two ways in which readers and audiences learned about the horrific potential of nuclear weapons. By definition, the making of the atomic bomb was a secret. Dropping it, and later testing it, was a shock—a shock that had to be managed. Dropping the bomb on Hiroshima on August 6, 1945, was thus also a news bomb. Around two hundred thousand died in one detonation. The US military sought to maintain control of the message. The first reportage was bland and lifeless. The photographs issued to editors consisted of air force aerial shots—which conveyed the impression that the first victim was the cloud cover pierced by the massive mushroom that erupted into the skies over the unseen (and invisible) city below. Thereafter, the image of the mushroom cloud would become a dominant impression of the new weapon's lethal potential. Getting the human story from the ground was a challenge, not least because once Japan did surrender, the occupying allied forces under the US military maintained their control over who and what was published. This did not stop intrepid efforts. In May 1946, the editors of the *New Yorker* magazine dispatched John Hersey to the scene of the first atomic blast. He and his editors were seasoned enough to know that timing was of the essence; Hersey slipped into Hiroshima and spent three weeks in the wreckage interviewing helpers and survivors. The result was an issue of the magazine devoted to a single story, simply called "Hiroshima." When it hit the stands on August 31, a year after the blast, it was a sensation. In 1949, it was released in translation in

Japan. "Hiroshima" conveyed to readers in a new way what it was like to be bombed. The key was giving to the survivors, the *hibakusha*, voice and chronicling those first days in which humans collapsed in puddles of their own vomit, blood, and excrement from diarrhea, nausea, and fevers. Hersey's was not the only account. How others got their information stories out also tells us about message management. On August 9, at the military base at Hakata, one Japanese propagandist photographer, Yosuke Yamahata, was ordered to the scene of another bombing, this time in Nagasaki, to shoot images for the military. Driving through the night, he had to wait till dawn for there to be enough light to start shooting. As the sun rose, the scale of the ruin appeared. Stepping through the smoldering fires—he would later recall the macabre horror as "a strangely beautiful scene"—Yamahata spent the next twelve hours shooting the day-after wreckage. His was the most comprehensive visual record of the aftermath of the bomb. Within two weeks, his images appeared in the Japanese newspaper *Mainichi Shimbun* (Daily news). To staunch the controversy, the occupying American military shut it down. With the end of US occupation, censors finally lifted restrictions in 1952. In September of that year, *Life* started to print Yamahata's work. Bordered by Pepsodent and Westinghouse ads, the lunar black-and-whites and freeze-framed images of the aftermath hit the stands of middle America. On the twentieth anniversary of the Hiroshima bombing in 1965, Yamahata started to vomit and turned violently ill. He died a year later from cancer caused by the radiation he absorbed while shooting the wreckage of Nagasaki.

Controlling the way the Japanese learned about how Americans bombed and burned them continued to be a matter of contention and diplomatic conflict. Indeed, getting information and news about civilian and military uses of nuclear capabilities of states anywhere has remained a point of standoff between officials and investigative reporters.

The Broken Hourglass

The hourglass regime depended on how print technology, telegraphy, and oligopolies mediated millions of consumers and their sources. It was layered over with the idea that reporters were committed to objective reporting, which would make the news worthy. It was sustained by a delicate balance of mass advertising and ambivalent government regulation, at once adhering to principles of press freedom while trying to control the message. Both sides of the regime, the technological foundation and reportorial distance, took a hit in the 1960s and occasioned a full-blown crisis of the fourth estate in the 1970s. Television drained away advertisers. A new generation of journalists and photographers cast aside their professional identities as neutral witnesses to become advocates for the voiceless and the powerless in an adversarial world.

The first hit to tele*graphy* came from the advent of tele*vision*. The radio was not a blow to the print news business, though in areas where papers were expensive and literacy rates lower, the radio did take a bite out of potential demand for print news. Unlike radio, television was much more concentrated than the print industry. It also developed a more global programming reach. Early broadcasting systems relied on partnerships across borders and the import of entertainment product—*I Love Lucy* for Asian markets, Argentine soap operas for the vast Spanish-speaking markets—in a scramble for viewers and advertisers. In the mid-1950s, America's NBC and CBS took in well over half the profits of the entire television industry. The BBC had a grip on Britain. These providers called themselves "networks"—a bland term for oligopoly. In most of Europe, governments simply added television broadcasting to existing state communications monopolies, keeping the new medium under government authority. Beyond Europe, countries bereft of nascent television industries in the 1950s offered a new commercial frontier as far as American television interests were concerned. During the 1950s, Latin America, noncommunist East Asia, and Turkey established US-style private broadcast systems and abided by US broadcasting standards to facilitate imported products. In some cases, American interests worked with foreign governments and invested in local media conglomerates (as in Brazil, Mexico, and the Philippines). Elsewhere in the world, television industries conformed to colonial legacies. Francophone and Anglophone Africa, for example, inherited the centralized state broadcasting bureaucracies of their former colonizers.

TV changed the production and circulation of news. The daily television newscast became morning and evening rituals. By 1960, network news was broadcast daily from 7 to 9 a.m. and early on Sunday evenings, with half-hour "specials" common in the wake of major news events. In Britain, the BBC's *Tonight* news program drew an average of seven million evening viewers, blending "hard" news with "human interest" stories to attract viewers. The turning point of the crisis was, one might say, 1960. In that year, Americans bought more news emitted from television sets than from the printed page. A national poll in 1959 showed that 57 percent of respondents got their news from papers; by 1963, a majority had turned to television. The TV shock was almost instantaneous. New York City's four evening newspapers in 1950 had been halved by 1960 and halved again—to one—in 1970. Hallmark magazines also got whiplashed. Between 1969 and 1972, three of the most widely read news-magazines in America (the *Saturday Evening Post, Life,* and *Look*) closed down. The neck of the hourglass became tighter. Advertisers slipped away and poured their resources into the more vivid potential of television.

The crisis was more than economic and technological. The concept of objectivity that had nurtured journalistic professionalization and global re-portage, bolstered by the notion of the camera as the "eye of history" (as the American Civil War photographer Mathew Brady put it), came under assault. I won't go into detail on this except to note that the 1960s brought a new generation of reporters to the fore. They relied on the old networks and still dispensed their reporting into the same old (increasingly beleaguered) outlets. But the stories and montages were taking a decisive turn, making reporters into advocates of justice or defenders of the weak. The most famous was of course the way in which reporting on the Vietnam War unfolded to make it less and less an episode of Yankee heroism and more and more a tale of hubris, peasant killing, and jungle burning. Eddie Adams's shot *Saigon Execution,* mentioned at the start of this chapter, was one lurid episode—though, to be true to Adams, he was unhappy with the way his picture was then framed as an indictment of the South Vietnamese puppet state. But there was the report-ing on the clamor for *free speech in Czechoslovakia, the photos of Gilles Caron of the stately rue Saint Jacques in Paris torn up by student demonstra-tions and littered with charred vehicles, and the efforts of the Mexican govern-ment to suppress the massacre of students gathered in the center of the capital to demonstrate against the one-party state's lavishing resources on the Olym-pic Village. Indeed, 1968, the year of these uprisings, was something of a sym-bolic turning point. Don McCullin was already making himself famous as the photographer of Cold War Berlin, London gangs, and Vietnamese bloodlet-ting. The year 1968 had him shooting the Beatles during their *White Album* recording and flying off to Nigeria to shoot the savagery of the Biafran civil war in unflinching black and white, as if to draw the observer's eye to the dis-tortions of the famished human body and to the flies preying on sores and eyes. McCullin, heir to Capa's gritty realism, threw aside Capa's avowed non-involvement. For McCullin, chronicling the suffering of the poor was political, and he meant to play a political role. He, and his Nikon F, became celebrities in a new style of committed reporting. His imagery of Vietnam invited news consumers to wonder whether the GI was not just another victim of warmon-gers in Washington.

By the end of the 1960s, a paradox loomed over the global news business. Torn from the threat of television competition, it was also the stage for a new idyll of heroic reporting. It was no coincidence that the notion of embedding went by the wayside—and that reporters were increasingly shot in the crossfire or going down in helicopter crashes—as Gilles Caron, a close friend of McCullin's, did in 1970 on Route 1 between Cambodia and Vietnam in territory controlled by the Khmer Rouge. The lens of McCullin's own Nikon deflected a bullet that was meant for him. There was a problem with this new style of advocacy reporting, though it took some time to pan out. Less committed even to the illusion of objectivity, the news threatened to become a matter of interpretation, a battle over the narrative, and from there, the *facts themselves. Anyone with an active memory of how fascists or TASS throttled the news business to produce stories to suit their agenda could warn progressive activists that this was a dangerous game; those who did get the message were in turn reminded that it was always in the interests of business to depoliticize the message. Between competition and heroism, print media was under assault and under fire.

Advocacy journalism was one response to the dissolving postwar consensus. Another form of adversarial stance taking by the print media was fueled by the spectacle of state violence—and reporters' commitment to informing publics about hidden truths about repression. This form disavowed partisan loyalties. Instead, truth tellers claimed to be objective and found themselves in conflicts with authorities. In France, exposés of torture and civilian casualties during the Algerian War embarrassed the government. There was already a furious debate over whether the *presse de la trahison* (traitorous press) had betrayed the nation in Indochina. But Algeria was worse: closer and more intractable, the state clamped down on television and radio, over which it still had direct regulatory powers—but it had less power over print media, which (like the leftwing *Libération*) documented repressive counterinsurgency and (like *Algérie française*) reported bombings by Algerian militants in a bitter feud over national loyalties. The Charles de Gaulle administration looked ever weaker and more ham-fisted in its efforts to control the reporting by seizing newspapers and magazines or threatening legal actions on trumped-up charges about, for example, finances, as in the case of the highbrow *Le Monde*. The effect was to provoke even more hostility between the press and the Fifth Republic.

If the war in Indochina let loose French truth seeking in the 1950s, it also unleashed a contest over information in the United States a decade later. As the Vietnam War worsened, members of the government of Lyndon B. Johnson began to despair. The secretary of defense, Robert S. McNamara, in June 1967 secretly commissioned a lengthy report on how the country had gotten into the quagmire. But instead of disclosing what was learned, the government kept a lid on it—until 1971, when an insider named Daniel Ellsberg released the three-thousand-page top-secret narrative on the US role in Indochina (and another four thousand pages of appendixes). The *Washington Post* and the *New York Times* proceeded to publish what would be called the Pentagon Papers to an already frustrated and polarized public.

Ellsberg represented a new type in the history of information. The *leaker had always been around. For as long as media existed, politicians and the powerful had used such figures surreptitiously to convey news that served their interests; leaking was an effective way to manage the circulation of news. It was also, by definition, a métier reserved for the insider. Very occasionally, there would be a sensational announcement. But so long as the press had a cozy relationship with power, it more often colluded and covered up. The wars of the 1960s changed the balance. Insiders fed secret information to outsiders, using the press as the medium, setting in motion a long process that culminated in entire organizations—exemplified above all by WikiLeaks formed in 2006—devoted to disclosing secret information by using insiders and leaky vessels of state. A military analyst in the Defense Department and later RAND Corporation, Ellsberg had what was called "privileged access" to information. Like others in the intelligence community, he had become disillusioned with the war and especially what he considered the systematic misinformation and lying by the government and the high command. He approached the *Times* reporter Neil Sheehan, who took the scoop to his editors. The aspect of the Pentagon Papers that caused the most uproar and street protests was the degree to which the public and Congress were kept in the dark about key decisions that led to escalation and disaster. It was hard to pinpoint any single incident in what was an astonishing catalog of deliberate dis- and misinformation. But the cover-up of clandestine provocations against North Vietnam that led two patrol boats to attack a US vessel (the USS *Maddox*) in the Gulf of Tonkin in August 1964, and which was used as a pretext for a congressional resolution to authorize the president to take any actions "necessary" to defend the United States against attacks, was pivotal. It was this resolution that triggered formal involvement. The White House used it as a legal means to escalate the war. Within twelve hours, bombers were en route to shower the North with their payloads. Eight years later, the newspapers were revealing to the public that the whole Tonkin "incident" had been manufactured.

Distrustful of the press and wanting to control the narrative about the war, the government of Richard M. Nixon in 1972 sought to clamp down on the publication of the Pentagon Papers by issuing restraining orders. In the end, the US Supreme Court freed the newspapers to continue printing the documents—arguing that the First Amendment freedom of speech and press trumped the arguments about national defense.

Meanwhile, Ellsberg surrendered to authorities in Boston. "I felt that as an American citizen, as a responsible citizen, I could no longer cooperate in concealing this information from the American public. I did this clearly at my own jeopardy and I am prepared to answer to all the consequences of this decision," he declared. A Los Angeles grand jury indicted him on charges of stealing and holding classified documents. But in a case that would only intensify the hostility between the press and authorities—and would illustrate the paranoid style of the Nixon White House—the judge announced a mistrial. It turned out that the White House had sent agents, illegally, to break into the office of Ellsberg's psychiatrist to steal files and thus "leak" information that would stain his reputation. The slippery slope continued. Members of Nixon's administration approached the trial judge with a job offer: directorship of the FBI. The government's lawyers were then caught with illegal wiretaps on Ellsberg—which they claimed to have lost. It was a fiasco. And it was all public information. So it was that the cycle of leaking, breaking, *hacking, smearing, and more effort to leak and indict seeped into journalistic practice.

Indeed, while the Pentagon Papers rocked world opinion about the US conduct of the war in Vietnam and the bizarre trial against the leaker unfolded, the Nixon circle would not be deterred from relying on secret dirty tricks. On June 17, 1972, White House "plumbers" were sent to break into the Watergate Hotel in Washington to obtain confidential information on the Democratic presidential campaign. They got caught. The White House scrambled to cover up the story in an increasingly ornate pile of lies. A few journalists, most notably Bob Woodward and Carl Bernstein of the *Washington Post*, with congressional staffers and ultimately some key leakers on the inside, brought the saga to light—which eventually helped lead to the president's resignation. Watergate became a metonym for official skullduggery and journalistic exposé.

Torn between advocacy and objectivity, and faced with the mounting competition of television in particular, the press again entered into a furious debate—and gathering anxiety. It took decades, but the pressure had compound effects on the business. Closing print sources and shrinking newspaper budgets meant less work for staff photographers. Working on tight margins, editors increasingly turned to wire services for distant images. Nowadays, five image providers dominate the picture industry: Getty Images, Corbis (Microsoft), AP, AFP, and Reuters. With the advent of *digital images and the billowing volume, editors review thousands of photographs a day (as opposed to a few dozen per day in the predigital photography age), hunting for the most riveting, if not always the most complex or subtle, shot. The effect is a tilt toward simple, tightly focused compositions over wider contextual frames. Speed and affective shock value are prized over complexity and accuracy. Framing and photoshopping have only accentuated this trend. Some photographers have lashed out against the quest for the "too-perfect picture" and advocate a return to film to spend more time on composition, perspective, and exposure—slowing things down to be more creative with the shots than spending time on a laptop and relying on Adobe software.

The same fate befell the writer. Belt-tightening editors cast off their stringers. Newspapers had to rely ever more on wire services. In recent decades, the notion of a "week's" digest in an age of acceleration was becoming an anachronism. In the United States, weekday newspaper circulation peaked in 1973 at 63 million daily sales, declined slowly after 1980, and plunged after 2008 to 20 million. One of the remaining popular mass-circulation news (as opposed to entertainment or general interest) weeklies, *Time*, has threatened to go belly up more than once. With readers wanting around-the-clock reportage—or more, instant notification with a headline "feed" or a digital "gram" of news— the magazine's circulation plunged to two million. Newsstands—even in Paris and Buenos Aires, where sidewalks were decorated with curtains of magazines, comics, and popular history—became rarer. The glossy for global mercenaries, *Soldier of Fortune*, closed in 2016, no doubt due to the avalanche of online militia chatter. Digital editions are only a small fraction of the circulation, in Britain accounting for only 5 percent of sales. Indeed, of the total online circulation in the UK, 40 percent comes from one magazine alone: *The Economist*. The British writer Nick Davies levied a devastating blast against his industry, charging modern journalism with repackaging unverified, secondhand material gleaned too often from dubious, unchecked sources, to line the profit margins of the commercial interests who produce and circulate what passes as "news." The new regime is no longer an hourglass. It is, in his words, "Flat Earth News"; gone is the art of double-checking, of editing; churnalism masquerades as journalism. In their place are information brownouts and news deserts. It is important to note, though, that the current malaise about truth and news has been gathering for decades.

Despite the appearance of rising and falling hegemony of print media and telegraphic circulation, there has been an underlying continuity. Even considering the transformation with digital media, a few names remain uncannily familiar. Some are family names with cunning staying power: Murdoch, Getty, McClatchy, or Hearst. Others are household institutions: the BBC, the Associated Press, Reuters, or NBC, all of which predate the first Wall Street crash of 1929.

In 1962, two scholars published pathbreaking books about the media, especially print media, and the modern condition. The German philosopher Jürgen Habermas wrote a book about what he called the *bürgerliche Öffentlichkeit*, the bourgeois public sphere, in 1962. Its translation into English, *The Structural Transformation of the Public Sphere*, had to wait for another fateful year, 1989 (see also chapter 11 for discussion of this work). Habermas made the case for the rise and fall of an autonomous domain of journalism, reading *salons, and *coffeehouses, where the literate and "polite" classes would gather and debate information from and about the world in spaces reserved apart from the marketplace and the polity. Print culture played a vital role in informing and influencing with information and learned opinion. He lamented the way in which mass print media became a new technology for managing consensus and promoting sales. This pessimistic narrative was at odds with the other pathbreaking book of 1962, by the Canadian Marshall McLuhan. *The Gutenberg Galaxy: The Making of Typographical Man* became a cult classic. It announced the arrival of what he called "the Global Village," laced together by wires— hence "Typographic Man"—and electronic interdependence. In this account, print media and news circulation had cleared the stage for a higher order of intervisibility; instead of depending on two-dimensional, static print, consumer-villagers could tune in to their television sets. This hot media mobilized more senses to intensify the awareness of what was going on elsewhere. Hence the making of a global village.

Habermas and McLuhan stood at either end of the spectrum of debate about the media. But they did share a sense that an age of commercialized and integrated public information was ending. For reasons in part technological, in part economic, in part resulting from new practices of production and consumption of information about distant happenings, the media became the stage and the source of an *epistemological mayhem that would gather force in the 1960s. One might say that the informational upheaval has ripened in our day. McLuhan and Habermas could look back on a century in which it appeared to be the other way around. The printed word and image claimed to speak as self-evident truths. Yes, some accused photographers of staging their shots. Yes, others charged writers with putting words into the mouths of subjects. But on the whole, the long century of print was one in which the hourglass created the medium for managing the flow of information from sources to consumers worldwide.

Further Reading

Gerald J. Baldasty, *The Commercialization of News in the Nineteenth Century*, 1992; Jeremy Black, *The Power of Knowledge: How Information and Technology Made the Modern World*, 2014; Oliver Boyd-Barrett, "'Global' News Agencies," in *The Globalization of News*, edited by Oliver Boyd-Barrett and Terhi Rantanen, 1998, 19–34; idem, *The International News Agencies*, 1980; Oliver Boyd-Barrett and Terhi Rantanen, eds., *The Globalization of News*, 1998; Robert W. Desmond, *The Information Process: World News Reporting to the Twentieth Century*, 1978; Juan Gonzalez and Joseph Torres, *News for All the People: The Epic Story of Race and the American Media*, 2011; Daniel R. Headrick, *The Invisible Weapon: Telecommunications and International Politics, 1851–1945*, 1991; Carol Sue Humphrey, "Coming of Age: The Growth of the American Media in the Nineteenth Century," in *The Rise of Western Journalism, 1815–1914: Essays on the Press in Australia, Canada, France, Germany, Great Britain and the United States*, edited by Ross F. Collins and E. M. Palmegiano, 2007, 173–201; Richard R. John and Jonathan Silberstein-Loeb, eds., *Making News: The Political Economy of Journalism in Britain and America from the Glorious Revolution to the Internet*, 2015; Simon J. Potter, *News and the British World: The Emergence of an Imperial Press System, 1876–1922*, 2003; idem, "Webs, Networks, and Systems: Globalization and the Mass Media in the Nineteenth- and Twentieth-Century British Empire," *Journal of British Studies* 46, no. 3 (2007): 621–46; Matthew Pressman, *On Press: The Liberal Values That Shaped the News*, 2018; Tehri Rantanen, "The Globalization of Electronic News in the Nineteenth Century," *Media Culture Society* 19, no. 4 (1997): 605–20; idem, "The Struggle for Control of Domestic News Markets (1)," in *The Globalization of News*, edited by Oliver Boyd-Barrett and Tehri Rantanen, 1998, 35–48; Donald Read, *The Power of News: The History of Reuters*, 2nd ed., 1999; Dana Schwartz, "Objective Representation: Photographs as Facts," in *Picturing the Past: Media, History, and Photography*, edited by Bonnie Brennen and Hanno Hardt, 1999, 158–81; Jonathan Silberstein-Loeb, *The International Distribution of News: The Associated Press, Press Associations and Reuters, 1848–1947*, 2014; Anthony Smith, *The Newspaper: An International History*, 1979; John Steel and Marcel Broersma, "Redefining Journalism during the Period of the Mass Press 1880–1920: An Introduction," *Media History* 21, no. 3 (2015): 235–37; Heidi Tworek, "The Creation of European News: News Agency Cooperation in Interwar Europe," *Journalism Studies* 14, no. 5 (2013): 730–42; Dwayne R. Winseck and Robert M. Pike, *Communications and Empire: Media, Markets, and Globalization, 1860–1930*, 2007; Timothy Wu, *The Attention Merchants: The Epic Struggle to Get Inside Our Heads*, 2016.

11

Publicity, Propaganda, and Public Opinion

FROM THE *TITANIC* DISASTER TO
THE HUNGARIAN UPRISING

Richard R. John & Heidi J. S. Tworek

THE *TITANIC* DISASTER is an unlikely landmark in the history of information. Yet a landmark it was. The world's largest and most opulent oceangoing vessel, the *Titanic* unexpectedly collided with an iceberg and plunged into the frigid North Atlantic in 1912, drowning over fifteen hundred passengers and crew. No one seriously believed the *Titanic* could sink. But it did. Some interpreted the disaster as a Greek tragedy, a Dickensian social commentary, or a love story. For others, it became a parable about the power of information: a portentous warning about the terrible things that could happen when a message failed to reach its intended destination, or, even more ominously, when access to information was denied.

The presumption that something as ephemeral as information could be invested with world-historical significance is a modern invention. For much of human history, contemporaries rarely regarded information as an agent of change. This was largely because so much of what we today would define as information remained tightly controlled. Priests, political leaders, merchants, and government officials enjoyed privileged access to time-specific updates on religion, politics, commerce, and public life. Each would have regarded the idea of broad access to information as strange, if not downright dangerous. Not until the eighteenth-century *Enlightenment would it become commonplace, at least in Europe and North America, for moral philosophers, social theorists, and statesmen (an apt turn of phrase, since political leaders were almost all men) to embrace the daring presumption that improvements in popular access to information would promote the public good. In some circles, it would even become fashionable to credit technical advances in what we would today call information technology with hastening moral progress, an assertion familiar to today's digital utopians, social media enthusiasts, and smart phone advertisers. Ours is not the first age when visionaries proclaimed that "information wants to be free."

For the US sociologist Charles H. Cooley (1864–1929), the influence of technical advance on moral progress was an article of faith. Innovations in information technology, such as the mail, telegraph, or telephone, Cooley confidently predicted in his landmark 1909 exploration of "social organization," would inexorably usher in a new era of "moral progress" (his phrase) in which "the public consciousness" would expand outward from the locality to the nation and beyond, until eventually the "world itself" would be included in "one lively mental whole."

Cooley's identification of technical advance with moral progress shaped the popular understanding of the *Titanic* disaster. Not until 1900, a mere dozen years before the *Titanic* sank, would it become possible to send or receive messages through the air. This technical advance was known as wireless telegraphy to distinguish it from wire-based telegraphy, an innovation first popularized in the mid-nineteenth century. Wireless telegraphy in 1912 remained a one-to-one narrowcast medium whose proper operation demanded a high level of technical expertise. Only after the First World War would it become the one-to-many broadcast medium for speech and music that is today known as radio.

The movie director James Cameron did not cast the *Titanic*'s wireless operator as his hero, let alone make a blockbuster film about him (almost all wireless operators were male). Yet he might have. For the *Titanic* wireless operator's frantic calls for help hastened the arrival of a nearby ship that rescued almost half of the ship's passengers. Had circumstances been different, even more could have been saved. For on the night of the disaster, the ships best positioned to rescue passengers stranded in lifeboats had all turned off their wireless receivers. To make matters worse, the Marconi Company (then the leading supplier of wireless equipment) limited access to its network. Had information flowed more freely, or so many contemporaries quite plausibly believed, fewer passengers might have drowned.

This essay traces the shifting understanding of the Enlightenment truism that improving popular access to information is a public good. It spans the "age of radio"—an epoch that can be said to have begun in 1912, the year of the *Titanic* disaster, and to have ended in 1956, the year in which US-backed radio broadcasts failed to catalyze a political revolution in communist Hungary. Technical advances in information technology, of course, continued after 1956; they included, in particular, the widespread commercialization of the digital computer, the technical advance most central to today's information age. In some quarters, the Enlightenment faith in the emancipatory promise of information never died.

Yet the age of radio remains a watershed in the history of information. For it challenged, without entirely undermining, the Enlightenment faith that technical advance in information technology could bring moral progress. This challenge can be traced by examining the evolution of three media *genres— publicity, propaganda, and public opinion—and three media organizations— the metropolitan newspaper, the government messaging agency, and the radio broadcasting station. In particular, we examine how media insiders— political leaders, government officials, business elites, journalists, and social scientists—understood the relationship between publicity, propaganda, and public opinion.

This understanding changed over time. Early on, many if not most media insiders presumed that public opinion was shaped by, and often identical with, the information published in the press. Beginning in the 1910s, a small but influential group of social scientists challenged this premise. The audience for news, they demonstrated, was often unpersuaded by the information it read in the newspaper or heard on the radio. Building on this insight, they transformed an amorphous phenomenon that was familiar to the Enlightenment political theorists and that was known variously as the "public," "public opinion," or "public sentiment" into a theoretical construct that could be precisely measured using quantitative techniques. In so doing, they invented the modern concept of public opinion.

In the age of radio, the production and distribution of international news, as well as its systematic analysis by social scientists, was the work of a tiny elite. Almost entirely excluded from this process was the vast majority of the world's peoples—women, the illiterate, the colonized, the nonwhite. Sadly, but perhaps not surprisingly, journalists only rarely depicted these groups with sympathy or insight. This elitist bias did not go unremarked. The Indian anti-colonial activist Mahatma Gandhi challenged prevailing assumptions about news management, as did government officials in Japan and the Soviet Union. These critiques notwithstanding, international news remained dominated by a relatively small number of Western organizations that enjoyed close ties to political leaders, government officials, business elites, and journalists. In the United States, the United Kingdom, and Germany, their ranks included a constellation of social scientists who set the terms for a mid-twentieth-century debate about the relationship between publicity, propaganda, and public opinion that remains influential today. The information-related organizations, individuals, and ideas that shaped this debate are the main focus of this essay.

The United Kingdom, the United States, and Germany each had distinctive national histories, institutional arrangements, and intellectual traditions. Yet in all three countries, media insiders shared a surprisingly similar understanding of the relationship between information, power, and social change. Intellectual developments in one country often crossed national borders, and in some instances, academics physically relocated from one country to another. Of these intellectual migrations the most consequential was the exodus of social scientists from Germany to the United States in the 1930s following the Nazis' rise to power.

The Information Infrastructure

The metropolitan newspaper and the government messaging agency each took advantage of technical advances that predated their emergence. Among the most important was the vast network of undersea (or "submarine") telegraph cables that by 1914 encircled the globe. The best-known and most intensively utilized cable network spanned the North Atlantic, beginning with the first successful Atlantic cable in 1866. Contemporaries hailed this network for annihilating time and space, fostering sociability, and promoting world peace. While historians sometimes assume that this language was unique to electrical communications, identical claims had been previously advanced to characterize the steamship, the railroad, and the mail.

The novelty of the cable network is easily exaggerated. The North Atlantic cables followed the same route, and served the same market, as the Cunard steamships that the British post office had relied on since 1840 to carry the mail. Though the Atlantic cable was faster, it was really more of an incremental change than a fundamental rupture. Cable rates were extremely high, discouraging the transmission of long messages. The vast majority of merchants active in the Atlantic trade in the early 1900s continued to rely on the mail—just as they had before 1866.

Cables were big business. The most important cable lines were owned and operated not by governments, but by a relatively small number of companies that ranked among the world's largest and most powerful multinational corporations. Cable company managers assumed that they would earn more by keeping prices high and volume low. As a consequence, cables were used primarily by government officials, journalists, and the global commercial elite—the Victorian equivalent of today's 1 percent. Prior to the post-1970 restructuring of global telecommunications, it was extremely rare for ordinary people to send a telegram overseas. If you wished to stay in touch with a distant friend or a family member, you posted a letter. The "Victorian *internet" was not the telegraph, but the mail.

The landline telegraph network, in contrast, was often government owned and government operated. This made landlines even more nation-centric than submarine cables. In many countries, landlines were administered by the same government agency that coordinated the mail, in an arrangement that was popularly known as a PTT. This was true not only in the United Kingdom and Germany but also in France, Switzerland, and Japan. These institutional arrangements profoundly influenced the rate structure for long-distance intranational communications. This was because, in these countries, it was almost always cheaper to send a telegram a long distance inside the country's borders than to send it even a short distance to a neighboring country. In some countries—spurred by nationalization of the landline telegraph network and the emergence of a robust transnational reform movement known as "postal telegraphy"—it became almost as cheap in the late nineteenth century to send a telegram as a letter. Despite this reform, for most people the posted letter, whether handwritten or typed, retained—as a telegram did not—a palpable reminder of the sender's presence, making it a superior medium for the conveyance of personal information.

In the United States, in contrast, the postal telegraph movement failed, and the telegraph would not be configured as a popular medium for in-country messages until 1910, several decades after the postal telegraph movement had lowered in-country telegraph rates in the United Kingdom and Germany. The telephone, in contrast, had by 1910 already been configured for a decade as a low-cost way to circulate information over short distances. The popularization of the telegraph and telephone was coordinated not by the government but, rather, by a nexus of corporations that was dominated by a vast combine popularly known as Bell. Bell leaders touted this combined low-cost long-distance-telegraph–short-distance-telephone service as "universal service," an arrangement that they were forced to abandon in 1913 after the Justice Department instituted a lawsuit on behalf of a rival network provider. The popularization of the telephone in the United States was much remarked on by British visitors; it set the United States apart from the United Kingdom and France, though not from Germany and Sweden.

Cables had politics. By far the largest and most extensive cable network operated out of the United Kingdom, a fact well understood by British imperial officials, who used their dominant position in the information infrastructure to project imperial power overseas. Other countries with a sizable cable network included the United States, whose government subsidized cable-laying projects in Latin America to try to bolster US political influence and promote overseas trade. The German government also looked to information technology to bolster its international standing. Intent on challenging the British, the French, and the Americans, it invested heavily in wireless telegraphy, then the newest *new media of its day.

The close relationship between cable corporations and national governments dated back to the 1890s. Prior to this period, though nominally British, the world's largest cable corporation—the Eastern and Associated Company, which linked the United Kingdom with its colonies in India and East Asia—operated largely independently of political control. The one vital exception concerned landing rights. Every cable corporation needed government permission to land its cables on the shoreline of another country, a seemingly minor issue that became increasingly salient as governments tightened their control over the transnational flow of information.

In the 1890s, everything changed. It was in this decade, but not before, that the Great Powers came to regard the cable network as a strategic asset in international relations, military planning, economic policy, and geopolitical prestige. In recognition of this fact, the British, German, and US governments each began to invest heavily in laying new cables. The British government, for example, subsidized a cable connection between Vancouver, Canada; Australia; and New Zealand that opened in 1902. The Vancouver-Australia cable completed the final link in an imperial "All-Red Route"—a global network of cables that landed only on British or imperial soil. British government officials no longer needed to fear that a rival power could tap their cable lines and intercept messages cabled between London and their imperial possessions.

Henceforth, the cable network became a tool of empire, and not an open market, a distinction that would loom large in the interwar debate over the emerging information order. To put it differently, the British government was committed to improving the information infrastructure within the British Empire, rather than around the globe. (British postal policy in this period had a parallel goal: when imperial postal officials championed "universal" penny postage, they had in mind cheap postage within the British Empire, and not cheap postage anywhere in the world.)

The All-Red Route deeply troubled German government officials, who feared that the British government could mobilize it in wartime to control the informational environment. The widespread conviction that the British government had censored cables between South Africa and Europe during the Second Boer War (1899–1902) lent credibility to this concern. Further confirmation came in 1903, when the British government denied a German cable promoter the right to land a transatlantic cable in Great Britain.

Any lingering questions about the political significance of the cable network were decisively answered when the First World War began in August 1914. Within days, the British government had cut every important cable linking Germany to the United States. For the duration of the war, the cable network became an "invisible weapon," a key military resource in what historian Jonathan Reed Winkler has aptly dubbed the "information warfare" that pitted Germany against the United Kingdom and its allies, which after April 1917 included the United States.

British control over the cable network led directly to one of the greatest publicity coups of the period. To counteract the negative effect of the potential entry of the United States into the war as an ally of the United Kingdom and France, German secretary of state Arthur Zimmermann sent a top-secret telegram in January 1917 to a high-ranking Mexican government official over hostile telegraph lines (the German lines having already been cut). In this telegram, Zimmermann offered Germany's support for returning territory to Mexico that the country had lost to the United States in the Mexican-American War (1846–48), should Mexico declare war on the United States in response to the anticipated US declaration of war on Germany. The British government intercepted Zimmermann's message and decoded it, a major triumph for British intelligence. When the decoded message became public, it outraged many Americans, a sentiment that intensified when, a few months later, Zimmermann acknowledged its authenticity. In combination with Germany's resumption of unrestricted submarine warfare, the Zimmerman telegram contributed to President Woodrow Wilson's decision, in April 1917, to seek and obtain congressional support to declare war against Germany.

Here is one example, of many, when information technology brought war, not peace. US president James Buchanan had hopefully predicted in 1858 that a transatlantic cable would ensure "perpetual peace" between the United Kingdom and the United States. Buchanan could not have been more mistaken. Had an Atlantic cable linked the United Kingdom and the United States in 1861, or so contended the British minister to the United States shortly thereafter, near-instantaneous communication would have heightened the mounting diplomatic tensions between the two countries and almost certainly led to war.

The consequences of the cable network extended far beyond its role in diplomacy, espionage, and surveillance. It also fostered a new kind of news broker: the international news agency. The first international news agencies were founded in the mid-nineteenth century to gather news from around the world and to supply it directly to newspapers. The vast majority of newspapers could not afford correspondents in their nation's capital, let alone foreign correspondents. International news agencies solved this problem by saving newspapers the cost of foreign correspondents and of transmitting news by cable to the press.

Just as the cable network was a tool of empire, so too were the most important international news agencies. For in addition to greatly increasing the volume of information on world affairs, they promoted the interests of the nations with which they were linked. Each had close ties with one of the world's major powers: Reuters with the United Kingdom; Agence Havas with France; Wolff's Telegraphisches Bureau with Prussia and, later, Germany. The dominant US international news agency was the Associated Press, the successor to a Chicago-based news agency that dated back to the Civil War. Each of these news agencies cooperated with the others in a cartel that lasted from the mid-nineteenth century until the outbreak of the Second World War. (The principal exception was the Associated Press, which pulled out of this arrangement in 1934.)

The Metropolitan Newspaper and Its Critics

The rise of international news agencies owed much to the concurrent rise of metropolitan newspapers, a new medium that emerged more or less simultaneously in the late nineteenth century in the United Kingdom, Germany, and the United States. The metropolitan newspaper, with its growing readership for international news and large and growing advertising base, would provide the international news agencies with a large and steady revenue stream, while elevating publicity to an unprecedented prominence in public life.

The ubiquity of the metropolitan newspaper was one of the wonders of the age. Though its predecessors dated back to the seventeenth century, they contained relatively little content and rarely reached more than a few thousand copies. Almost no single issue exceeded four pages (one sheet of paper folded once). In the late nineteenth century, everything changed. Printed in an attractive format, profusely illustrated with engravings and cartoons, sometimes with multicolor supplements, individual issues ran to eight, sixteen, or even more pages filled with original content written by a permanent staff of full-time reporters. All were dailies, with hefty Sunday editions; the most successful published as many as six editions at least five days a week. Some stories originated with beat reporters or out-of-town correspondents. Others reached the newsroom by wire. If an unusually important news story broke, *publishers interrupted their regular press run to print a one-page extra, sometimes within ten minutes of receiving the information.

This new medium was, by definition, urban. Small towns, villages, and rural districts had to make do with less. Here daily newspapers remained unusual, with local coverage spottier, and original news stories fewer and less varied.

The most successful metropolitan newspapers reaped large profits from advertisements, subscriptions, and street sales. Rapid urbanization had increased the size of their readership, making them an attractive advertising medium for the many new businesses that had begun in the late nineteenth century to churn out a multitude of branded, packaged products. Flush with revenue, editors invested in high-speed machinery that could print thousands of copies in minutes on cheap paper made from wood pulp rather than rags.

The novelty of metropolitan newspapers was obvious to contemporaries. In the United Kingdom, they were called the "new" journalism, a phrase coined in 1887 by cultural critic Matthew Arnold. In Germany they became known as "boulevard papers." In the United States, they were the "yellow press," a phrase that derived not from the supposedly lurid content of their articles, but from the popularity of a cartoon character known as the "yellow kid."

Journalists dubbed the publishers of the most successful British and American metropolitan newspapers "barons." The feudal barons of medieval Europe commanded the labor of a legion of retainers; fin de siècle publishers presided over media fiefdoms in which they had become a new aristocracy. Perhaps the most celebrated British newspaper baron was Alfred Harmsworth, the first

Viscount Northcliffe (1865–1922). Among Harmsworth's US-based counterparts were William Randolph Hearst (1863–1951) of the *New York Journal,*
Joseph Pulitzer (1847–1911) of the *St. Louis Post-Dispatch* and *New York World,*
Adolph S. Ochs (1858–1935) of the *New York Times,* and Robert R. McCormick
(1880–1955) of the *Chicago Tribune.*

Northcliffe rose from a humble background to found a media empire that
targeted newspapers at new kinds of readers. The *Daily Mail,* which he founded
in 1896, catered to a lower-middle-class audience. Priced at half the cost of its
London rivals, it swiftly became the largest-selling newspaper in the world—a
million copies daily by 1902. The following year, Northcliffe created the *Daily
Mirror* to reach female readers. After a rocky start, Northcliffe changed its
format to incorporate more visual material, including photographs. Six years
later, Northcliffe bought and revived the prestigious London *Times,* a testament to his emergence as one of the most influential press barons of the age.

Less ambitious than Northcliffe, yet no less influential, was W. T. Stead
(1849–1912). As editor of the *Pall Mall Gazette,* Stead pioneered the exposé, a
demanding literary form that combined ethnographic detail, florid language,
and religious fervor. Buoyed by an unshakeable faith in the redeeming power
of publicity, Stead piled up *fact upon fact in emotionally riveting, morally
charged, and often lurid prose that chronicled urban evils ranging from pros-
titution and police corruption to unsanitary housing.

Stead was fascinated by the United States and crossed the Atlantic frequently to report on its industrial expansion and urban squalor. Among the
most celebrated of his exposés was *If Christ Came to Chicago* (1894), a percep-
tive and deeply reported investigation of everyday life in a metropolis that
many contemporaries, including Stead, regarded as the most revealing "shock
city" of the modern world. Though Stead would not have considered himself
a sociologist, his block-by-block diagrams of Chicago's slum neighborhoods
bore a family resemblance to the information-packed monograph, *Hull-House
Maps and Papers,* that Jane Addams compiled the following year on her Chicago neighborhood or that W.E.B. Du Bois published in *The Philadelphia
Negro* (1899). Like the municipal socialist Delos Wilcox, each regarded publicity as a key to social reform.

Stead's zest for original reporting proved his undoing. Intent on expanding
his coverage of the United States, he booked a ticket on the *Titanic*—and per-
ished in the mid-Atlantic. Yet his pioneering form of information-intensive
reporting would be emulated by the rising generation of investigative journalists, popularly known as "muckrakers," that included, in the United States,

Ida B. Wells, Lincoln Steffens, Ida Tarbell, and Upton Sinclair. These journalists combined in-depth reporting with compelling story lines to reach large audiences. Like President Theodore Roosevelt, who gave the muckrakers their name in a 1906 speech in which he criticized their excesses, they believed in the power of publicity as an agent of reform. Each marshaled reams of information to inspire people to action.

"Facts, facts piled up to the point of dry certitude, was what the American people then needed and wanted," declared the journalist Ray Stannard Baker in 1945 in assessing the early twentieth-century popular fascination with information-packed prose. Publicity, or so contemporaries assumed, was the handmaid of reform. "'Let there be light!'" proclaimed President Woodrow Wilson in his political testament—"The New Freedom"—in 1913: "Publicity is one of the purifying elements of politics. The best thing you can do with anything that is crooked is to lift it up where people can see that it is crooked, and then it will either straighten itself out or disappear. . . . There is no air so wholesome as the air of utter publicity." For progressives of all stripes, information and reform seemed inextricably linked.

Wilson's words serve as a reminder that, in the period before the First World War, publicity had a broader, and more positive, meaning than it would after 1918. Today publicity often refers to the subjective presentation of information to cast a favorable light on a person, organization, or cause. Should a corporation find itself confronted with negative news coverage, it might mount a publicity campaign. Prior to the First World War, in contrast, publicity retained its close association with the core Anglo-American journalistic value of transparency. In a 1901 message to Congress in which he called for the investigation of big business, President Theodore Roosevelt made this identification of publicity and objective information explicit: "The first essential in determining how to deal with the great industrial combinations is knowledge of the facts—publicity." Though Roosevelt admired facts, he recognized that they had a limited ability to shape public opinion. To reach the public, Roosevelt sardonically observed, the most relevant art form was not the finely wrought "etching" but the flamboyant "circus poster." Over time, the boundary between publicity and transparency blurred, and publicity became identified with the overtly promotional appeals later known as "public relations." Among the pioneers in this field were two journalists: George Michaelis, who in 1900 founded the Publicity Bureau in Boston to burnish the image of railroads, public utilities, and universities, and James E. Ellsworth, who in 1907 became a publicity agent for Bell, which was well on its way to becoming one of the largest corporations in the world.

The late nineteenth-century press baron was a familiar figure in Germany too. The most famous German press barons were Leopold Ullstein (1826–99) and Rudolf Mosse (1843–1920). Ullstein purchased his first newspaper in the late 1870s. In the early 1900s he founded the first German tabloid, *B.Z. am Mittag* (B[erlin] n[ewspaper] at noon); shortly thereafter, he purchased the prestigious *Vossische Zeitung* ([C. F.] Voss's newspaper), a decision reminiscent of Lord Northcliffe's purchase of the London *Times* in 1908. Mosse founded a number of successful German newspapers, including the long-lived *Berliner Morgen-Zeitung* (Berlin morning newspaper), which he operated in conjunction with a highly successful advertising business that he used to increase the page counts of his publications.

Ullstein and Mosse were liberal and Jewish. During the First World War, they were joined by Alfred Hugenberg, an industrialist who created a publishing empire that featured more conservative content. During the Weimar Republic (1919–33), their ranks included the communist Willi Münzenberg, who briefly became the second-largest publisher in the country, before being driven out of business by the Nazis.

While metropolitan newspapers in the three countries had much in common, national variations remained. Per capita newspaper readership was much higher in the United States and Germany than in the United Kingdom. London was the metropolitan newspaper hub in the United Kingdom, while metropolitan newspapers originated in many cities in the United States and Germany. The United Kingdom did boast a flourishing provincial press whose ranks included the *Manchester Guardian*, the *Liverpool Echo*, and the *Birmingham Post*. Yet this press remained, as its name implies, provincial compared to London. In the United States, metropolitan newspapers flourished not only in New York City but also in Chicago, St. Louis, and San Francisco. In Germany, similarly, metropolitan newspapers thrived not only in Berlin but also in Frankfurt, Munich, and Cologne.

The training of journalists also differed from country to country. In the United States, Joseph Pulitzer championed the founding of specialized journalism schools to train new reporters; British publishers, in contrast, remained committed to hiring journalists who learned their trade on the job. In Germany, a third journalistic tradition emerged. In the United Kingdom and the United States, journalists regarded the reporting of information to be their primary task. In Germany, journalists subordinated reporting to interpretation. Many newspapers had political or religious affiliations, and journalists were expected to hew to the party line. One example was *Germania*, a Berlin-based newspaper founded in 1871 to support the Catholic Center Party. *Germania* played a critical role in mobilizing German Catholics during the Kulturkampf, the anti-Catholic campaign that Chancellor Otto von Bismarck would launch in the following year. Exceptions existed. Following the abolition of newspaper taxes in the 1870s, a new kind of newspaper—the *Generalanzeiger* or general advertiser—emerged in many cities. Intended to appeal across the political spectrum to a rapidly growing urban audience, these newspapers relied heavily on advertisements.

The metropolitan newspaper prompted an outpouring of commentary, positive and negative. Much focused on the sheer volume of information. Each morning, remarked the British journalist Ford Madox Ford in 1911, the newspaper reading public was "overwhelmed" with a "white spray of facts" that were "more or less new, more or less important, more or less veracious."

Newspaper reading did not necessarily render the public well informed. "The [prewar] inhabitant of London," the British economist John Maynard Keynes nostalgically observed in 1919, "could order by telephone, sipping his morning tea in bed, the various products of the whole earth, in such quantity as he might see fit, and reasonably expect their early delivery upon his doorstep." For this inhabitant, Keynes elaborated, the "projects and politics of militarism and imperialism" and the "racial and cultural rivalries" that divided the world were "little more than the amusements of his daily newspaper, and appeared to exercise almost no influence at all on the ordinary course of social and economic life," a remark that revealed the inhabitant's—and Keynes's—obliviousness not only to the precariousness of the international order, but also to the violence wrought by British imperialism on its colonial subjects.

German press critics fixed their sights on the influence of commercial considerations on newspaper coverage. Too many publishers ran their newspapers like a schnapps distillery in order to intoxicate their audience by blunting awareness of pressing social issues, complained the German media scholar Robert Brunhuber in 1907. German newspapers had an obligation, contended a prominent journalist eight years later, to reject their alliance with a profit-seeking news agency that was linked to the government. As an alternative, they should fund a news broker modeled on the Associated Press, an organization owned by newspapers and operated on their behalf. Economic autonomy, or so the journalist elaborated, would free the metropolitan newspaper from government intervention in news supply. Though the news broker model was much discussed, it would not come to fruition until 1949, with the founding in West Germany of the Deutsche Presse-Agentur (dpa).

The relative importance in German journalism of interpretation, as distinct from reporting, set it apart from journalism in the United Kingdom and the United States. In looking back on his years as a journalist in the Weimar Republic, the Hungarian-British journalist Arthur Koestler reflected on this distinction. Anglo-American journalists, Koestler reminisced, believed in "impersonal and objective reporting of facts." German journalists, in contrast, had a "tendency towards subjectivity." One German editor, Koestler scathingly recalled, had proclaimed facts not to be "fit for the reader when served raw." Instead, "they had to be cooked, chewed and presented in the correspondent's saliva." Such an outlook, Koestler believed, predisposed German readers to reject fact-based journalism in favor of the Nazis' deliberately slanted propaganda.

Whether or not voter behavior correlated so directly with newspaper reporting was a question that a later generation of social scientists put high on its research agenda. Yet the relationship that Koestler identified was real. Journalists *had* undermined Weimar democracy by scandal mongering and indicting the "system" as corrupt. In so doing, they unintentionally helped to bolster nationalists who insisted that only a strong leader could save Germany from economic ruin.

US journalists echoed the British and German critique of the metropolitan press. The subservience of journalists to advertisers was deplorable, contended the editor and publisher Hamilton Holt in 1910. As an alternative Holt called for a foundation-based "independent" press. Upton Sinclair's *The Brass Check* (1919) was a blistering exposé of journalists' willingness to publish false and misleading information to protect vested interests while undermining the public good. Like Brunhuber, Sinclair accused journalists of bowing to the profit motive in their coverage of the news.

While journalists penned the most acerbic press criticism in this period, they were hardly alone. Academics quickly followed, spurred by the simultaneous rise of the metropolitan newspaper as a popular medium and sociology as an academic discipline. Germany in the late nineteenth century had emerged as a world leader in the social sciences; it was hardly surprising that German scholars led the world in this field too. Though Max Weber is best known as a sociologist of religion, science, and politics, he was also fascinated by journalism and urged his colleagues to analyze its character and significance. Following Weber's lead, social scientists founded the Institute for Newspaper Science in Leipzig in 1916, a mere eight years after the University of Missouri established the first professional school of journalism in the United States.

German scholarship on the press proliferated in the interwar period with dozens of books and doctoral dissertations. While politicians continued to regard the citizenry as gullible and easily manipulated, academics knew better. In this debate, the critique of mass culture popularized by sociologists like Ferdinand Tönnies (1855–1936) anticipated later arguments about communications and public life advanced by the Austrian émigré Paul Lazarsfeld.

German scholarship on the press found a receptive audience in the American academy. Social scientists should investigate the "natural history of the newspaper," declared the University of Chicago sociologist Robert Park in 1923. Park's interest dated back to the prewar period, when he had toiled away as a graduate student in Germany. The influence on the American academy of this German tradition would soon be eclipsed by a second German tradition—known as the Frankfurt school—that would be pioneered by a talented generation of German-speaking refugee scholars who had fled Germany for the United States in the 1930s. Park focused on the relationship of journalism and democracy. Members of the Frankfurt school, in contrast, had witnessed the collapse of democratic institutions in Germany and Austria; not surprisingly, they found it more compelling to analyze the press as a tool of mass persuasion and to devise novel techniques to measure its effects.

Government Propaganda and the Legacy of the Great War

The First World War marked a watershed in the history of information. The catalyst was not technological: radio broadcasting had yet to emerge, and wireless remained important primarily for military communications. Rather, governments on both sides of the war mobilized the press to get their message across. These messaging campaigns generated an enormous volume of information, often labeled propaganda, that in the postwar period would be widely criticized for hastening the rise of fascism.

Propaganda was hardly new. To defend itself against the heresy of Protestantism, the Catholic Church in the early seventeenth century established an organization that it officially called the Sacra Congregatio de Propaganda Fide, which became in English the Congregation for the Propagation of the Faith, or, simply, "the Propaganda." The effectiveness of this clerical organization impressed government leaders, who borrowed freely from its methods in times of crisis to buttress their authority. The British government led the way, using its control of the cable network to spread (and suppress) atrocity stories during the Boer War (1899–1902).

Government messaging campaigns reached unprecedented heights of sophistication during the First World War, when all the major belligerents established agencies designed specifically to rally the troops and stiffen civilian morale. It is sometimes assumed that journalists in the Anglo-American world operated independently of the state. In fact, they worked covertly or overtly with the governments in their respective countries. To keep the public informed, government agencies relied on two very different techniques: censorship and messaging. Sometimes governments suppressed information about the war; sometimes they shaped coverage. In the United States, government messaging was coordinated by the aptly named Committee on Public Information (CPI), a bit of nomenclature that reflected the intimate linkage (forged in the prewar period by the metropolitan press) between information and publicity. The CPI was led by a pair of crusading journalists: George Creel (1876–1953), who oversaw domestic messaging, and Walter S. Rogers (1878–1965), who coordinated the circulation of US-based press coverage outside of the country.

Creel won the admiration of President Woodrow Wilson for his earnest disparagement of publicity bureaus, which Creel regarded as morally suspect. Like the muckrakers, with whom he can be profitably compared, Creel told stories to move minds. CPI-generated messaging, Creel insisted, was not propaganda, but advertising: the marshalling of facts to shape public opinion.

The CPI prepared newspaper copy, designed posters, and commissioned movies and public talks. Rogers's mandate was to expand US-based messaging overseas, with a focus on positive news stories that he hoped would crowd out the often-unflattering coverage in the foreign press of race riots, lynchings, and sensational crimes. The US government, in Creel's view, did not circulate propaganda, a word he deplored. Rather, it trafficked in truth. Not everyone agreed, a conflict that would prove highly contentious following the war.

In the United Kingdom, the relationship between the metropolitan press and wartime government messaging was equally tight. Eager to run British government messaging, the press baron Lord Northcliffe turned down Prime Minister David Lloyd George's offer to run the air ministry. Following brief stints on a succession of government advisory committees, Northcliffe got his wish and served during the final months of the war as the director of government messaging for enemy countries. A second press baron, the British Canadian publisher Max Aitken (1879–1964)—better known as First Baron Beaverbrook because of the knighthood that he received just before the war—was tapped in March 1918 to head the British government's new Ministry of Information.

Only belatedly would the Germans follow suit. Although the German high command understood the importance of propaganda to counter enemy messaging and bolster civilian morale, its initial foray into government messaging was bureaucratically disorganized. Not until 1917 would it establish a centralized government press bureau.

The different approaches that the three belligerents adopted to government messaging were reflected in the nomenclature they adopted. The British and American messaging agencies included the word "information" in their official name. The German ones did not. The agency responsible for much of the German government's messaging, including its surveillance of enemy propaganda, was the emergent German Secret Service, the Nachrichtendienst (intelligence service). The word *Nachrichten* refers not only to "news," in the sense of messaging, but also to "intelligence," in the sense of espionage. The Germans used both tools in the Middle East, where they tried to undermine British imperial rule by fomenting anticolonial sentiment. For the Germans, messages could be not only broadcast, but also censored, and even surveilled.

This conflation of news and espionage was by no means unique to Germany. Though the British and American wartime messaging agencies were purportedly in the information business, like their German counterpart, they combined broadcasting, censorship, and surveillance. This conflation of news and espionage continued long after 1918. The Office of War Information established by the US government in 1942 to coordinate US domestic and international messaging during the Second World War would be dissolved and folded into the Central Intelligence Agency (CIA) in 1947.

The German defeat in 1918 led to much soul searching about the ineffectiveness of the German government's wartime media policy. Right-wing critics of the postwar Weimar regime bitterly complained that the war had been lost not on the battlefield but in the press, pointing their fingers incorrectly at journalists and publishers, of whom several were Jewish. Military leaders also found much to deplore. Colonel Walter Nicolai, chief of the German Secret Service between 1913 and 1919, contended that the German government could not communicate effectively with its population because of the widespread popular confusion between the Nachrichtendienst (intelligence service) and the Pressedienst (press service). Germany's poor wartime messaging, contended the German journalist Edgar Stern-Rubarth in 1921, had been a "political instrument" critical to Germany's defeat. Stern-Rubarth even blamed Anglo-American messaging for demoralizing Germany's Austrian ally in 1918 so effectively that Austria's troops summarily surrendered. The widespread conviction that Anglo-American propaganda had won the day was reinforced by the translation into German of a number of English-language books such as Sir Stuart Campbell's *Secrets of Crewe House* (1922) that detailed the allies' wartime media policy.

Germany was not the only country to entertain sober second thoughts about the relationship between its government's messaging and the war. In both the United Kingdom and the United States, contemporaries derided their governments' messaging campaigns as "propaganda," a term that in the prewar period had a largely neutral, or even affirmative, connotation. The policy implications of this rapidly shifting intellectual terrain troubled the US political scientist Harold Lasswell (1902–78). Propaganda, Lasswell sardonically observed in the introduction to *Propaganda Technique in the World War* (1927), had come to acquire an "ominous clang." In response, Lasswell countered that every government had an obligation to channel in a positive direction the "mighty rushing wind of public sentiment." Propaganda, Lasswell elaborated, deliberately using the now-suspect word with pride, was an indispensable—and ethically unobjectionable—political resource: "Propaganda as a mere tool is no more moral or immoral than a pump handle. . . . The only effective weapon against propaganda on behalf of one policy seems to be propaganda on behalf of an alternative." Building on the work of the German Edgar Stern-Rubarth and the Briton Sir Stuart Campbell, Lasswell elaborated that the purpose of propaganda was to convince the public that its military opponents were "incorrigible, wicked, and perverse" and that by "a circularity of psychological reaction the guilty is the satanic and the satanic is the guilty." Defeated countries like Germany, Lasswell perceptively added, were "predisposed" to attach "very great importance" to foreign propaganda in explaining their defeat.

Lasswell was right. Postwar German governments *had* invested heavily in new media to try to influence populations abroad. British and US insiders also learned lessons from the war. Buoyed by the apparent success of their government's media policy, each derided propaganda as a dirty word, and, misleadingly, as a failed media policy that neither government had pursued. The governments of the United Kingdom and the United States had purportedly circulated not propaganda, but information. This distinction was not entirely spurious: the German government *had* intentionally spread falsehoods during the war more than the British or the Americans. Yet no government had a monopoly on truth. A few like Lasswell strenuously resisted this seemingly incontrovertible proposition. *Only* the enemy had deliberately set out to mislead, Lasswell contended, a failed messaging policy that demoralized its audience by persuading it that news was inherently false and unreliable.

The discrediting of wartime messaging proved so successful that, in the 1920s, few public figures other than Lasswell proved willing to defend propaganda explicitly. Among the outliers was the American public relations and marketing pioneer Edward Bernays (1891–1955). Bernays, like Lasswell, recognized the utility of propaganda as a tool for mobilizing public support in domestic politics. In *Crystallizing Public Opinion* (1923) and *Propaganda* (1928), Bernays did his best to salvage the concept of propaganda as an analytical tool. Echoing Lasswell's premise that propaganda was not necessarily malign, Bernays defined it in *Propaganda* as nothing more than "the establishing of reciprocal understanding between an individual and a group." Bernays justified his defense of the concept by appealing to psychology, which was perhaps not surprising, since he was a double nephew of the psychologist Sigmund Freud. In so doing, Bernays evaded the larger ethical issues that government propaganda raised for liberal champions of democratic institutions such as the philosopher John Dewey and the journalist Walter Lippmann. Only when, to his horror, Bernays discovered that Hitler's propaganda minister Joseph Goebbels owned a copy of *Crystallizing Public Opinion* would he reluctantly "speak up for democracy"—publishing a book of this title in 1940.

Dewey and Lippmann differed in occupation, temperament, and perspective. Dewey never lost his faith that journalists could elevate the tone of public debate by cultivating in the public an aptitude for the free and full discussion of the leading issues of the day. Lippmann, in contrast, in two important books—*Public Opinion* (1922) and *Phantom Public* (1925)—came to believe that the fundamental task of journalism was not to engage the many, but to provide accurate information for the few. "There seems to be no way of evading the conclusion," Lippmann wrote just after the war, "that liberty is not so much permission as it is the construction of a system of information increasingly independent of opinion. . . . The administration of public information toward greater accuracy and more successful analysis is the highway of liberty."

Dewey found much to admire in Lippmann's critique. Lippmann's reformulation of democratic theory, Dewey memorably declared in a famous book review of *Public Opinion*, was "perhaps the most effective indictment of democracy as currently conceived ever penned." Yet Dewey faulted Lippmann for presuming that, in a democracy, the purification of information at its source could substitute for the ongoing nurturing of civic engagement. For Dewey, information became consequential only when it engaged the entire citizenry in forums that reached far beyond the corridors of power. The solution was to revive bottom-up civic engagement, informed by the best scientific knowledge. For Dewey, journalists were high-profile players in an ongoing contest to interest the public in the public interest. For Lippmann, in contrast, journalists should remain discreetly on the sidelines and patiently counsel elites.

While Dewey and Lippmann differed in their prescriptions concerning the role of information in public life, it would be a mistake to contend—as have, unfortunately, many social theorists, media scholars, and historians—that they were antagonists in an epochal public debate over the possibilities and limitations of democratic institutions. No such debate occurred. Both Dewey and Lippmann championed liberalism, democracy, and pluralism—value commitments that distinguished them not only from the pro-Nazi German political theorist Carl Schmitt, but also from the avowedly Nietzschean Baltimore newspaper columnist H. L. Mencken, an unabashed pro-German monarchist who built an enormous popular following with his searing take-downs of American political ideals. Both were skeptical of the pre–First World War assumption that if the citizenry were sufficiently well informed, it could make wise decisions about public affairs. And both were relentless in their condemnation of information that had been intended to deceive, a common definition of propaganda. Nothing angered Lippmann more than the deliberate misreporting in the 1910s of the Russian Revolution by the *New York Times*, the subject of his pioneering indictment in 1920 of what might today be called "fake news." Dewey, for his part, enthusiastically defended the scientific method, a process that, almost by definition, valorized the judgment of a meritocratic elite. For both, it was, in the end, a relatively straightforward task to distinguish between public opinion, which they approved of, and propaganda, which they did not.

While Dewey and Lippmann remained wary of what Lasswell and Bernays persisted in calling propaganda, German, French, and Soviet policy analysts championed aggressive government messaging as an effective tool for promoting a positive national image abroad, an initiative that they rebranded as "cultural diplomacy." French interwar diplomats launched cultural initiatives to boost the country's public image, such as establishing educational institutes in Poland and other newly created eastern European nation-states. Not to be outdone, Soviet diplomats invited travelers from the West to tour Soviet factories and power plants. Following one such Soviet-sponsored tour, the American journalist Lincoln Steffens famously remarked that he had seen the future and that it worked.

The interwar debate over propaganda shaped the messaging agencies of the belligerents in the Second World War. The Nazis embraced the term *propaganda* and created a Ministry of Public Enlightenment and Propaganda. Convinced that Germany had lost the last information war, the Nazi propaganda minister Joseph Goebbels unleashed a torrent of information to embolden its population and demoralize its foes. While Weimar scholars such as Ferdinand Tönnies had tried to refine the concept of "public opinion" as an analytical tool, the Nazis rejected the concept outright as a "rallying cry of liberalism." To explain how people understood the world, Goebbels posited that their mental outlook could be divided into two categories: *Stimmung* (mood) and *Haltung* (attitude). Stimmung was fleeting and idiosyncratic and could be influenced by daily fillips of information. Haltung, in contrast, was rooted in a person's deeply ingrained habits and could be changed only slowly over an extended period of time. Nazi propaganda relied on this distinction to cultivate and sustain a pro-Nazi frame of mind. Among the Nazis' most effective policies was their systematic denigration of all non-Nazi information outlets as false and all non-Nazi information providers—including journalists, public figures, and even celebrities—as liars.

To spread their message, the Nazis relied on newspapers, films, posters, speeches, and radio, a rapidly evolving new media in the 1930s whose potential had yet to be tapped. For radio listeners at home and abroad, Nazi-approved broadcasts supplied an alluring mix of news and entertainment. German radio was so effective that, in 1938, the American radio executive César Saerchinger published an essay in *Foreign Affairs* entitled "Radio as a Political Instrument" in which he characterized the German shortwave radio station at Zeesen as the "most terrific agency for the spread of political doctrine that the world has ever seen." When Germany negotiated the surrender of France in the summer of 1940, Nazi radio broadcasts in thirty-one different languages could be heard in Europe, Asia, Africa, and the Americas: German radio, alongside the German army, seemed poised to conquer the world.

The British government stepped up its messaging as well. To maintain British imperial cohesion while preempting the colonization of its radio audience by rival Italian and German broadcasters, the BBC established a shortwave radio network in 1932. Originally called the Empire Service, this network is known as the BBC World Service today. To shape public opinion in the United States and cultivate support for Britain should it find itself once again at war, British officials built a sophisticated radio broadcasting office in Rockefeller Center in New York City. In addition to overseeing the BBC's North

American Service, this office secretly planted stories in the US press to outrage public opinion against Germany. Before long, both the Rockefeller Center office and the North American Service would be folded into the British Information Service, a prototype for the US government's own overseas broadcaster, the Voice of America (VOA).

Mindful of American hostility toward propaganda, British government officials took care to conceal their penetration of the US media market. The effectiveness of British propaganda during the First World War was by this time well known through books such as James Duane Squires's authoritative *British Propaganda at Home and in the United States, from 1914 to 1917* (1935). Many Americans were highly skeptical of British intentions, convinced, not entirely implausibly, that Britain had duped the United States into declaring war on Germany in 1917. British officials shared the American fascination with the lessons of the First World War. To understand Germany's burgeoning information empire, for example, British government officials in the 1930s resurrected their own assessments of German news agencies from the First World War.

The US government was no less determined than the Germans or the British to avoid the mistakes of the past. Troubled by the capacious mandate of Creel's Committee on Public Information, President Franklin Delano Roosevelt deliberately parceled out authority over government messaging to a panoply of government agencies. Of these agencies, perhaps the one closest in spirit to Roosevelt's own ideas about government messaging was the Office of Facts and Figures. Under the leadership of Archibald MacLeish (1892–1982), the librarian of Congress, this government agency helped generate information relevant to the war effort following the Japanese attack on Pearl Harbor. MacLeish pursued a "strategy of truth." "A democratic government," MacLeish explained in a 1942 public radio debate with Lasswell, is "more concerned with the provision of information to the people than it is with the communication of dreams and aspirations. . . . The duty of government is to provide a basis for judgment [on the part of its citizens]; and when it goes beyond that, it goes beyond the prime scope of its duty."

Critics charged that Roosevelt needed an American Goebbels to maintain civilian morale and countermand Nazi propaganda. "If democracy is to endure," Lasswell wrote in 1941, "democracy must make propaganda in favor of itself and against propaganda hostile to itself. This is the propaganda aspect of civic education." In 1942, MacLeish set up a study group, the Committee on War Information, to devise a way forward. In Lasswell's view, MacLeish's "strategy of truth" had proved to be woefully inadequate as a policy goal. To be effective, Lasswell believed, government messaging had to have a "large element of fake in it."

Roosevelt had committed the United States to countering German propaganda even before Pearl Harbor pushed the country into the war. To push back against Nazi radio broadcasts in South America, US lawmakers in 1940 established the Office of the Coordinator of Inter-American Affairs (CIAA). In the following year, CIAA would broadcast the US government's first international direct radio programming. Voice of America (VOA) followed shortly thereafter. Intended to counter German propaganda and supplement the BBC, VOA had been established with a mandate that was unusually expansive. By 1945, it was broadcasting around the world in forty languages, a remarkable achievement for an organization with such a short history.

The most important US wartime messaging agency was the Office of War Information (OWI). Established by Roosevelt in June 1942 under the direction of the popular radio broadcaster Elmer Davis, the OWI boasted a talented staff that included Milton Eisenhower, the brother of the general. In Eisenhower's view, the OWI should not set policy, as many believed the CPI had in the First World War. On the contrary, Eisenhower contended, it should "continue to be thought of primarily as an *information* agency." MacLeish left the OWI the following year. "I hated information work," he later reminisced, having found it virtually impossible to walk the fine line between publicity and propaganda: "I suppose in times of peace . . . you could probably devote yourself to information, trying to help a self-governing people to govern themselves. By seeing that they got the information they had to have. But in war you were always on the verge of propaganda."

The Office of War Information outlasted the war and, in 1953, was rechristened the United States Information Agency (USIA). The primary mission of the USIA was to combat propaganda originating in the Soviet Union, which had emerged as the country's principal postwar ideological rival. To counter the Soviet threat, the USIA relied on a battery of social-scientific techniques known as "psychological warfare." To streamline its operations, it absorbed the Voice of America and collaborated with the Central Intelligence Agency, which covertly funded a number of information-related organizations that included Radio Free Europe and the Congress for Cultural Freedom.

Not everyone approved. Psychological warfare, warned Walter Lippmann, compromised journalistic integrity and undermined democratic values: diplomats, and not radio broadcasters, should communicate the government's message overseas. The pollster George Gallup disagreed. The Soviet threat had become so dangerous, Gallup warned in 1952, that lawmakers had no choice but to establish a "Department of Ideological Warfare." Though Gallup never got his agency, the postwar contest between the United States and the Soviet Union that Lippmann had foreseen, and that he would label the "Cold War" in 1947, severely restricted journalists' ability to obtain freely the information they had customarily used to report on public affairs. This problem would become so serious that, in 1954, the *New York Times* columnist James Reston, a consummate Washington journalistic insider, complained to Congress about the executive branch's "news management" of the press.

Wireless, Radio Broadcasting, and the Free Flow of Information

The new Cold War rivalry was not the only impediment to Reston's idealized free flow of information. Another was the ability of radio broadcasting to transcend the traditional geographical constraints that had limited the circulation of print. Newspapers could be impounded at national borders. While radio broadcasts could be jammed, they crossed borders invisibly and without permission, making information warfare far harder to contain.

The emergence of radio in the 1920s as a broadcast medium was an event that no one could have predicted. The Italian-Irish wireless promoter Guglielmo Marconi had originally intended to build a business around real-time point-to-point communication, for which a ready market existed, rather than one-to-many broadcasting, a medium with uncertain commercial prospects. Marconi was an Edwardian Steve Jobs, an image-conscious promoter who crafted a public image of himself as a lone-wolf genius inventor. Yet he was no fool. Though the share price of his business fluctuated wildly in response to rumors floated in the press, Marconi had by 1914 found a niche in the lucrative business of maritime logistics—a service of self-evident utility to merchants, shippers, and naval officers. In many countries, navies had invested heavily in the new medium to coordinate from afar the movement of their ships at sea.

Under different circumstances, radio might have remained point-to-point. Instead, it emerged in the 1920s as a broadcast medium, an innovation with far-ranging implications for the history of information, journalism, and public policy. In the United Kingdom and Germany, lawmakers devised regulatory safeguards to limit commercialization. In the United States, in contrast, regulatory safeguards gave way to wide-open commercialization, an outcome backed not only by radio promoters and Bell, which hoped to profit from its ownership of the nation's most sophisticated long-distance wire network, but also by advertisers and the many amateur radio buffs who did not want to be shut out of the spectrum. Just as many lawmakers remained wary of a government-operated radio network, so, too, promoters and radio buffs looked to the nation's long commitment to antimonopoly to guarantee their continued access to the radio spectrum.

It is a historical truism that old media does not expire following the advent of new media in an irreversible death spiral. For the technological determinist, it might seem foreordained that radio broadcasting would swiftly supersede the metropolitan newspaper. Yet this did not happen. In most countries, the metropolitan newspaper remained the primary outlet for breaking news until the Second World War, when it would be supplemented, though rarely rendered obsolete, by radio.

Radio proved useful to journalists long before Germany invaded Poland in 1939. For the most part, however, the medium was deployed in this period less to broadcast information from radio stations to their audience than to circulate information from reporter to publisher. Even here, radio's role was limited. Of the news items that found their way into European newspapers in 1934, fully 70 percent had arrived by mail—with the rest arriving via cable, radio, or telephone.

The regulatory framework for radio broadcasting that emerged in the 1920s built on precedents for regulating not only wireless but also municipal public utilities such as gasworks and electric power plants. Though the US government had in the 1900s sent delegates to the world's first two international radio conferences, the new medium was regulated primarily by the courts. Following the *Titanic* disaster in 1912, this all changed. Lawmakers and journalists deplored Marconi's refusal to interconnect with his rivals and found it outrageous that amateur radio operators had flooded the airwaves with misleading and possibly fraudulent information about the doomed ocean liner's final hours. The *New York Times*, for example, had published a false news story, based on a wireless report, that the *Titanic* had survived its collision with the iceberg, and was being safely towed to Halifax with all its passengers aboard.

To bring order to the electromagnetic spectrum, Congress required every wireless operator to obtain a license. Following US entry in the First World War, the navy purchased Marconi's US assets, including its manufacturing facilities and patent rights, so that it could build out a government-owned and government-operated wireless network to facilitate wartime naval communications. Commercial radio broadcasting emerged only in 1919, following the navy's transfer of control over its radio assets to the Radio Corporation of America, a commercial venture founded to manufacture radio equipment. Henceforth radio broadcasting in the United States would be not only US owned and US operated, but also regulated in accordance with a principled antimonopolism that rested in municipal utility law.

The influence of municipal public utility law on radio regulation is often overlooked. In the 1920s, and for many decades thereafter, almost all the most powerful and influential commercial radio broadcasters in the United States were based in New York City, Chicago, and other leading metropolitan centers. US radio policy was *not* shaped by a lack of regulation, as is often assumed. In fact, it was molded by an antimonopoly regulatory tradition, rooted in municipal utility law, that privileged civic ideals over private profit. Antimonopoly did not necessarily lead to the atomization of big business. On the contrary, in radio broadcasting, as well as in telecommunications, and, eventually, television broadcasting and even digital platforms, it helped to enshrine the bedrock presumption that corporate management and not government administration was not the exception but the rule.

The negative example of the United States decisively shaped British radio regulation. The most important British broadcaster in the 1920s was the British Broadcasting Corporation (BBC), a government-owned and government-operated content provider funded by user fees. The British government had chartered the BBC not only to forestall the nightmare scenario that the British radio spectrum might come to resemble the commercially driven, advertising-drenched chaos that had prevailed in the United States, but also to slow the importation of cheap German-made radio receivers.

Radio regulation in Germany took a somewhat different path. Just as US wireless promoters derided Marconi as an obstacle to progress, so did German government officials. From their perspective, Marconi's primary threat was not to naval communications, but to foreign policy. Troubled by the dominant position of the United Kingdom in the global cable network, they hoped to build a global wireless network that could circumvent the All-Red Route. Spurred in part by the fascination of Germany's Kaiser Wilhelm II with new media, government officials pushed two private companies in 1903 to launch a joint subsidiary named Telefunken, a high-tech start-up devoted to cutting-edge innovations in wireless equipment. Telefunken quickly became a major rival to Marconi. For a decade, however, its commercial expansion was frustrated by Marconi's refusal to interconnect. To solve this problem, the Telefunken executive Hans Bredow lobbied at a 1912 London wireless conference to draft *protocols obligating rival wireless networks to interconnect. With the *Titanic* disaster grabbing headlines, Bredow prevailed, and, before long, Telefunken and Marconi entered into various patent-sharing agreements, a business strategy that hastened the integration of the global wireless network.

For the German government, a German-based global wireless network had the potential to liberate it from the British-dominated All-Red Route of globe-encircling cables. Finished in early 1914, the German "All-Wireless Route" linked Germany to its far-flung colonies in Africa and the Pacific. Both Germany's emerging wireless network and its rudimentary cable network proved highly vulnerable to attack. Within days of the first gunfire on the western front, the British cut the most important German overseas cables, while Australia made it a military priority to capture the Pacific islands housing German wireless towers. In response, the German government teamed up with Telefunken to build an alternative world wireless network, a venture that never quite got off the ground.

Wireless energized the decades-old vision of liberal postal reformers that information might one day flow freely and unimpeded around the world. Though Marconi was based in the United Kingdom, this vision had less appeal there than in Germany and the United States. The reason was simple. The United Kingdom already enjoyed a dominant position in the global cable network, reducing the lure of a rival network. In Germany and the United States, in contrast, wireless became a tool with which to bypass the British.

In Germany, this vision was embraced after the First World War by Bredow, who by this time had left Telefunken for a series of high-level positions in radio broadcasting and government radio regulation. Bredow's positions enabled him to shape the future of German radio. Skeptical of amateurs, Bredow lobbied for government control not only of wireless receivers but also of wireless information. Should wireless information remain privately held, he warned, speculators might trade on inside information regarding the fluctuation in exchange rates and security valuations to defraud the public. Bredow clamped down on private use of wireless, but that did not stop Germany's slide into hyperinflation in 1922–23.

The US journalist-turned-government-official Walter S. Rogers championed a sweeping vision of an information-abundant future in a rhetorically effusive, multipage memorandum that he prepared at the request of US president Woodrow Wilson in February 1919, four months after the cessation of hostilities, and twenty-one months before the first regularly scheduled US-based radio broadcast. Rogers was based at this time in Paris, where he was coordinating news coverage of the US delegation to the Paris Peace Conference, a logical follow-up to the work he had performed in New York City for the CPI during the war. "Barriers to the flow of news from nation to nation," Rogers declared in his preamble, should be "removed in the general public interest": "The ideal is a world-wide freedom for news, with important news going everywhere."

Under existing conditions, Rogers elaborated, the unimpeded global flow of information had become an indispensable prerequisite for world peace: "The steady extension of democratic forms of government and the increasing closeness of contact between all parts of the world point to the conclusion, that the ultimate basis of world peace is common knowledge and understanding between the masses of the world. Hence the distribution of intelligence in the form of news becomes of the utmost importance." To hasten the free flow of information across national borders, Rogers looked to the League of Nations, which, he hoped, would become a center for the exchange of technical information on wireless and radio, and the promulgation of the international protocols necessary to transform global news into a single integrated market.

Radio Broadcasting and the Crisis of Democracy

Radio broadcasting evolved differently in the United Kingdom, Germany, and the United States. It was, thus, perhaps surprising that, in the 1920s, commentators in all three countries hailed radio as a savior of the nation. By creating an imagined community of listeners, or so they assumed, the new medium could combat parochialism, foster common understanding, and encourage a laudable spirit of civic engagement. This project would only gradually come to be associated with the broadcasting of news.

The rise of radio news popularized a new way of gaining access to time-specific information about the outside world. For the first time, it became possible to learn about current events by listening to them as they unfolded—or "broke," a bit of nomenclature that radio broadcasting helped to popularize in the 1920s—rather than merely by reading press reports. Radio bulletins announcing breaking news predated the emergence in the late 1930s of regular radio news broadcasts. Not everyone approved. In the view of Sir John Reith, the first director of the BBC, the new medium was best suited to the broadcast of classical music and similar kinds of high-toned entertainment and popular lectures aimed at uplifting the masses. News broadcasts did not fit comfortably into either category. At least in the 1920s, relatively little news found its way onto the BBC. When news did find its way onto the air, it was almost always morally salubrious, or, as the phrase went, "worthy." Newspaper accounts of fires, deaths, and motorcar accidents were deemed insufficiently weighty. On Good Friday in 1930, for example, a BBC announcer reported, regretfully—though, conceivably, not without a touch of sacrilegious irony—that there was simply no news to report that night. Beginning in the 1930s, a combination of circumstances prompted the BBC to begin to gather and broadcast its own news inside the United Kingdom, throughout its empire, and, increasingly, to radio listeners around the world, including those in the United States, Asia, and Latin America who might have been otherwise tempted by broadcasts from fascist countries.

Radio news proved, if anything, even more controversial in Germany. In the 1920s, German radio expert Hans Bredow had warned that radio news broadcasts might stoke panic among German listeners, given the divisiveness of the political landscape in the Weimar Republic. To limit political instability, Bredow lobbied successfully in the late 1920s and early 1930s for government supervision of radio broadcasting, including radio news. Bredow was a principled critic of the Nazis and resigned his government post when Hitler came to power in January 1933. Ironically, however, the radio regulations that Bredow had backed to limit political controversy during the Weimar era proved to be a huge boon for the Nazis, since they made it relatively easy for Nazi publicists to silence their critics, once their party had gained control of the state.

Nazi publicists made full use of radio to get their message across. Hitler's speeches were routinely broadcast on the air, as was pro-Nazi news. In addition, they enlisted the British fascist William Joyce to broadcast German propaganda to a British audience. Lord Haw-Haw, as Joyce would be derisively nicknamed by the British press, reached a large audience in the United Kingdom.

Before long, however, radio listeners who were not true believers found the Nazis' radio fare monotonous and unreliable. During the Second World War, Nazi officials waged an information war to block foreign news reports from reaching German listeners—primarily by jamming their signals—and to do everything they could to ensure that domestic and foreign news reports that originated in Germany or German-occupied lands toed the party line. German radio listeners quickly caught on to the deception. In fact, during the Second World War millions of ordinary Germans increasingly tuned in to radio stations that originated in enemy countries—particularly the BBC—to hear more reliable information about the war.

The challenge of radio news extended beyond issues of form and content. An even more basic question confronted regulators, station managers, and listeners: Who was the audience? The publishers of metropolitan newspapers had begun in the late nineteenth century to answer this question by providing data on the size and demographic makeup of the publication's readership to the advertising agencies that purchased newspaper space for their clients. The resulting information, which would become widely accepted as a proxy for consumer preferences, helped to rationalize the newspaper advertising market, stabilizing a critical revenue stream for the publishers and, not incidentally, the job security of the journalists who reported the news.

Radio was different. Though station managers did their best to persuade advertisers that their audience was large, well-to-do, and consumption minded, it was notoriously difficult to determine just who was listening in. This conundrum was particularly vexing in the United States, where advertising was the primary revenue stream. In the absence of audience data, it was hard to calculate advertising rates. Newspaper publishers, working in conjunction with advertising agencies, had devised a workaround. Radio stations had not. To help solve this problem, a new industry—public opinion polling—emerged.

Public opinion pollsters built on and helped to promote a new way of thinking about human nature. In the United States, the new thinking was popularized by advertisers who questioned the presumption that consumers based their purchasing decisions on rational criteria. Consumer decisions, in their view, were often influenced by emotional appeals that tapped into irrational and, in some instances, unconscious fears and desires. The "product" of advertising, declared one US advertising man shortly after the war, was "public opinion." In Germany, similar assumptions, drawn in part from academic research on group behavior, informed specialists in the emerging field of *Werbepsychologie* (advertising psychology).

In the United States and Germany, advertisers built on the disparaging analysis of crowd behavior that had been popularized in the late nineteenth century by the French social theorist Gustave Le Bon (1841–1931). Le Bon's critique met with a responsive audience in the United Kingdom, where elites had warned for decades that metropolitan newspapers might inspire "irrational" crowd behavior. In 1920s Germany, this critique became a staple of the anti-Semitic journalism of the right-wing newspaper magnate Alfred Hugenberg, who castigated Jewish publishers as a pack of manipulative Pied Pipers guilty of "deluding" a gullible German public into rejecting conventional assumptions about politics and culture.

Public opinion, like propaganda, has a venerable history. The origins of the concept went back to ancien régime France, where political economists invoked it to monitor shifting attitudes toward public finance. Originally, the concept referred to the attitudes not of the many, but of the few—and, above all, to well-informed bourgeois men. In their quest to understand what a later generation would call mass society, the concept would be swiftly embraced by political theorists ranging from David Hume and James Madison to Alexis de Tocqueville and John Stuart Mill.

Interestingly, none of these political theorists devoted more than passing attention to the technically demanding, and conceptually fraught, question of how public opinion might be measured. When contemporaries considered the issue, they were mostly content to sample newspaper articles. In the United States, for example, the Baltimore journalist Hezekiah Niles clipped articles from hundreds of publications in compiling *Niles's Weekly Register*, the most influential news digest of the early republic, while in the 1880s the editors of *Public Opinion*—a magazine that, as its title implied, tried to gauge the popular mood—reprinted editorials from publications espousing different points of view. In Germany, similarly, journalists routinely conflated public opinion with the pronouncements of contemporaries that they had gleaned from the press—pronouncements that they would then reprint or summarize in their own columns. To streamline the process, newspaper clipping services sprang up to provide their clientele with articles on particular topics of interest.

In the interwar period—hastened by the rise of radio—public opinion would cease to refer to the considered judgments of a discerning, and presumably well-informed, elite. Instead, it would be reconceptualized as the cultural beliefs of the many. Two modes of cultural analysis proved to be particularly influential. The first traced public opinion to material conditions that rested ultimately in economic power; the second to the subjective preferences of the audience itself. Both were pioneered by a small but influential group of German émigré scholars who fled Nazi Germany for the United States.

The materialist mode of cultural analysis originated at the Institute for Social Research in Frankfurt, Germany. Founded in the interwar period, the Frankfurt school—as this movement became known—critiqued institutional arrangements and cultural norms from a neo-Marxist perspective. The Frankfurt school produced a body of scholarship on new media that remains influential today. Siegfried Kracauer explored why working-class German shop girls flocked to the cinema. Walter Benjamin analyzed how the "mechanical reproduction" of famous works of art—for example, through photography—destroyed their ineffable aura of authenticity.

While modern technical contrivances devalued certain modes of cultural expression, they amplified others. The desacralization of art, Benjamin argued, would enable propagandists to aestheticize politics—rendering the masses vulnerable to fascist appeals. Information, Benjamin contended in an essay on Russian storyteller Nikolai Leskov, was a new literary genre, created by the metropolitan newspaper for the middle class to consume. Spawned by the "fully developed capitalism" of modernity, it challenged such venerable storytelling forms as the epic in a "more menacing way" than had other older literary forms, such as the novel: "This new form of communication is information."

Benjamin's work intertwined with certain ideas of Theodor Adorno and Max Horkheimer. Like Benjamin, Adorno and Horkheimer were Jewish, which obliged them to flee Germany for the United States after the Nazis came to power. Horkheimer had been the head of the Institute for Social Research in Frankfurt. When the Nazis came to power in 1933, he moved the Institute first to Geneva, and then New York City, where it found a home at Columbia University.

Adorno's first project following his arrival in the United States was a Rockefeller Foundation–funded study of the relationship between radio broadcasting and Hitler's rise to power. Like the first generation of public opinion pollsters, Adorno drew on social psychology to probe the relationship between form and content. Radio broadcasts, Adorno provocatively concluded, predisposed certain listeners to become fascists, including, in particular, those individuals who harbored what he would famously label an "authoritarian personality." While Adorno would later be faulted for psychological reductionism, his analysis of the authoritarian personality generated an innovative tradition of scholarship on the relationship of culture and politics.

The most influential of Adorno's publications on the relationship of media and society was the *Dialectic of Enlightenment* (1944), which he coauthored with Horkheimer. *Dialectic* traced the origins of present-day "culture industries"—a capacious conceptual category that included radio broadcasting, movies, and popular music—to the Enlightenment belief in reason, a faith that they presumed, somewhat paradoxically, would inexorably undermine the promise of rational thought.

Neither Adorno nor Horkheimer had much confidence in the objective measurement of subjective preferences. This task would fall to their sometime colleague Paul Lazarsfeld, an Austrian Jew who helped to found the new field of communications research. Shortly after his arrival in the United States, La-zarsfeld obtained funding from the Rockefeller Foundation to investigate radio listening habits—the same project on which Adorno had briefly worked. Lazarsfeld originally based his research center at Princeton, before moving it to Columbia University, where it would become the Bureau for Social Research, a center that still exists today.

The most influential contribution of central European émigrés to US communications research was methodological. Though Lazarsfeld was not the first to rely on focus groups and longitudinal panel surveys to measure public opinion, he would become their most devoted champion. Similar techniques would soon take root in the United Kingdom. The longitudinal panel survey, for example, would be used extensively by the Mass Observation project, a British social research organization, founded in 1937, that was best known for its three-decade-long investigation of the living conditions of the British working class.

No comparable methodological innovations in communications research would originate in Germany until after the Second World War. A key figure in German postwar media scholarship was Elisabeth Noelle-Neumann, who is best known for *The Spiral of Silence: Public Opinion—Our Social Skin* (1980; English translation 1984). Noelle-Neumann completed a PhD dissertation at the University of Missouri in 1940 on US public opinion research. Following her return to Germany, she wrote widely for Nazi publications. In a newspaper article entitled "Who Informs America?," for example, she blamed Jewish publishers for monopolizing the American press. Following the Nazis' defeat, Noelle-Neumann built on her American training in public opinion research to establish in 1948 the Allensbach Institute, the first center for quantitative communications research in West Germany.

The Frankfurt school would remain an influential center for communications research following the Second World War, especially after its return to Germany in 1953. A key figure in the postwar generation was the philosopher Jürgen Habermas. In his *Structural Transformation of the Public Sphere* (1962; English translation 1989)—discussed also in chapter 10—Habermas built on his predecessors' long-standing interest in the influence of communications media on public life to trace the rise and fall of the "bourgeois public sphere," a social form, he contended, that originated in the *coffeehouses and cafés of early eighteenth-century England in which men could rationally exchange information on public affairs.

Habermas's characterization of this novel social space as "bourgeois" paid homage to the Frankfurt school's materialist mode of cultural analysis. So too did his mordant, and at times despairing, assessment of the political consequences of modern media. Like Adorno, Habermas criticized the "cultural industries" of the nineteenth and twentieth centuries for debasing public life by commercializing domains that had formerly fostered the rational exchange of information.

The translation of Habermas's *Structural Transformation* into English in 1989 helped to popularize the concept of the "public sphere" in the English-speaking world. For the next two decades, this concept helped set the agenda for communications research in both the English-speaking and the German-speaking worlds. The resulting information exchange was a two-way street. Only after *Structural Transformation* had been translated into English would historians, philosophers, sociologists, and media scholars join together to publish a critical reassessment—*Habermas and the Public Sphere* (1992)—that faulted Habermas for idealizing a communicative realm that marginalized women, nonwhites, and the poor. Habermas himself would join this transnational information exchange, contributing an essay to that volume in which he acknowledged his critics.

Conclusion

The history of information in the first half of the twentieth century was profoundly shaped by three media organizations: the metropolitan newspaper, the government messaging agency, and the radio broadcasting station. The popular fascination with the sinking of the *Titanic* in 1912 fit neatly into an oddly optimistic, resolutely progressive morality play as old as the Enlightenment. Had the distress signals broadcast by the *Titanic*'s wireless operator been more widely circulated, the disaster could have been averted. Limited information imperiled; abundant information saved. An analogous logic shaped the popular understanding of the metropolitan newspaper: publicity was good; more publicity was better.

Following the First World War, when the British, German, and American governments fought an information war alongside the war on the ground, thoughtful observers in all three countries came to regard this prewar faith in publicity as misguided and naive. No one could possibly possess the intellectual bandwidth—or so Walter Lippmann observed in *Public Opinion*, pointedly including himself—to process intelligently the information that would be necessary to pronounce competently on all the issues of the day. By deliberately manipulating the public through propaganda, messaging agencies only made a bad situation worse. No longer was the citizenry omnicompetent; no longer could information save. No longer did public opinion bear any relationship to the carefully calibrated judgment of the few. Henceforth, it would become increasingly conflated with the often-inchoate preferences of the many.

The prewar faith in the free flow of information persisted, especially in the United States. Yet with the rise of radio broadcasting, it became obvious to media insiders in the United Kingdom, Germany, and the United States that the new medium challenged basic assumptions about the relationship between information, freedom, and power. No longer could the beneficence of information be taken for granted.

The Hungarian uprising of 1956 furnished a fitting epilogue to the often-extravagant expectations that accompanied the long-standing US commitment to the free flow of information. Though the leaders of the Hungarian resistance were driven primarily by internal considerations, CIA-backed Radio Free Europe broadcasts emboldened protesters to overplay their hand by demonizing the Soviet-backed regime and raising the possibility of outside military support. Few events better symbolized how the Enlightenment dream in the salvific power of information could become a nightmare. For the Hungarian rebels, information was not freedom and the CIA's news management was a death sentence for an audience primed to listen in.

Though US-backed radio broadcasts had not instigated the uprising, and figured little in internal Soviet decision making, they helped to fan the flames of a failed insurgency that left as many as twenty thousand dead. The reputation of Radio Free Europe never entirely recovered. Even sympathetic observers termed its conduct in the uprising a "debacle." It was not the ethereal airwaves, but the tangible presence of Soviet tanks, that won the day, at least for the time. What had changed since 1912? Not only the absence of information, but also its abundance, could be a harbinger of disaster. Nothing was as simple as it seemed.

Further Reading

Theodor W. Adorno, *The Culture Industry: Selected Essays on Mass Culture*, 1991; Jonathan Auerbach and Russ Castronovo, eds., *The Oxford Handbook of Propaganda Studies*, 2013; Colin B. Burke, *America's Information Wars: The Untold Story of Information Systems in America's Conflicts and Politics from World War II to the Internet Age*, 2018; John Dewey, *The Public and Its Problems*, 1927; David Greenberg, *Republic of Spin: An Inside History of the American Presidency*, 2016; Julia Guarneri, *Newsprint Metropolis: City Papers and the Making of Modern Americans*, 2017; Jürgen Habermas, *The Structural Transformation of the Public Sphere: An*

Inquiry into a Category of Bourgeois Society, 1962, translated by Thomas Burger with the assistance of Frederick Lawrence, 1989; Daniel R. Headrick, *The Invisible Weapon: Telecommunications and International Politics, 1851–1945*, 1991; Andrew Hobbs, *A Fleet Street in Every Town: The Provincial Press in England, 1855–1900*, 2018; Max Horkheimer and Theodor W. Adorno, *Dialectic of Enlightenment*, 1944; Richard R. John, *Network Nation: Inventing American Telecommunications*, 2010; Richard R. John and Jonathan Silberstein-Loeb, eds., *Making News: The Political Economy of Journalism from the Glorious Revolution to the Internet*, 2015; Walter Lippmann, *Liberty and the News*, 1920; idem, *The Phantom Public*, 1925; idem, *Public Opinion*, 1922; Simone M. Müller, *Wiring the World: The Social and Cultural Creation of Global Telegraph Networks*, 2016; John Nerone, *The Media and Public Life: A History*, 2016; Elisabeth Noelle-Neumann, *The Spiral of Silence: Public Opinion—Our Social Skin*, 1980, English translation 1984; Marc Raboy, *Marconi: The Man Who Networked the World*, 2016; Paul Starr, *The Creation of the Media: Political Origins of Modern Communications*, 2005; Heidi J. S. Tworek, *News from Germany: The Competition to Control World Communications, 1900–1945*, 2019; idem, "The Savior of the Nation? Regulating Radio in the Interwar Period," *Journal of Policy History* 27, no. 3 (2015): 465–91; Jonathan Reed Winkler, "Information Warfare in World War I," *Journal of Military History* 73, no. 3 (2009): 845–67.

12

Communication, Computation, and Information

Paul Duguid

SURROUNDED AS WE ARE BY INFORMATIONAL devices such as smart phones, watches, and speakers, along with computers, tablets, and similar *digital devices, all interlinked through *internet connections, it is generally uncontentious to assert that we live in the "information age." Such an assumption distinguishes this chapter, bringing this book up to the present, from its predecessors. They principally use modern notions of information to explore the past. From such a perspective, as the historian Robert Darnton notes, "every age was an age of information." But this chapter centers on an age whose inhabitants regularly invoke "information" to distinguish their age from every other, often citing information technologies of the sort mentioned above as the cause of the age's distinctiveness. Indeed, some see these as making our age so distinct that history is irrelevant. Anthony Levandowski, a prominent Silicon Valley engineer, told a *New Yorker* journalist in 2018, "The only thing that matters is the future. . . . I don't even know why we study history. . . . In technology, all that matters is tomorrow." Yet such claims, paradoxically, must assume some knowledge of the past in order to be able to dismiss it, for in asserting that the current age is so distinct they presume some idea of what the past was like, how we got here from there, and when that transition occurred. As Steve Jobs, a better-known Silicon Valley guru, put it, "You can't connect the dots looking forward, you can only connect them looking backwards." The same might be said for disconnecting the dots, as Levandowski and *born digital champions try to do, for that too needs an understanding of the past. Connecting the dots, as this chapter (and, indeed, this book) seeks to do, helps reveal the extent to which our age is (or is not) distinct. The chapter investigates, in particular, the way in which over time the realms of computation and communication were combined to form the "information technology" that is assumed to have shaped the new age.

Change and Continuity

Breaking history into ages has a long history itself. In the eighteenth century, the economist Adam Smith identified his own society as having reached the "state or age" of commerce, distinguishing this from prior ages of hunters, shepherds, and agriculture, while, infused with similar ideas of progress, his contemporary George Washington distinguished their era from a prior "gloomy Age of ignorance." Of course, Smith's age of commerce and Washington's "Auspicious period" certainly relied on what we might now classify as "information technologies," such as printing, *bookkeeping, timekeeping, and the postal service that carried Washington's "circular." But it is our age that conceptually connected such a diverse array into a unitary category of devices that are together seen as creating an entirely new era by, on the one hand, underwriting new kinds of labor, production, distribution, and consumption, as well as particular kinds of goods or commodities; and, on the other hand, instigating new kinds of connectivity and sociality to support communication in the "public sphere" and develop unprecedented forms of "social network."

To investigate the attendant claims about the new age, we need first to explore when it is seen as beginning, and by extension when its distinctive technology is seen to emerge. For the first, we might explore when the occupants themselves began to claim "information" as a marker of their own age.

In July 1977, IBM ran an advertisement in *Fortune* magazine asserting "Information: there is growing agreement that it is the name of the age we live in." IBM supported its claim by noting "changes in our perception of information itself" driven by an "explosion" in the "volume of information" before consoling readers with the promise that there "exists today remarkable technological capacity for dealing with it," capable of turning information from a threat into "an inexhaustible resource." IBM then highlighted its own contribution to such technological capacity, invoking its machines from "computers to copiers" and including a "vast array of electronic techniques."

As IBM's own history can, as we shall see, be traced back into the nineteenth century, its advertisement, while recognizing a certain level of self-awareness, fails to mark a cutoff. For instance, its invocation of distinctive technology pushes us back two decades to an article in *Harvard Business Review* in 1958 that noted that the "new technology" that had "begun to take hold in American business" largely after World War II "does not have a single established name." The article decided to call it "information technology." (A little later, IBM called its contribution to the 1964 World's Fair the "Information Engine.") This definition pushes us back in turn yet another decade to 1949, when *Scientific American* claimed a revolution was taking place, "based on the transformation and transmission of information" and enabling "information processing," driven by "mathematical machines." In giving primacy to such accounts from the world of business and science, we should not overlook the claim of the literary critic Marshall McLuhan, who announced the "age of information" a decade before IBM's advertisement, but similarly claimed this age was driven by electrical machines through which "commodities themselves assume . . . [the] character of information."

Such observations reflect a coming together in the postwar years, and no doubt in part as a result of wartime innovation, of ideas about computation and communication, resulting in IBM's "growing agreement." But IBM's long history in making "machines," *Harvard Business Review*'s imprecise "largely after World War II," *Scientific American*'s claim that its revolution succeeded a prior one in the nineteenth century, and McLuhan's vagueness about "electrical" machines all make it tricky to know when to look for the origin of the transformation they all want to mark. Indeed, their own decade-by-decade regression illustrates how claims to historical antecedents can prod us back indefinitely, so that, investigating "information technology," we slide irresistibly toward such devices as the ancient Greek Antikythera device or the Chinese abacus. To limit such a slide, we might invoke those smart devices, portable computers, and the internet that, as I suggested above, are regularly offered as unproblematic indicators of our distinctive age, and explore their roots and commonalities. These exemplars embrace communication and computation in ways many would agree transformed access to and use of information. Thus homing in on generally accepted antecedents of such tools, particularly those explicitly cited by developers in that postwar period that *Harvard Business Review* portrayed as critical, might plausibly allow us to stop an indefinite if not infinite regression.

In tracing such a path, however, we should not assume that those three notions—communication, computation, and information—were always as readily associated as they are today. For example, if we were to say "calculation" rather than "computation," the connection would be far less clear, yet the ancestors of modern computers were, as we shall see, primarily calculating devices. Consequently, until quite recently, communications and computation were for many fundamentally distinct. McLuhan's work, for example, focuses almost wholly on the former while IBM's advertisement involves primarily the latter, yet each assumes that it embraces the devices that produced the "information age." Similarly, in the early 1980s, the software pioneer Joe Weizenbaum disputed an account of the rise of the "information society" offered by the sociologist Daniel Bell. Bell, in Weizenbaum's words, saw the "information society" as the "child of the marriage between modern communication and computer technologies." Weizenbaum, by contrast, like many before (and after), argued that these two were fundamentally distinct species.

Nonetheless, today it can be hard to see the two as anything other than interrelated. And one critical notion making such confidence possible may be their shared identity as "information" devices. Thus, connecting some of the dots that brought communication and computation together, as I attempt in what follows, will I hope tell us something about our claims to a distinctive "age" marked by information.

Computing Engines

From the 1949 *Scientific American* article to the issue of *Time* magazine that nominated the computer as the "machine of the year" in 1983 to contemporary TED talks, Charles Babbage (1791–1871) is widely portrayed, in *Time's* terms, "as the first man to conceptualize a true computer." As so often with technology heroes (e.g., Gutenberg, Morse, Jobs), Babbage is perhaps not quite as original as conventionally portrayed. Nonetheless, he conceptualized two distinct types of machine, the "Difference Engine" and the "Analytical Engine," in which later computer pioneers saw the roots of their own work. (Accounts of Babbage are limited to "conceptualization" because, continuously enticed by new possibilities, he failed to complete a version of either.)

With the Difference Engine, Babbage sought to automate the production of reliable mathematical tables. Such tables of figures could turn complex mathematical calculations into more simple and so more manageable ones. Logarithms, for example, transformed baffling multiplication and division into straightforward addition and subtraction. Unfortunately, the work of calculating and printing such tables required challenging mathematics and tedious typesetting, both of which contributed to published tables being notoriously error strewn. Babbage sought to produce more reliable figures, driven by the hope "that all these tables . . . might be calculated by machinery," which, with automated printing, would overcome human frailties. Surveying earlier table-making attempts, he found that one of the best, devised by Gaspard de Prony (1755–1839) for the French government, was quite machine-like. Drawing on Adam Smith's famous "division of labor," Prony had broken down the calculating task into columns of people working together, the more proficient disassembling difficult calculations into manageable subtasks that they passed to their less proficient colleagues. Developing Prony's insight, Babbage sought to build a "mechanism for assisting the human mind in executing the operations of arithmetic" with columns of calculating cogs replacing the columns of calculating people and taking up the disassembled tasks and passing partial results to neighboring columns for completion.

The British government funded Babbage's work, but when Babbage lost interest, the government withdrew support, and the project dwindled. A major distraction for Babbage was that engine's more sophisticated sibling, the Analytical Engine, with which he hoped to bypass many of the assisting human minds required for the earlier engine by "teaching the engine to see and then act [with] foresight." This theoretically self-controlling machine relied on "operations," driven by a "mill," whose results could be put in a "store" until needed. Babbage appropriated these terms from the industrial production of grain, but with them he envisaged the programming, central processing, and memory of modern computers. Moreover, as Prony's division of labor had inspired Babbage to divide computational tasks, so another Frenchman, Joseph Marie Jacquard (1752–1834), who had developed punched cards to control elaborate silk-weaving machines, inspired Babbage's card-fed input system. In essence, by reworking insights and tools of the industrial era, Babbage foreshadowed its end, which his intellectual heirs would help to instantiate.

Babbage's work cultivated the attention of eager enthusiasts who were more capable than he of addressing a broader audience. These included the Italian mathematician (and later prime minister) Luigi Menabrea (1809–96) and the English mathematician Ada Lovelace (1815–52). Menabrea wrote an enthusiastic account of the potential of both engines in French, which Lovelace then translated into English and annotated with insightful notes twice the length of the original. These commentaries revealed, perhaps even to Babbage, unanticipated possibilities for his engines.

Machines that presage the future tend to provoke thoughts of "technological determinism," suggesting that once envisaged, such machines irresistibly push forward and transform society in the process. Yet, despite the support of his enthusiasts and the accolades of our contemporaries, rather than pushing forward, Babbage and his work sank into oblivion. Intermittently, engineers stumbled upon the work and attempted to complete one or the other of his engines. During Babbage's lifetime, a Swedish father and son, Georg and Edvard Scheutz, supported by the Swedish government, built a version of the long-abandoned Difference Engine, receiving a gold medal (and Babbage's approval) at the Great Exhibition in Paris in 1855. Nevertheless, in 1871, *Scientific American* allotted Babbage a cursory one-paragraph obituary, dismissing the "calculating machine" as "valueless for general use."

Despite this limited contemporary appreciation, more recent historians and computer scientists have seen essential precursors of the modern computer in Babbage's devices. They have, however, revealed no similar anticipation of the communication aspects of modern technologies, despite Babbage's living in the era of transformational communication systems, such as trains, steamships, telegraphs, and telephones. Babbage was well aware of these. Indeed, he blamed "railway mania" for making it hard to find engineers for his engines, while the ability of the telegraph to convey "information over extensive lines with great rapidity" impressed him. But though Babbage saw communication devices dealing with "information," that concept had, for him, no bearing on his engines or on his idea of computation. If we see the computer as critical to an "information revolution," Babbage and his supporters almost certainly did not. Billed as "father" of the computer, he evidently was not aware of what Daniel Bell and others saw as the inevitable suitor for his child.

As Babbage and his machines sank, another central figure in histories of computation, Herman Hollerith (1860–1929), rose to prominence in the United States. Not only did advances in engineering make building his machines easier, but Hollerith, unlike Babbage, found customers for them, first in the government, then in corporations, both of which, as populations, workforces, and industrial production grew, found keeping track of their charges more challenging and looked to machinery for help.

Hollerith began with the government. After leaving university, he had gone to work on the 1880 US decennial census. Though mandated by the country's constitution, US census work was disorganized. (That other countries were better organized probably made them less interested in developing innovative machines.) Faced with a growing population, tabulation of the 1880 census was slower, more demanding, and more expensive than ever before, and the task barely finished when work on the 1890 census began. The difficulty of extracting accurate statistics inspired a colleague of Hollerith's to insist, with a vision reminiscent of Babbage's, that "there ought to be a machine for doing the purely mechanical work of tabulating population and similar statistics." Hollerith designed such a machine and won a government competition to automate the 1890 census. Though the population had grown by some 25 percent and the census asked twice as many questions as in 1880, Hollerith's calculator made the 1890 tabulation both faster and cheaper, saving two years in time and $5 million in costs.

Previous attempts at automation in the Census Office had used a machine fed by a paper strip that was indefinitely long and consequently made access to particular points cumbersome. Hollerith's major insight was to feed in data with discrete cards. Where Babbage took inspiration for his cards from the silk industry, Hollerith took his from the railways, where tickets were issued as cards printed with a selection of identifying features that an inspector's punch would perforate to create a "punch photograph" of individual travelers ("light hair, dark eyes, large nose"). Hollerith adapted the idea, using more census-like characteristics (sex, age, birthplace, conjugal status, occupation) for a census "photograph." The machines made electrical connection through the punched holes, allowing indicated data to be selected, sorted, accumulated, and enumerated.

Though Hollerith's preeminent biographer refers to him as a "forgotten" giant, his recognition was more immediate than Babbage's. Census offices in Europe and Russia and manufacturing, railway, insurance, and finance corporations on both sides of the Atlantic sought his machines. To meet demand, Hollerith formed the Tabulating Machine Company, which, in the early twentieth century, transformed itself, via the Computing-Tabulating-Recording Company, into International Business Machines, or IBM. This transformation can make the transition from the nineteenth century to IBM's advertisement about the "information" age seem inescapable. Yet, while Hollerith's company explicitly invoked "computing," notions of "information" and "communication" played little role in his work, nor, for a long time in IBM's. By the time of its 1977 advertisement, IBM was eager to embrace "information," as that had by then come to be seen as a facet of computing, but the company still did not associate its machines with communication.

Moving from Babbage to Hollerith and from there to IBM, the story inescapably seems another of Anglo-Saxon men advancing technology. The "second industrial revolution," which, as James Beniger's influential *Control Revolution* argues, spurred the development of modern computers, took place primarily in Britain and the United States in an era of white male dominance, so it is not surprising that a tale connecting the conventional dots should reflect these privileged features. But this preponderance should not allow us to underestimate women's contributions, from Ada Lovelace as a critical interpreter of Babbage's work to the anonymous female "computers" who ran Hollerith's machines, each processing up to ten thousand cards per day and overcoming the inevitable challenges and failings of emerging technologies that early workers have to surmount but retrospect tends to hide. Nor should the Anglo-Saxon focus allow us to ignore Hollerith's German heritage, the critical contributions from France of Jacquard and Prony, nor the Italian Menabrea and the Swedish Scheutzes. Further, conventional championing of market entre-preneurialism in the information age should not obscure the critical role of government in this history, funding Babbage and then Hollerith, building infrastructure, and overseeing standards. And while the story also resembles whiggish accounts of irresistible, emancipatory forward progress, applauded by Beniger, as society found ways to gain control over information, we should note ominous foreshadowing of the technology's converse control over people: Babbage's work anticipated Frederick Winslow Taylor's (1856–1915) "Scientific Management," which from the nineteenth-century factory to Amazon warehouses has treated people themselves as cogs in machines, while Hollerith's "punched photographs" point to later forms of surveillance, from IBM's role in helping the Nazis monitor their population and impose race law to India's use of biometrics to avoid railway ticket scalpings.

Communications and Information

The nineteenth century primarily saw "information" as an aspect not of machine calculation, but of human communication, in particular of writing, books, and libraries. Hence to see the trajectory of information and communication we need to look at this alternative context. Moreover, there is an intriguing link between the two. The colleague of Hollerith's at the Census Office who raised the Babbage-like idea of a tabulating machine fed with cards was John Billings (1838–1913), a doctor working on census "vital statistics." Previously, Billings had conducted research at the US surgeon general's office and, overwhelmed by its resources, attempted to reorganize its library. Such challenges were common at the time. Scientific endeavor increasingly suffocated under its growing output, with new articles, reports, commentaries, and books accumulating at unprecedented rates. Scientists and librarians desperately sought ways to make this output accessible. Billings played both roles, and in the surgeon general's library he pioneered a card catalog for books and articles while also developing the scholarly *Index Medicus* in 1879, a still-published, innovative monthly index of new medical research. Both projects relied on library cards, no doubt inspiring Billings's suggestion to Hollerith. (In 1896, Billings became the first librarian of the consolidated New York Public Library.)

The explosion of research in the late nineteenth century prompted numerous such attempts to make scholarly output accessible. One of the most adventurous, again organized around cards, was undertaken by the Belgian scholar Paul Otlet (1868–1944), who pioneered the field of "documentalism." While history recognizes Babbage for foreshadowing the computer, applause is often as loud for Otlet presaging the *World Wide Web. Like Billings, whose work he knew, Otlet sought to track the content of publications. But rather than merely pointing to the source, as Billings's cards did, Otlet attempted to liberate the *facts, ideas, and information, as he variously referred to these (in French, *faits, idées, information*), from books and the like, which, to Otlet, an enthusiast of telegraph, telephone, radio, television, and cinema, appeared as outdated physical constraints on the communication of information. Otlet envisaged the product of such liberation as "informations sans préoccupation d'ordre" ("[pieces of] information without any concern for order") and began to accumulate the key facts of human knowledge extracted from books and inscribed on cards so that they could be easily reordered. Extracted facts were indexed for author and source by another set of cards, creating "informations documentées" ("documented [pieces of] information"). All these cards (later, microfiches) were organized in files that were in turn collected in a library-like center, the Mundaneum, to be replicated in, connected to, and distributed from similar venues throughout the world. For the Mundaneum, Otlet planned a multimedia, desk-like device, the *mondothèque*, to give users means to access this atomized information and reassemble it into new structures of knowledge. Information and communication were, in this view, inseparable aspects of human knowledge, and Otlet's grand notion of "documentalism" envisioned technology (some admiringly modelled on Hollerith machines) to further all three across the world. In the process, Otlet idealistically hoped to liberate not only information but humanity.

Otlet's vision embraced extant notions of information and communication and in the process revealed many assumptions that would become critical as these two embraced computation. People had come to see information as a

fundamental, countable, and transferable unit of human knowledge accumulated in books—since the eighteenth-century *publishers' advertisements had
regularly boasted that there was "more" information in their books than in
their rivals'—and Otlet by extension sought the independence and subsequent reassembly of such units in new forms connected by networks of links
into what he envisaged as a "mechanical brain." While his dream of a worldwide network was never fulfilled, he built nodes of this vision in Belgium,
stocking them with hundreds of thousands of indexed and conceptually
interconnected cards.

Over time, librarians took up such views of "information" from Billings,
Otlet, and also the influential library scholar Melvil Dewey (1851–1931), the
proponent of *decimal classification for library books. Subsequently,
the worlds of documentalism and librarianship would claim the identity of
"information science," a trajectory that can be traced in the successive names
of one journal from *Journal of Documentary Reproduction* (1938), to *American
Documentation* (1950), to *Journal of the Association of Information Science*
(1968), to *Journal of the Association of Information Science and Technology*
(2001). Yet librarians' work had little direct influence on computer science,
which reached its views of "information" and "communication" from other
directions. The resilient distance between these two worlds is indicated in an
article from the early 1970s in the *Journal of Librarianship* that, echoing Weizenbaum's insistent separation noted earlier, inveighed against the "erroneous
notion that computers were able to handle or even to produce information
(when all they can ever do is manipulate data)."

Information Defined

In many ways a visionary, Otlet imagined the world of information networked
through the Mundaneum as leading to world peace. As if in response, the two
world wars of the twentieth century helped to sideline his work. Turning attention back to calculating machines, the wars played a central role in advancing computing, where development was once more driven by government
investment and national interests, as we shall see. But the evolution of modern
technology and the concept of "information" nonetheless took a significant
nonmilitary turn between the wars, guided by corporate research with little
direct interest in either library science or computation, in particular in the work
of a major communications company, AT&T, seeking to address challenges of
the wired network whose potential, as we have seen, Babbage admired.

In the 1920s at Bell Laboratories, AT&T's research center, the engineer Ralph Hartley (1880–1970), exploring the "manufacture of telephone apparatus" and "long distance telephone lines," sought to measure "the capacity of the physical system to transmit information." Hartley saw information as the common underpinning of telegraphy, telephony, and television, which forward-looking eyes could see converging on telephone lines. That idea of "information" may seem unproblematic today, but Hartley was cautious about it, noting that "information is a very elastic term," that elasticity making objective measurement difficult. Consequently he decided to "eliminate the psychological factors" and "establish a measure of information in terms of purely physical quantities." Thus his research was deliberately and profoundly separated from discussions of information and knowledge at play in, for instance, documentalism and libraries.

In his search for an objective measure, Hartley echoes the French engineer Émile Baudot (1845–1903), who in the 1870s recognized that in using "long" and "short" pulses (as well as a "medium" gap to mark the separation of letters and a "long" gap for the separation of words) to compose messages, Morse had introduced subjectivity into telegraphy (one person's long might be another's short) and thus the system often required that the recipients of a signal guess at the meaning of the message under transmission in order to interpret the *code. Baudot replaced *Morse code with Baudot code, a mathematical cipher that antedated modern *binary codes (for which Baudot is still recognized in the use of *baud* as the unit of measurement for the speed of a signal along a channel). Baudot signals were particularly significant for international telegraphy. First, they could be transmitted accurately to recipients who did not understand the message. And second, they could handle nonalphabetic writing more easily than Morse code. Baudot's work resembled experimentation with numerical codes, which were being developed in China to suit its nonalphabetic script at the same time (see Gitelman and Mullaney, chap. 9).

Hartley's more celebrated AT&T colleague Claude Shannon (1916–2001) developed Hartley's insights, leading to Shannon's enormously influential "mathematical theory of communication" (often erroneously referred to as the "mathematical theory of information"). Shannon defined communication as "reproducing at one point . . . a message selected at another." To measure the accuracy of that reproduction without reinvoking the psychological factors that troubled Hartley, Shannon dismissed "meaning" as irrelevant to the task, further distancing semantic understandings of communication. (As his colleague Warren Weaver noted, the mathematical theory was indifferent to whether the signal indicated "the text of the King James Version of the Bible" or the word "Yes.") With such assumptions, Shannon was able to calculate the most efficient way to send "information" over a line. Where Hartley's model had also had to ignore "noise" or interference on the line, Shannon was able to incorporate that and deduce optimal ways of dealing with it. More significantly, Shannon's meaning-neutral account of information was also able to address the computer: "This case has application not only in communication theory, but also in the theory of computing machines," he noted at one point. Shannon mentioned this only in passing and clearly felt that the connection was not obvious; nonetheless, influenced by Shannon's work, the notion of "information" as autonomous signal started to connect dots between "computation" and "communication." With psychology, meaning, and semantics omitted, however, the notion of information in play is self-evidently a restricted one. Nevertheless, Shannon's theory spread from the telephone to any domain willing to claim "information" as part of its provenance, particularly those looking for mathematical validation. This wide embrace (implicitly assuming that more information was more informative) troubled Shannon, who remained ever conscious of the restrictions of his definition and feared that in many appropriations of his work these were being ignored.

The adoption of Shannon's work for "computing machines" became central to the growth of those machines following military-supported research of World War II, in which Shannon himself took part. Indeed, Shannon's theory in part developed from his attempts to design impenetrable encryption. Among other things, wartime research helped rediscover Babbage: Alan Turing (1912–54), who worked on the innovative Colossus computer at Bletchley Park to crack the German Enigma encryption machine, reported that Babbage was regularly discussed there. Turing himself went on to instantiate ideas behind Babbage's Analytical Engine in the development of stored-program digital computers, naming his machine the "Automatic Computing Engine" in tribute to the "engines" Babbage and Lovelace had described. (Turing's US contemporary John von Neumann [1903–57] also drew on Babbage for what he called his "Electronic Computing Instrument.") These engines or instruments were number crunchers, having little to do with conventional interhuman communication. Fittingly, Bletchley interoffice communication relied on paper messages pulled on wires along underground tunnels rather than the advanced computation machines being built above ground.

Animal and Machine

As wartime insights developed in the postwar years, however, the new "computers" fostered increasing elision between descriptions of people and of machines. Following wartime work on the "feedback" needed to track moving targets, Norbert Wiener (1894–1964) developed the concept of "cybernetics," which saw information feedback as common to "communication in the animal and the machine." Turing took computation in a similar direction with his attribution to machines of information-related concepts formerly reserved for animals, such as "memory," "stimulus," and "search." Attributions of this sort, leading to concepts like *"artificial intelligence" and "thinking machines," raised questions about when such usage was primarily metaphorical, indicating similarities between two worlds, and when, rather, it assumed a single, homogeneous world in which the same concepts could be applied unproblematically to both man and machine. Information's elasticity, which Hartley and Shannon sought to limit, helped foster this elision.

The influential computer scientist Vannevar Bush (1890–1974) made similar assumptions. Before the war, working to make power lines more efficient (much as Hartley and Shannon had worked with telephone lines), Bush, though unaware of Babbage, built a Babbage-like machine. During the war he supervised scientific research for the military and after helped to found the US National Science Foundation (NSF) to propagate that research in the peacetime world. Apparently unaware of Otlet, too, Bush's celebrated postwar essay "As We May Think" raises similar issues. Like Billings, Bush displayed a heightened sense of scholarly anxiety, noting that wartime military funding had produced a surge in scientific discovery that, without better means of storage and access, would probably be lost. Bush proposed that a "record" be made of such findings. "To be useful to science," he argued, this record must be "continuously extended" and "stored." In response, he conceptualized a small camera (a little like Google's infamous Glass) to be worn on the forehead for scientists to record whatever they encountered, and the *memex, rather like Otlet's mondothèque, a machine to store and sort such records, giving people "access to and command over the inherited knowledge of the ages" and allowing them to build links between previously unconnected ideas to produce new insights or "creative thought." The memex, Bush argued, would relieve the intellectual burdens of humanity because "whenever thought for a time runs along an accepted groove—there is an opportunity for the machine."

Again, I should pause to acknowledge that the conventional story continues to revolve around white males in the Anglo-American world—though figures from Baudot to Otlet, Wiener, and von Neumann challenge those geographical boundaries. Equally, the invisible but essential women that ran Turing's machines, and the "girls" that Bush can barely bring himself to acknowledge running his, faced and survived demanding work to make these machines viable. Indeed, despite their significant contribution, the highly productive work of wartime women "computers" was suppressed in postwar years as they were pushed to one side to give precedence to returning male soldiers. Hence, as scholarship such as Marie Hicks's *Programmed Inequality* (2017) has shown, even those who did pioneering work with early computers, programming the pathbreaking ENIAC and UNIVAC machines, writing the COBOL language, or developing Smalltalk, among them Marlyn Meltzer, Betty Holberton, Jean Bartik, Grace Hopper, Adele Goldberg, and many others, remained almost invisible.

Switching

Both inside the military and out, the machines and the organizations that used them tended to instantiate centralized, hierarchical structures. Over time, however, changing designs of computers challenged these structures, and with them dominant concepts of communication and information. The first digital machines, huge assemblies of interdependent vacuum tubes, were inherently centralizing. Organizations that adopted them allocated "computer rooms" to hold the machines and the people that ran them. Those requiring their services went to the machine, into which, for the most part, their calculating needs were fed on punched cards. One of the first corporate machines, LEO, developed in the early 1950s by J. Lyons and Co. in England, was used to centralize the firm's control over a supply chain that stretched from tea fields in India to teahouses in London.

Limitations of such centralization provoked the idea of time-sharing, enabling several people to use the same machine simultaneously, a far more efficient use of expensive machine time (and, usually, of people's time too). Time-sharing took advantage of the Babbagean process of breaking down tasks into subunits. These ran independently, amid the work of other users, to be reintegrated and reassembled when the subtasks were completed. This alternative approach also prompted a shift from cards to keyboards for the input, which allowed access points to be distributed more widely. In turn, distributed access raised the possibility of long-distance use, allowing people without local machines to seek access to and run programs on computers far away. As Hartley and Shannon had shown, the lines both had studied could support reliable access from remote terminals, further decentralizing computer use and introducing "communication" as a term for interaction with a computer.

Designers sought the most efficient way to arrange this. The answer turned out to be "packet-switching": once again, breaking down messages into elemental units (or "packets") to be sent independently across communication lines. This idea emerged at two separate venues, and their different paths to a similar conclusion reveal yet more about the changing relationship of computers and communication.

One version developed in the early 1960s at the Research and Development or RAND Corporation in California, under the eye of the electrical engineer Paul Baran (1926–2011) and funded by the US government at the height of the Cold War. Researchers addressed the problem of "survivable communications": how branches of the military might communicate in response to attack if their lines of communication, still of the sort that Hartley had studied, were vulnerable. Baran and colleagues proposed "distributed communications," building networks of multiple lines between any sender and receiver, thus providing multiple paths for a message to take. The message would be broken down into numerous subunits, each able to travel by different routes to the destination, where they would be reassembled. Which route each part would take could be decided at interconnected "store and forward" nodes along the way, depending on the state of the network at the time. The system could thus route around trouble: if one path was impassable at some point, packets could be sent along another. Only if the entire network was destroyed would communication collapse. "Survivability," Baran proposed, "is a function of switching flexibility." Both military and nonmilitary communication systems took on the structure Baran had envisaged, less to avoid bombing than, as with time-sharing, for the efficiency and flexibility it promised for the system as a whole.

Simultaneously, another "communication" project was getting underway at the National Physical Laboratory (NPL), a British standards institute. Donald Davies (1924–2000), who had worked with Turing, oversaw the project. Where RAND was investigating interhuman communication networks, the NPL was responding to the spread of computers and the challenge of "real-time communication" among them. The strategy was to replicate aspects of time-sharing and batch-processing or "methods used in multi-access computers" in order to allow what Davies called "a conversation between the user and the computer." Where Baran sought to avoid destruction, Davies sought to avoid congestion, but both came to a similar conclusion, now known under the name given to the NPL work, "packet-switching."

Both Baran and Davies made predictions for what Baran called the "wired city" that such networks would enable. The differences between these predictions reflect some of the differences between their initial assumptions. Along with "computer-aided school instruction," Baran foresaw users managing "bus, train, and air scheduling" and "person-to-person" communication, whereas Davies envisaged, among other things, "editing and typesetting of text," "booking of transport," "banking," "remote access to national records," and, reflecting British proclivities, "betting." Overall, where Baran was building networks that allowed interpersonal communication, Davies focused more on "computer to computer conversations" and the "communication needs" of "remote on-line data processing." These differences reflect ways in which information as an aspect of interpersonal communication was still in the early 1960s seen as distinct from "information-processing" computation.

"The Computer as a Communication Device," a 1968 essay by Joseph Licklider (1915–90) and Robert Taylor (1932–2017), each of whom played seminal roles in developing the internet, recognizes these distinctions while envisioning their pending merger. The authors saw themselves engaged in a struggle to portray the computer not "as a mathematical device, but as a communication device," as Taylor later put it in an interview. This portrayal was a challenge because, as the two wrote, a "communications engineer thinks of information from one point to another in codes and signals," which is very much in the spirit of Hartley, Shannon, and Davies. But, Licklider and Taylor insisted, "to communicate is more than to send and receive." In the process of pulling ideas of communication, computation, and information together, while building on send-and-receive models, they implicitly started to add back issues of psychology and meaning, which Hartley and Shannon had explicitly extracted to make their theories work. Licklider and Taylor, however, saw the separation as primarily historical and institutional: "Information transmission and information processing have always been carried out separately and have become separately institutionalized." Their new vision predicted the beginning of the end of such separation and projected the idea of new social communities emerging "face to face through a computer" from this united but enlarged notion of "information."

Licklider and Taylor exemplified their vision by describing an online meeting they had taken part in organized by Doug Engelbart (1925–2013) of Stanford Research Institute. In 1968, Engelbart caused a sensation with what became known as the "Mother of All Demos," in which he demonstrated real-time communication with remote colleagues through a computer and for which one of the key devices was the computer "mouse," on public display for the first time. The amalgamation of notions of "information," supported by the combined insights of Baran, Davies, Licklider, Roberts, and Engelbart, was leading toward what would be called the "internet," a packet-switching network using computers and related devices to transmit and process "information" not only among machines but among communities of people. Distinct ideas developed by Babbage, Hollerith, Otlet, Hartley, Shannon, and Bush began to coalesce in modern "information technology," but the commonalities, taken for granted now, were not, as this history suggests, self-evident then. Bernard Strassberg of the US Federal Communications Commission acknowledged twenty years later that "the first awareness that we had of the fact that computers and data processing had something in common with communications started in early '65." In all, Licklider and Taylor's title, "The Computer as a Communication Device," was designed to envision the future provocatively rather than describe the present complacently.

Layering

The internet as we know it today is the outcome of these multiple attempts to interconnect different types of device. (The word *internet* indicates that the initial goal was to *inter*connect multiple, different *net*works with one another, though the term today tends to invoke an all-embracing, single network.) Interconnections require common standards: a telegraph message written in Morse code but sent on a network built to expect Baudot codes, for example, would fail. Telecommunications companies, computer companies, governments, and militaries all had interests in what sort of networking should evolve, but each had different priorities.

Consequently, it proved difficult to find acceptable common standards. After complex and contentious battles, most parties eventually converged around a pair of standards or *"protocols" known as "Transmission Control Protocol" and "Internet Protocol" or TCP/IP, features of almost every connected device today.

The TCP and IP standards developed under the aegis of the Advanced Research Projects Administration (ARPA), a branch of the US military. Through the 1970s, ARPA had sought to interconnect a set of computing research centers it had established at different sites (mostly universities), primarily to allow Davies-like time-sharing among them. The central challenge was to enable Davies's "data communications" not only among different sites but also between computers built on different principles. For this, protocols standardized the means of "translation" from different "layers" of different machines and across different networks so that each contributor, rather than needing to understand the diverse workings of the whole network, only had to know how to use the "application layer" of the local device and how to transfer files produced there up to the shared "transport layer" (TCP) and "network layer" (IP), which could remain indifferent to all that happens locally below in much the same way that the post office does not have to understand what goes into producing a particular letter, but only how to take that to the address on the envelope, on the condition that the address conforms to protocol. Many different sets of protocols were suggested, some claiming to be superior to ARPA's. ARPA had the advantage, however, that the military could command all who wanted access to its network to use its protocols. It delivered such a command, demanding all those already on or aspiring to join its network to accommodate TCP/IP by January 1, 1983. Conformity was not quite so instantaneous, but ARPA protocols became the de facto international standards.

ARPA's focus remained machine-to-machine communication and its users primarily researchers. Lawrence Roberts, one of the early proponents of email, noted that personal communication was "not an important motivation for a network of scientific computers." From the early 1970s, however, users designed various systems to make interhuman communication easier. The engineer Ray Tomlinson transformed a time-sharing messaging protocol into a forerunner of email in 1971, in essence combining Baran's network vision with Davies's (and in the process introducing the now-familiar "@" for addresses). But he told his colleagues to keep his innovation secret as it was not what he was meant to be working on. Similar improvisation led to the development in 1981 of SMTP, a widely accepted, IP-compatible mail transfer protocol. In the eyes of Janet Abbate, the preeminent historian of the internet, email was the "smashing success" that reinvigorated languishing networks and encouraged private corporations to set up and interconnect subnetworks, leading ultimately, in the mid-1990s, to the internet being privatized as a communications network, supporting person-to-person, machine-to-machine, and person-to-machine exchanges all embracing the term "information." Privatization reflected the increasing participation of commercial companies in the networks, whose rise to dominance is signaled by the prevalence of ".com" addresses. The first of these was acquired in March 1985, just before the NSF created its own network, NSFNET, an initial step away from the military control of ARPA and toward the privatization of the internet in the 1990s, during which time the number of connected computers grew from about two thousand to two million. Initial purchasers of the ".com" addresses were computer companies. A decade later they were companies offering public access, usually via subscription, to the range of services Baran and Davies had envisaged.

The initial failure of network designers to see the potential for both types of communication seems plausibly to rest on the two distinct "institutions" of "communication" and "information" that Licklider and Taylor described. Actual users, like Tomlinson, by contrast, pragmatically ignored this separation, adapting networks for both intermachine and interpersonal connection.

A similar story of user interests and adaptations transformed another packet-switching network, Transpac in France. In 1976, fearful of falling behind the United States in computer development, the French government commissioned a report to outline a competitive strategy. (The NPL packet-switching work in the UK was driven by similar concerns.) The report, *L'Informatisation de la Société*, introduced the term *télématique* (telematics) to recognize the "mariage entre les ordinateurs et les réseaux de transmission" or that, as Daniel Bell, who as we have seen would go on to claim such a "mariage" as critical to the birth of the information society, put it in his introduction to the US edition, "the computer is not only a computational machine, but a communication device." (The US edition was entitled *The Computerization of Society*, which suggests that some US scholars still did not recognize the "mariage.") In pursuit of broader "informatization" and well ahead of the United States, the government-owned French telephone service developed a packet-switching network to connect consumers rather than, as with ARPANET and NSFNET, to connect researchers and deprecate communication. The service provided free MINITEL (Médium Interactif par Numérisation d'Information Téléphonique) terminals to households throughout France. These keyboard-driven terminals supported *videotext*, bridging typewriter, telephone, and television, which Hartley had sought to combine. The initial service offered a relatively unexciting digital telephone book. But private corporations were encouraged to offer other services over the network and soon gave users the opportunity to engage in many of the activities that Baran and Davies foresaw—telebanking, online bookings, grocery shopping, and newspaper reading. Consequently, through the 1980s, France was probably the best exemplar of Baran's "wired world." The most popular MINITEL service were its *messageries*. These, precursors of internet "chat rooms" that later reached similar levels of popularity elsewhere in the world, were built initially by users who, rather like the early email protagonists, *"hacked" the system to enable users to interact with one another rather than just with banks or betting shops.

For all its success, MINITEL was a closed network controlled from above. Elsewhere, as network protocols spread, different public and private networks were interconnecting. One of particular importance developed across the border from France at a nuclear research center, CERN (Conseil Européen pour la Recherche Nucléaire) in Switzerland. An international collaboration, CERN confronted many of the problems faced by NPL and ARPA, because, despite shared goals, researchers were often isolated from colleagues who worked on different, incompatible machines. To address this problem, CERN created its own internal network in the 1970s. It changed to TCP/IP in the mid-1980s, becoming by 1990 the largest European internet site. Despite this push toward interconnection, an English engineer at CERN, Tim Berners-Lee (b. 1955), remained frustrated with the difficulty of finding out what his colleagues were up to. He believed that "once someone somewhere made available a document, database, graphic, sound, video . . . it should be accessible (subject to authorization . . .) to anyone . . . [with] a link." Equally, he saw value in allowing people to build new associations between documents and the like, something, he noted, "that the brain can do easily." Pursuing such thoughts he became aware of earlier ideas from Bush and Engelbart and the computer maverick Ted Nelson, who had introduced the notion of *"hypertext" as a way to link digital objects without having to go through a centralized machine or institution.

With an international group of CERN colleagues, Berners-Lee developed a system that fulfilled many of the goals espoused by these early proponents of linked systems. He initially thought of his as something like a phone book, providing addresses of fellow researchers and their documents, which makes his path a little like MINITEL's. And as with MINITEL, the ultimate system developed far beyond this idea, producing the World Wide Web, whose protocols standardized document formats and provided unique addresses for each document with the links to reach them from any computer on the network. The outcome was in many ways a digital instantiation of Otlet's worldwide vision from some ninety years before of decentralized connectivity. Stanford University's Linear Accelerator Center (SLAC) established the first US web server in 1991. One champion there was the laboratory's librarian, Louise Addis, who saw the potential for opening access to SLAC's online documents. Her contribution implicitly recognized a convergence of the semantic sort of bibliographic information of Otlet's vision with the signal-based sort of Shannon's.

Going World Wide

While the development and spread of the internet can occasionally appear as an irresistible, technologically driven force emerging primarily from Silicon Valley entrepreneurs, the contributions of ARPA, MINITEL, and CERN indicate that the forces at play were more complex and more diverse. Among these three pioneers alone, we see the power of the military in ARPA, of state telecommunications systems in MINITEL, and of international scientific research in CERN. Equally, not only did MINITEL develop in France, but the web, while developed in Switzerland, was a truly international effort: the first paper its developers published had Belgian, Danish, English, Finnish, and French coauthors. And it was in this work that the interhuman communications potential of these networks was more directly explored. Moreover, while ARPA and the web drew on government funding to address a specialized audience, MINITEL, while launched with state funding, was designed to draw on French corporations and consumers for funds. The different ways of developing software have been opposed as the "cathedral" versus the "bazaar," to suggest hierarchical versus market forces as alternative structures. For the spread of the internet, we have to consider these two not simply in opposition, but in complex combinations of "top-down" and "bottom-up" forces, as governments sought to retain political stability while keeping pace with developments elsewhere, and to encourage markets and enjoin or resist "natural monopolies" in telecommunications, while being pushed to respond to the demands of an inventive and adaptive public. This transition is perhaps best exemplified in the standards of the internet, which as we have seen were first issued from on high, by ARPA, taking advantage of what the historian Andrew Russell calls the "advantages of autocratic design," but increasingly were "opened" to democratic decision making within standards organizations, of which the NPL was a precursor.

Similarly contending forces were evident as the networks spread worldwide. Japan, where in the 1970s perhaps the earliest discussions anywhere of an "information society" (*joho shakai*) appear, also adopted ideas of "informatization" (*johaka*), a notion that became popular throughout Asia, with the establishment of its Center for the Informatization of Industry in 1985. Japan's telecommunications monopoly, however, made illegal the sorts of improvisation that, as we have seen, pushed popular development elsewhere. Consequently, insular, proprietary, unconnected subscription networks developed first. It took time (and the disbanding of the monopoly) to produce an open, interconnected network. In China, the state controlled developments, but, seeking like others to keep up with the West, it introduced a program of popular "informatization" at the beginning of the twenty-first century. Elsewhere, developing countries explored the idea that information and informatization could produce economic development, for which, it was assumed, what the French had called *télématique mariage* was necessary and thus increasingly adopted, though control from above, which drove many such developments, often had to contend with desired autonomy from below (manifest in such things as the development of internet cafés). Political structures played a curious role in these developments. As Benjamin Peters argues in *How Not to Network a Nation*, a Soviet internet project failed because, where "the capitalists behaved like socialists . . . the socialists behaved like capitalists." In these different contexts, the elasticity of terms like *information* and *informatization* helped different sociopolitical circumstances accommodate local desires to join the networks that were visible elsewhere. In India, for instance, scientific research initiated packet-switching developments, but state monopolies restricted broader access. Enthusiasts returning from other countries and determined to replicate their more open networked systems, however, gradually forced state and corporate accommodation.

Stretching Information

In the international adoption of "informatization," we literally see the idea of "information" being stretched, despite both Hartley's and Shannon's resistance. It can be useful to think of this elasticity being achieved less by stretching than by layering, deploying the structure on which the internet and the web were built, and which has roots reaching back through much of the work discussed above.

Berners-Lee called layers "simple rules for global systems." More elaborately, Abbate describes the internet as a "layered system . . . organized as a set of discrete functions that interact according to specified rules . . . arranged in a conceptual hierarchy . . . from the most concrete . . . (such as handling electrical signals) to the most abstract functions (e.g., interpreting human language commands from users)." Overall, this structure represents for Abbate a "division of labor." That phrase takes us from the World Wide Web back to Babbage and his insights from Prony and Smith that the way to build a calculating machine was to divide it into layers, with each layer able to execute its own task and pass the result down to the next, which could in turn perform its tasks while remaining usefully ignorant of what went on above. Such a structure, from Babbage to Berners-Lee, provided efficient coordination among both devices and people. Similar assumptions can be seen in the economics of Shannon's time. The economist Friedrich Hayek, a Nobel laureate, had argued in the 1930s that markets work efficiently by providing consumers with prices for goods, "information" that allows consumers to make rational decisions without needing to understand the complex forces that produce the goods or bring these to the market. The "information" encoded in price is a product of but also efficiently excludes the information carried by people active in the market.

In such arguments, "information" is used at different levels, but the notion of information differs with the layer. We can see such layering in Hartley's and Shannon's work, as each isolated signals for machine communication by excluding human dimensions of psychology and semantics. Shannon portrayed this process in his famous "Schematic diagram of a general communication system" (figure 12.1).

In Shannon's account the *"information source* . . . produces a message."

Then a *"transmitter* . . . operates on the message . . . to produce a signal suitable for transmission." The *"channel* is merely the medium used to transmit the signal." The *"receiver* . . . performs the inverse operation of that done by the transmitter,"* and the *destination* is the person (or thing) for whom the message is intended" (italics in original). It would not be unreasonable to use *information* at each layer: as the input, as the stripped-down message, as the signal transmitted, and as the outcome at the destination. But it would not be the same notion at each layer.

At its heart, with psychology and meaning stripped out, all that counts for successful communication in Shannon's terms is for the destination to end up with the signal sent. Reception is the mirror image of transmission. Transmission is predictable, and anything unpredicted a malfunction. Licklider and Taylor classified this as the "engineer's" view of communication. "But to communicate," they argued, "is more than to send and to receive." So saying, they

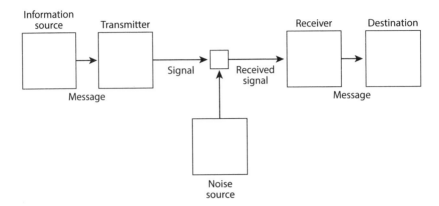

FIGURE 12.1. Schematic diagram of a general communication system. Figure 1 in Claude Shannon's "Mathematical Theory of Communication," *Bell Systems Technical Journal* 27, no. 3 (1948): 379–432. Reused with permission of Nokia and AT&T Archives.

take information to another level. At this level we do not always condemn the unpredictable as malfunction or failure (what Babbage was trying to overcome in human "computers") but sometimes see that as understandable, and sometimes even laudable "interpretation" (this was often required, for instance, of Morse's telegraph operators), something we might even classify as insight or innovation. From this we get the originality that prompts Otlet, Bush, and Berners-Lee to extoll connections made through links that have never been made before. Yet, as Licklider and Taylor themselves show, we tend to use this same term, *information*, across the different levels, sometimes using it to denote something objective, independent, autonomous, and countable, while sometimes using it for something context bound and consequently subjective and interpretable.

Moreover, while layers may help to separate people from machines, they can also contribute to ideas of people as themselves layered systems. At times "information" is the stuff of thought, ratiocination, and conscious decision making. At other times, it is the stuff of signals, something that lies beyond our consciousness and reflection. Vannevar Bush, for example, used *information* the latter way, arguing that "when the eye sees, all the consequent information is transmitted to the brain by means of electrical vibrations in the channel of the optic nerve." (Bush even suggested these signals could fruitfully be intercepted and understood by machines.) For the products of ratiocination, by contrast, he reserved words like *knowledge* and *record*. Where Hartley removed psychology and Shannon meaning, Bush thus extracted awareness, self-consciousness, and reflection from human information, which is reduced to signals along channels, sounding very like electric impulses along power lines, the focus of his early work. And as with those lines, he assumed that the impulses in the nervous system are unproblematically and unreflectively received. From these perspectives, "communication in the animal and the machine," as Wiener had put it, start to look the same, with "information" helping to unite the two. If "information" allows us to pull together computation and communication, by extension it can also allow us to pull together people and machines. Thus von Neumann started to account for both as kinds of "automata."

Stretched to the Limit?

Our "age of information" has inherited these elastic accounts. In his book on advertising, *The Attention Merchants* (2016), for instance, the lawyer Timothy Wu notes at one point that "information cannot be acted upon without attention" while, at another point, noting that "every second, our senses transmit an estimated 11 million bits of information." It is hard to see us giving attention to 11 million *bits a second. Yet the assimilation of computation and communication, with information as the common factor, is generally seen as unproblematic.

"Information processing" is often taken as common to both and seen as a mechanical process. With "information" as the key ingredient of exact and correct calculation, the abundance of information has offered an optimism that arose with the age and is evident in the areas of economics and the public sphere mentioned earlier as critical venues for appraising the age's distinctive use of information. Economics, which helped propel ideas of an "information economy" and "information work" to vindicate claims for an "information age," embraced notions of "complete" or "perfect" information, the former in particular suggesting that with more information people's decision making will improve and as a result markets will become more efficient, coordinating the needs of all involved through welfare "optimization." Similarly, the economic idea of "asymmetric information" as the reason for market failure has implicitly assumed that "symmetrical information" will lead to success, implying that if everyone has the same information their behavior will synchronize into Shannonian mirror images, leaving aside concerns about whether people who have the same information might interpret it differently. Context, history, personal reflection disappear in these visions just as they did in Shannon's, though he was more explicit about the move in his models. Invisible, too, are innumerable assumptions about the commodification of information, and alternative assertions that "information wants to be free." These have spurred fights over *open access and *open source, with some asserting that the public sphere depends on uninhibited circulation of information, while others assert that commodification is essential to innovation and market-driven progress.

Such modern notions of "information" underwriting the democratic public sphere have led to assumptions that increases in availability of information will lead to increased democracy. From here arise enthusiasms for social media as means to overcome undemocratic control, and claims that they will lead irresistibly to freedom follow. These views build on ideas of Licklider and Engelbart that technology would set us free, which in turn echo earlier views of Otlet's. Moreover, Otlet's notion (echoed later by Bush) that information was sufficiently autonomous that it could be isolated from its source and recombined with other pieces of information reflects ideas, emphasized by the historian of the public sphere Jürgen Habermas, that democracy feeds on information independent of its source. Ideally, we don't enter the Habermasian public sphere, but rather our information goes in alone and is judged on its merits, not its source or context. Here we can see similarities once again to Hartley's and Shannon's attempt to atomize and isolate units of information. Related assumptions can be found in the libertarian, anti-institutional streak that runs through many modern champions of the information age, who unquestioningly link computation and communication. The cyberlibertarian John Perry Barlow, for instance, declared the "independence of cyberspace," renouncing the old world for a new world in which computation strips information from institutional control (much as Otlet sought to strip it from books), and so doing underwrites the autonomy of both information and individuals. Similar anti-institutionalism can be read in prophecies that the "quantified self" will allow people to manage their own health and so bypass the institutions of medicine, that "blockchain" will do away with central banks, or that MOOCs (massive open online courses) will eviscerate schools and universities.

Through all such accounts runs a pervasive "techno-optimism" that has heralded control over information as giving us control over the world in which we live. Thus we see a lot of "info-solutions" in which information is offered as a solution to our problems based on the assumption that those problems can be coherently and comprehensively diagnosed in terms of information. If education is the delivery of information, for example, schools can be replaced with computers. Not only do such solutions play the informational equivalent of the "man with a hammer," but they also tend to overlook, while nonetheless depending on, the elasticity of the use of the notion of *information* used in such diagnoses, an elasticity that has allowed us to weave very different ideas of information, communication, and computation into an apparently harmonious whole.

The optimism that runs through these claims has to confront contrary feelings that rather than more information being a good thing, it can be highly problematic; and that while control over information may be beneficial, we are often in danger of being controlled by information and the algorithms it feeds. Both the optimistic and the pessimistic views have a curiously long history. Though we may claim information as a distinctive feature of the twenty-first century, the phrase "age of information" first appeared in the eighteenth, at the height of the *Enlightenment, just as Smith was declaring the age of commerce and Washington denouncing the age of ignorance. And then, too, it supported a unifying and optimistic view of that period's social, political, and economic transformation. Declaring his to be an "age of information," the essayist Vicesimus Knox assumed, like some today, that the book, as the fount of communicable information, would probably kill the university and claimed that if people were given the right information, they would do the right thing. Hence, at the end of that century as at the beginning of this one, people enthusiastically embraced information as both uniting and transformative, weaving society into an egalitarian network of autonomous individuals. Critics, however, then as now, cautioned that different ideas of information were in play, some of which espoused information as the necessary ingredient for open deliberation and debate and the convergence of different people into a harmonious society; and others of which took information as an autonomous force to which people were irresistibly subject. Perhaps, after all, the dots of our "information age" are more closely connected to the past than those who deem history irrelevant realize.

Further Reading

Janet Abbate, *Inventing the Internet*, 1999; Kenneth J. Arrow, "Information and Economic Behavior," in *Collected Papers*, edited by K. Arrow, 1984, 136–52; Geoffrey D. Austrian, *Herman Hollerith: Forgotten Giant of Information Processing*, 1982; James R. Beniger, *The Control Revolution: Technological and Economic Origins of the Information Society*, 1986; Tim Berners-Lee and Marl Fischetti, *Weaving the Web: The Original Design and Ultimate Destiny of the World Wide Web by Its Inventor*, 1999; M. K. Buckland and Z. Liu, "History of Information Science," *Annual Review of Information Science and Technology*, no. 30 (1995): 385–416; Vannevar Bush, "As We May Think," *Atlantic Monthly* 176, no. 1 (1945): 101–8; Martin Campbell-Kelly and William Aspray, *The Computer: A History of the Information Machine*, 1996; Robert Darnton, "An Early Information Society: News and Media in Eighteenth-Century Paris," *American Historical Review* 105 no. 1 (2000): 1–35; Paul Duguid, "The Ageing of Information: From Particular to Particulate," *Journal of the History of Ideas* 76, no. 3 (2015): 347–68; Gerard Goggin and Mark McLelland, *The Routledge Companion to Global Internet Histories*, 2017; Marie Hicks, *Programmed Inequality: How Britain Discarded Women Technologists and Lost Its Edge in Computing*, 2017; Richard John, "Rendezvous with Information? Computers and Communications Networks in the United States," *Business History Review*, no. 75 (Spring 2001): 1–13; J.C.R. Licklider and Robert W. Taylor, "The Computer as a Communication Device," *Science and Technology* 76 April (1968): 21–41; Julien Mailland and Kevin Driscoll, eds., *MINITEL: Welcome to the Internet*, 2017; Armand Mattelart, *The Information Society: An Introduction*, 2001; Marianna Mazzucato, *The Entrepreneurial State: Debunking Public vs. Private Sector Myths*, 2014; Benjamin Peters, *How Not to Network a Nation: The Uneasy History of the Soviet Internet*, 2016; Andrew L. Russell, *Open Standards and the Internet Age: History, Ideology, and Networks*, 2014; Claude Shannon and Warren Weaver, *The Mathematical Theory of Communication*, 1964 [1948]; Joseph Weizenbaum, "Once More, the Computer Revolution," in *The Microelectronics Revolution: The Complete Guide to New Technology and Its Impact*, edited by Tom Forrester, 1981; Hans Wellisch, "From Information Science to Informatics: A Terminological Investigation," *Journal of Librarianship* 4, no. 3 (1972): 157–87; Norbert Wiener, *Cybernetics: Or Control and Communication in the Animal and the Machine*, 1948; Shoshana Zuboff, *In the Age of the Smart Machine: The Future of Work and Power*, 1988.

13

Search

Daniel Rosenberg

AT A CONFERENCE IN AUSTRALIA IN APRIL 1998, two Stanford University graduate students described the challenge of searching for information on the *World Wide Web and a new tool called "Google" that they had designed to address it. The challenge of search in this evolving domain, as Sergey Brin and Larry Page explained it, reflected at once the size, dynamism, and character of the web. Though not even ten years old, the web was already big, and its growth was rapidly accelerating. One could foresee a time in the near future when it would dwarf even the largest electronic database then extant. This was the problem to which Brin and Page nodded when they named their search engine Google, evoking the mathematical term "googol," meaning ten to the one hundredth power. Google was designed to process what would later come to be called *big data. It was built specifically to scale with the web. It was also built to mirror the web's dynamism. In contrast to the *structured data found in traditional databases, information on the web was heterogeneous, conforming to no predetermined subject categories. Older techniques of information retrieval designed for searching databases foundered in this new environment. In 1998, Brin and Page wrote, only one of the top four commercial web search engines could find even itself.

In hindsight, it is bracing to reread Brin and Page's paper, "The Anatomy of a Large-Scale Hypertextual Search Engine." It offers a remarkable snapshot of the world just before the emergence of Google and the web as we know it, that last fleeting crepuscule of the twentieth century before search became ubiquitous in everyday life. Their paper is full of details that now feel either charmingly quaint, terribly ominous, and sometimes both. When Brin and Page unleashed their first crawler onto the web to collect and index everything it could find, many system administrators had no idea what to make of the hits it was giving them. "It turns out," Brin and Page write, "that running a crawler which connects to more than half a million *servers, and generates tens of millions of log entries generates a fair amount of email and phone calls. . . . Almost daily, we receive an email something like, 'Wow, you looked at a lot of pages from my web site. How did you like it?'"

And it is not just those perplexed administrators whose voices echo from a former world: Brin and Page, too, sound like time travelers. Unlike commercial search engines of the day such as Lycos and Altavista, which kept their algorithms and data closely guarded as proprietary secrets, Google was to be open and noncommercial. "We believe," Brin and Page write, "the issue of advertising causes enough mixed incentives that it is crucial to have a competitive search engine that is transparent and in the academic realm." That was April 1998. Google incorporated in September of the same year. It went public in August 2004. By 2018, its parent corporation, Alphabet, was valued at over one trillion dollars. The algorithms that Google uses today are as closely guarded as any corporate secret.

What is search? What role does it play in our information culture? Where did it come from? Consider what made Google's first algorithm distinctive. As Brin and Page observe in their paper, in 1998 existing approaches to web search worked, if just barely. At that time, the various strategies of information retrieval used by the major search engines were all showing strains in handling the unstructured data of the web. Because the information content of the web was not organized by categories, representing it as such was both difficult and limiting. Yet, in one way or another, this was what the state-of-the-art search engines were doing. At the time, one of the most popular search portals, Yahoo!, still employed human indexers to make categorized lists of websites. These were often useful, but, in addition to imposing categories that might differ from those of both creators and consumers of information on the web, it was hard to see how this approach could scale with the web as it grew. The word-indexing techniques favored by other search engines were automated, but at scale even vector space models and similarly sophisticated statistical approaches overlooked important references and produced a lot of irrelevant hits. These "tended to prefer results that were textually similar to query terms, regardless of their thematic relevance," so, for example, a search on the phrase "Bill Clinton" using a popular search portal produced as its top result the "Bill Clinton Joke of the Day" page. Another engine gave a top ranking to a page that said only, "Bill Clinton sucks," while entirely missing the website www .whitehouse.gov. To use terms from the field of information retrieval itself: when applied to the web, the Yahoo! approach offered precision at the expense of recall, while the word-indexing approach offered recall at the expense of precision. Neither reflected the inherent logic of the web itself.

According to Brin and Page, the difference between web search and database search came down to two main factors: scale and heterogeneity. Whatever advantages there were in existing approaches to web search, most operated on *taxonomic principles that had characterized the field of electronic data processing since its emergence a century earlier with the punch cards and machine tabulators applied to the US Census of 1890 by Herman Hollerith. Such systems could process large volumes of data efficiently, so long as that data fell into rigidly delineated categories. Indeed, historically, it was the control of categories itself that transformed otherwise heterogeneous information into data in the first place, going back all the way to mortality rolls, censuses, and other ambitious enumerative enterprises dating to the *early modern and medieval periods. In contrast to this structured universe of data, write Brin and Page, "the web is a vast collection of completely uncontrolled heterogeneous documents." Yet, as they well knew, the problem of uncontrolled heterogenous documents endemic to the web was in no way original to it. To the contrary, it was a problem that scholars and other searchers had been dealing with continuously since the beginning of documentation itself in fields quite different from those in which the database had grown up. The approach to web search proposed by Brin and Page was derived not from an earlier development in electronic data processing but from the history of scholarly notation techniques.

The specific formula for web search that Brin and Page first proposed—an algorithm they called "PageRank"—drew from a tradition that extended as far as that of the data roll, running parallel to it, sometimes interacting, but remaining through it all distinct. To determine relationships among pages on the web and to determine the value of particular pages as responses to a given query, Brin and Page made an analogy between the *hyperlinks that connected web pages and the notes and bibliographies that connected traditional scholarly texts to one another. In traditional print scholarship, Brin and Page observed in their 1998 paper, writers use footnotes to point to the prior research and argumentation on which their own work relies. In doing this, they also ratify the value of these sources. A footnote, they said, is a kind of vote for the relevance of a specific source to the matter at hand. Compare the notes in a few related books, and you begin to get a picture of who the authorities are in that field. And it is not just general importance to which these references attest; they also indicate the specific relevance of a source to a given subject, which is, of course, the precise aim of a web search. The geneticist may never have considered the possibility of DNA computing, but repeated citation of earlier genetics research in articles on DNA computing by biochemists and computer scientists confirms the relevance of the earlier work to the subject.

To achieve a view of this network of references, Google used its crawler to follow links all over the web and to map them. Borrowing an idea from academic citation analysis, its PageRank algorithm characterized a web page according to its so-called back links—not the list of links found on that page but rather the list of links to that page from others—and the link graph accounting for the network of such connections across the web. Of course, assembling a comprehensive list of back links for the web, to say nothing of mapping them, was no trivial task, but as it emerged at Google, the assembled graph offered a metric for establishing the importance of web pages as well as characterizing their subject matter. Using this approach, Google would need no predetermined categories. Those would write themselves.

From a conceptual point of view, Google's break with received approaches in information retrieval was decisive. And yet, what Brin and Page were proposing drew directly on long-standing tradition. The most immediate precedent was Eugene Garfield's bibliometrics, from which also derives the so-called *impact factor often employed today as a quantitative measure of the influence of academic publications. Through this, their approach drew on very old traditions of commentary and interreference. In effect, they treated the web as a kind of literature, but this should not be surprising: the notion that the structure of the web might look something like the referential structure of a literature was baked into the enterprise from the start.

This was axiomatic for the gadfly computer theorist Theodor Holm (Ted) Nelson, who, already in the early 1960s, envisioned an electronic network of documents that encompassed much of what would eventually be realized in the World Wide Web and more. In his 1974 samizdat manifesto *Computer Lib/ Dream Machines* and his 1980 *Literary Machines*, Nelson argued that a web of documents such as he imagined would create new possibilities for writing, while also bringing into view and activating nonlinear structures implicit in *analog text. *Hypertext*, Nelson's term for the cross-linking, associative, nonlinear, and nonhierarchical aspects of texts and collections, was thus a new name for a basic and pervasive textual structure. In Nelson's words: "Many people consider [hypertext] to be new and drastic and threatening. However,

I would like to take the position that hypertext is fundamentally traditional and in the mainstream of literature. Customary writing chooses one expository sequence from among the possible myriad; hypertext allows many, all available to the reader. In fact, however, we constantly depart from sequence, citing things ahead and behind in the text. Phrases like 'as we have already said' and 'as we will see' are really implicit pointers to contents elsewhere in the sequence." And elsewhere, "Hypertext can include sequential text, and is thus the most general form of writing. (In one direction of generalization, it is also the most general form of language.)" To Nelson, literature was not a collection of independent works, but a docuverse, "an ongoing system of interconnecting documents." In his own proposal for an electronic document network, these interconnections were paramount. Quotations would offer dynamic windows into source texts, intellectual property would be traceable, and content creators could take advantage of a decentralized micropayment mechanism incorporated into the underlying exchange *protocol.

Both backward- and forward-looking, Nelson's would have been a very different web from the one that was implemented by the World Wide Web Consortium in the 1990s. For historians, the backward-looking aspects of Nelson's vision have particular resonance: over the course of many centuries, Nelson argued, textual scholars had worked out systems for connecting heterogeneous fields of inquiry into a great web of knowledge, in which factors such as importance and interrelationship were constantly represented and evaluated, and through which practiced readers could move fluidly and with intelligence. While the old paper universe had limitations that electronic media might mitigate, the basic principles at work should be considered all that much more robust for that very fact. The old media could not do everything that electronic media would be able to, but over centuries the scholarly traditions of manuscript and print worked. This was something that had not yet been shown for the electronic word. Nelson insisted on attention to precedent. Why? "Literature is debugged," he said.

All this is notable for several reasons. First, it helps to clarify what was new about Google when it was introduced: as Brin and Page explain it, the basic insight behind PageRank was the realization that in its link structure, the web provided its own *metadata; that is, in its network of links, the web expressed its native relational structure. As a consequence, PageRank was able to do autonomously what Yahoo!, for example, was using human readers to accomplish. Second, it illuminates a fundamental tension in the application of Brin and Page's technique to the accumulated wealth of information accessible on the web. While Google took its inspiration from time-tested traditions of bibliographic interreference, at the same time, it systematically disregarded the metadata that this tradition had generated and preserved over a long period of time. Third, it shows how centrally the project of the web reiterates old and persistent problems of information seeking. Brute-force solutions common in the digital era were mostly impractical if not out-and-out impossible in analog media. Predigital systems of interreference were, by force of necessity, models of elegance.

There are exceptions. In the early 1940s, for example, before he had regular access to a computer, the digital *humanities pioneer Roberto Busa composed a dissertation on the use of the Latin preposition "in" found in the works of St. Thomas Aquinas, itemizing by hand on notecards each instance of "in" among the roughly thirteen million words that Aquinas wrote. For his next feat, the fifty-six-volume *Index Thomisticus* (Index to Thomas), Busa used an IBM computer to apply a similar method to every word in Aquinas's works. The example of Busa—and that of other early adopters including Paul Tasman (working on the Dead Sea Scrolls) and David W. Packard (working on Livy)— makes clear how directly certain kinds of analog research models could be adapted to the context of the computer and what becomes possible once a computer is unleashed on repetitive tasks of this sort.

We should note that in many cases, and this was certainly true in the 1940s when Busa began his *Index Thomisticus*, the image of the computer working autonomously is misleading. Much computer processing takes place without human intervention, but even in today's world of data processing, a great deal of repetitive data labor, ranging from the sorts of tasks done by gold farmers in online gaming to the piecework one finds through Amazon's Mechanical Turk, is still performed by people. Some of this labor, such as the image recognition processing we perform each time we decode a captcha or the unannounced A/B testing constantly implemented by web services, we barely notice, if at all. Busa himself employed a large staff of women to key in Aquinas's texts. He explained that he employed women in these tasks because they were more reliable and accurate than men. (And surely they could be paid less too.) On these lines, it is worth noting that even in the 1940s, the term *computer* was still mostly used to name a human worker whose job was to perform mathematical calculations, and that this particular job was frequently done by women. The persistence and intensification of this kind of work in the age of the web, as well as its outsourcing to various locations in the developing world, has led to an emergent critique of the digital sweatshop.

PageRank is only one expression of a common pattern in the history of information of implementing and transforming old techniques using new technologies. Other statistical search strategies have similar genealogies. The practice of alphabetical indexing fundamental to electronic search, for example, is quite old. It significantly predates the printed book, though in the West its efflorescence came in the first decades of movable type print in the fifteenth century. In printed books, mechanical reproduction brought with it standardized pagination. This, in turn, allowed for standardized page indexes. As Ann Blair has noted, such indexes were often selling points for new books. And, of course, new editions required new pagination, and new indexes, and potentially new purchases (see chapter 4.)

Even in the era before print, very important books—in Europe, this meant especially the Bible—were already indexed with microscopic precision. As early as the thirteenth century, the French Dominican friar Hugh of St-Cher produced a *concordance index containing nearly every word in the Bible. In 1445, the Jewish scholar Isaac Nathan completed a concordance to the Hebrew scripture, printed first in Venice in 1523, along similar lines. Nathan's work listed not only the words that it indexed but also those that it excluded by rule. In the 1950s, IBM engineer Hans Peter Luhn would recommend the same practice, the application of what he called a stop list, in automated concordance indexing systems. Created in two different languages five hundred years apart, Nathan's and Luhn's lists, both of which contained mostly so-called function words such as articles, prepositions, conjunctions, closely resemble one another.

Early on, Google explicitly signaled which words its searches were stopping. Users had to take an extra step if they wished to search certain very common words including those on Luhn's and Isaac's lists. At the start of 2007, a Google search on a phrase that included common function words such as "the Fourth of July" or "A Room with a View" would elicit a set of results along with a message that the search had been conducted only on the words "Fourth July" or "Room View." Google wagered that in most cases the result of searching the shorter phrase would be close to that of searching the longer one and that the savings thereby achieved in processing power and time favored searching the stopped phrase rather than the complete one. This was precisely the reasoning that Luhn had employed when he composed his first sixteen-word stop list for his electronic Keyword-in-Context (KWIC) indexing system and that Nathan had used in composing his concordance to the Hebrew scripture. In Luhn's case, the economy could be measured in boxes of paper punch cards and machine time, just as, in the case of Nathan, it could be measured in paper and scribal labor.

Because the Bible and the Bible concordance are both books, it is easy to overlook just how substantial a technical intervention the latter represents. In the concordance format pioneered by Hugh of St-Cher, the words of the source text are disassembled and then reassembled as an alphabetical word list. Hugh's concordance contains the full text of the Bible and nothing but that text. And yet, his concordance is not the Bible. In it, the text of scripture appears in an entirely different order from the source text. As the early concordance format developed in the thirteenth century, it came to include the presentation of contextual passages—what we would today call snippets—so that users could see immediately how words were being used and could evaluate whether those instances were relevant to their search. A passage that contained two or more words deemed significant might appear in the concordance more than once, resulting in a work that, though it contains only words from the Bible, would be longer than the Bible. It also, very importantly, resulted in a text that could be read on its own.

Over time, Bible concordances proved enduringly popular. After nearly three centuries, Alexander Cruden's 1737 *Complete Concordance to the Holy Scriptures*, for example, has still never been out of print. Concordances have also remained a terrain of scholarly innovation, offering a notable variety of formats and schemes of linguistic stemming. And after Cruden, the concordance approach was applied increasingly to texts other than the Bible. In 1741, Cruden himself published a "verbal index" to John Milton's *Paradise Lost*. In time, other writers including Dante and Shakespeare got their own concordances, each in itself an indicator of their cultural significance. Among the most notable modern concordance systems is the one published in 1890 by the American Methodist scholar James Strong, providing an alphabetical index to every word in the King James Bible along with a numerical reference system—"Strong's Numbers"—assigning to each English word in the King James Version a corresponding Hebrew or Greek word.

Of course, readers understood concordances as reference tools. No medieval reader would have imagined that Hugh's concordance meant something independent of the Bible. Its purpose was to aid in reading scripture, but the very fact that medieval Christian scholars knew the text of the Bible so well facilitated the relative independence of the concordance in use. Leaving aside the theological question, from the point of view of the history of information, the practice of reading a concordance, or, to generalize, the practice of reading an index, is distinctive, just as is the practice of scanning the snippets presented as the result of a Google search. These come from the web pages that Google indexes, but they are not those pages, and reading Google results is not equivalent to reading web pages, a fact that is reinforced with some intensity each time it turns out that a Google result links to content hidden behind a pay wall. Reading a Google results page is an information practice of a different sort, a kind of scanning or mapping operation similar to what Hugh hoped his concordance would allow biblical scholars to perform. In our culture, however, the place of this kind of index reading is transformed. What in the Middle Ages was a rarified scholarly practice serves us increasingly, in our age of search, as the very model of reading itself.

The practice of information seeking is as old as any historical record we have. It is a fundamental concern for any library, archive, or repository. Among the most famous losses in that most famous information catastrophe, the destruction of the Library of Alexandria, was that of the *pinakes* or tables of categories composed by the scholar-poet Callimachus in the third century BCE. This catalog of sorts, as much as the texts in the library, contained precious information, metadata, as we would say today. Self-evidently, the larger a given collection, the more complex a problem search becomes; hence the composition of the pinakes for what was said to be the world's largest library; hence too, Brin and Page's shorthand, ten to the one hundredth power, in their name for Google. So, we should not make the mistake of thinking that the amount of information to be searched nor the rapidity of its growth is a new concern in our period.

The contemporary docuverse is indeed large and rapidly growing. But the problem of scale is endemic to the world of documents, and both the worry about it and the fantasy of mastering it have reappeared with regularity throughout the long history of information, inspiring new cataloging systems and devices in each era, including a kaleidoscope of what Markus Krajewski has called "paper machines," ranging from the "literary closets" of Thomas Harrison and Vincent Placcius in the seventeenth century (Blair, chap. 4) to the "Mundaneum," the card-based "Universal Bibliographical System" of the Belgian documentalist Paul Otlet at the start of the twentieth (Duguid, chap. 12). If there is a point somewhere back in history before which scholars fretted about it, it must have been very long ago indeed. Socrates famously worried about the corrosive effects of writing: in his age memorization was understood to be a crucial technical and intellectual skill. Having information memorized allowed a thinker not only to access but to spontaneously interrelate different ideas. For him, the prospect of a society in which important knowledge was committed to writing but not to memory presented a serious danger. Of course, his admonition did nothing to slow down the offloading of memory onto external media such as manuscript scrolls, even by his own acolytes including Plato and Xenophon. Had it, we likely would know little if anything about Socrates today. (In fact Socrates also acknowledged the value of writing in preserving what had been lost to memory, notably when he praised in the *Timaeus* the Egyptians' written records of events that the Greeks, dependent on memory, had forgotten.)

Nor, for that matter, was the idea of a mechanical search engine itself novel in the twentieth century. The great visionary of search Vannevar Bush, who headed the US Office of Scientific Research and Development (OSRD) during World War II, the same agency that oversaw the Manhattan Project, described his work as extending a tradition of information machines going back to those proposed by the German philosopher Gottfried Wilhelm Leibniz late in the seventeenth century and the English mechanical engineer Charles Babbage early in the nineteenth century. Each envisioned a kind of computer. Babbage actually designed two, one called the "Difference Engine" and another, the "Analytical Engine," for which the mathematician Ada Lovelace wrote programs. But in the cases of both Leibniz and Babbage, writes Bush, "the economics of the situation" were against bringing the designed machines into existence. Before the age of mass production, the labor necessary to build and run such machines exceeded what they could save the user. Even in July 1945, when Bush published his classic essay "As We May Think," describing a hypothetical search machine called the *"memex," the mechanical computer was still a relative novelty. Hollerith's tabulating machines were only a half a century old. The ENIAC computer at the University of Pennsylvania, which used punch cards for input and output, would not debut publicly until early the following year.

Bush's moment was one of enormous technical innovation in the area of electronic computing. For this, ENIAC is emblematic. And yet, the important insights in Bush's great article on search did not rely fundamentally on that technology. Tellingly, his own system would have mostly employed analog photographic technology such as microfilm rather than the electronic technology such as was found in ENIAC, to *compress libraries into a desk-sized device. Tellingly, too, some of the key features of Bush's proposal, including a ubiquitous, forehead-mounted wearable visual recording device, remain embryonic some seventy-five years later despite efforts in multimedia life logging by experimenters such as Gordon Bell and Stephen Wolfram, and innovations in wearable devices such as Google Glass.

The idea of applying technology to problems of information search was fundamental to Bush's project, but the specific technologies of his day were less so. More important to his thinking was a problem, sometimes referred to as *information overload, for which there are abundant precedents in the history of information. For Bush himself, the pressing problem, as well as the unique opportunity, emerged directly from the technical research that flourished during the Second World War. In the article in which he described the memex machine, Bush argued that with the war now over, scientists could and should turn their attention to the "mountain" of knowledge that society had amassed but not mastered. "The summation of human experience," he wrote, "is being expanded at a prodigious rate, and the means we use for threading through the consequent maze to the momentarily important item is the same as was used in the days of square-rigged ships." To address the problem Bush proposed a kind of Manhattan Project of the mind.

Elevated as were the goals that he articulated, the instigating problem for the director of OSRD was military and industrial. Indeed, at war's end, in addition to taking account of its own burgeoning literature in science and technology, the United States was faced with the felicitous problem of absorbing parallel literatures captured from its defeated adversaries. In the following decades, Cold War competition too would figure centrally in the imperatives of information retrieval. As scientific journals multiplied and industrial reports piled up, information pioneers such as Douglas Engelbart, whose Augmentation Research Center at the Stanford Research Institute (SRI) was responsible for crucial early work on both the computer mouse and the graphical user interface, framed their work in this light. In a 1958 article on the "information problem," Engelbart and his collaborator Charles Bourne articulated the need: "Recent world events have catapulted the problem of the presently unmanageable mass of technical information from one that should be solved to one that must be solved." The Soviet approach, they continued, was to throw bodies at the problem, including twenty-three hundred dedicated translators and abstractors "who publish over 400,000 abstracts of technical articles from more than 10,000 journals originating in about 80 countries." The American response, they said, ought to both match and advance on what the Soviets were doing. On the one hand, it was incumbent on the United States to establish its own National Technical Information Service parallel to the Soviet All Union Institute of Scientific and

Technical Information. On the other, it would be essential to deploy within it a "highly mechanized" system of information search. As Engelbart and Bourne wrote, "Technology, so adept in solving problems of man and his environment, must be directed to solving a gargantuan problem of its own creation. A mass of technical information has been accumulated and at a rate that has far outstripped means for making it available to those working in science and engineering."

Many of the influential technical information systems developed in this period imposed controlled vocabularies and prefabricated systems of classification on their subjects. That is to say, they applied precisely the kinds of approach that Brin and Page considered typical of the field of information retrieval prior to Google. These systems enhanced the slip and card systems of earlier innovators such as Placcius and Otlet, allowing more search factors to be coordinated, but as Brin and Page argue, in the end, they could be only as good as the categories around which they were constructed. And even in their time, they were put in question by more flexible indexing approaches such as those proposed by Bush and Luhn.

The urgency of Engelbart and Bourne's language reflects the real demands of the moment—not least among these, that of garnering funding from US government defense agencies—yet, in the longer history of information, the postwar context of Engelbart and Bush appears epiphenomenal, as does the specific technological character of both the challenge and the proposed solution that each articulates. Consider another statement of the "information problem" from two centuries earlier when the broadside and the newspaper represented the bleeding edge of new media, when an explosion of published books worried researchers as much as did the explosion of technical literature that concerned Bush, Luhn, and Engelbart.

That world, at the midpoint of the eighteenth century, argued the French philosopher Denis Diderot, was poised at the edge of a fundamental and irreversible transformation of knowledge and media. In his words, "As long as the centuries continue to unfold, the number of books will grow continually, and one can predict that a time will come when it will be almost as difficult to learn anything from books as from the direct study of the whole universe." Perhaps for Diderot, that time had not yet quite arrived, but the forces at work appeared both intensifying and inexorable. Diderot's proposed solution to the problem was technical. With his collaborator, the mathematician Jean le Rond d'Alembert, he would create a new kind of *encyclopedia that would make it practical to navigate this flood of books.

Diderot and d'Alembert were not alone in their concerns: to illustrate the problem, their contemporary the French journalist and critic Louis-Sébastien Mercier invented a new literary form, the novel of the future. Mercier's 1771 book, *The Year 2440: A Dream If Ever There Was One*, described politics, society, and knowledge in a speculative world located seven centuries in the future. In one of the most famous scenes in that book, the narrator, a time traveler from the eighteenth century, makes his way to the building that in his day housed the Royal Library of France. The traveler finds the building still there, looking much as it did in his own time. But when he enters, he gets a shock: the great halls that had once been filled with printed books are now empty, or nearly so. All that remain are a few volumes.

The time traveler, knowing the stories of the great Library of Alexandria, approaches a librarian and ventures to ask if some "fatal conflagration" had not devoured the king's collection. To this, the librarian replies, "Yes, it was a conflagration; but we lit it with our own hands." Faced with a crushing, ever-growing accumulation of books, "what remained for us to do, but to rebuild the structure of human knowledge?" From shelves and shelves of books, the good information was sorted out from the bad and, in the end, not much was left. This was condensed into clear language and assembled.

Book burning aside, Mercier's plan echoes that of Diderot and d'Alembert. They gathered the best writers they knew and made an encyclopedia that contained key knowledge from a wide range of technical and humanistic fields that could serve as a kind of index to all. The resulting work, one of the great monuments in the history of information, also contained eleven volumes of illustrations that set a standard for contemporary information graphics. The organization of the work was novel, and, for its creators, as much as for Bush, Engelbart, or Brin and Page, it was this technical dimension that distinguished it. Diderot and d'Alembert believed that in their explosive information environment, above all, knowledge had to be searchable so that it could be found and accessed quickly and then reassembled creatively according to the changing needs of the user and the demands of the moment.

To achieve these search capabilities, the *Encyclopédie* of Diderot and d'Alembert combined several older technical strategies. The typical encyclopedia of the time, according to Diderot and d'Alembert, was organized thematically and in a general sense hierarchically. They called this kind of organization *encyclopedic order. In a work organized this way, discoveries in natural history and in the study of language, for example, would occupy entirely different sections of the work. Moreover, within each thematic section, information was often deeply buried. A researcher interested in one specific aspect of natural history, perhaps bird calls, might need to read everything about birds to learn anything useful on the subject, and a researcher interested in somehow connecting information about bird calls to information about human language was in a still greater bind. This was, of course, part of the problem that Socrates had envisioned resulting from the abandonment of the ancient arts of memory, but for Diderot and d'Alembert, three centuries into the age of print, the solution had to emerge from print itself.

As with many such innovations, the full implications of Diderot and d'Alembert's adaptation of the encyclopedia format were not all immediately apparent. Indeed, the publisher's 1745 prospectus for the *Encyclopédie* promised readers little more than a translation of the English *Cyclopaedia* published by Ephraim Chambers in 1728. By 1751, when the first volume of the work appeared, the project had changed fundamentally. Chambers's book remained an inspiration, and some of its features were emulated in the new work including its alphabetical organization and its cross-references; his text, by contrast, was abandoned. By 1755, when the fifth volume of Diderot and d'Alembert's work appeared, including the self-reflexive entry ENCYCLOPÉDIE, the encyclopedia embodied a fully conceptualized *epistemological program.

Diderot and d'Alembert's work turned out to be an encyclopedia of a new kind. Unlike a thematic encyclopedia, theirs was divided into discrete chunks—articles—each placed under a headword—what today we would call a keyword. The information in these articles was sourced from a crowd of writers selected for their knowledge and special perspective, a *société de gens de lettres*, as Diderot and d'Alembert put it, though the gendered English translation, *society of men of letters*, was in fact more accurate. In their argument and presentation, these different contributions were not to be integrated. Instead, they would be interlinked through a web of embedded cross-references operating according to several different logics. The idea that knowledge could be usefully grouped into hierarchical categories, a branching tree of the sort suggested by Francis Bacon's classification of knowledge, was not abandoned. To the contrary, in his preliminary discourse, d'Alembert sketched his own version of Bacon's tree. But instead of organizing the text around this tree, Diderot and d'Alembert embedded its logic in the network of cross-references woven throughout.

In an important way, this move strengthened the tree of knowledge, because it unburdened it: now that it could be understood to represent only one possible projection of complex and overlapping fields of knowledge, problems of hierarchization disappeared. Trees of different kinds could be imagined, as could linking structures that were horizontal rather than hierarchical. Diderot, ever the wit, even described a satirical style of cross-reference familiar in today's world of hashtags, in which the reference itself serves as a form of commentary. He counseled his readers to look out for these signals, "carefully weighing" the significance of each cross-reference. For example, says Diderot, at the end of one article in the *Encyclopédie* (on Grey Friars), the attentive reader will notice an incongruous cross-reference to MONK'S COWL. The reader who follows that cross-reference will be amused to discover an account of a pointless sartorial debate that once (for a century) raged among the Franciscans. Put the two entries together, and the reader will understand that what looked like praise for the argument in the first article "was meant ironically." References of this sort, Diderot suggests, allow the *Encyclopedia's* authors to criticize "ridiculous customs," afford "a delicate and amusing way to pay back an insult," and offer "an excellent means of snatching off the masks from the faces of certain grave personages."

The way into Diderot and d'Alembert's *Encyclopédie* was distinctive, too. Here again, the French editors borrowed from the Englishman Chambers, who, two decades before, had eschewed encyclopedic order in favor of a more humble dictionary order. Like him, Diderot and d'Alembert organized their encyclopedia alphabetically. In the perspective of electronic information technology, this hardly seems much of an innovation, but the implications were substantial and the significance enduring. What Diderot and d'Alembert noticed in their reading of Chambers was that individual words shorn of syntactic context were excellent tools for search.

In retrospect, the *Encyclopédie* appears a visionary document. But we should not be taken in by what looks like foresight in Diderot any more so than by the science fiction future of Mercier's *2440*. Rather, we should understand both the *Encyclopédie* and *2440* as telling documents of their time. The *Encyclopédie* of Diderot and d'Alembert *feels* modern because the imperatives and conditions—the feeling of overload, the sense of acceleration—that drove it resemble the imperatives that drive our own information society. Neither Diderot nor Mercier saw the future. What they saw, powdered wigs or no, was a media present that we are still living out. And, as they understood it, the core problem of modern information society was the problem of search.

This is also the deeper message behind Mercier's vision of burning books. Presented as it was, his account of the destruction of the books in the Royal Library was neither utopian nor dystopian. Mercier was a prolific writer who certainly did not want *his* books burned, but he really did believe, as did Diderot and d'Alembert, that a great encyclopedia could do more good in the world than a vault filled with mediocre, redundant, or unfindable books. His efforts were aimed at changing the perspective of the reader on the problem of knowledge in general. For all these *Enlightenment writers, more information ceased to be a useful objective. The goal was better and more accessible information, information that could be used and recombined in previously unimagined ways.

This brings us to what is the most striking observation made by Vannevar Bush in his famous article on the memex, one influential in both the design and the ultimate coming into being of the web itself. Bush's vision revolved around two key desiderata. First was a mechanical system providing access to an enormous amount of information from diverse sources through a single interface. Second was a way of traversing this information in crisscrossing associative trails. To achieve the first, Bush proposed microfilm. This turned out not to be the best technology for the application, although it took some time for this to become obvious: late in the twentieth century, vast archiving projects still employed microfilm. To achieve the second, Bush proposed something so simple that it harked back to early modern *commonplace books and the rearrangeable note slips and index cards of scholars such as Desiderius Erasmus, Conrad Gessner, and Vincent Placcius. As individual readers worked their way through the subject matter on the memex, they would create trails that would allow them to retrace their own paths through the forest of information and to share them with others. The tool for doing this would be a new, technical feature of the memex machine. But the underlying idea was as traditional as scholarship itself.

The notion of automating the process of association was more novel. Here, Luhn was an exemplary contributor. At IBM in the early 1950s, Luhn began work on what he called a "business intelligence system." His goal was to design a computer program to examine new technical literature, summarize it, and direct it to appropriate engineers at IBM. Like Diderot's *Encyclopédie* and Bush's memex, Luhn's system was meant to break out of the rigid categories of field specialization that would, for example, send articles on chemistry exclusively to chemists. Appropriately, Luhn's work in this area was eagerly followed not only by computer scientists but by a wider community of documentalists drawn from diverse institutions ranging from libraries to scientific societies to national security agencies for which the management and processing of information were central. This grouping of fields was represented, among other places, in the American Documentation Institute, later the Association for Information Science and Technology, or ASIS&T, where Luhn would for a time serve as president. In itself, this grouping was important, and the combination of approaches that it fostered is strongly echoed in the genealogy of PageRank.

Luhn's procedure was simple in concept. The computer first had to determine which words used in a text were most important. This was to be achieved statistically first through an analysis of word frequency: words that appeared often in an article were considered significant as long as they were not so frequent that they represented nothing more than the regularities of the language or of the present field of research. Thus, for example, the computer would be instructed to ignore function words such as the articles *the* and *a* as well as more content-laden terms such as *doctor* or *illness* when preparing an abstract from a medical journal. Words that were determined to be significant were ranked by the algorithm. High-ranking terms were then assessed to be the keywords of the source article and were used to characterize and to classify it.

Luhn proposed further that, following this approach, key sentences might also be identified, extracted, and arranged in order. What resulted would serve as an "automatic abstract" of the source article. Users of Luhn's "business intelligence system" would characterize themselves by selecting a set of keywords of interest to them. The system could then match abstracts to readers. On the basis of feedback gleaned as users accepted and rejected abstracts suggested by the system, keyword profiles for both users and articles could be refined. Notably, in Luhn's system, the reader and the text were *both* characterized by profiles made up of keywords: from the point of view of the system, the searcher and the searched were interchangeable.

Luhn worked for IBM, which had an immediate business interest in information retrieval both for its internal operations and as a commercial product that it could market to others. And much of early web search too was driven by commercial concerns. Yet some search projects emerged from academia as well. The most successful of these was Google itself, which began as a graduate student research project. Indeed, at the start of 1998, Google was still an academic project, and though that would soon change, it remained then a characteristic that its creators considered important. "Up until now," they write, "most search engine development has gone on at companies with little publication of technical details. This causes search engine technology to remain largely a black art and to be advertising oriented." By contrast, they continue, "With Google, we have a strong goal to push more development and understanding into the academic realm." In their paper, they envision Google as a "Spacelab-like environment" where "other researchers can come in quickly" and "process large parts of the Web." At the time, this was just a premise, but so, for that matter, was the entire project of making Google a tool for the everyday web user, which Brin and Page convey in what must be some kind of record-setting understatement: "we believe our solutions are scalable to commercial volumes with a bit more effort." Time would show that Google scaled very well to commercial volumes; at scale, it would come to dominate the field of web search, despite concerted, well-funded competition by Microsoft and other corporate rivals, and state-protected companies such as Baidu in China and Yandex in Russia. To say that the web grew exponentially in the following two decades barely hints at the pace of change. In 1998, Brin and Page's first crawler was able to collect and index a total of one hundred forty-seven gigabytes of data. A recent estimate put the size of Google's index at approximately one hundred million gigabytes, a growth of six orders of magnitude.

Of course, once reconfigured as a commercial project, Google would become expert in the same "black art" that Brin and Page had criticized. While the implications were enormous, the reasons were banal. Some were proprietary: once it was in the market, a search engine was competing with others, and not only other search engines, but also other interested parties such as site administrators who would attempt to *game* search engine results in order to obtain high rankings for their sites. Entire businesses emerged specializing in this kind of search engine optimization, and varieties of web spamming including link farming, redirection spamming, and visual cloaking became common. Search engines had a stake in preventing their results from being manipulated by outsiders, whether because they wanted to be able to offer better results, or because they wanted to be able to pick winners themselves. Other issues were technical: search algorithms were becoming more complex, and with the application of *machine learning to their optimization, the connection between specific intentionality on the part of engineers and the operation of the search mechanism became more distant and harder to fully comprehend, even for the engineers themselves.

Part of what allowed web search to become so ubiquitous to begin with is that, to the individual user of a search engine, search appeared to be a free service. From a certain perspective, it was: neither Google nor its main competitors charged individual customers for web search, and search is a powerful tool. Certainly, consumers of search experienced real costs, including charges by ISPs (*internet service providers) and by consumer electronics companies that make and sell the devices used to conduct searches. This is to say nothing of the many economic and environmental externalities of the communications infrastructure underlying the internet. But, remarkably, search itself, in the form provided by Google, Microsoft, and other commercial services in the early twenty-first century, generally incurred no direct charge.

For these companies, the incentive structure worked the other way around: when users searched, search companies made money, and the more people searched, the more money the search companies made. The same incentive structure led these companies to offer a variety of other products—including social media, document and spreadsheet software, web browsers, mobile phone operating systems, low-cost computer equipment, *cloud storage, and internet connectivity—that lowered barriers to participation and helped keep users within a given data ecosystem. In the case of Google, this included also massive absorption and service of web content, including from 2004, the Google Books text digitization project, and from 2006, the video streaming service YouTube, which quickly became the second most visited site on the web, surpassing Facebook, Amazon, and other web heavyweights, and ranking behind only its mother corporation, Google.

From the point of view of the history of the web, both YouTube and Google Books were enormously important. From the point of view of the history of reading and scholarship, Google Books was transformative. With it, Google leap-frogged the many digitization projects already being conducted by libraries and other information providers. In one fell swoop, it created the largest repository of books on the web and integrated it into a search environment shared by every-thing else that Google indexed. As Google presented it, Google Books was a realization of the age-old dream of the universal library. In its own words, Google's aim was to make "the full text of all the world's books searchable by everyone." That idea was reinforced early on by the agreement of several major research libraries including the New York Public Library and the libraries of the University of Michigan, University of Oxford, Stanford University, and Harvard University to participate in the project. Google would scan their holdings, process them using OCR (*optical character recognition), and make them searchable. The libraries too would get copies of the resulting electronic docu-ments, which they would then pool through the academic consortium Hathi Trust. Libraries and foundations, of course, continued their own digitization work and constructed valuable interfaces such as those for the manuscript col-lection in the Vatican Library's online DigiVatLib and the early books collection at the Bayerische Staatsbibliothek's Münchener DigitalisierungsZentrum. For most users, however, it seemed likely that the principal gateway to "the world of information contained in books" would be Google itself.

Google Books was a big idea and a big project, and its ambitions were amplified by enthusiasts such as technology theorist and *Wired* magazine founder Kevin Kelly. In Google, Kelly wrote, the world's books become "one very, very, very large single text: the world's only book," "a single liquid fabric of interconnected words and ideas." For him, "turning inked letters into electronic dots that can be read on a screen is simply the first essential step in creating this new library. The real magic will come in the second act, as each word in each book is cross-linked, clustered, cited, extracted, indexed, analyzed, annotated, remixed, reassembled and woven deeper into the culture than ever before. In the new world of books, every bit informs another; every page reads all the other pages."

In some respects, Kelly was undoubtedly right. In Google Books, and everywhere else on the web, too, the experience of reading was changing. Boundaries between texts were becoming more malleable, and the difference between reading and searching was increasingly blurred. At the same time, in the version of the web that emerged at the end of the twentieth century, and in the version of Google Books developed for it, none of these utopian longings was fulfilled. This was less a failure in innovation than in imagination, argued Theodor Nelson. The basic protocols on which the web was running—including HTTP (hypertext transfer protocol) and HTML (Hypertext Markup Language), proposed in 1989 by Tim Berners-Lee—limited the relationships among documents that could be implemented.

Not all visions of the universal library have been utopian. For Denis Diderot, as for many of his contemporaries, the idea of the universal library was as much cautionary as it was visionary. During the Enlightenment, as we have seen, the story of the destruction of the Library of Alexandria resonated strongly. When Enlightenment thinkers thought about the Alexandrian Library, they mostly thought about the fragility of knowledge and of media, a subject of renewed importance in our own age of digital ephemerality. For them, the Library of Alexandria represented an Icarian dream: the greatest library in the history of the world, and it went up in flames. In the charter for his encyclopedia project, Diderot alluded to that catastrophe, promoting his *Encyclopédie*, of which there would be many copies, as a kind of starter kit for a new world of knowledge after the next, ineluctable information holocaust: "The most glorious moment for a work such as this would be that which might come immediately in the wake of some revolution so great as to suspend the

progress of science, to interrupt the labors of craftsmen, and to plunge a portion of our hemisphere into darkness once again. What gratitude would not
be lavished by the generation that came after this time of troubles upon those
men who had discerned its approach from afar, and who had taken measures
to ward off its worst ravages by collecting in a safe place the knowledge of all
past ages!" As Tung-Hui Hu has argued, a related kind of apocalyptic, or
necropolitical, thinking underlay Paul Baran's original design for a distributed
and thus un-nuke-able ARPANET in the 1960s as well as the *data bunkers* that
today inhabit the husks of old fallout shelters deep below ground.

However comprehensive the Library of Alexandria in fact was, and however
precisely it came to its end, it must have been a remarkable resource. No physical library ever again made the same claim to universality. This has something
to do with the fact that over time, as Diderot pointed out, the world of books
kept expanding. It also has much to do with the history of empires. In the West,
after Alexandria and before Google, no political or commercial entity had the
wherewithal to engage in a comparable project. The Library of Alexandria was
impracticable apart from Egypt's military and infrastructural dominance.
When ships docked at Alexandria, they were meant to send any book on board
to be copied at the library. An ancient account describes books acquired this
way piled up in warehouses. The extent to which this actually happened is a
mystery, but the principle is illuminating. While Egypt's wealth and passion for
Greek culture gave it the power to make such a demand, it was its domination
of infrastructure that allowed it to channel information into its repository.

The Google Books project began in 2004 when Google proposed two book
initiatives, one aimed at contemporary *publishers and one aimed at libraries.
Google Print, announced at the Frankfurt Book Fair in October 2004, was to
allow digital search and access to current books through agreement with publishers. The Google Books Library Project, announced in December 2004, was
to do much the same with material obtained from libraries. In 2010, a Google
Book Search engineer estimated that since the beginning of print in the West,
approximately 130 million unique titles had been published—actually, the
number he gave was 129,864,880. Eventually Google intended to obtain and
digitize the vast majority of these. By October 2015, it had made a respectable
start by scanning twenty-five million books from its research library partners.
By that time, Google Print and the Google Library Project had been subsumed
under the common rubric of Google Books.

From the start, Google Books provoked controversy. Problems of *fair use
and *copyright had to be settled. A major legal issue was whether Google

would be allowed to operate its book projects on an opt-in or an opt-out principle—in other words, whether Google would have to ask authors and publishers for permission before or after digitizing their works. Google's preference and its initial approach were decidedly for opt-out: Google tried to hoover up everything it could first and to deal with the niceties later. And while publishers and writers initially sued regarding this approach to copyrighted materials, Google's partnership with research libraries allowed it to plunge into scanning headlong. Authors and publishers argued that Google's approach "shifts the responsibility for preventing infringement to the copyright owner rather than the user, turning every principle of copyright law on its ear."

Some governments, too, including those of France and Germany, argued that Google's approach placed "unchecked, concentrated power" over the shared fund of human knowledge, as well as the unique cultural heritage of nations around the world, in the hands of an unaccountable US commercial entity. The research libraries partnered with Google tried to find a middle ground. Harvard's librarian, the eminent book historian Robert Darnton, for example, made a case for using Google's scanning to build up digital materials for a network of noncommercial digital libraries, the DPLA or Digital Public Library of America, in order to guarantee access to out-of-copyright books, which are in the *public domain. Darnton found models for such networks of collective agreement in library initiatives developed in Europe and especially in Europeana, a pan-European network of networks. Others argued for even more ambitious, public efforts such as the Human Knowledge Project proposed by historian and media scholar Siva Vaidhyanathan.

For its part, Google defended the notion of amassing "the world's knowledge stored in books" in its own repository, arguing that digitizing books and then making them searchable through a single, unified interface transformed them fundamentally, using the legal term of art. In its legal arguments, Google focused on the claims of authors and publishers to works still in copyright. These, it argued, could be addressed by assuring that copyrighted items stored by Google would not be viewable except as permitted by copyright holders. It argued that its search product would provide specific benefits to authors and publishers by making their properties discoverable and by driving traffic to them, whether on the web, in a physical library or bookstore, through on-demand printing, or in some other way. It argued further that the public good that it would create relied on the comprehensiveness of its underlying data. That, in turn, demanded the opt-out approach. Though complex, a settlement agreement reached in 2008 affirmed Google's basic strategy. It also permitted

Google to monetize its collection of digitized books through a variety of mechanisms. And it affirmed the premise that the "world's knowledge stored in books" would be rendered searchable through Google's proprietary interface under terms mostly set by Google itself.

Many worried that the Google Books project would crowd out others. The scope and cost of its book digitization were enormous, and, despite dedicated efforts by a number of public and nonprofit entities, once Google had advanced to a certain point, these critics argued, it was hard to imagine another institution doing the same heavy lifting. Indeed, evidence to support these concerns was abundant: many likely competitors to Google Books, including the nonprofit Internet Archive and the library partners in the Google Books project themselves, had already opted to rely on Google to provide digitized texts for their own collections. This was, for the libraries, a principal incentive to participate in Google's project in the first place. Thus, whatever Google did in its digitization project was likely to endure and to propagate through many channels. Consequently, as readers relied increasingly on digital means to access books, their experience of books would be increasingly shaped by Google, by its selections, its scanning procedures, its treatment of bibliographic metadata, and so forth. The looming dystopian possibility was not a Google that dominated the treasury of world literature. Rather, it was a Google that for one reason or another never fully took the problem of books seriously, that abandoned the task only partway done, or both. And a decade or so in, many of these fears seemed more than justified. After a largely successful legal struggle to defend its approach to digitization, Google Books appeared to evolve rather little, and Google stopped saying much about it.

Early studies quickly demonstrated a wide range of problems and peculiarities in Google's approach. For example, the algorithms applied by Google Books frequently attributed to books the wrong publication dates. In a review in the *Chronicle of Higher Education*, Geoff Nunberg pointed out that according to Google Books, Raymond Chandler's *Killer in the Rain* was published in 1899, the same year as "*The Portable Dorothy Parker*, André Malraux's *La Condition Humaine*, Stephen King's *Christine*, *The Complete Shorter Fiction of Virginia Woolf*, Raymond Williams's *Culture and Society 1780–1950*, and Robert Shelton's biography of *Bob Dylan*." Classification was similarly problematic. "H. L. Mencken's *The American Language* is classified as Family & Relationships. . . . An edition of *Moby Dick* is labeled Computers; *The Cat Lover's Book of Fascinating Facts* falls under Technology & Engineering. And a catalog of copyright entries from the *Library of Congress is listed under Drama (for a moment I wondered if maybe that one was just Google's little joke)."

As Paul Duguid showed, Google Books had similar problems interpreting what was inside of books. It failed to read drop capitals, the large initial letters common at the beginning of book chapters; it mistook book illustrations for scanning errors; it read book plates as title pages; its optical character recognition functioned poorly on older books, particularly those published before 1800. Various features such as hyperlinked tables of contents worked inconsistently, and, depending on the quality of the initial digital scan, Google often failed to recognize entire sections of works. All this created serious problems for text search within the corpus and even greater problems using the corpus for quantitative analysis—including the briefly ballyhooed culturomics, or quantitative analysis of culture, emblematized by the Google Books Ngram Viewer—or anything else. Of course, Google had every intention to provide the best digitization possible at scale, and it had some very good reasons to want to do this. As Nunberg pointed out, the fact that in 2009 Google was still displaying ads for gardening supplies to readers of Walt Whitman's *Leaves of Grass* could not have particularly pleased ad buyers at Home Depot. Regardless, this was the situation.

In all this, most worrisome perhaps was Google's programmatic lack of interest in bibliographic metadata, the very stuff that makes a library a library rather than just a storehouse of books. This was an ironic development, since the catalog was in principle the aspect of the traditional library *best* adapted to the digital framework, as well as its most comprehensive tool for information search. Indeed, historically, the library card catalog was the very paradigm of the humanistic database, and massive digitization—retroactive *conversion, as it is called—of library catalogs had begun long before the advent of Google Books. Nicholson Baker's famous essay "Discards," a *cri de coeur* for the library card catalog and against the "national paroxysm of shortsightedness and anti-intellectualism" that had led to its devaluation and destruction, was published in the *New Yorker* in 1994, four years before the founding of Google and a full decade before the announcement of the Google Books Library Project. And Baker's essay was already belated: New York Public Library, for example, had microfilmed and disposed of its card catalog in the late 1970s.

Others followed. As Baker recounts in his essay, even Harvard University, with a massive catalog containing more than five million cards, was doing a retrocon, sending off boxes of cards, a week at a time, to OCLC, the Online Computer Library Center in Dublin, Ohio, which then rendered them in "machine-readable form," specifically the so-called MARC or Machine Readable Cataloging format developed in the early 1960s with the Library of Congress. In fact, the standardization of library catalogs had begun earlier still. At the very start of the twentieth century, the Library of Congress in the United States began selling printed copies of its own catalog cards. To create or augment their card catalogs, libraries in the United States and elsewhere could order cards from Washington. A 1969 study of the Rice University Library, for example, found that fully two-thirds of the library's catalog cards had been purchased from the Library of Congress. This system had many advantages: catalogers at the Library of Congress were skilled professionals, and their system was detailed, standardized, and represented the bibliographic state of the art. From the late 1960s, OCLC offered a similar service, printing cards for libraries on demand. But OCLC also offered another feature, exploiting the possibilities offered by MARC. The OCLC not only could send copies of individual cards to libraries, but it could sort those according to MARC fields, providing drawers for author, title, and subject, for example, or for more rarefied categories such as shelf list or catalog number when requested.

The OCLC approach was both bibliocentric and economically clever. A preprinted OCLC card cost more than a similar Library of Congress card, but in addition to the advantages offered by the automatic sorting that it could perform, OCLC offered libraries a way of offsetting their costs. While a library would pay to purchase a card that was already in the OCLC database, when it discovered an item for which OCLC had no record, it could earn credit by creating a new master record for OCLC through a dedicated computer terminal obtained through the OCLC consortium. As Baker writes, "there was plenty of incentive for all libraries, engaged in the creation of a kind of virtual community long before there were such things as Usenet and listservs, to pump up the burgeoning database. What began mainly as a handy, unilateral way of delivering the Library of Congress MARC files to member libraries turned into a highly democratic, omnidirectional collaboration among hundreds of thousands of once isolated documentalists." When libraries began shifting from card catalogs to OPACs (Online Public Access Catalogs) from the late 1970s, the existing OCLC database provided the foundation.

For many libraries, then, the shift to online catalogs was both welcome and intuitive. While a library employing duplicate OCLC cards might hold card sets representing *several* MARC fields, a library employing a computerized catalog could sort records according to *any* MARC field down to the most obscure. Even so, there were difficulties. Some problems endemic to the

OCLC approach even before OPAC were intensified by it. In the OCLC system, for example, the master record that governed what was on a given OCLC card was determined the *first* time that data was entered. If the first record contained an error, omission, or idiosyncrasy, it would be perpetuated in every catalog that employed that record. Additionally, OCLC lacked a good system of authority control, a major issue for any database. If one catalog used the name Mark Twain and another Samuel Clemens, an OPAC might end up with conflicting records or overlooking a work entirely. In general, OCLC was resistant to variation. If a Harvard card contained information that was either more detailed than what was in the OCLC record or particular to the Harvard Library, this information was at serious risk of being lost in translation. Even if OCLC's error rates were low, irreplaceable information was always at risk, and along with it, aspects of the unique scholarly history embodied in every library.

By the time that Google Books started up, many of these concerns seemed comparatively minor. After all, the digital retroconversion of card catalogs was meant to preserve and enhance their traditional functionalities, and the path from MARC to OCLC to OPAC was conducted within the institutional framework of libraries. Something very different was happening in Google Books. From the beginning, as Brin and Page stated, their system was meant to work in a way distinct from catalog-type search. Google Books would itself have no catalog. Not even an accession list. So there was no simple way to even determine what books Google Books contained. And when Google absorbed the textual content of libraries, it did not do the same for their indexing systems. Rather, it expected readers entering its corpus to rely on the same kind of search tools that it applied to the web more generally.

Consistent with the big data ethos that governed its search strategies, in Google's digitization projects, quality mattered, but quantity mattered more. Thus, the difficulties Baker pointed to in the digital retroconversion of library catalogs in the 1980s and 1990s were amplified in the digitization of the books enumerated therein. A digitized book, whatever its virtues, simply was not the same variety of object as a printed book or manuscript; having multiple copies of one digital scan was not the same as having multiple books; and the convenience offered by remote access was often paid for by an inferior product.

The result of all this—though it became more difficult to perceive as libraries themselves increasingly relied on electronic tools—was a search experience unlike what libraries had until then provided. Without question, Google's search was powerful and the advantages many, particularly when, to use Nunberg's words, one's purpose was only to "find a chunk of a book that answers our needs." In such cases, a Google-type search offered a means to enter books "sideways." But this was very often at the expense of knowing exactly what it was that one was entering, why one ended up there, or where that there was. Was a searcher looking at a first edition, a revised edition, an extract, a compilation, a plagiarism, a parody? These sorts of questions were of particular importance for scholars, but, in fact, they were issues for every reader, and, in an age of widespread digitally generated *disinformation*, all the more so. In traditional libraries, the curation provided by librarians and the metadata provided by catalogs served these ends, even if most readers never noticed. In the framework of Google Books, these services were absent.

At all events, by the second decade of the twenty-first century, as readers relied increasingly on the web as a principal source of information, algorithmic search displaced structured approaches to search to a great extent. Unlike the pinakes of Callimachus, versions of the old library catalogs—or at least their digital shadows—remained available through libraries, but the seamlessness of the delivery of textual content in Google, the great extent of its reach, and its integration into the ubiquitous environment of search increasingly made the web a likely first stop, and for the same reason, often also a last stop in information search in the world of books.

What Wendy Hui Kyong Chun called the "conflation of memory and storage" also presented new problems for the history of information. As digital media increasingly supplanted analog media, and as the web increasingly connected to everything around it, old archival mechanisms faced new threats. Digital media became obsolescent quickly, and the graveyard of *dead media grew crowded as paper punch cards were replaced by magnetic tapes and tapes by magnetic disks and these by optical disks and these by solid state memory and this by cloud storage and so on. Archives in the digital era began requiring that donors provide, along with digitally stored materials, the computer equipment necessary to read them; and this was often not enough, as old computer systems themselves often failed when they could not be virtualized or emulated on a newer system. Ironically, many archives began asking for paper versions of anything delivered digitally. Only decades into the digital era, foundational works of interactive digital art were already disappearing into the ether. In the condition that Chun referred to as "the enduring ephemeral," curators debated how to preserve an experience of (now old) new media art without altering it substantially.

Even bigger problems of preservation were presented by the link graph of the web and by the interactive structures of web search. Organizations such as the Internet Archive and rhizome.org made efforts to address the first of these challenges. Recognizing that the web had no self-archiving function, the Internet Archive set out to take snapshots of it every day and to make these available through what it called the Wayback Machine, allowing users not only to view individual stored pages but also to *surf* a stored version of the web on a given date in the past. Rhizome.org, focusing on the problem of viewing art rather than information, provided a tool for viewing the web through virtualized historical *web browsers* going all the way back to Marc Andreesen's *NCSA Mosaic*, first issued in 1993. The second problem, that of archiving search itself, proved less tractable. While the Internet Archive could make available the websites that Google or AskJeeves or another search engine might in the past have recommended as well as the links among them, it could not emulate the generation of search results as such. For the early decades of the web, these results, crucial information artifacts in and of themselves, proved as ephemeral as any expression of traditional oral culture had ever been.

This situation was of immense concern to activists such as the creators of the Long Now Foundation including the writer Stewart Brand and the computer engineer Danny Hillis. Brand writes,

> "Back when information was hard to copy," said Hillis, "people valued the copies and took care of them. Now, copies are so common as to be considered worthless, and very little attention is given to preserving them over the long term." He noted that thousands of years ago we recorded important matters on clay and stone that lasted thousands of years. Hundreds of years ago we used parchment that lasted hundreds of years. As a result, Hillis suggests, we are now in a period that may be a maddening blank to future historians—a Dark Age—because nearly all of our art, science, news, and other records are being created and stored on media that we know can't outlast even our own lifetimes.

To achieve their goal of encouraging long-term, "generational" thinking, the Long Now Foundation produced a number of compelling artifacts including Hillis's Ten-Thousand-Year Clock, "the world's slowest supercomputer," and the Rosetta Disk, a durable three-inch nickel plate micro-etched with over one hundred thousand pages of culturally important texts readable under a microscope. In 2004, one Rosetta Disk was launched into space. Others have been readied to survive an information apocalypse here on earth.

As Brin and Page noted in their 1998 paper, in the first years of the web, the principal financial basis of search was advertising. A user searching the web with a major search engine would get results relevant to query terms along with advertisements the system determined to be relevant and that sponsors paid for through programs such as the AdWords auction that Google launched in 2000. As we have seen, this model had the great virtue of making search nominally free, but as Brin and Page argued at the time, it also produced incentives for "search engine bias" and "poor quality search results." In part, Brin and Page suggested, the market would take care of these. Obvious examples of bias, such as "selling companies the right to be listed at the top of the search results for particular queries," were likely to cause "an uproar." However, products of "less blatant bias are likely to be tolerated by the market. For example, a search engine could add a small factor to search results from 'friendly' companies and subtract a factor from results from competitors. This type of bias is very difficult to detect but could still have a significant effect on the market." And studies of search, particularly in the e-commerce sector, bear out this hunch.

At the same time, as Brin and Page predicted, the market did a reasonably good job of clearing out search engines that provided obviously distorted results or that failed to adequately defend against spammers. Actually, the market did a reasonably good job of clearing out *everyone* except Google. Surviving search engines including Google promoted their results as objective and unbiased by human judgment. In fact, they found the principle of algorithmic neutrality so valuable that they were willing to defend it even in the face of strenuous public protest, as in 2004 when Google was criticized for allowing an anti-Semitic website to achieve a top ranking in response to the search query "Jew." But, as Tarleton Gillespie has argued, the implications of algorithmic neutrality are equivocal, and the fact that an algorithm is unsupervised does not mean that it is value-free. Some algorithmic values are explicit. As we have already seen, Google's algorithms are designed to promote search results of high quality and relevance and filter out or demote fraud and spam. In Safe-Search mode, Google's algorithm filters pornographic material. And there are large parts of the web including the so-called dark web that Google does not search at all. As Siva Vaidhyanathan has argued, Google has an important stake in making the web that its users experience as safe as possible. Users who trust Google and the web use both more. But "safe" and "trustworthy" are not the same as "complete," "enlightening," or "urgent."

The principle here is a general one: algorithms pick and choose by rule not by whim, but that does not mean that their selections lack character. When the algorithm is black boxed, that character becomes hard to determine and hard to critique. From time to time, one gets a view of just how particular a search engine's interpretations can be. In 2013, UN Women published a series of public service ads entitled "The Autocomplete Truth," to demonstrate how pervasive sexism remained in the world and in the world of information. Each ad from the United Nations group featured a photograph of a woman's face. Over her mouth was superimposed the image of a Google search box (along with the note "Actual Google search 9/3/13") and a partial query phrase including "Women shouldn't . . ."; "Women cannot . . ."; "Women should . . ."; and "Women need to . . ." Below each query was the list of suggestions made by Google's autocomplete feature. After "Women need to . . . ," for example, the list read, "be put in their place"; "know their place"; "be controlled"; "be disciplined." None of these suggestions represented the editorial views of the corporation, just as the anti-Semitic link that Google suggested in 2004 for the query "Jew" did not represent anti-Semitism on Google's part. At the same time, together they show that, depending on how it is tuned, a search engine may reflect and even amplify common prejudices and presuppositions.

On some points, Brin and Page's 1998 critique of the "mixed incentive" structure produced by the advertising revenue model proved durable, but after they wrote their paper, that model substantially gave way to a new approach centered on harvesting and analyzing data on user habits and preferences. This newer model in turn reinforced the incentive for search companies to offer still more products. Google's Gmail and Google Maps services, for example, collected data on individuals at a level of detail rivaling or exceeding that of social media services such as Facebook whose entire premise was user profiling. In the first decades of the twenty-first century, profiling of this kind enabled web search companies to offer increasingly personalized results. For consumers, this was convenient, and many welcomed it, authorizing web services to read and store great volumes of personal data such as location histories, calendars, and contact lists, in order to get better results. But as data on individuals became available from more and more sources, explicit permission to access any particular data stream diminished in importance. Predictive analytics became both more powerful and more intrusive as users increasingly engaged entities such as Google through portable and wearable technologies, AI assistants, and ubiquitous sensor technologies communicating through the internet of things.

In the era of personalization, search became increasingly bidirectional. As users searched the web, they accumulated data profiles that were themselves cross-referenced and searched. By 2018, the Google personalization algorithm, for example, considered more than two hundred factors or signals. And

Google's approach in this regard was less extraordinary than exemplary. Still in 2018, how such data were assembled and shared remained mostly obscure and unregulated, despite some important legislative efforts, especially the robust General Data Protection Regulation of the European Union, which became enforceable that same year.

As these changes took place, public awareness came along only in fits and starts. Not long before, in 2011, German Green Party politician Malte Spitz could still make headlines in the German weekly newspaper *Die Zeit* (The time) by revealing that his cellular telephone provider, Deutsche Telekom, was automatically creating and storing records of his geolocation history. Within a short span of time, it became clear that Spitz's discovery only scratched the surface of what data were being captured, stored, and shared on a routine basis by commercial and government entities. In 2013, former US National Security Agency contractor Edward Snowden *leaked documents detailing the NSA's enormous arsenal of data collection instruments, as well as its powerful internal tools for searching that data.

And the revelations kept on coming. In 2018, a whistle-blower revealed how the political data mining firm Cambridge Analytica acquired the data it used to target individuals for messaging during the 2016 US presidential election campaign. The data came from a third party who had offered a seemingly innocuous quiz app on Facebook. More than 250,000 users signed up for the app and, in ticking off its EULA or end-user license agreement, intentionally or unintentionally provided the app permission to access much of their Facebook data, as well as that of more than eighty-seven million of their Facebook friends, even those who had not themselves signed up for the app.

Each of these cases provoked public outcry, and each highlighted just how much was still left to do to regulate the use of *personal data*. In most, no laws were broken. Lawsuits, such as the one filed by Spitz against Deutsche Telekom, and leaks such as Snowden's mostly served to shed light on the voracious appetite for data among large commercial and state actors. All this, as Matthew Jones has argued, reflected quickly changing attitudes toward data itself. As recently as 1996, the US National Security Agency identified the exploding volume of data that it had to handle as one of the top three problems it faced. About the same time, Microsoft research engineer Usama Fayyad framed the issue this way:

> If I were to draw on a historical analogy of where we stand today with regards to digital information manipulation, navigation, and exploitation, I find myself thinking of Ancient Egypt. We can build large impressive

structures. We have demonstrated abilities at the grandest of scales in being able to capture data and construct huge *data warehouses. However, our ability to navigate the digital stores and truly make use of their contents, or to understand how they can be exploited effectively is still fairly primitive. A large data store today, in practice, is not very far from being a grand, write-only, data tomb.

Under the old information retrieval regime, too much data, and particularly too much miscellaneous data, only made the system more unwieldy. But, as Jones explains, in the regime of big data, the problem was reversed: in 2006, a top-secret memo circulated within the NSA opened with the words, "Volume Is Our Friend."

Of course, none of this was entirely without precedent. In the twenty-first century, government surveillance was not new. In fact, the word *statistics* itself was coined originally to name the science of data analysis developed by the eighteenth-century bureaucratic state. And businesses, too, had long taken an interest in customer behavior and preferences. Beyond the scale of the data collection, what made these newer projects so striking was that now individuals were donating their data directly to the institutions that were surveilling them, and they were doing it incessantly. Indeed, in some cases, as for example in genetic genealogy services such as 23andme.com and ancestry.com, individuals were paying to have their most immutable, personally identifiable data decoded and made searchable with few guarantees about its eventual use.

Beyond the question of privacy, personalization changed the way search itself functioned. It influenced the ranking of standard search results so that users in different locations and with different search histories saw different results for the same query. Different ads were displayed. News feeds featured different stories. Again, the convenience was real. A regular *New York Times* reader was more likely to be served a story from the *Times* than from the *Daily News*. A basketball fan was more likely to be served basketball stories than stories about hockey. But this development was widely criticized. The activist and critic Eli Pariser, for example, argued influentially that personalization tended to build walls between people, what he called filter bubbles, reinforcing prior experiences, preferences, and beliefs at the expense of surprise and learning on the one hand and of common culture on the other.

In some respects, search was always personal. The "literary closets" of Thomas Harrison and Vincent Placcius allowed scholars to assemble, preserve, and share textual finds. Bush's memex machine was meant to standardize and to automate the process. But the black-boxed personalization employed by the major web services operated differently, simultaneously centralizing the service of information and fragmenting—narrowcasting—its presentation in unprecedented ways. What one user saw as the result of search was different from what was seen by their neighbor. And as the Cambridge Analytica affair made clear, the accumulated effect of serving targeted information to targeted audiences could be substantial, not least in reinforcing, by providing common information to subgroups, the groupings that resulted in the differential service of information in the first place.

In the environment of big data, the importance of words, which had been the lifeblood of search technology, changed too. On the front end, users increasingly gained the ability to search using nonlinguistic representations including maps, images, and music, for example. Meanwhile, on the back end, search services such as Google acquired the ability to combine many different kinds of data with user queries. For entities such as Google, words were precious, yet they had always been proxies for something else, such as desires, behaviors, or identities. In this new environment, proxies were everywhere.

Search in the early twenty-first century differed importantly from search in preceding epochs. Pixels replaced paper. Data became big. Searchers themselves became the subject of search. Search was everywhere integrated into everything. Yet, somehow, the big transition from "looking something up" to "googling it" seemed to happen quite naturally. A long history of search helps us understand how a technology so world changing as Google could be so quickly and thoroughly assimilated into information culture and practice: in fact, Google was something that users had at least a millennium to prepare for. At the same time, this history helps clarify how great was the cultural change the modern search engine effected. While a search engine such as Google employed a format strongly reminiscent of the indexes that preceded it, implemented as it was, it enabled a style of reading so extensive and aleatory—so deeply rooted in the experience of the *index*—that even peak print did not foreshadow it. Ironically, in some ways, it produced an experience more similar to that of a medieval textualist such as Hugh of St-Cher than to that of a typical reader of the late twentieth century.

The history of information was always also the history of information search. This was no less true at the advent of the *codex book or of movable-type print than at that of the web. Like those earlier changes in the mediascape, the emergence of the web produced tensions between tradition and innovation. Old practices did not go away. Instead, web search contributed new tools to

an existing repertoire including indexes, concordances, file systems, encyclopedias, and others, many of which were enhanced and extended through their
implementation on the web. Nor was the era of Google the first in which designers of search systems sought alternatives to older hierarchical taxonomies.
Hugh of St-Cher and Denis Diderot both aimed to flatten information hierarchies. Vincent Placcius and Vannevar Bush innovated techniques of navigating
through text corpora by creative association rather than by categorical rule.

Yet, by the second decade of the twenty-first century, web search had become more than one kind of search among others; it had become the paradigm
of search in general, even as search had integrated itself into nearly every aspect of daily life. The benefits were enormous. When you could hold up your
smart phone, camera on, and layer a contextual search over the world before
you, *reality*, the boosters said, was *augmented*. But the trade-offs were substantial too. Many of these were already suggested in Brin and Page's original charter
for Google. There, they had argued for a transparent, accountable, not-for-profit
search engine. There, they had argued for the application of principles deeply
embedded in the traditions of humanistic scholarship. There, they had warned
about the incentives that the market imposes on a search company driven by
profit. Two decades into the twenty-first century, Brin and Page's 1998 paper
had become both a telling artifact in the history of search and a promising
launch point for future critique.

Further Reading

Ann Blair, *Too Much to Know: Managing Scholarly Information before the Modern Age*, 2010;
    Sergey Brin and Lawrence Page, "The Anatomy of a Large-Scale Hypertextual Web Search
    Engine," in *Computer Networks and ISDN Systems* 30, nos. 1–7 (April 1, 1998): 107–17; Vannevar
    Bush, "As We May Think," *Atlantic Monthly* 176, no. 1 (July 1945): 101–8; Wendy Hui Kyong
    Chun, *Updating to Remain the Same: Habitual New Media*, 2016; Robert Darnton, *The Case
    for Books: Past, Present, and Future*, 2009; Dennis Duncan, *Index, A History of the: A bookish
    Adventure* (2021); Tarleton Gillespie, "The Relevance of Algorithms," in *Media Technologies:
    Essays on Communication, Materiality, and Society*, edited by Tarleton Gillespie, Pablo J.
    Boczkowski, and Kirsten A. Foot, 2014; Anthony Grafton, *The Footnote: A Curious History*,
    1999; Tung-Hui Hu, *A Prehistory of the Cloud*, 2015; Matthew Jones, "Querying the Archive:
    Data Mining from Apriori to PageRank," in *Science in the Archives: Pasts, Presents, Futures*,
    edited by Lorraine Daston, 2017: 311–28; Hans Peter Luhn, *H. P. Luhn, Pioneer of Information
    Science: Selected Writings*, edited by Claire K. Schulz, 1968; Theodor Holm Nelson, *Computer
    Lib / Dream Machines*, 1974; Eli Pariser, *The Filter Bubble: How the New Personalized Internet
    Is Changing What We Read and How We Think*, 2011; Frank Pasquale, *The Black Box Society*,
    2015; Daniel Rosenberg, "An Archive of Words," in *Science in the Archives: Pasts, Presents*,

Futures, edited by Lorraine Daston, 2017, 271–310; idem, "An Eighteenth-Century Time Machine: The Encyclopedia of Denis Diderot," in *Postmodernism and the Enlightenment*, edited by Daniel Gordon, 2001, 45–66; Trebor Scholz, *Uberworked and Underpaid: How Workers Are Disrupting the Digital Economy*, 2017; Nanna Bonde Thylstrup, *The Politics of Mass Digitization*, 2019; Siva Vaidhyanathan, *The Googlization of Everything (and Why We Should Worry)*, 2012.

GLOSSARY

analog/digital. Terms to describe the operating character of mechanisms. *Digital* describes mechanisms that offer particular, preset states—such as a light switch that can be on or off, or a keyboard that can be set to all capitals or all lowercase. *Analog*, by contrast, indicates devices with continuous settings—such as a light dimmer or a thermostat that can be turned up or down across an undivided spectrum. Most modern computational devices are underpinned by a binary digital system, where the fundamental settings are either 0 or 1, which nonetheless allows them to produce apparently continuous settings. The terms are also used, by extension, for a broad division of history into two eras. The phrase "digital age" is used to describe the era of widespread digital computing, often assumed to coincide with the growth of the public internet. All that comes before is then treated as if it shared traits of a contrastingly "analog" era.

archival thinking/consciousness. An approach to historical research that assumes that historians should ask questions about how archives, as collections or institutions with their own histories and realities, determine the understanding of the pasts for which they not only provide evidence but also shape the stories told.

artificial intelligence (AI). A branch of science and research that focuses on producing computer systems that are assumed to respond with human-like thinking when addressing human tasks.

big data. A set of data that owing to its enormity requires special computing power and analytical attention to be manipulated or understood. A key goal of big data collection and analysis is to unearth underlying patterns or trends that are invisible to other research approaches.

binary. The foundational system of os and 1s that is used to make information readable for computers.

bits. A term coined by the mathematician John Tukey for binary digits, the fundamental units of digital encoding. Made of 1s and 0s, they originally reflected whether a switch was on or off or a signal was "long" or "short." Computers are designed to work with groups of bits. The conventional grouping is made of eight bits and known as a "byte."

book hand. A formal script used in copying books or documents, usually by trained scribes.

bookkeeping. The practice of maintaining accounting records of debits and credits that allow for future access and use.

born digital. A qualifier used to describe texts that were first produced for a digital platform, as opposed to those that might be translated into a digital form from their original analog state.

cabinet of curiosities. An early modern collection of items considered interesting or valuable, including natural specimens and items created by human crafts. Whether formed by monarchs or private collectors, cabinets of curiosities offered materials and models for the development of museums.

canon. A body of religious works, literature, or artistic productions (e.g., sculptures, films, paintings) that is considered culturally authoritative or of exceptional quality.

catechism. A religious text, typically in question-and-answer form, containing important doctrinal positions and often used in an educational setting.

cloud, the. A metaphor commonly used to invoke a ubiquitously accessible system in which large volumes of data are stored in centralized *data banks, linked by the internet, rather than on individual computers. The ethereal term *cloud*, it is often pointed out, obscures the physical reality of thousands of miles of cables, and vast, energy-consuming and heat-producing *data warehouses, all of which require frequent physical maintenance.

code. A set of rules for inscribing information, usually to promote more efficient transmission or resist unwanted recipients. Code could refer to the translation of information for communication (e.g., "Morse code") or to a secret cipher, such as ones that governments have long used to encrypt information. It can also refer to the underlying symbolic representation of information in a computer system or program, that is, machine code.

codex. A book constructed of a number of quires of paper, or similar writing surface, bound together at the spine. The term derives from the Latin *caudex* for "trunk of a tree" or "block of wood."

coffeehouse. An establishment, formed in the early modern Ottoman world and then in Europe, where people (at first only men) gathered to drink coffee, read, and talk about news. As a location for the interchange of political views, the coffeehouse has been used as an emblem for the early "public sphere."

colophon. A short statement placed at the end of a manuscript or printed work, announcing some details about the text, such as title, author, producer (e.g., scribe or printer).

commonplace book. An early modern notebook in which users stored textual excerpts under topical headings to facilitate retention or retrieval. The excerpts were often copied from books (e.g., by famous authors) but could also include personal observations.

commonplaces (*loci communes*). Fixed turns of phrase to be committed to memory. In the early modern period, the term designated selected topics, exempla, and sayings. The commonplace book was the storage medium for loci communes.

compression. The practice of producing a digital representation of information, often by eliminating redundancy, to achieve more efficient storage or transmission. The process is said to be either "lossless" or "lossy" depending on whether the result sacrifices some of the quality of the original.

concordance. A reference tool, first developed in the thirteenth century for the Bible, that collects in alphabetical order all the occurrences of the words in the text so they can be found easily without reading the whole work. A variety of concordances, many of them digital, also exist for examining word usage in classical Latin and Greek texts and in works in many other traditions, such as the Talmud, the Quran, and the corpus of Vedic Sanskrit texts.

conversion. The means of representing a communication in a new medium, such as translating written letters into electric signals for transmission over telegraph lines.

copia. Meaning "abundance" in Latin. The ability to write abundantly was highly valued as a sign of education in the European Renaissance. In order to achieve copiousness in writing and speaking, students were taught to gather phrases and information from their reading into their notebooks and memories, so that they could insert many examples and quotations into the texts they produced.

copyright. A legal construct that gives exclusive rights, usually for a limited time, over authored "works" understood as an "expression," typically on condition that the expression is "original," that is, in some (minimalist) sense "creative."

cursive. A manner of writing that conjoins adjacent letters within a word. By eliminating the spacing between individual letters, cursive saves a writer space on the page, as well as time spent writing.

data warehouses/data banks. Repositories of valued digital content, usually with highly restricted access. Given the value of the data, they are often subject to attack by people seeking illicit access. Consequently, the strength of security and upkeep for these databases faces continuous and constantly changing challenges. It is in these storage centers that the data accessed through the "cloud" is managed and made accessible to users.

dead media. Media forms that have been superseded and so present significant barriers to access (e.g., the contents of a floppy disk cannot be easily accessed by a modern-day laptop).

decimal classification (DC). A bibliographical system developed in the late nineteenth century to categorize content internationally using numeric categories to classify library holdings by content and location.

digital/analog. *See* analog/digital.

early modern period. The period of history from roughly 1400 to 1800, thus named on the notion that various features of "modernity" originated then, including new intellectual movements, religious schisms, the formation of nation-states, voyages of exploration and colonization, and early global capitalism. Though this periodization originated as a way of describing European history, its use has expanded to cover a more global context.

encyclopedia. A term that nineteenth-century European scholars applied to works of large scope with various ordering principles from around the world, including examples from East Asia and the Middle East. Although the term was formed from the Greek for "all-around education," it was associated from its first use in the Renaissance with the "circle of learning" and works that covered a large range of topics, often with a systematic arrangement to match the order of the disciplines as each author conceived it. The *Encyclopédie* of Diderot and d'Alembert (1751–75) gave the term a new set of associations with a large and usually alphabetically ordered reference book.

encyclopedic order. An arrangement of knowledge into a hierarchical scheme by discipline or another system of classification, typically contrasted with alphabetical order.

enlightenment. A term used to describe a period of increased or especially noteworthy intellectual and philosophical activity. "The Enlightenment" often refers specifically to eighteenth-century France, while "the early Enlightenment" refers mostly to late seventeenth-century thinkers like Isaac Newton, John Locke, and Pierre Bayle.

ephemera. Common objects created for a particular, brief purpose, typically designed to be disposed of afterward, with a focus on printed materials on paper. Examples are advertisements, catalogs, pamphlets, theater programs, and tickets.

epistemology. A branch of philosophy that examines the foundations and properties of knowledge, and a central concern of philosophers since ancient Greece. Among other questions, epistemology examines how humans know when something is true or false.

exegesis. The practice of critically examining, interpreting, and explicating a text. Practitioners of exegesis, called exegetes, in ancient as well as contemporary times have most often focused on sacred scriptures or canonical literary texts.

fact. From the Latin verb *facere* meaning "to make" or "to do." A fact is that which was done, occurred, or exists.

fair use. A common-law principle that under certain circumstances (e.g., educational use) allows copyrighted text to be used without the explicit approval of the copyright holder.

florilegium/florilegia. From the Latin for a "collection of flowers," florilegia were collections of authoritative sayings organized by topics and alphabetically arranged for easy retrieval.

free speech/freedom of speech. A legal principle that protects, within certain limits, an individual's ability to express ideas and opinions. Within the US legal system, this protection is enshrined in the First Amendment to the Constitution.

gazetteer. A textual compilation concerning the geography, peoples, history, and other features of a particular locality, culled from texts, in situ observations, or conversations.

genre. A category to describe a kind of text or artwork with certain shared characteristics of form or content. Mysteries and romances are examples of genres for novels. Outside of literature, the term can also refer more broadly to a specific form or style of text.

glossary. A reference element, often at the end of a book, that features brief definitions of selected terms.

guild. An association of skilled workers that regulated the practice of their trade. This kind of organization was the norm in medieval and early modern Europe. In England, for example, the printing trade was controlled by a London guild, the Stationers' Company, which was granted a monopoly by statute allowing it to prevent nonmembers from operating printing presses and to force members to conform to certain norms.

hacking. In the pejorative meaning of the word, the unauthorized engagement with a digital system or data repository, often with the goal of gathering or destroying privileged or personal information. "Hack" also has a positive meaning as an unauthorized or unexpected solution to a difficult problem.

House of Wisdom. A palace library founded in eighth-century Baghdad and staffed mainly by officials of Iranian descent, responsible for collecting books about Persian heritage and ancient Arabian lore. Recent scholarship has rejected the view that it served as a research academy and translation hub; instead it probably designated a library modeled on those of the Sasanian Empire and reflects the influence of the bureaucratic traditions of Iran on the new Islamic empire.

humanities. A set of disciplines that was thought to foster ethical qualities in leaders, and which derived from the Renaissance pedagogical program known as the *studia humanitatis* (humane studies). These disciplines included classical and modern languages, history, philosophy, and literature.

hypertext. Interlinked digital text that allows a reader to navigate to preselected and interrelated information. Hyperlinks are markers within digital documents that allow users to connect to other documents. Connections are usually achieved by clicking on the link. The related document then appears on the screen. Hypertext is text that relies on such links and the interrelated documents to fulfill the purpose for which the document was designed. The word was coined by Theodor (Ted) Nelson, an early internet pioneer.

illumination. The ornamentation using colored and gold pigments of a manuscript or printed work.

impact factor. A measure of supposed academic worth built around the number of citations that each article receives in a particular journal. The measure assumes that journals with higher impact factors are more widely read and thus the articles they contain more important than journals with low impact factors.

indulgence. Remission of temporal punishment for sin, often recorded in a certificate issued by the Catholic Church and attesting to an act of charity, a pilgrimage, or the use of a rosary or other devotional objects. Indulgences were printed in great numbers (including by Johannes Gutenberg) as single sheets, which have a very poor survival rate.

information overload. The sense or feeling that there is simply too much information for one to grasp and recall given the resources available. Complaints about overload are not unique to the so-called digital age but can be found in various premodern contexts.

Internet. An interconnected network of computers and related devices to transmit and process digital communications. The modern internet is the outcome of a vast number of connections among multiple different networks, though current use of the term evokes an all-embracing, single network.

Jesuit. *See* Society of Jesus.

leak. The unauthorized disclosing of information classified as private or secret.

learned societies. Associations of the learned around a shared interest, such as poetic performance, or the study of language, or of science. Three principal examples still active today, the English Royal Society, the French Académie des Sciences, and the German Academia Leopoldina, were formed in the late seventeenth century and disseminated findings of their members in the form of a periodical.

lexicon. A reference book devoted to explaining terms in a foreign (mainly classical) language or terminology specific to a particular field of knowledge.

libel. A legal term used to designate false or defamatory statements that are recorded in writing or other fixed form. Libel differs from slander, which encompasses verbal, gestural, or unrecorded defamation.

Library of Congress. A major research library in Washington, DC, maintained by the US government, which aims to hold a copy of every book published in the United States. The Library of Congress developed and maintains a cataloging system that assigns subject headings to every publication entering its purview following a controlled vocabulary widely adopted in other libraries. These headings first appeared in the late nineteenth century and are still in active use today.

literacy. The ability to read and write. Historians distinguish many types of literacy. "Pragmatic literacy" was sufficient for managing basic legal and business affairs. "Mercantile literacy" involves reckoning and reading in the vernacular. In Europe, before the modern period, to be "literatus" meant to possess the ability to read Latin, which was expected of all clergy and students.

longue durée. Literally "long duration," a term introduced into historical practice by the French historian Fernand Braudel and now widely used. It refers to a historical method that emphasizes developments that take place over the very long term, such as changes in climate, which both shape human society and are shaped by it. Cultural phenomena may also act on long time scales.

machine learning. A statistical and computer-based method that uses inductive algorithms trained on large data sets to extract patterns and adapt machine behavior in response to these patterns. In particular, when used in the fields of artificial intelligence or natural language processing, it enables machines to infer the judgments of human reasoners with no pretense of reproducing the thought processes and somatic judgments of human beings. More generally machine learning algorithms are designed to "improve automatically through experience" (Tom Mitchell, 1997).

marginalia. Annotations left by readers in the margins of a written or printed text. Marginalia can be studied as records of one person's reading but also of methods of reading typical of a given context.

memex. A contraction of either "memory extended" or "memory index," referring to a photoelectric machine envisioned by the engineer Vannevar Bush to link documents (on microfilm) chosen by the owner, thereby superseding both index cards and library classification. As such, it was a precursor of hypertext systems and the World Wide Web.

metadata. From the Greek *meta-* for "behind." These data "about data" record details about the items being cataloged. Book metadata, for example, usually include the place and year of publication, the format, and authorship. Metadata help structure the data in a collection according to items' relationships with one another.

Morse code. A telecommunication system developed in the nineteenth century by Samuel Morse and Alfred Vail that used combinations of electric pulses (dots and dashes) to encode letters and numbers.

new media. A term applied to digital media, with the implication, not always correct, that they either displace or replace older forms.

notary. A person invested with the authority to create, authenticate, and store documents with legal significance.

open access. A form of publication committed to making documents, including scholarly research in peer-reviewed journals, open to any interested user to read, copy, or circulate, without the need for permission, payment, or proof of institutional affiliation.

open source. Both a principle and a practice according to which a piece of computer code is open to adoption and adaptation. Open source codes, programs, or scripts are not controlled by any company or person. Instead, all are free to use the code for their own purposes, on the understanding that what is produced is also made available on similar terms.

optical character recognition (OCR). The process by which a machine "reads" a document, converting the analog lettering on a page into digital bits and bytes that can then be, for instance, digitally searched or reorganized.

palimpsest. A manuscript in which an initial layer of writing has been either partially or completely erased, often through scraping, and a more recent text inscribed over it.

papyrus. The dominant writing material used in ancient Egypt, Greece, and Rome, made from the pith of a plant native to the Nile delta. Texts written on papyrus rolls often required re-copying owing to the fragility of the medium. Nonetheless, thousands of papyrus fragments have survived (particularly in dry desert conditions) and are studied by papyrologists.

paratext. Textual material, usually but not always at the front and back of a book, that refers to the main text, such as the frontispiece, table of contents, dedication, prefaces by author or printer, commendatory odes, illustrations, alphabetical indexes, and errata lists.

parchment. A writing surface made from animal skin, including calf skin (vellum) but also the skin of sheep, goat, or pig. Even after the availability of paper, parchment was used for tran-scribing particular types of documents (e.g., classical texts, charters, bulls) deemed espe-cially important. *See also* vellum.

philology. From the Greek for "love of words," a discipline devoted to studying the histories, contexts, and developments of ancient or classical languages and literatures.

polymath. A scholar who studies a variety of disciplines and makes original contributions to several of them, such as Gottfried Wilhelm Leibniz (1646–1716), whose interests included history, theology, linguistics, and sinology as well as the philosophy and mathematics for which he is best known.

protocol. A standardized set of rules allowing different machines within a network to com-municate with each other. Rather than needing to accommodate the diverse workings of all the machines in a network, each machine has only to respond to the agreed-on protocols to transmit and receive communications.

public domain. The cornerstone of copyright law designating those materials to which no legal restrictions on use or reproduction apply. The public domain denotes what is left over after all other rights have been defined and distributed.

publishers. The person(s) or company that manages publication or the public dissemination of a text (in print, digital, or another format). Though not a universal phenomenon, certain rights have historically been reserved to publishers, including, to varying degrees, copyright and the control over reprinting a work.

publish or perish. A colloquial academic expression that communicates the expectation that scholars must publish their work in articles and books in order to advance their academic careers.

Reformation. A movement of religious reform, begun by Martin Luther in 1517, that resulted in a schism of the Western Christian church into Roman Catholic and many Protestant branches.

Renaissance. From the French for rebirth. The term describes a revival of learned and artistic culture. In the European context, the Renaissance refers to the period circa 1300–1600, dur-ing which humanists, with their focus on classical antiquity, recovered and studied not only texts but also architecture (e.g., the dome) and art (sculptures large and small), coins and inscriptions, and other cultural remains. The term also occurs in the "Carolingian Renaissance" (around 800 CE), noted for the foundation of new schools offering instruction in Latin; and the "twelfth-century Renaissance," which featured the transmission of Aristo-telian philosophical works to the Latin West from the Arabic translations circulating in Spain. The term has also been applied to other cultural contexts.

reproducibility. The extent to which material can be copied and then disseminated. Reproducibility presupposes that information is independent of its source and does not change as it travels.

Republic of Letters. An international and self-described network of early modern scholars, philosophers, and thinkers who communicated with one another via letters and personal contact.

research library. A library, often but not always associated with a *research university, devoted to supporting research in a wide range of specialized academic fields by an active acquisition policy.

research university. A model for a university developed in late eighteenth- and early nineteenth-century Germany and widely adopted around the world since then that places a high emphasis on research. Today, the professor at such a university not only teaches but is expected to generate new knowledge and train others to do so.

salon. A private gathering of literati, often hosted by women in seventeenth- and eighteenth-century France. Some historians consider salons crucial spaces for the discussion of ideas under fewer constraints than were common in public settings; others see them more as forms of sociability dominated by the aristocrats who assembled them.

scholasticism. A method of analysis practiced in medieval universities in Europe, focused on disputation about and logical commentary on authoritative texts, including Christian theology and Aristotelian philosophy.

scriptorium/scriptoria. Site(s) in which scribes copied texts, whether in medieval monasteries or in the commercial enterprises that sought to create multiple copies of manuscripts for sale in urban centers, in late medieval and early modern Europe among other contexts.

semiotics. The study of signs, which proved important for understanding and developing nineteenth-century communication technologies. It features in multiple disciplines, from philosophy to computer science and marketing.

server farm. A massive collection of computing devices, often located in a remote location, that stores and processes digital information. Server farms are usually built to provide data to a particular organization, whereas the "cloud" is more commonly used to describe data storage that serves internet users more generally.

shorthand. A method of recording speech in abbreviated form through different symbols and notes.

skeuomorphism. The presentation of content or an interface that aesthetically resembles an older medium. The majority of online books and electronic resources, for example, resemble the page-based and paratextual forms of codices, with traditional formatting parameters.

Society of Jesus/Jesuits. A Catholic order founded in the sixteenth century famous for its secondary schools and for the system of regular reports generated by its missionaries in Europe, the Americas, and Asia.

structured data. Data organized and stored as information in certain specified classes. In contrast, **unstructured data**, like materials on the web, are heterogeneous, conforming to no predetermined subject categories.

taxonomy. A means of structuring the world or its representation hierarchically. In biology, for example, the taxonomy of Carl Linnaeus (1707–78) sorted the organic world into a nested hierarchy of categories (families, genera, species, etc.) that to some degree have a real, if abstract, existence.

vellum.   A writing surface manufactured from calfskin. Vellum was the medium of choice for manuscripts in medieval Europe. A text could also be printed on vellum, but this was done only occasionally during the early decades of printing to create a copy of special value. Vellum was also used in book bindings, as it was more flexible, more durable, and less expensive than alternatives like boards covered in leather.

vernacular.   A language used in daily life as one's primary means of communication. The vernacular is often contrasted with so-called dead or world languages (e.g., Latin), or older variants of a mother tongue usually reserved for particular ceremonial or religious occasions (e.g., Classical Arabic vs. Modern Standard Arabic).

World Wide Web.   The networks developed within the internet that use shared protocols to standardize document formats and provide unique addresses for documents or other dynamically generated content, allowing users to reach those resources from any computer on the network.

CONTRIBUTORS

JEREMY ADELMAN is Henry Charles Lea Professor Emeritus of History at Princeton University and Director of the Global History Lab at the University of Cambridge. He is the author of *Worldly Philosopher: The Odyssey of Albert O. Hirschman.*

ANN BLAIR is Carl H. Pforzheimer University Professor in the Department of History at Harvard University. She is the author of *Too Much to Know: Managing Scholarly Information before the Modern Age.*

PAUL DUGUID is an Adjunct Full Professor Emeritus at the School of Information at the University of California, Berkeley. He is coauthor, with John Seely Brown, of *The Social Life of Information.*

DEVIN FITZGERALD is Curator of Rare Books and Global Print Culture in the UCLA Library, Special Collections. His publications include "The Early Modern Information Revolution," coauthored with Ann Blair, in *The Oxford Handbook of Early Modern European History,* and "Chinese Papers in the Early Modern World" in *Ars Orientalis.*

JOHN-PAUL A. GHOBRIAL is Professor of Modern and Global History at the University of Oxford and Lucas Fellow and Tutor in History at Balliol College. He is the author of *The Whispers of Cities: Information Flows in Istanbul, London, and Paris in the Age of William Trumbull.*

LISA GITELMAN is Professor of Media, Culture, and Communication at New York University. She is the author of *Paper Knowledge: Toward a Media History of Documents.*

ANJA-SILVIA GOEING is Professor of the History of Education at the University of Zurich and Program Coordinator and Associate in the Department of History at Harvard University. She is the author of *Storing,*

Archiving, Organizing: The Changing Dynamics of Scholarly Information Management in Post-Reformation Zurich.

ANTHONY GRAFTON is Henry Putnam University Professor of History at Princeton University. He is the author of *Magus: The Art of Magic from Faustus to Agrippa.*

RANDOLPH C. HEAD is Professor of History Emeritus and Professor of the Graduate Division at the University of California, Riverside. He is the author of *Making Archives in Early Modern Europe: Proof, Information, and Political Record-Keeping, 1400–1700.*

RICHARD R. JOHN is Professor of History and Communications at Columbia University. He is the author of *Network Nation: Inventing American Telecommunications.*

ELIAS MUHANNA is Associate Professor of Comparative Literature and History at Brown University. He is the author of *The World in a Book: al-Nuwayri and the Islamic Encyclopedic Tradition.*

THOMAS S. MULLANEY is Professor of History and Professor of East Asian Languages and Cultures, by courtesy, at Stanford University. He is the author of *The Chinese Typewriter: A History.*

CARLA NAPPI is Mellon Professor of History and codirector of the Humanities Center at the University of Pittsburgh. She is the author of *Translating Early Modern China: Illegible Cities.*

CRAIG ROBERTSON is Professor of Communication Studies at Northeastern University. He is the author of *The Filing Cabinet: A Vertical History of Information.*

DANIEL ROSENBERG is Professor of History at the University of Oregon. He is the coauthor, with Anthony Grafton, of *Cartographies of Time: A History of the Timeline.*

WILL SLAUTER is Professor of American History in the English Department at Sorbonne University. He is the author of *Who Owns the News? A History of Copyright.*

HEIDI J. S. TWOREK is a Canada Research Chair and Professor of International History and Public Policy at the University of British Columbia. She is the author of *News from Germany: The Competition to Control World Communications, 1900–1945.*

INDEX

Page numbers in italics refer to figures

A NOTE ON THE TYPE

This book has been composed in Arno, an Old-style serif typeface in the classic Venetian tradition, designed by Robert Slimbach at Adobe.